Kentucke's Frontiers

A History of the Trans-Appalachian Frontier

Malcolm Rohrbough and Walter Nugent, editors

Kentucke's Frontiers

Craig Thompson Friend

Indiana University Press   Bloomington & Indianapolis

This book is a publication of

Indiana University Press
601 North Morton Street
Bloomington, Indiana 47404-3797 USA

www.iupress.indiana.edu

Telephone orders 800-842-6796
Fax orders 812-855-7931
Orders by e-mail iuporder@indiana.edu

⊗ The paper used in this publication meets the minimum requirements
of the American National Standard for Information Sciences—
Permanence of Paper for Printed Library Materials, ANSI Z39.48-1992.

Manufactured in the United States of America

Library of Congress Cataloging-in-Publication Data

Friend, Craig Thompson.
Kentucke's frontiers / Craig Thompson Friend.
p. cm. — (A history of the trans-Appalachian frontier)
Includes bibliographical references and index.
ISBN 978-0-253-35519-5 (cloth : alk. paper) 1. Kentucky—History—To
1792. 2. Frontier and pioneer life—Kentucky. 3. Kentucky—History,
Military. 4. Indians of North America—Kentucky—History. 5. Indians
of North America—Wars—Kentucky. 6. Kentucky—Race relations.
7. Kentucky—Social conditions. 8. Patriarchy—Kentucky—History.
9. Political culture—Kentucky—History. 10. Religion and culture—
Kentucky—History. I. Title.
F454.F75   2010
976.9'01—dc22
2010021943

1 2 3 4 5 15 14 13 12 11 10

For my partner
Roderick Glenn Turner,
a native Kentuckian

Lie still and go to sleep, or the Shawnees will catch you.
　　　　　—Elizabeth Shotwell Drake to her children, 1780s

⊫ Contents

Illustrations

Figures

Maps

Foreword

For most Americans, the phrase "the American West" conjures up the western half of the nation. From the Great Plains across the Rockies and the Intermontane Plateaus to the Pacific Ocean came a flood of popular images, from trappers, cowboys, miners, and homesteading families to the "Marlboro Man" and country-western music. This has been "the West" since the California Gold Rush and the migration of '49ers propelled this region into the national consciousness.

But it was not always so. There was an earlier American West, no less vivid and dramatic. Here the fabled figures were not John Charles Frémont but Daniel Boone, not Geronimo but Tecumseh, not Calamity Jane but Rachel Jackson, not "Buffalo Bill" Cody but Davy Crockett. This earlier West ran, geographically, from the crest of the Appalachian Mountains to the Mississippi River, from the border with Canada to the Gulf of Mexico. It was the West of Euro-American expansion from before the American Revolution until the middle of the nineteenth century, when the line of frontier settlement moved through it toward that next, farther West.

In its initial terms, the story of the First American West involved two basic sets of characters: first, the white people of European origin (and, south of the Ohio River, many African American slaves), who spread relentlessly westward; second, the original settlers, the Native Americans, who retreated grudgingly before this flood. These first Europeans, French and Spanish, appeared on this landscape in the 1600s and early 1700s, where their interactions with the original native peoples involved both cooperation and conflict. The English arrived a half-century later. In numbers, the Europeans were almost always a minority, and so both sides sought not conquest or annihilation but mutual accommodation, a joint occupation of the land and joint use of its resources, a system of contact allowing both sides to survive and even to benefit from one another's presence. Trade developed and intermarriage followed; so did misunderstandings and violence. But a delicate balance, supported by mutual interests, often characterized relations among Europeans and native peoples.

When Anglo-Americans began moving through the Cumberland Gap from Virginia into what hunters called the Kentucke country in the 1750s, they soon tilted the balance of the two cultures, occupying large portions of Kentucky and pressing against native groups from Ohio south to Georgia. By 1780, the Anglo-Americans had also occupied the former French settlements of Cahokia in Illinois and Vincennes in Indiana. Despite strong resistance by several native groups, the seemingly unending reinforcements of white families made their gradual occupation of the trans-Appalachian frontier inevitable.

In the 1780s the infant American government issued ordinances spelling out how the land between the Great Lakes and the Ohio River was to be acquired, subdivided, and sold to the citizens of the new republic, and how a form of government organization would lead to statehood and equal membership in the Union. A parallel process was soon set up for Kentucky, Tennessee, and the lands south to the Gulf.

In the 1830s and 1840s, the remaining native groups east of the Mississippi were removed to the West. The expansion of settlement into the trans-Appalachian frontier now continued unchecked into Illinois, Wisconsin, Michigan, and the great cotton lands and hill country of Alabama, Mississippi, and Florida. The frontier period had been completed—as early as the 1820s in Kentucky, and within the next twenty years over much of the Old Northwest and in the Old Southwest.

In brief terms, this is the story of the trans-Appalachian frontier. Over scarcely three generations, the trickle of settler families across the mountains had become more than four million, both white and black. Beginning with Kentucky in 1792 and running through Florida in 1845 and Wisconsin in 1848, a dozen new states had entered the American Union. Each territory/state had its own story, and it is appropriate that each should have a separate volume in this series. The variations are large. Florida's first European arrived in 1513, and this future state had both Spanish and American frontier experiences over 350 years. Missouri had a long French and Spanish history before the arrival of American settlers. Kentucky and Ohio did not, and Americans in large numbers came there quickly through the Cumberland Gap.

The opening and closing of the settlement frontier is the subject of each of these volumes. Each begins with the world that existed when Europeans made contact with native peoples. Each describes and analyzes the themes associated with the special circumstances of the individual territory/state. And each concludes with the closing of the frontier.

We editors have selected these authors because of their reputations as scholars and interpreters of their individual territories/states. We believe that you will enjoy this and other volumes in the Trans-Appalachian Frontier series.

Of all the places on the trans-Appalachian frontier that captured the attention of native peoples, early Anglo-American settlers, and later historians, the place that we know as Kentucky had two dominant features: it was the most violent, and it was the settlement experience most surrounded by myth and fantasy. In his fine study, Craig Thompson Friend has identified and analyzed these two strands of Kentucky's frontier experience with great insight and fluency. As he writes in his preface, Kentucky "remains the inspirational vision of our frontier past." He reminds us that on no other American frontier did fear and terror play such an important role. Intercultural violence became a central feature of the Kentucky frontier. Friend's nuanced analysis displays the traditional Kentucky historical figures—Native Americans and Anglo-Americans, women and men, black and white—with new and expanded roles.

Friend's study is also remarkable for coming to terms with another central theme of Kentucky history, namely, the early adoption and increasingly widespread use of slave labor in what would become the commonwealth. His discussion shows us how the open-ended nature of the first generation of Anglo-American (American after 1783) settlement—with its public chorus of freedom and opportunity—was perfectly compatible with the institution of slavery. Indeed, slavery spread rapidly in the commonwealth, particularly in the central Blue Grass region. Slavery would become a salient feature of the trans-Appalachian frontier south of the Ohio River. Friend's study shows us its beginnings in this first frontier experience.

Amidst the violence of the "dark and bloody ground" of wars against native peoples, Kentuckians never lost sight of the economic advantage that had brought them west. This economic advantage had two dimensions: land and slaves. They fought native peoples for the first. They adopted the second freely of their own choice. Not all Kentuckians agreed with that choice, and Friend describes the considerable opposition to the emergence of a slave commonwealth. In the end, however, the most influential Kentuckians saw economic and social stability as grounded in the institution of slavery. In this fashion, the violence of the wars against Indian peoples would be replaced by the violence of a system incorporating lifelong servitude.

The struggle, and the story, starts in the 1720s. From then until the close of the War of 1812, the author stirs a pot full of political and military narrative, race and gender relations, legal and constitutional patterns, and the role of a range of religious groups. Before 1790, there were open questions about Kentucky's future. It was already clear that Anglo-Americans would replace Native Americans, but would the region be slave or free, socially stratified or egalitarian, Federalist or Jeffersonian? The answer to each question would be "both."

Craig Thompson Friend has written or edited several books on Kentucky and southern history, notably *Southern Manhood: Perspectives on Masculinity in the Old South*; *Southern Masculinity: Perspectives on Manhood in the South since Reconstruction*; and *Along the Maysville Road: The Early American Republic in the Trans-Appalachian West*, among others. A member of the history faculty at North Carolina State University since 2005, he is a fine teacher and a leader in the public history movement, having developed courses in local and community history and trained students for careers in the field. He is also an engaging

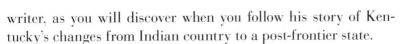

writer, as you will discover when you follow his story of Kentucky's changes from Indian country to a post-frontier state.

Malcolm J. Rohrbough
University of Iowa

Walter Nugent
University of Notre Dame

Preface

"There are two ways of being American," expounded English writer D. H. Lawrence in 1926: "by recoiling into individual small-ness and insentience, and gutting the great continent in fren-zies of mean fear. It is the 'Puritan way.' The other is by *touch*; touch America as she is; dare to touch her! And this is the he-roic way."

Since 1784, when John Filson published *The Discovery, Settle-ment, and Present State of Kentucke*, trans-Appalachian pro-moters and historians alike have celebrated the heroic way of being American. White men who encroached upon and settled Kentucke became (and have remained) cultural heroes imbued with greater character than many actually enjoyed. Consider es-teemed historian Robert V. Remini's thoughts of 1992: "Because of my research into early Kentucky history, I came to recognize the extraordinary number of genuine heroes who decorate its history. Probably, this is true of many other states as well. I just don't know. But I do know it is true of Kentucky." Well, of course it is just as true of other states, but the pioneer hero—as embod-ied in Filson's story of Daniel Boone, in the ideal of the "Hunt-ers from Kentucky" memorialized in song following the War of 1812, in Lord Byron's celebration of the "back-woodsman of Ken-tucky," in the character of Natty Bumppo who hunted and fought his way through James Fenimore Cooper's *Leatherstocking Tales* of the 1830s, in George Caleb Bingham's 1852 painting of *Boone Escorting Settlers through the Cumberland Gap*, in the pioneer farmers celebrated by Frederick Jackson Turner in 1893 for over-coming the stubborn American environment, in the 1939 movie *Drums along the Mohawk*, and in coonskin caps of the 1950s and 1960s that identified viewers of Walt Disney's *Davy Crockett* and *Daniel Boone* TV series—was and remains a prototype of the xviii ♦ P_{REFACE}

Kentucke frontiersman, of the "genuine hero" who, as Remini put it, "took fantastic personal risks to realize a dream, a dream that ultimately benefited millions of others."

Celebration of the heroic way has led to a misperception that Kentucke embodied *the* American frontier experience, one that was uniformly and primarily a progression of (white American) civilization that repeated itself on each successive frontier as Americans continued westward. It is an ideal that was created by nineteenth-century historians determined to establish Kentucky's colonial lineage, that was made sacrosanct by Turner's "frontier thesis," and that continues to permeate national history and popular memory. Frontier heroism provides a cultural marker against which we measure our own national character. "We think back to the pioneers of an earlier century," Ronald Reagan remarked on the occasion of the space shuttle *Challenger* disaster, "and the sturdy souls who took their families and their belongings and set out into the frontier of the American West. Often, they met with terrible hardship. . . . But grief only steeled them to the journey ahead." A quarter-century earlier, John F. Kennedy prefaced the "New Frontier" by appealing to the heroism of an older one: "From the lands that stretch three thousand miles behind us, the pioneers gave up their safety, their comfort and sometimes their lives to build our new West. They were not the captives of their own doubts, nor the prisoners of their own price tags. They were determined to make the new world strong and free—an example to the world, to overcome its hazards and its hardships, to conquer the enemies that threatened from within and without." Boone and his peers have long represented the sturdy, determined, heroic qualities of the American frontiersman, and Americans have long celebrated the ways in which their forebears connected with the grandeur of the North American continent and *physically* mastered it and its indigenous inhabitants. This was, and remains, the inspirational vision of our frontier past.

Yet, heroism did not manifest in a vacuum. The heroic way required the other way of being American—the frenzies of mean fear shaped in an atmosphere of random violence, large-scale war, and both real and imagined terror that inspired violent reaction and imbued martial manliness. This "Puritan way" was far more pervasive and insidious than we have allowed in our retelling of the past. As on contemporary frontiers such as those in Pennsylvania where, according to historian Peter Silver, "horror and fear flowed from the attacks that Indians and Europeans made on one another," panic permeated the Kentucke frontiers. One could argue that Americans needed the heroic idea of the frontier to push beyond their fears. Faced with the unremitting possibility of losing one's family and one's life, Americans took up the "Puritan way" of being American, attacking the terror in frenzies of mean fear and allowing themselves to be socially traumatized in ways that had significant cultural consequences.

Acting out in the "Puritan way" bound early white and black Kentuckians to the violence and terror faced by ancestors on earlier colonial frontiers. As historian Richard Slotkin described, in the late seventeenth century, King Philip's War and Mary Rowlandson's captivity immersed New England colonists in an "atmosphere of terror," trapping them in an "Indian-haunted dreamland." One hundred years later, in the 1780s, when Elizabeth Shotwell Drake put her children to bed with the words "Lie still and go to sleep, or the Shawnees will catch you," she ensured that they—like all Kentucke settlers—persisted in that Indian-haunted dreamland, whether Indians lurked at their cabin doors or not.

Initially, my objective in *Kentucke's Frontiers* was to provide a readable narrative of Kentucke's transformation into Kentucky,* one that synthesizes much of the scholarship produced over the past quarter-century. Many, many historians have told the story of frontier Kentucke, making it difficult for anyone to offer new insights and analysis. Still, as I worked through the narrative, I

---

* With statehood in 1792, the name of the region officially became Kentucky, with a "y." But throughout most of the earlier period, there was inconsistent use of the "y." Settlers, surveyors, and observers wrote of the region as "Caintucky" or "Kentucke," which one might imagine had a long e (ē) as the final syllable. In the eastern backcountries, the final syllable was occasionally dropped, and the region was simply "Kentuck" or "Caintuck." I have opted to use "Kentucke" to refer to the region prior to statehood and the Americanized "Kentucky" upon the region's entry into the union.

came to realize that the Kentucke frontiers have a more contemporary relevance than one might grasp at first. I hope that readers will consider how frenzies of mean fear made and unmade Kentucke, shaping the future not only of this trans-Appalachian region but of the American nation as well.

I define Kentucke's frontier period rather narrowly, from the 1720s through the first decade of the nineteenth century. In the 1720s and 1730s, the Shawnees led allied Native Americans into the Ohio River valley as pioneers, having been pushed out a half-century earlier by the Iroquois. Theirs was an uneasy settlement: the new multinational villages struggled against continued pressures from the Iroquois, worked to hold both French and British imperial interests at bay, and tried to negotiate a comfortable relationship with the American colonists. As those colonials began to breach the Appalachian Mountains in the 1760s, they comprised another wave of pioneers, one that would not find cultural commonalities with their new neighbors. Indeed, only a few hunters appear to have bridged that divide. Instead, Kentucke instantly became a frontier of intercultural violence. As in any environment in which terror emerges as a dominant theme, within both Native American villages and colonial stations, frenzies of mean fear and a search for security drove decision making. They were forces that could not subside until one side was eliminated. For that reason, not until the mid-1790s, with significant defeats over the Shawnees and their allies, did white Kentuckians turn from their search for security and stability to society building.

One is tempted, then, to draw Kentucke's frontiers to a close in the 1790s with its admission as a state in 1792 and the Treaty of Greenville in 1795 that dramatically reduced the threat of Indian attacks on the lands south of the Ohio River. Yet, the fear spawned by frontier violence did not abate and proved influential as Americans transformed Kentucke into Kentucky. As Native Americans exited Kentucky's stage in the mid-1790s, white Kentuckians found it difficult to rewrite the script of their daily lives. There had to be others who could assume the sinister roles once reserved for Indians; others who lurked in the woods, watching for opportunities to upset the stability and security that white Kentuckians had paid for with the blood of parents, children, siblings, friends, and neighbors. Even before Virginia's Gabriel's Rebellion in 1801, rumors of slave insurrection circulated throughout the United States, and in Kentucky, the threat of slave rebellion replicated rumors of Indian attack. African Americans became the dark, uncivilized Others. In 1799, one white Kentuckian declared them "Ignorant Savage Heathens" who represented not only the absence of but the negation of "civilized" values. Kentucky did not have to be a slave state: its patriarchs chose to make it so. Any other narrative—one of racial cooperation or of daily life without fear—just did not correlate with the terror that had framed nearly three decades of white trans-Appalachian experience.

While I remember as a child watching Fess Parker confront both "good" and "bad" Indians in the television show *Daniel Boone*, it was as a graduate student that I first intellectually engaged frontier Kentucke through Malcolm Rohrbough's *The Trans-Appalachian Frontier.* In two chapters entitled "The Search for Security" and "The Search for Stability," Rohrbough examined Kentucke and its southern neighbor Tennessee between 1775 and 1795. At the heart of his analysis was the evolution of a region from one of sporadic white settlement to one with sufficient institutions—stations, militias, courts, schools, and churches—to stabilize society. As Rohrbough concluded, "a New World emerged with an institutional framework much like the Old. The institutional structure that evolved assisted materially in the preservation of property rights. The new trans-Appalachian settlements had conferred benefits on thousands of families in the form of land. Not surprisingly, some had benefited more than others." I appreciate Rohrbough's paradigm, but I also read those lines differently than what I suspect Rohrbough intended. A new world did emerge as Kentucke transformed into Kentucky, but far more was at stake than land.

White men always had the greatest advantages on the frontiers, and many came to Kentucke to prove themselves "big man" patriarchs who, through courage, craftiness, and skill, led extended families in the pursuit of land and sustenance. Michael Rowan, a fictional father and settler in Robert Schenkkan's 1992 Pulitzer Prize–winning *The Kentucky Cycle*, best sums up the ambitions of thousands of white men who migrated westward during and after the Revolutionary War to stake their claim to a piece of Kentucke and establish their patriarchal status: "Take a lesson from your old pa here, boy, on how to get ahead in the world. You got to think further than your own nose; further than your neighbor's nose. You don't get ahead just thinkin' about tomorrow or the day after. You got to think years down the road. (*He drinks.*) With a slave, we can work half again as much land. More land, more corn. More corn, more whiskey. More whiskey, more slaves. More slaves—more *land!* I'll own those damn mountains before I'm through." Land, slavery, and the market became symbiotic on Kentucke's frontiers and the foundations upon which white frontier manhood (and later white southern patriarchy) was established. Land was significant, then, only in relationship to its agricultural output and the availability of markets at which those productions could be sold.

But frontier Kentucke also offered majoritarian political participation, more fluid gender roles and responsibilities, and the potential abolition of slavery. With statehood, white men sought ways to strengthen patriarchy against these more egalitarian forces. Through courts, churches, stores, and the state legislature, Kentucky institutionalized patriarchy, and gendered and racial inequality. All were cultural choices made to alleviate terror and stabilize the uncertain and fragile societies of an emerging Kentucky. By the War of 1812, Kentucky arrived as an Old South state, fully controlled by and rooted in the honor-driven culture of white southern manhood, and benefiting white men by negating opportunities for blacks, Indians, and white women.

At the heart of this "southernization" was the entrenchment of slavery, although the institution could never fully be separated from the region's past. "It is impossible to conceive the great South as being, on the whole, more than a few steps removed from the frontier stage at the beginning of the Civil War," commentator W. J. Cash once observed. Early-nineteenth-century Kentucky, like the rest of the South, reflected the influence of its frontier origins, sustaining a context for terror and fear that, having once been directed toward the Indians, was turned upon black slaves, who posed a constant but largely imagined threat of insurrection. Whites responded by codifying restrictions and violence against enslaved African Americans, and even extending those restraints over free blacks, who theoretically shared in Kentucky's promise.

Even as Kentucky became southern in the early 1800s, remnants of the frontier went unresolved: the Chickasaws held fast to their claim over the westernmost reaches of Kentucky; the economic and social isolation of the Appalachian communities continued to hinder settlement and growth; and an Indian confederacy forming in the Illinois territory under the leadership of Tecumseh and his brother Tenskwatawa resurrected the threat of Indian attack. But these problems no longer framed Kentucky's narrative. The frontier had passed. As the War of 1812 erupted and Kentuckians clamored to attack the Indian confederacy, Humphrey Marshall published the state's first history, marking the end of frontier and the beginning of remembrance.

* * *

Kentucke's frontier story has been told many times, and I am greatly indebted to those scholars who created the evidentiary and interpretative foundations for future authors like me. Foremost is Thomas D. Clark, whose work on early Kentucky defined the field throughout most of the twentieth century. In 1999, I sat in a booth adjacent to Dr. Clark's at a Kentucky book fair. He was in the twilight of his career; I was pushing my first book. He had a long line of people awaiting his autograph most of the day, some of whom wandered over to my booth. Yet, during breaks and in the late afternoon lull, he and I sat and talked about our scholarly interests. I received a great education that day.

I was honored to be invited by Walter Nugent and Malcolm Rohrbough to write *Kentucke's Frontiers*, and I value their guidance as I revised it. I appreciate their patience, as well as that of Robert Sloan of Indiana University Press. I have been privileged to have shared an interest in the early American frontiers and early American republic with a cohort of thoughtful and thought-provoking scholars, including Judy Kertész, Lorri Glover, Stephen A. Aron, and Andrew R. L. Cayton, who read and offered suggestions for the manuscript. Sherry Hardin produced the maps for this book, and I appreciate her fine work. I am grateful as well for Neal O. Hammon's sharing of his own research and thoughts.

Finally and most importantly, I come to Rod Turner, to whom this book is dedicated. Through sixteen years, Rod has shared my life and my interest in Kentucky. As I have completed this book, he has been a great inspiration and, occasionally, a wonderful distraction.

Kentucke's Frontiers

I.

THE INDIANS' FRONTIERS

Autumn ushers gray skies into the Ohio River valley. In the mid-eighteenth century, the shift in weather inspired regional peoples to prepare for the cold days ahead by completing the harvests, gathering the last of the berries and firewood, and organizing hunting parties that characterized winter life among many Native Americans. European traders and the few other whites living among the Indians similarly stocked up on supplies in anticipation of the cold and snows of winter. In 1755, Mary Draper Ingles made different plans as autumn arrived. As she, several other European colonists, and their Shawnee captors moved southward across the Ohio River and turned westward toward the Big Bone Lick to gather salt for the hunting season, Ingles and an older German woman quietly vanished into the forests of northern Kentucke.

Ingles had been uprooted from her Virginia home over two months earlier. In late July, Shawnees had attacked Draper's Meadow, a small outpost of white settlers in the foothills of the Appalachians on Virginia's New River frontier. Six years earlier, two families—the Drapers and the Ingleses—had created new lives there, culminating in Mary Draper's marriage to William Ingles. The couple had two sons and expected a third child. But

the New River frontier, like those farther to the north, was about
to explode.

In the late 1740s and early 1750s, tensions between the French
and British over influence among northern Indians and control
of the Ohio River valley put colonial settlers at risk. Shawnee
leaders both at Chillicothe on the upper Scioto River and at the
lower Shawnee Town at the mouth of the Scioto purposefully
played the imperial powers against one another. It was a dangerous game at which they were quite adept: the art of negotiation was a staple of Shawnee diplomacy, evidenced by their success in safeguarding their autonomy from the British and the
French, as well as the powerful Iroquois to the east.

The art of war was equally central to Shawnee international
relations. Throughout the 1740s and early 1750s, they fought the
Cherokees for access to and usage of Kentucke's hunting lands,
and they regularly battled the Catawbas over past hostilities.
Branches of Athiamiowee (what colonials knew as the Great Warriors Path), which Shawnee, Miami, and Wyandot warriors traveled to attack the southern Indians, coursed southeastward from
the Ohio River along the Kanawha River and Big Sandy River
valleys through the Appalachians into the eastern foothills, where
they forked. One major route turned northeastward, following the
valley of the Shenandoah River; the other turned southwestward
through the eastern Cherokee settlements, including Echota, Tellico, and Hiwassee, then forked again with one trail headed northward toward the Cherokee Overhill towns and the other continuing southwestward to the upper Creek villages. Northeast of
where Athiamiowee branched after entering the eastern foothills,
it passed close by Draper's Meadow.

By 1755, Shawnees had allied tenuously with the French in the
imperial contest for North America, and antagonisms against the
Cherokees were replaced by resentment of intrusive English colonists. In the colonial Pennsylvania and New York backcountries,
conflict had erupted already, but isolated in their corner of the Virginia frontier, the Ingleses and Drapers had no news of the ominous developments. In early July, Shawnees traveled along Athiamiowee, arriving in Draper's Meadow on the 8th, attacking
homesteads, killing most of the settlers, setting fire to the crops,

and taking captive Mary Ingles, her sons, and her sister-in-law. Thus began a twenty-nine-day journey to lower Shawnee Town. Ingles's mental and physical anguish is unfathomable: unaware of her husband's fate, giving birth on the third evening of the journey, separated from her sons and Betty Draper as the party reached its destination, and being adopted into a nation of people with whom she could only minimally communicate.

As Draper's Meadow burned and Mary Ingles stumbled through the Appalachian forests, to the north in the wilds of western Pennsylvania, Major George Washington and his Virginia militia joined Major General Edward Braddock's British regiments in crossing the Monongahela River to seize Fort Duquesne from the French. On July 9th, as Washington recalled, "We were attacked (very unexpectedly) by about three hundred French and Indians. Our numbers consisted of about thirteen hundred well-armed men, chiefly Regulars, who were immediately struck with such an inconceivable panic that nothing but confusion and disobedience of orders prevailed among them." Within three hours, Braddock lay dying, his troops were in chaos, and the French and Indian War had begun.

Juxtaposed against the historical gravity of Braddock's defeat—significant not only to the history of the backcountry but to the course of world history—the raid and destruction of Draper's Meadow seem rather inconsequential. But to the residents of Draper's Meadow and to thousands of settlers in equally small worlds along the Virginia and Pennsylvania frontiers, the events in western Pennsylvania evidenced contention between two powerful yet remote governments. That struggle could seemingly go on for decades, as indeed it had since the mid-1600s. Indian raids upon white settlements more immediately threatened the westward march of American colonists. If successful, the French and their Native American allies would have made settlement of the British colonial frontiers, including Kentucke, impossible.

The Origins of Kentucke

Native Americans long inhabited the region that one day would be known as Kentucky. For over twelve millennia, prehistoric peoples used the land as a hunting ground. Around 9,000 BC, small groups of Paleoindians tracked wooly mammoths and mastodons through the frigid climate zone. Over the next two thousand years, the regional climate tempered, making human survival more viable and allowing for a more sedentary society. Between 7,000 and 1,000 BC, native peoples formed larger living groups dependent upon hunting, fishing, and gathering, and gave rise to what has been called the Woodland culture. To stimulate growth of berry-producing shrubs and canebrakes, by which they enticed bison and other game, they burned out underbrush and created expansive barrens where larger mammals could graze. The richness of barren soils supported lush meadows and thick canebrakes that the descendants of Woodland peoples would discover to be prime hunting grounds. Additionally, salt licks peppered the landscape, attracting bison, deer, and elk. The weight of the herds compacted soils, trampled small trees and underbrush, and enlarged the barrens.

The fecundity of regional soils also supported simple gardening that native peoples used to complement hunting. By 1,000 BC, the reliability of food production—both farming and hunting—allowed for more permanent villages and the development of ceremonial life, including construction of burial mounds and a wide-ranging exchange network that provided ritual goods. Circa AD 1,000, increasing complexities within native life led to cultural divisions and distinctions. Along the floodplains of the Mississippi River, large towns arose among the smaller villages typical of Woodland culture. Characterized by fortifications, large ritual plazas, temples atop large mounds, and village populations that sometimes exceeded one thousand people, this Mississippian culture had extensive trade relations with southeastern and midwestern peoples. Mississippian farmers relied on occasional flooding to replenish soils. Consequently, agricultural production was fruitful, providing a primarily maize-oriented economy. Even as they continued to hunt, Mississippian peoples abandoned ancestral reliance on large mammal hunting and targeted much smaller game—turtles, fish, wild turkeys, and whitetail deer—to supplement corn-based diets.

Simultaneous with the development of Mississippian culture, to the east in the region bisected by the Ohio River, the Fort Ancients arose. Smaller than Mississippian centers but still often exceeding five hundred residents, their towns were vibrant primarily in the summers. The residual ash of Woodland-era burnings had replenished topsoils and allowed continued dependence on large mammal hunting. In winters, as the hunting season began, inhabitants gathered as small, temporary parties that dispersed throughout the region in search of whitetail deer, elk, turkey, bear, and bison. Still, as populations grew, hunting was not enough to support the sustenance needs of Fort Ancient villages. Employing a shifting-field agriculture that required families and their farms to relocate frequently from exhausted lands to more fertile fields, the Fort Ancients developed an agriculture of corn, beans, squash, and sunflowers, supplemented by the gathering of nuts and berries. They also raised tobacco, both for personal consumption and for trade.

Cultural differences between Mississippians and Fort Ancients became increasingly apparent as the fifteenth century ended. The former had created more sedentary societies, while the latter depended on long-distance hunting parties and temporary fields. Year-round permanence stabilized Mississippian society, resulting in centralized political and religious structures. The large Mississippian temples and burial mounds found in Cahokia (Missouri), Aztalan (Wisconsin), and Moundville (Alabama) never manifested among Fort Ancients, who, although nucleated, did not congregate in such critical mass as to warrant elite structures. Instead, Fort Ancients buried their dead within villages, clustering corpses in small mounds and distinct mortuary areas, and ornamenting graves with limestone, ceramics, stone and bone tools, and marine shell beads.

The presence of marine shells reveals that the Fort Ancients enjoyed a rather vast trade network. Indeed, what became known as Athiamiowee was only one of many trail networks connecting the Ohio River valley to disparate peoples and trade. Beginning at the mouth of the Scioto River, a trail ran southward across the hunting lands, through what would be known as Cumberland

Gap, and on to the Holston River valley where it intersected Athi-amiowee. Another trail originated at the juncture of the Ohio and Licking Rivers, leading southward to cultures forming along the Gulf of Mexico. Still other trails sprawled northward to the Great Lakes region. The webs of trails that stretched across the Ohio River valley evidenced the trade and mobility central to Fort Ancient life by the 1500s.

The Fort Ancients and Mississippians also developed within a temperate climate that, since AD 1,000, had averaged a few degrees above the temperatures of preceding centuries. Circa 1400, however, a "Little Ice Age" enveloped Europe and North America. Climatic change most dramatically affected Mississippian populations, undermining the rich agricultural foundation on which their culture was formed and scattering peoples in search of more reliable farming environments. Muskogean-speaking peoples, now identifying themselves as Creeks, Chickasaws, and Choctaws, moved southeastward and formed a confederation around the town of Coosa. Only the Chickasaws maintained lands on the eastern banks of the Mississippi River (once part of the mighty Cahokian realm) as their traditional territories.

By the mid-1500s, Spanish forces began to infiltrate the southeast. Hernando de Soto landed in Florida in 1539, and with troops numbering over six hundred, he wandered northward and westward on an expedition headed for Spanish Mexico. His route apparently took him as far north as a series of concentrated Indian populations in the southern Appalachian mountains, where the Spanish demanded food, information, and even women from the Muskogean peoples who resided in Chiaha, Coste, and other confederation villages. By the fall of 1540, the expedition reached Coosa, where de Soto quickly established control by kidnapping the chief. After a month of tense relations, the Spanish moved on toward the Mississippi River, along the banks of which de Soto died in 1542.

Twenty-five years after his countryman's death, Juan Pardo's expeditionary force arrived in the region. Yet, again, the Spanish had neither the stamina nor the military abilities to reach Mexico. Near the Little Tennessee River, they met an angry Indian force that threatened attack unless Pardo retreated. The

Spanish returned to Chiaha, where they constructed a small fort that remained manned until the larger contingent had safely escaped to the Carolina coast.

As impotent as the Pardo and de Soto expeditions appeared to the Spanish Crown, they were most effective in alarming native cultures. The Creeks, Choctaws, and Chickasaws worked to fortify their respective nations and carve out distinct territories for themselves. The Creeks created a confederacy in the southernmost foothills of the Appalachians, absorbing lesser Muskogean-speaking nations like the Alabamas, Yuchis, and Natchez. The Choctaws moved southward along the Gulf Coast. And the Chickasaws stayed to the west, along the Mississippi and Tennessee Rivers.

To the northeast, the Cherokees emerged as a distinctive national group as well. Having migrated southward after a defeat at the hands of the Iroquois and Lenni Lenapes, the Cherokees had been an identifiable cultural group for a considerable time and laid claim to the region as their ancestral homeland. By 1540, when de Soto's expedition marched through their lands, the Cherokees were a settled, agricultural people living in approximately two hundred large villages.

By the time Charles II bestowed the Carolina colony upon seven proprietors in the 1670s, British colonial traders had found their way into the Appalachians and the Cherokee villages. They offered iron pots, blankets, beads, guns, and other goods that Cherokees had never enjoyed, and they knew how to manipulate the emerging trade relationship. In 1673, they inspired the Cherokees to raid Spanish settlements in Florida that had provided alternative trade for southeastern Indians. Yet the British also armed other Indian peoples, destabilizing the region and threatening Cherokee security. The Cherokees warred against several coastal tribes of the Carolinas that had strong trade ties to the British. But Cherokee security could be secured more easily by fortifying villages and guaranteeing a reliable supply of guns. Hence, in 1684, the Cherokees agreed to supply South Carolina authorities with deerskins and Indian slaves in exchange for manufactured European goods. With ready access to the hunting lands on the western side of the Appalachians and the British colonials eager to profit from this trade, the Cherokees were situated to become a powerful military and trade nation. As warriors became deer hunters, the entire perspective of Cherokee life shifted from people who followed their tribal priests and the wisdom of their ancestors to a people who followed their trade allies and the pursuit of profit making.

The Catawbas were also coalescing as a national group. Theories abound as to their origins, but by the sixteenth century, the Catawbas had migrated into the eastern foothills of the southern Appalachians. As Siouan-speaking people, they had little in common with various Algonquians to the east or with the Cherokees to the west. Pardo's expedition of 1567 encountered the Iswa, a Catawba tribe, but little is known about them until Virginia traders established contact in the 1650s. Cultural differences and the emerging competition over trade with British colonials made the Cherokees and Catawbas natural enemies.

While the Little Ice Age decimated Mississippian culture and gave rise to new patterns and identities among southeastern Indians, its impact on Fort Ancient culture was quite different. Because the Fort Ancients had not adopted agriculture as the primary food source, they were less affected immediately by climatic change. Fort Ancient culture, then, did not disappear from history: shifting-field agriculture and long-distance hunting that had once dominated the Ohio River valley remained as prominent characteristics of what became Shawnee culture.

Shawnees enjoyed a strong national identity, but with summer villages located along waterways north of the Ohio River and winter hunting camps constantly relocating throughout the hunting lands to the south, the Shawnees did not invest much effort in developing central political organizations. Unlike the Creeks, they offered no confederation to surrounding Indians, and unlike the Cherokees, they did not function as a singular nation. The Shawnees comprised five divisions, each acting as an almost autonomous unit. Division leaders and even village chiefs were selected for character and achievement, and most held those positions for life. Their primary responsibility was to assure order by resolving disputes, allying with other villages and divisions, and negotiating intra- and international trade.

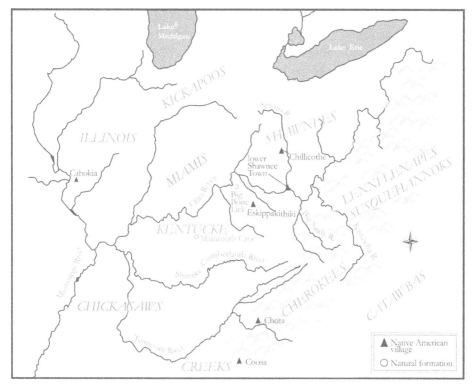

Map I.I. The Hunting Ground. Drawn by Sherry Hardin.

The Shawnees also enjoyed good relations with other Indians in the Ohio River valley. They shared an oral tradition with the Kickapoos who, living in the southern Great Lakes region, had anointed their neighbors "Shawnee," meaning "southerner." To the east lived the Lenni Lenapes, whom the Shawnees considered the ancestors of all Algonquian-speaking peoples. To the west were the Miamis, another Algonquian-speaking people with whom the Shawnees often allied militarily.

Villages, both Shawnee and those of other regional peoples, lined the Ohio River and its tributaries by the seventeenth century. Each typically contained a central plaza surrounded by burial and residential sites. In the winter months, kin groups from the villages set out on winter hunts, not returning until early spring when it was time to plant. As soils and resources were depleted over a generation, populations often uprooted their homes and families to reconstruct their villages on new grounds.

Thus, as the seventeenth century opened, Kentucke, a territory that the Fort Ancients had cultivated as hunting lands and that a multitude of Indian nations surrounded, was largely unoccupied. The Shawnees and the Cherokees were most active in the region: the former temporarily relocating most of their people and material goods into its hunting grounds each winter; the latter using the Great Warriors Path and other trails through the Appalachians to access the region for the Carolina deerskin trade. So too did the Miamis and Lenni Lenapes hunt in Kentucke, as did the Chickasaws, who entered in the western end of the region, along the Cumberland River. Still, while the region was only lightly inhabited, and that being primarily in winter months, the remnants of its Indian heritage remained: Mississippian mounds in its western and southern reaches; shelters in the mountains; less impressive mounds from the Woodland and Fort Ancient eras across the central and northern parts of the region; barrens and canebrakes created by intensive burning; and evidence of temporary hunting camps scattered throughout.

Exodus

And so it might have remained for some time had it not been for three events that brought dramatic change to the world the Indians had made: an onslaught of European diseases, the arrival of European colonists, and the growing hegemony of the Iroquois. While disease certainly did not singularly lead to the demise of aboriginal cultures, it did force decimated populations to seek out more stable villages, nations, and alliances. Indeed, the eagerness with which many southern Indians joined the Creek confederacy suggests their need to consolidate in order to survive. The Spanish introduced diseases among the southeastern Indians in the mid-1500s; the French spread bio-organisms into the Great Lakes region and Ohio River valley in the early 1600s; and English colonists brought more into the mid-Atlantic region in the mid-1600s. Many ethnographers estimate that epidemics sparked by Spanish contact alone killed 75 percent of the southeastern Indian population. Those who lived on the periphery of Kentucke's hunting lands endured their share of that holocaust, although those to the south suffered substantially more loss: the Creeks may have declined by as much as 90 percent, while the Shawnees lost approximately 40 percent of their population. These larger, more stable, and sedentary nations maintained regional dominance by absorbing refugees from decimated neighboring nations.

Foreign populations in North America were also on the rise. Arriving Europeans—the French along the St. Lawrence River, the Dutch in the Hudson River valley, the Spanish along the Gulf Coast, and the English in New England, the Delaware River valley, Virginia, and the Carolinas—not only contributed to the spread of disease but disseminated European material goods among their new neighbors. The extensive network of trails that had facilitated Indian-Indian trade over the previous millennia opened the way for Europeans to infiltrate Indian villages. Iron kettles and pots, pewter plates, teacups, glass mirrors, flannel breeches, silk handkerchiefs, candlesticks, guns, eyeglasses, and alcohol circulated into and around Indian villages, and then on to other native peoples as part of the pan-Indian trade culture. In return for their fine goods, European traders expected middleman status in the fur and deerskin trades. Indian hunters consequently depleted local deer and beaver populations, spurred on by merchant-traders who settled in Indian villages and set up shop.

Colonials' desire to profit off the western wilds incidentally brought the first Virginians to the edge of Kentucke. As commander of the trading post at Fort Henry, Abraham Wood was intrigued by the web of Indian trails that stretched into the Blue Ridge and Appalachian Mountains. In 1654, he explored and named the New River in western Virginia. Seventeen years later, he financed Thomas Batts and Robert Fallam's expedition farther west into the Blue Ridge Mountains and along the Tug Fork, a tributary of the Big Sandy. The two men marked trees along the Tug Fork, laying claim to the region for King James II, Governor William Berkeley of Virginia, Wood, and themselves.

Wood had invested in western lands before, but his purpose in sending Batts and Fallam westward was not land acquisition.

Instead, it was the fur trade for which he lusted. The Cherokees regulated the trade on the eastern side of the Appalachians,
providing their South Carolina trade partners with beaver furs
and deerskins from the hunting lands of Kentucke. Finding it
difficult to establish direct trade relations with the Cherokees,
the Virginians had negotiated with the Occoneechi Indians to
serve as middlemen in the fur economy. A small nation of Siouan
speakers who lived along the Roanoke River, the Occoneechis
served as a buffer between the Cherokees and the enlarging Iroquois empire to the north, and between the Cherokees and the
growing British populations of Virginia. Because of their relative isolation, the Occoneechis also provided safe haven for other
nations uprooted by the tremendous disruptions of seventeenth-
century disease and violence. By the 1670s, dislocated Saponis
and Tutelos had moved into the region; and by 1676, the Cones-
togas arrived from Pennsylvania, fleeing the Five Nations of the
Iroquois.

In order to circumvent the Occoneechis, Wood proposed establishing direct relations with the Cherokees and, in 1673, hired
James Needham and an indentured servant, Gabriel Arthur, to
find the most direct routes into the Overhill Towns. With an Occoneechi as their guide, the men traveled across the southern Appalachians, eventually arriving in a village of the Tomahitans,
a band of the Cherokees who had extensive trade connections to
Carolina merchants in Charles Town. Upon securing an agreement with the Tomahitan Cherokees, the Virginians started back
toward Fort Henry. Possibly aware of the adverse consequences
posed by the agreement, however, the Occoneechi guide turned
on the men, killing Needham. Arthur fled to the Tomahitans,
who adopted him into the village. Over the following months, he
accompanied Tomahitan Cherokees on war journeys, one campaign of which traveled northward along the Big Sandy River to
attack the lower Shawnee Town at the mouth of the Scioto River.
For a year, Arthur survived Indian wars and another attempt on
his life by the Occoneechis. In the summer of 1674, he finally returned to Fort Henry, probably the first Virginian to have wandered Kentucke.

The Cherokees' attack on lower Shawnee Town was most likely among the last of the seventeenth century. In the 1670s, the Shawnees, weakened by recent wars with the Eries and Neutrals to the north and the Cherokees to the south, were forced out of the Ohio River valley by the Iroquois. By 1656, the Iroquois had conquered and assimilated most of their Iroquoian-speaking neighbors, and were eyeing the trans-Appalachian hunting lands, which, according to Wyandot oral tradition, were called "Kentucke," meaning "land of tomorrow." The Iroquois certainly expected it to become their future territory. Even as they remained at war with the Susquehannocks in central Pennsylvania, they turned many of their resources toward clearing Algonquin-speaking tribes from the Ohio River valley and lower Great Lakes region. The Miamis, Kickapoos, and other midwestern Indians fled to the west of Lake Michigan. The Shawnees, however, allied with the Susquehannocks and held firm in the Ohio River valley. In 1658, the western Iroquois (Senecas, Cayugas, and Onondagas) escalated war, forcing the Susquehannocks to concentrate on defending their homelands in the eastern foothills of the Allegheny Mountains, and the Shawnees quickly lost what little security they had gained from the alliance. Three years later, smallpox ravaged the Susquehannocks, and the epidemic soon spread to neighboring Lenni Lenapes. By the mid-1660s, incapable of staving off Iroquois forces on their own and unable to call upon their allies to help, the Shawnees began to abandon the Ohio River valley in search of security.

Probably in a tactical effort to ensure long-term survival of the nation, but also indicative of the splintered political organization that characterized their society, the Shawnees split into four distinct refugee groups. The first, comprising those from Chillicothe and Kispoki, moved southward into an extensive basin of a river that became known as the Shawnee River, just west of the Cherokees. Although relations had not been friendly between them, the Shawnees and Cherokees found a common enemy in the Iroquois, who were beginning to intrude on Cherokee lands and trade as well. Additionally, Shawnee settlement provided the Cherokees a buffer against another traditional enemy—the Chickasaws to the west. When the French began to explore trans-Appalachia in the 1670s, expecting to find Shawnees along the Ohio River, they were surprised and a bit confused to instead meet them in the Shawnee River valley.

Another group, the Hathawekela Shawnees, crossed through Cherokee lands and settled along the upper Savannah River. Again, the Cherokees permitted this buffer settlement between themselves and a traditional adversary, the Catawbas. In fact, Cherokee actions throughout the 1660s evidenced a determination to reduce threats from the south and west as they faced the powerful Iroquois. In 1674, British traders encountered these Shawnees, whom they called the Savannahs. Still, the Hathawekela Shawnees faced trying circumstances in the southern Appalachians. Animosities with the Catawbas grew into outright war, one that would rage for nearly a century. Because the Iroquois were determined to either control or eliminate the Shawnees, the Savannahs also faced regular raids by Senecas who traveled southward along Athiamiowee. Ironically, the Shawnees' Catawba enemies proved their salvation. Indiscriminate in attacks on southern tribes, Senecas who were determined to wage war on Savannahs often also engaged Catawbas, who, better situated than the Savannahs to strike back, routinely chased the Senecas northward into the Pennsylvania backcountry.

A third group of Shawnees retreated westward into the Illinois country. By 1683, these Chaskp Shawnees numbered nearly three thousand, living on the western reaches of the Ohio River. The Iroquois were not satisfied, and two years later, Senecas attacked the Miamis who had allowed the Chaskp to relocate into the region. The Shawnees and Illinois joined in defending the neighboring Miamis, and with the Senecas distracted by a 1687 assault by Jacques-Rene de Brisay, the Marquis de Denonville and governor of New France, the Iroquoian offensive died. Still, the threat of the Five Nations worried the Miamis and Illinois, and by 1689, tensions were high between the Shawnees and their protectors. The Chaskp Shawnees abandoned the Illinois country, joining their kin from Chillicothe and Kispoki in the Shawnee River valley.

THE INDIANS' FRONTIERS 15

In the meantime, the Iroquois war against the Susquehannocks was drawing to a close by 1675. The fourth Shawnee refugee group traveled eastward in the aftermath of the collapse of Susquehannock society, allying with the Lenni Lenapes and settling at the confluence of Piqua Creek and the Susquehanna River in southern Pennsylvania. While the Iroquois allowed the Piqua settlement as part of their peace with the Susquehannocks, they also required the Lenni Lenapes to pay annual tribute beginning in 1677, making them participants in the Covenant Chain, an unequal confederation in which only the Iroquois exerted power and voice. The Iroquois needed these clients, not only for tribute but as warriors in their longstanding struggle against the Hurons of the upper Great Lakes region. The Lenni Lenapes, Piqua Shawnees, and dozens of other smaller nations living along the upper Susquehanna crowded onto what amounted to a reservation under the control of the Iroquois.

By the turn of the eighteenth century, then, the Shawnees had largely abandoned Kentucke and the Ohio River valley. Only a few hunting camps, most notably the one at Eskippakithiki in north central Kentucke, survived as seasonal reminders that the Shawnees once had occupied and dominated the seventeenth-century Ohio River valley. While permanent and long-term settlement at Eskippakithiki before the 1730s is not supported by archaeological evidence, the significance of the village as a regular temporary village is unavoidable. Even as they abandoned the homeland of the Ohio River valley, Shawnees did not forget the abundant hunting lands of the region and returned occasionally to the camps.

While the splintering of the Shawnees weakened their cultural unity, it expanded their commercial relations. Those who settled along the Savannah River became entrenched in the Carolina trade networks centered in Charles Town and extending through the Cherokee and Creek nations. But English traders unscrupulously enslaved Indians, gouged prices, trapped Indians in debt, and watered down the rum. These activities so outraged the Yamasee Indians of South Carolina that, by 1715, resentment against Carolina traders and encroaching colonial settlements ignited

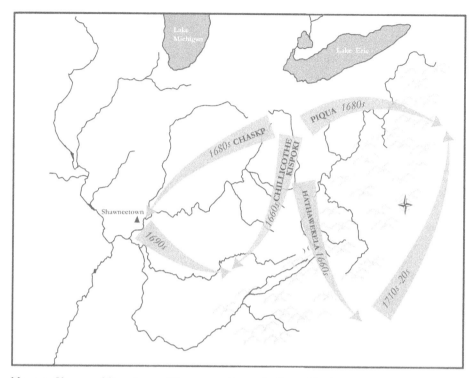

Map 1.2. Shawnee Migrations, 1660s–1720s. Drawn by Sherry Hardin.

outright rebellion. The Yamasees approached other Indians as allies, including the Cherokees and the Savannah Shawnees. But only the Shawnees joined in attacking outlying South Carolina settlements and instilling such fear among the colonists that it would be a decade before English settlement would again move westward. Enchanted by colonial promises of weapons and other goods, the Cherokees rejected Yamasee proposals and instead joined with the Carolinians, turning the tide of war. The Yamasees were pushed out of Carolina and forced westward, where prolonged war against the Creeks nearly annihilated them. On the losing side of the struggle, the Savannah Shawnees fled northward to join their kin in the Pennsylvania backcountry.

By the mid-1710s, other Shawnees discovered as well that they had outlived their welcomes. In the Shawnee River basin, the Cherokees had tolerated Shawnee settlement as a buffer against the Chickasaws, but the Shawnees betrayed the Cherokees, raiding a Cherokee village in 1692 while its warriors were absent on a winter hunt, and taking captives to sell as slaves to the English. Both the Shawnees and Cherokees still had common enemies in the Iroquois and Chickasaws, but the raid undermined loyalty between the two nations. Additionally, as Carolina merchants demanded more furs, the Cherokees looked to the abundant Shawnee River basin. Joining with their enemies the Chickasaws, who were being pushed as well by French traders in New Orleans to acquire more furs, the Cherokees turned on the Shawnees. In 1715, under the pretext of the Yamasee War, they forced the Shawnees to flee the Shawnee River basin for Pennsylvania as well.

Look Back toward Kentucke

The Iroquois became increasingly anxious with each wave of Shawnees that moved into their empire. When one Shawnee party received a warm welcome from New York's colonial council, it infuriated Iroquois leaders, who interpreted the negotiations as a threat to their hegemony. The Iroquois "do not mind that they come here," recalled Albany mayor Peter Schuyler about their reaction to the Shawnees' reception, "but for that they first want to get the whole house in order."

That would have been difficult. By the early eighteenth century, the Iroquois were losing control over the Covenant Chain and the peoples of the Susquehanna River valley. Colonial Pennsylvania administrators became more assertive in gathering and distributing land to settlers. The Indians of the Pennsylvania backcountry also exerted a bit of autonomy as well. The Iroquois favored English trade, but the Shawnees of Piqua were more attached to French trader Martin Chartier. An apparent deserter from LaSalle's 1680 expedition along the Illinois River, Chartier had established a trading post among the Shawnees when they were still in the Ohio River valley, married a Shawnee wife by the end of the decade, and enjoyed the protection of his Shawnee customers. He joined the Shawnees as they moved eastward, eventually setting up shops at Conestoga and Dekumeagah. When he died in 1718, his son, Peter, inherited the business. While the elder Chartier had avoided trade problems with the British, the younger was less successful. When confronted by Pennsylvanian authorities over unpaid debt, Peter lost a trading post and a three-hundred-acre tract that he had acquired only months earlier. As surveyors arrived in the region, Shawnees complained, to no avail. Instead, Chartier was evicted. He and many Shawnees retreated westward, into the upper Susquehanna River valley of western Pennsylvania.

Yet, by 1726, Shawnee anger toward the Pennsylvanians was not great enough to join the Iroquois in a full war against the English. They and their Lenni Lenape allies rejected Iroquois demands upon the Covenant Chain to aid in a proposed attack on the colonials, inspiring the Six Nations (the Tuscaroras had joined in 1722) to respond: "Since you have not hearkened to us not regarded what we have said, now we will put petticoats on you, and look upon you as women for the future, and not as men." Categorizing the Shawnees as women was meant not only to challenge their notions of manhood but also to reassert Iroquois authority over them. The Iroquois continued, "You Shawnese, look back toward Ohio, the place from whence you came, and return thitherward; for now we shall take pity on the English, and let them have all this land." Why the Six Nations suddenly chose to repopulate the Ohio valley with the very peoples who had been so troublesome over the past half-century may seem enigmatic. But the Iroquois had new plans: the Shawnees would resettle west of the Appalachians, creating a series of villages that would provide supplies and repose to Six Nations warring parties en route to the West.

Much of the reason for renewed Iroquois interest in the Ohio River valley was a resurgence of French influence in the region. Until the 1720s, Pennsylvania merchants had monopolized the Indian trade in western Pennsylvania and the upper Ohio River basin, with the blessing of the Iroquois, who had enjoyed substantial recognition and authority from the colonials in return. While Shawnee anger was not great enough to warrant war against the English in Pennsylvania, it was sufficient motivation to look elsewhere for European goods and relations. In 1728, Canadian officials invited Shawnees to Montréal in an effort to reverse French trading fortunes. French diplomats traveled the upper Ohio valley and met with Shawnees, promising greater and more profitable trade. While the Shawnees did not fully accept French offers, many did begin trading at Detroit even as they maintained a vibrant trade with the Pennsylvanians.

With the Six Nations eager to extend the influence of their empire, the "land of tomorrow" became the land of today for the Iroquois. By 1744, as they negotiated with colonial Virginians and Pennsylvanians at Lancaster, the Iroquois were so certain in their hegemony that Chief Tachanoontia boasted that "all the world knows we conquered the several nations living on the Susquehannah, Cohongowntown (Potomac), and on the back of the great mountains in Virginia . . . as to what lies beyond the mountains, we conquered the nations residing there, and that land, if the Virginians ever get a good right to it, it must be by us." But the Iroquois did not realize that, despite their understanding of the Treaty of Lancaster as one that recognized their national authority, they had signed a deed that granted the British king "all the lands within the said colony as it is now or hereafter may be peopled and bounded by his said Majesty." As the colonials interpreted it, the Iroquois gave away the West.

Even as negotiators met at Lancaster, the Shawnees busily made arrangements to move westward. In 1743, they had signed a treaty with the French to migrate into the Wabash River region. In fact, English negotiators at Lancaster were quite concerned that only one Shawnee participated in their negotiations, suspecting that the Shawnees were plotting something else. So, the Ohio River valley became a frontier for the Shawnees, Lenni Lenapes, and other tributaries of the Covenant Chain relocating westward.

It was not only the directives of the Iroquois or the enticement of the French that drew them out of Pennsylvania; within months after the Treaty of Lancaster, malaria raged among populations along the Susquehanna River. People took flight, looking westward for new homelands away from European settlers and their diseases. The Mingos and Piqua Shawnees were among the first to leave, heading into western Pennsylvania, where the Chartier party and other Shawnees had relocated along the Allegheny and Monongahela Rivers over the previous twenty years. By the late 1740s, Lenni Lenapes joined the Shawnee settlements, creating truly multicultural villages. Then, in 1751, French Canadians convinced the Wyandots to invite these diverse peoples into eastern Ohio, initiating a flood of second-generation migrants who, as they moved across the Alleghenies, returned to a region that their parents and grandparents had known as homeland.

The Shawnees' return to the Ohio River valley was not welcomed by all. The territory to which these peoples migrated was a vaguely defined region, bounded by the Kentucke hunting lands to the south, the *pays d'en haut* to the north, and stretching from the Alleghenies to the Illinois country, where the French had established strong trade and diplomatic ties. Despite their invitation to the Shawnees to repopulate the Wabash territory, Canadian officials fretted that most of the Indian migrants settled farther to the east along the Miami and Scioto Rivers, far from French economic and diplomatic reach. They suspiciously watched the rise of these new villages, each a "sort of republic, with a fairly large number of bad characters of various nations." Most certainly, the characters were "bad" because they had already begun to assert some independence. Freed from the constraints of the Covenant Chain and the encroachments of the Pennsylvanians, the creators of these new "republics" had little interest in becoming pawns for the French.

Also, among those "bad" characters were Pennsylvania traders such as George Croghan, a barely literate man of questionable business ethics who nevertheless gained widespread trust from the multicultural villages. He operated a vast commercial empire that extended from his base at the confluence of the Allegheny and Monongahela Rivers in the Pennsylvania mountains through lower Shawnee Town at the mouth of the Scioto River and ultimately Pickawilliny on the Wabash River. The villages formed a southern trade route along the Ohio River. Croghan also designed a northern/Great Lakes route to Sandusky. In 1748, he oversaw construction of the palisades at Pickawilliny, hoping to provide some security for his latest trading post, intended to serve the western Ohio River valley and challenge French trade dominance in the region. Thus, while independent, multicultural, and multinational, the villages that sprang up throughout the region were parts of larger trade networks, either Croghan's, which extended westward from Pennsylvania, or that of the French, which oriented Indians toward Detroit and French Canada.

Of course, none of these villages were really *new*. Few had been fully abandoned over the decades: as early as the 1680s, Shawnees allied with the Miamis had trickled back into the Ohio River valley, inhabiting villages abandoned by the Miamis as the latter nation moved westward. Occasional hunting parties had returned to the region as well, keeping village locations viable. As early as 1736, Shawnees had resettled into and reconstructed Eskippakithiki, and as might be expected, their old enemies the Catawbas attacked it soon thereafter. In the 1740s, a flood of Indian peoples populated that village and others, turning them into permanent towns. In 1745, Peter Chartier's party left the Alleghenies and temporarily stopped in lower Shawnee Town before moving on to Eskippakithiki, by then a reinvigorated settlement that covered over three thousand acres, where Chartier, along with Croghan, established trading posts.

North of the Ohio River, other permanent towns emerged as well. By 1749, lower Shawnee Town was a village of over one hundred houses scattered along bluffs on the north side of the Ohio River, overlooking the floodplains, the fields, and the forty houses situated on the south side of the river. Two years later, over three hundred warriors lived in the village. Pickawilliny arose in 1747 under the leadership of Memeskia, a Twightwee Miami chief who embraced Croghan's trade overtures and quickly transformed the village into the most significant trading post in the region, angering the French. And on the western reaches of the Ohio River, an old Chaskp village known as Shawneetown had at least two hundred warriors and their families by 1750. Dozens of other villages, including Chillicothe, Piqua, Wakatomica, and Maquachake, completed the resettlement of the Ohio country.

The flight westward posed problems, however. The Iroquois and English had never trusted Peter Chartier, who in the early 1740s rediscovered loyalties to the French. His 1745 migration into Kentucke partially resulted from accusations that he had instigated the murder of a Seneca chief and was openly encouraging the Shawnees to revolt against the Six Nations and the En-

glish. Only two years after his arrival at Eskippakithiki, Chartier
faced Iroquois pressure to abandon the village and region. The
threat of hundreds of angry Shawnees following their leader out
of Kentucky panicked colonists and Native Americans alike. Uncertain of what Chartier and his party would do, Carolina trader
John Ellis wrote to the Virginia governor on behalf of the Catawbas among whom he lived, requesting guns to "stand the brunt
of Peter Chartier and his five hundred men, and the other troops
which he expects to assist him." Chartier set his sights elsewhere,
however: the party descended the Tennessee River, unsuccessfully attacked the Chickasaws, then fled northward, where they
populated Shawneetown until 1761.

As the Six Nations demanded, the new villages served as resting places for Iroquois warriors: Senecas were early and almost
permanent residents. But in all of these places, the villages' multicultural natures dominated community life. The Lenni Lenapes
and Mingos were matrilineal; the Shawnees were patrilineal.
Some Shawnees, Miamis, and Wyandots preferred trade with
the French at posts in Vincennes, Miami, and Detroit. Mingos,
Lenni Lenapes, and other Shawnees were attached to the English, particularly Croghan and other Pennsylvania traders who
had moved westward with them. The mixed character of these
villages generated instability, and just as quickly as the Shawnees and their allies repopulated the region and constructed their
villages, differences among village leaders began to unravel the
Indians' frontier.

Impatient with these multicultural republics, the French decided to challenge their economic allegiances to the British. In
1748, the governor general of Canada sent a 230-man military
force under Pierre-Joseph Celeron de Bienville to secure French
claim to the Ohio River valley. The expedition left Fort Niagara
and traveled down the Allegheny and Ohio Rivers into trans-
Appalachia. Along the way, troops buried lead plates inscribed
with France's claim to the region. Many of the Indians they met
were friendly and welcoming, but others were unimpressed and
occasionally hostile, as Celeron de Bienville discovered in Pickawilliny. Twightwee Miamis' enmity angered the French who
had been trying to sway their chief, Memeskia, into abandon-

ing Croghan and the English and embracing French trade. In 1751, French patience waned: they raided the village, killing two Twightwee Miamis and capturing two English traders. Still, Memeskia refused to budge, so in the summer of 1752, Ottawas and Chippewas joined the French in attacking Pickawilliny again, burning the village, killing five Twightwee Miamis, taking six English traders as prisoners, and torturing Memeskia, eventually ripping his heart out and boiling and eating his body in a ritual intended to increase the consumers' power by devouring the flesh of their enemy.

To reinforce this example of French military might, months later the new governor general of Canada, the Marquis de Duquesne, sent more than two thousand French troops southward to carve a road from Lake Erie toward the headwaters of the Ohio River, where they were to construct a fort. The episode exhibited such military force that villages throughout the region began to expel English traders.

The Land Companies

Ironically, even as events turned against an English trade presence in the region, prospects for English settlement were on the horizon. Inspired by the Iroquois' agreement to the Treaty of Lancaster, Virginia officials began awarding transmontane lands to speculators, doling out over 2.5 million acres between 1745 and 1754. To facilitate the surveying and sales of these lands, the British Board of Trade chartered the Ohio Company in 1747. Among its stockholders were Thomas Cresap, Thomas Lee, George Fairfax, and Lawrence Washington. Initially, the company received a grant of 200,000 acres with the promise that upon settling one hundred families in the territory, there would be an additional 300,000 acres. The company commissioned Christopher Gist to explore the Ohio River valley and produce notes on trails, rivers, soil qualities, and the Indian presence. Gist delayed his survey, however, in order to invite Indian leaders to Loggs Town in 1752 for new negotiations with the Virginians.

Shortly after the chartering of the Ohio Company, the Virginia House of Burgesses, resenting the Board of Trade's claim of authority over western lands, chartered the Loyal Company and granted it 800,000 acres. A number of prominent Virginians, including Peter Jefferson, Edmund Randolph, and Joshua Fry, invested in the company and hired Thomas Walker to survey its tracts. A veteran surveyor with some experience in exploring Tennessee's Holston River region, Walker set out on a four-month expedition in 1749 along the Holston and Clinch Rivers before passing through Cave Gap along a branch of an old Indian trace. When he came upon the Shawnee River, he renamed it in honor of the Duke of Cumberland, a popular British military leader; it was a name that would spread beyond the river to the mountains and the gap through which the party traveled.

While it has been popular to identify Walker as the first white man in Kentucke, or more appropriately the first white to realize he was in a new territory, Walker himself knew otherwise. As the party traveled through the mountains northwest of the gap, he found "Laurel Trees marked with Crosses, others Blazed and several Figures on them. . . . A Beech stands on the left hand, on which I cut my name." In a ritual common among white pioneers as they explored new lands, Walker merely added his name to the list of those who had preceded him.

On the northeastern banks of the Cumberland (previously Shawnee) River, Walker's party built a cabin and planted a field of corn and some peach trees, the traditional method by which English settlers laid claim to land. Three men remained behind as Walker and two others explored the area for over a week without finding good soils or promising opportunities. The party returned to Virginia, pessimistic in its report to the Loyal Company about the lands of Kentucke, and without having met any Indians.

In early autumn 1751, Gist set out on his expedition for the Ohio Company, traveling down the Ohio River and recording his observations throughout a seven-month trip. He first visited lower Shawnee Town. Several days after he left the village, Gist came upon Robert Smith, a trader who supplied the surveyor with two mastodon teeth found at the Big Bone Lick, artifacts that Gist would subsequently hand over to the Ohio Company. By March 18th, Gist had crossed the Ohio River and journeyed along a well-beaten buffalo trace across northern Kentucke toward the center of what would become the Bluegrass region, passing by the lower Blue Licks and finally arriving at the Kentucky River. He then turned southeastward, incidentally traced part of Walker's route, and crossed through Pound Gap at Pine Mountain to return home. Gist's explorations around and into Kentucke were far more extensive than Walker's, and he traveled through the heart of the region's choicest lands. But like Walker, Gist was unenthusiastic about investment and settlement of trans-Appalachia. He reported to the Ohio Company that the region's inhabitants, particularly the increasing number of Indians allying with the French, would prove unreceptive to Virginian encroachments on the hunting grounds. Accordingly, the Ohio Company turned its attentions to the Kanawha River region on the eastern slopes of the Appalachians, eventually establishing one small settlement of eleven families at Redstone Old Fort.

Both men went back to their homes—Walker to Albemarle County, Virginia, and Gist to Yadkin County, North Carolina—with tales of abundant game in Kentucke. But beyond inspiring imaginations, neither expedition proved successful. Disappointed by the unenthusiastic reports, Virginia governor Robert Dinwiddie decided at the least to secure the lands of the Kanawha and upper Ohio Rivers. He appointed James Patton, Joshua Fry, and Lunsford Lomax to meet with Mingos, Lenni Lenapes, and Shawnees from the Ohio country to ratify the agreement made by the Six Nations in 1744. There was some urgency in arranging the negotiations. A year prior, Croghan had met with many of the same people and with Iroquois representatives as well to bind them to Pennsylvania's interests. During that meeting, a French agent unsuccessfully tried to intervene, demanding that the Indians turn the English traders away. Yet, the Virginians were not much more effective. When they called for negotiations in 1752, the Iroquois refused to attend, noting their allegiance to Pennsylvania and New York. The Shawnees, Lenni Lenapes, and Mingos who arrived in Loggs Town received £1,000 of goods meant to prime them for the news that the Virginians planned to make "Settlements of British Subjects on the Southern or Eastern parts of the River Ohio called otherwise Allegany." The Indians agreed to the arrangement but insisted that they were not handing over lands west of the mountains.

While the Indians of the Ohio River valley struggled with pressures from the Virginians and Pennsylvanians, the Cherokees had their own problems. In the months between Croghan's 1751 negotiations and the Virginians' 1752 meeting, a council of Wyandots, Lenni Lenapes, Shawnees, and Mingos hosted a contingent of nearly seventy Cherokees at the lower Shawnee Town. The guests requested Six Nations' permission to hunt in Kentucke for the season. But the Cherokees also wished to repair relations with the Wyandots, who had been raiding Cherokee and Catawba villages via Athiamiowee. Pressured by encroaching Carolina settlers and officials angered by an attack on several traders, the Cherokees hoped to make allies rather than enemies. At another lower Shawnee Town council a year later, they appeared desperate, proclaiming that "fourteen hundred of our men will be here in two months, to live amongst you, for we can live no longer in our own country, for the English are angry and refuse to supply us with powder and lead, because they say we kill their Traders."

Yet the Cherokees did not move into the Ohio River valley. Much of the reason was that Cherokee tensions with French-allied Indians were intensifying. The French demanded that their Indian allies undermine the alliances between other Native American nations and the British. Given their military might and their location adjacent to the powerful Carolina traders, the Cherokees became a prime target. In late January 1753, a party of over seventy Conewagos and Ottawas traveled southward to attack the Cherokees and Catawbas. South of Eskippakithiki, they collided with a caravan of Pennsylvania traders. When they attempted to take captive a Cherokee servant, the chance meeting erupted into battle. The Conewagos and Ottawas defeated their opponents, and while they had not reached the Overhill Towns, they started their return trip with six captured English traders and a Cherokee servant, who they believed would satisfy the French.

As the party reached Eskippakithiki on its return, it met John Findley, a Pennsylvania trader who had first explored Kentucke only a year previously. He had traveled the Ohio River to its falls and, upon finding no Indians, had wandered toward the Big Bone

Lick, where a small Shawnee hunting party met him and encouraged him to move farther east into Eskippakithiki. There he constructed a small station and store. When the northern Indians came upon him in early 1753, Findley tried to intervene on behalf of the captives. In retaliation, the Conewagos and Ottawas killed several of his servants, took many of his supplies, and burned the village. The displaced inhabitants probably joined Shawnee towns north of the Ohio River. Findley and a servant fled into the forests and eventually back to Pennsylvania.

The episode only compounded Virginian governor Robert Dinwiddie's anger over French influence in the Ohio valley. The French had built Fort Presque Isle near Lake Erie and Fort LeBoeuf in a part of the country claimed by Virginia's Ohio Company. Dinwiddie sent twenty-one-year-old George Washington and very small contingent to warn the French, but of course, the words of a young militiaman did little to dissuade them. The governor then plotted to preempt the French by constructing a fort at the confluence of the Allegheny and Monongahela Rivers. Offering western lands as payment to men willing to serve in the project, the governor appointed William Trent to oversee construction.

The stockade was still incomplete in April 1754 when nearly five hundred French troops arrived to construct a fort of their own, forcing Trent to flee back to Virginia. They demolished the colonial fort and built Fort Duquesne. As he and his men fled western Pennsylvania, Trent came upon a military force of 150 Virginians under George Washington headed to the area to reinforce his work. Although aware of the presence of the French, Washington decided to continue. A French force marched out to meet him but was surprised in an early morning attack by the Virginians, who killed the French commander and, anticipating retaliation, quickly built Fort Necessity. On July 3, 1754, the French attacked the camp, easily defeating the colonial troops, and agreeing to allow Washington and his men safe passage to Virginia in return for two British officers left behind as captives. Within a year, what had begun as a clash between Virginians and the French escalated into a trans-Atlantic war. In their first major offensive of the French and Indian War, the British sent Major General Edward Braddock and a large British force against

Fort Duquesne, but in April 1755, the French surprised the British, killing Braddock and capturing or killing nearly two-thirds of the force. One of the men who fought on the British side was the trader John Findley, who had lost his servants and trading post to the French-backed raid on Eskippakithiki.

As Braddock fell in Pennsylvania, Mary Draper Ingles wandered the trans-Appalachian forests with her captors. They were people with whom she was familiar: Shawnee warriors en route to terrorize the Catawbas had frequented the Ingles cabin in Draper's Meadow. Few settlers in the Virginia backcountry anticipated that their former friends, now in alliance with the French, would lay siege to their settlement. By mid-July 1755, however, Ingles was on her way to lower Shawnee Town, and Draper's Meadow lay in ruin.

Upon her arrival in the Indian village, Ingles faced a world much different from her own. Still, the presence of two French traders provided her an opportunity. In exchange for supplies for her baby, Ingles began sewing shirts from cloth provided by the traders, who then sold the clothing to Indians. The shirts became symbols of prestige and elevated Ingles's status, leading Shawnee chief Captain Wildcat to adopt her as a wife. But Ingles rebuffed his advances, angering Wildcat, who consequently adopted her two sons to raise as his own in his home village of Kispoki.

As part of their annual preparation for the winter hunts, the Shawnees packed many of their belongings and began to travel to the Kentucke hunting camps. Whether in a rock shelter or a narrow stream valley, each camp became home for about thirty members of an extended kin group. Corn accompanied the Shawnees, but the primary purpose of the journey was to find more food, either through gathering or through the hunt. In order to preserve venison and bison meat, the group distilled waters from local salt licks in order to use the salt. It was on one of these missions to the Big Bone Lick that Draper decided to escape and convinced an older German woman, probably captured in western Pennsylvania, to join her. Under the guise of gathering food, the two slipped into the Kentucke wilderness, leaving Ingles's newborn behind. It may seem a particularly harsh decision on the part of a mother, but the choice between leaving the child in a nurturing community and carrying the child along a rugged, dangerous journey through the wilds was really no choice at all.

On the sixth day, the women arrived back at the lower Shawnee Town. In mid-1753, a flood had destroyed that part of the village on the northern banks of the Ohio River, and its residents had recreated their village on the Kentucke side of the river. But the village was not active when Ingles returned for the last time; it had been largely abandoned for fall excursions. The two women hid in a cabin until daybreak, taking a horse and corn to survive the journey ahead. Still, they struggled for nearly two months; the corn did not last, and in autumn, while nuts were not hard to come by, more substantial food was scarce. Increasingly, the German woman became more desperate and, in one moment of madness, attempted to kill her companion. Somewhere near the headwaters of the Kanawha River, Ingles abandoned the old woman and headed southward, probably along an Indian trace through the Appalachians, where Adam Harman and his sons, old friends of the Draper family, found her. In time, they found the German woman as well.

Ingles's ordeal eventually became part of backcountry folklore, but in 1755, colonists interpreted it as another example of the increasing Indian threat. With settlers like the Drapers and Ingleses demanding protection, and with a promise from the Cherokees that they would aid Virginia in a campaign against the Shawnees, Governor Dinwiddie decided to form the Sandy Creek expedition under the leadership of Major Andrew Lewis. Nearly 250 men joined the force, but considering the distance of the journey and the strength of their enemies, settlers along the New River demanded more help. Gist, William Ingles, John Draper, and Matthias Harman successfully recruited over one hundred Cherokees to their cause. For over a year, Cherokees had been harassing French traders and French-allied Indians in the Ohio River region, so their willingness in joining the Virginians was very much in character. Setting out in early 1756, the expedition was to move up the Big Sandy River valley, the route so often traveled by the Shawnees when they moved southward against the Catawbas. The Virginians failed to travel the ridgetop paths so familiar to the Indians, however, and steep hills, torrential

rains, icy rivers, and a disastrous undersupply of food doomed
the mission. Starving soldiers deserted the force, many fleeing
into and dying in the mountainous wilderness. Lewis had little
choice but to turn back, leading what remained of the army in a
chaotic retreat. The Cherokees, disgusted by the utter incompetence of the Virginian effort, rescinded their promise to support
any efforts against the Shawnees and retreated from the war.

The Big Sandy expedition epitomized the colonial effort in the
first few years of conflict. Not until 1758 would the tide turn with
the appointment of William Pitt as British prime minister. He
reallocated resources, renewing British offenses against Québec,
Louisbourg, and specifically Fort Duquesne. The French had re-
assigned forces throughout North America, leaving the Alleghenies poorly defended. When attack was inevitable, the French
commander burned down Fort Duquesne and fled up the Allegheny River. Although fighting continued another four years, the
lynchpin of French control over the Ohio River valley was gone.
Those Indians who had allied with the French suddenly found
themselves forgotten and abandoned.

Even before the French and Indian War ended, the Ohio River
valley and Kentucke were no longer Indian frontiers. While the
Shawnees and their Indian allies continued to inhabit the region, they no longer enjoyed the relative freedom of having it
to themselves. The region had become a military frontier, with
the French exerting great influence through trade and military
might. With the Treaty of Paris in 1763, economic and military
presence merely shifted from one imperial power to another. But
the British did offer protection. In the Treaty of Easton in 1758,
Sir William Johnson, British Indian agent for the northern colonies, acceded to Iroquois requests that trans-Allegheny Pennsylvania be closed to English colonization and remain Indian hunting grounds. Three years later, as commander of British forces at
the newly constructed Fort Pitt, Henry Bouquet extended Johnson's concession to the Maryland and Virginia backcountries as
well. Finally, with Britain's acquisition of France's North American lands in 1763, King George III proclaimed trans-Appalachia
off-limits to settlement.

It was quite a setback for Virginia's land companies. The Ohio Company appealed directly to the crown; the Loyal Company had Virginia's governor intervene on its behalf. But despite their charters, and despite a promise made nearly a decade earlier that Virginia's soldiers would receive compensation for risking their lives to establish the colony's claim to trans-Appalachia, Britain refused to concede settlement rights. Instead, the veterans of the French and Indian War and their neighbors suspiciously, fearfully, and lustfully watched the West, awaiting an opportunity to transform trans-Appalachia into their frontier.

2.

COLONIAL KENTUCKE

In the winter of 1760, Jonathan Swift, a veteran of Braddock's doomed campaign into western Pennsylvania, led a caravan of packhorses and entrepreneurs into the Big Sandy region. They originally set out northwestward from Alexandria, Virginia, to Fort Pitt and then descended the Ohio River to the Kanawha River, crossing into the mountains until they came upon the Big Sandy River. Their destination was several "silver mines" that Swift had identified on a previous excursion. A furnace was constructed, and a company of fifteen investors was assembled. Over the next decade, these men mined in the Kentucke mountains and operated a fleet of ships in the Atlantic Ocean. Whether their treasures came from Appalachian caches or piracy against Spanish ships would be widely debated, but by 1769, when he returned to the Upper Yadkin River valley in North Carolina, Swift was rumored to be a wealthy man, although neither he nor his companions brought much wealth with them as they returned east. The proximity of their operations to a well-traveled branch of the Great Warrior's Path ostensibly forced the miners to hide their stores in pockets throughout the Appalachians.

By 1790, when the company met for the last time to gather silver from its mountain storehouses, only seven of the investors remained. The party assembled at the Great Cave, a mysterious

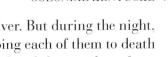

location where they had stored their silver. But during the night, Swift turned on his companions, stabbing each of them to death as they slept. The only thing that prohibited the murderer from taking all of the silver for himself was that he lost his eyesight, possibly in a gouge-and-bite struggle with one of his victims, although legend would have it that Providence had intervened.

Speculation over the Swift mines ran rampant and would continue to spark imaginations for another century. In 1800, local residents hired the Shawnee chief Blue Jacket to lead them to the mines. In the 1760s, Blue Jacket had lived in a Shawnee village that had arisen, probably as a respite for traveling warriors, at the confluence of Big Mud Lick and Little Mud Lick Creeks, tributaries of the Levisa Fork of the Big Sandy. Given his earlier proximity to the enterprises, the Shawnee chief claimed to know the location of the mines, but the party wandered for weeks without success. Blue Jacket blamed his failure on poor eyesight. But the legend did not subside, among either white pioneers or the Shawnees. In 1870, a Shawnee showed up near Little Mud Lick Creek with maps leading to the mines. Again, it was a futile enterprise.

In the 1760s, however, the story of Swift's silver mines was particularly pertinent. It was a morality tale denouncing the avarice of an increasingly materialistic colonial American society. In a decade in which imaginations about the trans-Appalachian West soared, sometimes beyond reason, many people of lesser status had to believe that what Kentucke and America offered could not be monopolized by only a few. Ancient peoples, pristine forests, and silver mines—rumors abounded, most fueled by only a few adventurers, some of whom made it their business to spark interest in the West on behalf of the land companies they represented. And with the Proclamation Line of 1763 in effect, most colonials wholeheartedly embraced the tales since very few were willing to go westward to find the truth for themselves.

Imaginations

Amidst French and British struggles over trade and military dominance in the Ohio River valley in the mid-eighteenth century there was a contest over bones. Nine years before Celeron de Bienville had led his military expedition across the region, another French military force had departed Québec for the southern Mississippi River valley, where the English-allied Chickasaws threatened French authority. Led by Charles Le Moyne, the Baron de Longueuil, an army of nearly 140 French soldiers joined by 320 Abenakis canoed down the Allegheny and Ohio Rivers, taking respite at the Big Bone Lick. Several Abenakis gathered fossils that somehow survived the expedition's journey down the Mississippi River and subsequent defeat to the Chickasaws. By the late 1740s, the relics found their way to Paris, where Count George Buffon, the great French naturalist, placed them on display; and that is where Louis Daubenton, another naturalist who specialized in quadrupeds, found them. Daubenton studied the fossils and presented his findings to the French Royal Academy, concluding that the tusks came from elephants and the molars from hippopotami. He anticipated that further exploration of North America would uncover the mammals living in its marshes and swamps.

The fossils' contributions to the evolution of modern paleontology, however, meant little to traders along the Ohio River valley. Instead, it was the ivory that enticed them. When Christopher Gist surveyed the region in 1751, he met an English trader who proudly claimed to have a five-foot-long tusk that he intended to sell and gave Gist two smaller samples to share with the Ohio Company. Inspired to find some ivory for his own profit, Gist headed toward Big Bone Lick before being turned back by rumors of a large party of French-allied Indians nearby.

George Croghan was more successful at retrieving fossils for profit. He learned of Big Bone Lick in the late 1740s, but increasing international tensions kept him from pursuing the trade until after the Seven Years' War ended. In 1765, he paid Shawnees to gather and deliver bones and tusks that Croghan then sold to interested parties in Philadelphia and London. Within a year, a fine collection had accumulated in the Tower of London's cabinet of curiosities. William Hunter, a fellow in the Royal Academy, speculated that the fossils belonged to a single type of mammal that he labeled the "unknown American," a carnivorous elephantine beast that, despite the desire of philosophers to study it, "as men we cannot but thank heaven that its whole generation is probably extinct!" Botanist Peter Collinson conjectured that similar bones found in Siberia actually had originated in southern Asia and been displaced by the biblical flood; but as to the fossils of Big Bone Lick, "what system, or hypothesis, can with any degree of probability, account for these remains of elephants being found in America, where those creatures are not known ever to have existed?" In Philadelphia, Benjamin Franklin examined the bones and determined that they came from an extinct herbivore. All of this scientific speculation only piqued intellectual curiosity in the western reaches of North America. What sort of place was the trans-Appalachian West, and more importantly, what type of place could it be expected to become?

While London and Philadelphia swirled in enlightened speculation, less contemplative colonists listened to the Indian lore pouring eastward over the mountains. About these great "unknown Americans," the Lenni Lenapes told a story that

> in ancient times a herd of them came to the Big-bone licks, and began an universal destruction of the bears, deer, elks, buffaloes, and other animals which had been created for the use of the Indians: that the Great Man above, looking down and seeing this, was so enraged, that he seized his lightning, descended to the earth, seated himself upon a neighbouring mountain, on a rock, on which his seat and the print of his feet are still to be seen, and hurled his bolts among them till the whole were slaughtered, except the big bull, who, presenting his forehead to the shafts, shook them off as they fell; but at length missing one, it wounded him in the side; whereon, springing round, he bounded over the Ohio, the Wabash, the Illinois, and finally, over the great lakes, where he is living today.

In 1766, a Virginia colonel visiting Big Bone Lick came upon a party of Iroquois and Wyandots heading southward to war against the Chickasaws. The head chief told another story of the bones, one that inverted whites' racial and natural order of things.

> [The Great Spirit] made man; but having formed him white, and very imperfect, and ill-tempered, he placed him on one side of it [the world] where he now inhabits, and from whence he has lately found a passage across the great water, to be a plague for us. As

the Great Spirit was not pleased with this his work, he took of black clay, and made what *you* call a Negro, with a woolly head. This black man was much better than the white man, but still he did not answer the wish of the Great Spirit, that is, he was imperfect; at last, the Great Spirit having procured a piece of pure, fine red clay, formed from it the Red Man, perfectly to his mind; and he was so well pleased with him, that he placed him on this great island, separate from the white and black men, and gave him rules for his conduct, promising happiness in proportion as they shall be observed. He increased exceedingly, and was perfectly happy for ages; but the foolish young people, at length forgetting his rules, became exceedingly ill-tempered and wicked. In consequence of this, the Great Spirit created the great buffalo, the bones of which you now see before us; these made war upon the human species alone, and destroyed all but a few, who repented and promised the Great Spirit to live according to his laws, if he would restrain the devouring enemy; whereupon he sent lightning and thunder, and destroyed the whole race, in this spot, two excepted, a male and female, which he shut up in yonder mountain, ready to let loose again, should occasion require.

In both the Lenni Lenape and Iroquois traditions, the great and terrible beasts remained in the region, hidden from human view but ready to strike when released.

It was only appropriate that Indian lore became entwined with the archaeological mysteries of the New West. Since Thomas Walker's 1750 discovery of Indian mounds at the headwaters of the Cumberland River, rumors had circulated throughout the East as to their origins and the types of peoples who once lived west of the Appalachians and their relationship to the peoples who still lived there. Colonials who had traveled down the Ohio River had seen two of the region's most impressive mounds. Along its eastern bank as the river flowed out of Pennsylvania towered a mound nearly seventy feet in height and three hundred feet in diameter, with a forty-foot-wide moat traversed by a single causeway. A nearby rivulet received the name Grave Creek in recognition of the mound's purpose. Farther downstream, on the northern bank of the river, was a mound nearly forty feet high and similarly surrounded by a moat. The future citizens of Mari-

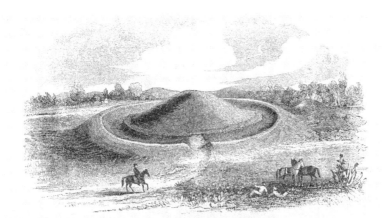

Figure 2.1. Smaller mounds, like this one found in modern Greenup County, peppered the Kentucke landscape and became objects of widespread speculation, first among backcountry Americans in the 1760s and 1770s and later among natural scientists in the early 1800s. From E. G. Squier and E. H. Davis, *Ancient Monuments of the Mississippi Valley* (New York: Bartlett and Welford, 1848), 82.

etta would situate their own town cemetery at its base. The two served as monuments to civilizations long past, but they also raised the curiosities of colonial Americans who measured mound heights and sketched images to be studied in the East. Two generations later, a Transylvania University professor counted 148 mounds in Kentucke alone. In the 1760s and early 1770s, the sheer presence of artificial mounds inspired imaginations.

Just who were the mound builders? A variety of creative hypotheses abounded. Benjamin Franklin theorized that de Soto and his men built the mounds during their wanderings in the 1500s. Another myth situated a Lost Tribe of Israel in the Ohio River valley. Among backcountry colonials, however, two other theories had particular relevance to their lust for trans-Appalachia. The more popular legend came from Lenni Lenape traditions. When their ancestors and those of the Iroquois had migrated eastward originally, ages before the forced migration of the seventeenth century, they collided with a fierce nation called the Allegewis, which claimed the hunting lands as its own by building mounds—for fortifications, for burials, and for temples. The

Allegewis refused to let the migrating nations pass farther. The Iroquois, capable warriors in their own right, pushed ahead, overcoming the Allegewis and moving eastward across the Appalachians. The Lenni Lenapes were weaker, however; they failed to breach the Allegewi resistance and called upon the Iroquois to help them. War followed, culminating in the last stand of the Allegewis at the Falls of the Ohio where, defeated and dramatically weakened, they retreated from the Ohio River valley and from Kentucke.

An even more intriguing and bewildering tale emerged from colonial backcountry tradition. In 1764, Shawnees took captive Maurice Griffiths, a Welsh migrant settled in Virginia's Roanoke River valley. Griffiths lived among them for several years and accompanied winter hunting parties to the trans-Mississippian west. On a trip up the Missouri River, he and his Shawnee companions were captured by white-skinned peoples who spoke Welsh flawlessly and spared the lives of the hunting party only because Griffiths could converse with them. Labeled the Madocs, they told Griffiths that their ancestors had come from a faraway country and had built mounds throughout the Missouri, Mississippi, and Ohio River valleys. The legend continued that those whom Griffiths met were merely the remnants of a great Welsh nation that had been almost exterminated in war against the darker-skinned Indians. Again, the contest between the mythic peoples and their Native American antagonists was fought on the hunting lands of Kentucke, and the climactic great battle occurred at the Falls of the Ohio.

Regardless of which myth was more appreciated, theories about the mound builders had several things in common. They conveniently invented an ancient and powerful civilization (usually ethnically distinct from contemporary Native Americans) that understood mound-building technology. The tales also translated the current Ohio River valley Indians as less-civilized peoples who had challenged more advanced peoples for control of Kentucke. The Falls of the Ohio more than once arose as the central geographical feature in these tales, reinforcing the importance of the river itself to regional identities but also making it an important destination for future settlers—whoever controlled the Falls of the Ohio would reign over the Ohio River valley. Finally, there was an implicit moral to these myths: the trans-Appalachian West had once been "civilized" and could be returned to that state with the elimination of the Shawnees and their allies. When contrasted with Native American tales about the great beasts of Big Bone Lick meant to discourage white settlement in trans-Appalachia, tales about the mound builders encouraged, even demanded, civilization's reclamation of the West.

The Emergence of Daniel Boone

The Indians were not going to be pushed out easily. Less than three months after the signing of the Treaty of Paris in 1763, Ottawa chief Pontiac convinced Mingos, Lenni Lenapes, and Shawnees to join his rebellion against the British, who, having replaced the French as the imperial power in the lower Great Lakes region, aroused Indian resentment by acting arrogantly and refusing to supply free ammunition. The Pennsylvania, Maryland, and Virginia backcountries immediately reverted to a state of terror. For nearly two years, Indian raids resulted in over two thousand colonial deaths and uncounted captures. Finally, after the British army defeated a multinational Indian force at Bushy Run and after Sir William Johnson secured Iroquois promises not to join the rebellion, British colonel Henry Bouquet and 1,150 men set out from Fort Pitt to take control of the Ohio River country. In October 1764, he negotiated with Lenni Lenapes, Shawnees, and Mingos on the banks of the Muskingum River, demanding a return of all captives, including some from the French and Indian War. Low on ammunition and unable to count on support from outside the region, the Indians agreed and turned over more than two hundred captives.

The end of Pontiac's Rebellion did not open the floodgates to trans-Appalachia. Instead, despite British inabilities to enforce the Proclamation Line of 1763, colonists seemed resigned to remaining east of the mountains. Only slowly and in small groups did a handful of backcountry hunters breach the Appalachians. George Croghan returned to the region in 1765. In 1766, James Smith, Joshua Horton, Uriah Stone, William Baker, and a young slave passed through the Cumberland Gap. That same year, five hunters from South Carolina traveled around the Kentucke wilderness, where they met two hunters who had descended the Ohio River into Kentucke: James Harrod and Michael Stoner. In 1767, John Findley revisited Kentucke and, upon returning to the Yadkin River valley of North Carolina, spun tales of the grandeur and abundance of the region. Hunters from Virginia—Casper Mansker, Henry Skaggs, James Knox, and Joseph Drake among them—wandered in and out of Kentucke in 1767 and 1768. On Christmas Day of the latter year, Knox celebrated near Raccoon Springs in the southeastern corner of the region by feasting on the marrow of bison bones.

Then, in 1768, British officials negotiated with Iroquois leaders at Fort Stanwix in New York. In return for a guarantee that their homelands were secure from colonial settlement, the Iroquois surrendered their claim to the lands of the Ohio River valley. Of course, while the Iroquois had declared control over the region for over a century, with the exception of occasional hunting parties, only small groups of Senecas and Mingos had actually occupied the valley, usually at multinational settlements like lower Shawnee Town. Through colonial eyes, however, the Six Nations had again given away the region, albeit without the consent of the Lenni Lenapes and Shawnees. News of the concession spread quickly along the backcountry. In that same year, the Treaty of Hard Labor sent another promising message to backcountry colonials. British Southern Indian superintendent John Stuart worked with Cherokee leaders to demarcate the eastern boundary of Cherokee territory, drawing a line from the Holston River northeastward to the Kanawha River and on to the Ohio. It was a significant concession by the Cherokees toward the ever-growing colonial populations pushing against the Appalachians, and it confirmed that Indian territorial boundaries were negotiable.

Almost immediately, longer and more extended excursions into Kentucke took place. In the spring of 1769, four Orange County, Virginia, hunters left for a long hunt into Kentucke and Arkansas. That same year, Benjamin Cleveland and four companions set out from the Yadkin country. Soon after they passed through the Cumberland Gap, a party of Cherokees robbed them of every-

thing, including their hats and shoes, and ordered them to leave
Kentucke. The episode was particularly harrowing for Cleveland,
who, on the return journey, had to kill and eat his hunting dog
to survive.

But it was John Findley and an inspired group of Yadkin River
valley farmers, better known as the "Long Hunters," who were
positioned best in 1769 to take advantage of the situation. Among
Findley's cohort was Daniel Boone, who had made an excursion
into the Big Sandy River valley the previous winter, leaving a bit
disappointed. In May, Findley's party set out, passed through
the Cumberland Gap, wandered northward toward the scene of
Findley's last visit to Kentucke at Eskippakithiki, and looked
out over the abundance of the "Great Meadow"—the lush rolling plains of central Kentucke. As Boone supposedly exclaimed,
"We found everywhere abundance of wild beasts of every sort,
through this vast forest. The buffalo were more frequent than I
have seen cattle in the settlements, browsing on the leaves of the
cane, or cropping the herbage on those extensive plains." They set
up Station Camp and over the next six months hunted between
the Red and Kentucky Rivers.

East of the Appalachians, colonial settlements had dramatically reduced wild mammal populations by destroying natural
pasturage, fencing off lands, and of course hunting. In particular,
Bison americanus (or what colonials called "buffaloes") were no
more than one per square kilometer by the mid-seventeenth century. In contrast, the Kentucke hunting lands were replete with
deer, elk, and bison. But the notion that this was a "virgin land"
was truly inaccurate. Centuries of Native American environmental engineering had produced a region of canebrakes, barrens,
and natural pasturage. Combined with the salt licks that bubbled
along most large waterways and many of the smaller ones, the
region's vegetation sustained huge bison, deer, and elk populations. In contrast to the meager large mammal populations in the
colonies, Kentucke had densities as thick as twenty per square
kilometer.

For men such as Boone and his companions, for whom the
hunt provided a means of demonstrating masculinity and leadership, the seemingly endless supply of bison and beaver proffered

a significant opportunity to profit from the fur trade and demonstrate manly dominance among the backcountry neighborhoods
of the Yadkin River valley. In the homosocial world of the long
hunts, acquisitions of skins signified hunting competence and
manliness. This interpretation of the hunt contrasted markedly
with that of the Shawnees, who condoned hunting for food, not
for pelts, as a telltale mark of masculinity.

Even as the Findley/Boone party wandered Kentucke, Shawnees were desperately trying to shore up their defensive alliances.
The collapse of Pontiac's Rebellion exposed the fragility of their
alliance with the weaker Lenni Lenapes, and they turned to Indians of the Great Lakes country: the Illinois, Piankashaws, Miamis, Kickapoos, Potawatomis, Ottawas, and Chippewas. They
also made overtures to the Cherokees and Chickasaws. But all
of these nations took time in considering Shawnee proposals,
leaving the Shawnees dependent upon the Wyandots and Lenni
Lenapes.

It was a band of Shawnees—angered over the Iroquois' sacrifice of the Ohio River valley, frustrated by the failure to bring
other nations to their aid, and quite unhappy to find North Carolina backcountrymen in Kentucke—that came upon Boone and
his hunting partner John Stewart in mid-December 1769. The
leader was Will Emery, a mixed-blood Cherokee who lived among
the Chillicothe Shawnees. He had to restrain the party's reaction
to the poachers. Instead, he demanded to see the hunting camp.
As they approached Station Camp, Boone noisily alerted his companions, who fled, leaving behind supplies and pelts, which the
Shawnees confiscated. Emery left Boone and Stewart behind,
each with a pair of moccasins, a small gun, some shot, and a
warning: "Now, brothers, go home and stay there. Don't come
here any more, for this is the Indians' hunting ground, and all
the animal, skins and furs are ours. And if you are so foolish as
to venture here again, you may be sure the wasps and yellow-
jackets will sting you severely." Hence, upon releasing Boone and
Stewart, Emery had ensured their abilities to hunt and survive—
to remain manly according to Indian definitions of masculinity—
by supplying ammunition, but he had severely impaired their
abilities to hunt for profit.

Figure 2.2. Daniel Boone became a legend in his own lifetime, especially after John Filson's biography of the frontiersman in 1784, a popular read among Americans and Europeans. Boone's adventures—real and legendary—contributed to creating the archetypal Western hero of American folklore. Courtesy of the Filson Historical Society, Louisville, Ky.

Boone and Stewart were not to be outdone, and as soon as the Shawnees departed, the two took off in pursuit. By nightfall, they found the Indians' encampment and, after the party fell asleep, stealthily reclaimed their horses and supplies and began riding southward. Almost comically, by sunrise the Shawnees had caught up with the two men, retaken the horses and pelts, and forced Boone and Stewart to march with them to the Ohio River. Before the crossing, the two men escaped. Two days later, they arrived at an abandoned Station Camp. Without supplies, they decided to return home, but a few days later came upon the original hunting party, which had been joined by Squire Boone and Alexander Neeley. Stewart, Neeley, and the Boone brothers turned back toward Kentucke; the others continued on to North Carolina.

Why did Daniel Boone survive this first of many interactions with Shawnees angered by his encroachment on the hunting lands of Kentucke? It is simple and rather traditional to imbue Boone with countless personal qualities that made him a quite capable "hero." Ultimately, however, it was the decision of the Shawnees and not Boone that spared his life. Had Boone come across a more radical Shawnee element, one determined to eliminate white colonial settlement in the backcountries, he most likely would have perished. Will Emery and his men, however, were more accommodating Shawnees who had resigned themselves to the inevitability of a shared hunting space, approaching Boone and his party as fellow hunters, and chastising them only to kill what was needed for food and not for profit. For accommodationist Shawnees, a flood of white migration could be avoided only by gaining the trust of the British government and depending on its enforcement of the Proclamation Line. King George III did not want to risk a renewed war on the trans-Appalachian frontier, and neither did the Shawnees with their weakened alliances.

In reality, however, the Proclamation Line of 1763 only heightened colonial curiosity. Intended to dissuade colonials' interests in the West and protect Native American territories, it instead had a dramatic psychological effect on colonial Americans. As we have seen, over the 1760s, rumors circulated throughout the colonies as to the awesome and even sinister nature of the West, giving rise to legends that became so powerful that they lingered for generations. At the turn of the nineteenth century, for example, Thomas Jefferson related a story about hunting parties in the late 1760s that heard horrible sounds in the forests of Appalachia. One party was stalked by a beast with "eyes like two balls of fire" and so fierce that "their horses were so agonized with fear that they crouched down on the earth, and the dogs crept in among them, not daring to bark." The party attributed its survival to the fires that were kept burning, but the hunters fled the country the follow morning. Trans-Appalachia was a terrifying but fascinating new world, and colonials desperately wanted to see it, touch it, and conquer it. With colonial interest piqued, the fragile scenario that allowed Will Emery and his men to react without significant violence would not last long.

Having set up a new hunting camp near the old village of Eskippakithiki, the Boone brothers and their companions continued to stalk the region for bison and beaver. Among their few amusements was a copy of Jonathan Swift's *Gulliver's Travels*, which Daniel Boone read to his friends around evening campfires. As Boone later recalled the story, one day Neeley returned to camp having shot two bison and quipping that he had "been that day to Lulbegrud and had killed two Brobdernags in their Capital," referencing the giant race of peoples found in the fictional city of Lorbrulgrud. The name stuck, albeit bastardized by Neeley's dialect, to the creek that flowed past the salt lick.

And thus Boone and his party began laying claim to Kentucke. Like others before them, and typical of thousands after them, the small hunting party sought comfort and familiarity with their new environment. After all, how do people, faced with the unknown, come to know it? If Benjamin Franklin were to have answered that question in the halls of the American Philosophical Society, an emphasis would have been placed on observation, experimentation, and categorization. For the less "enlightened," however, stripping the frontier of its mysteries and terror required less-scientific measures. In naming places, they connected with the land, almost in a manner reserved for the biblical Adam.

There was a more sentient way in which Boone related to the land as well—the way of touching the land and joining with it. By the spring of 1771, Stewart had disappeared in the wilderness and was feared dead, inspiring Neeley to return to North Carolina. Squire Boone had returned home as well to gather supplies, leaving his brother alone in the Kentucke wilds. Another party of Long Hunters under the leadership of Casper Mansker wandered into the Green River region and set up camp at Caney Creek. Assuming they were alone, they were startled one day to hear singing (albeit not very melodic) coming from the forest. They found Daniel Boone lying on the ground, bellowing at the top of his lungs.

This sort of enjoyment of the western wilderness was something that most colonials could not appreciate. Fear was a far more powerful force. Decades later, Boone supposedly waxed philosophically about his years in the hunting ground when Squire was gone and he was alone. "We were then in a dangerous, helpless, situation," he began, "exposed daily to perils and death among savages and wild beasts, not a white man in the country but ourselves." Thus, as for most whites who encroached on the Indians' hunting lands, fear was the foremost emotion. He continued, however, "I often observed to my brother, You see how little nature requires to be satisfied. Felicity, the companion of content, is rather found in our own breasts than in the enjoyment of external things: And I firmly believe it requires but a little philosophy to make a man happy in whatsoever state he is." Daniel Boone extracted more non-material happiness from Kentucke than most, but it was the joy of a man often touching Kentucke alone, away from his wife Rebecca and their children, away from large hunting parties, and routinely separated from Squire.

Despite the isolation of Kentucke, that Mansker's hunting party just happened upon Boone demonstrates that hunters did not stray too far from established paths. The many branches of the Great Warriors Path became fixed features of backcountry lore about trans-Appalachia and central routes for hunting parties, both colonial and Indian. Individuals knew the dangers of wandering from established paths and the security of remaining path-bound. There are many examples of lost individuals being found because they grasped this simple fact, beginning with Adam Harman's discovery of the escaped Mary Draper Ingles along an Indian path. A year after returning east, Alexander Neeley joined another hunting party into Kentucke, from which he was soon separated. Wandering aimlessly, surviving by killing and eating a stray dog, and gradually going mad, Neeley's only salvation was that the Boone brothers happened upon him. Some historians have labeled the meeting "strange coincidence," but it was neither strange nor coincidental. Even a man losing his sanity stayed on the beaten paths, making his rescue more plausible.

Boone was not one to stick to the paths, however. It was during these months of solitude between Squire's intermittent visits that Boone became a folk hero by blazing his own trails, although the tales themselves would take years to circulate. He wandered northward across the Kentucky River into the Great Meadow, beyond the Licking River to the Ohio River, which he traced westward to its symbolic falls. He followed the bison herds along an impressively worn trail that became known as the Old Buffalo Trace that directed him to the Lower Blue Licks, where he found hundreds of bison meandering around the salt licks. Then he traveled southward again, coming upon the confluence of the

Kentucky and Dick's Rivers, where he stood on bluffs overlooking the wilderness. Occasionally reckless in his appreciation of Kentucke (recall his singing!), as he examined the panorama of the Kentucky River valley, Boone was unaware of the approaching Shawnees until it was too late. He bounded over the cliff into the top of a maple tree below and slid some sixty feet to safety, reveling in the complaints of his pursuers above. The adventures of Daniel Boone in these solitary interludes made him an expert on Kentucke's geography, fauna, and dangers.

After two years of wandering Kentucke, Daniel and Squire Boone decided to return to the Yadkin country with a cache of furs and a fortune in stories. The evening after they passed through the Cumberland Gap, the brothers had pitched camp when a party of Cherokees approached. They asked for food and seemed harmless, but when the Boones refused to trade their guns with the group, the Cherokees turned hostile. The camp was demolished, the furs were stolen, and the Boones were lucky to survive. Daniel Boone had hunted in Kentucke for two years and had no furs to show for his efforts. All he had were his tales, and upon returning to the Yadkin River valley, he spent his first evening sitting around a campfire spinning "his hardships and adventures in the romantic land of Kentucky, where he had encountered bears, Indians, and wild cats—and had seen a country wonderful in its beauty to behold."

Only two months after the Findley/Boone party had left the Yadkin country for Kentucke in May 1769, Casper Mansker's party of forty Virginians from the New River region had ventured westward as well. Passing through Cumberland Gap, they traveled to Price's Meadow, where they established a base camp on the southeastern rim of the Great Meadow. Amazingly, they came across Daniel Boone only once over the next two years, and that instance was most certainly facilitated by Boone's caterwauling. On one hunting trip, however, they were met by a party of Cherokees. One of the colonials, Henry Skaggs, recognized the Indian leader, Captain Dick, so flattering the old man that he directed the Long Hunters to a rich hunting ground south of the Kentucky River that became known as the Green River valley. They were so pleased with the region's abundance that the party named the river near their stationary camp Dick's River after the Cherokee.

Like Will Emery and the Shawnees, Captain Dick willingly tolerated fellow hunters. But he gave stern counsel as well: "Kill it and go home." Some of the men took his warning seriously. After several successful hunts, they left the hunting party for Spanish-controlled Natchez to make a quick profit from their efforts. Others abandoned the party and went back to Virginia. In time, what had begun as a forty-man party was reduced to twelve. One day, while most of the hunters were away, Will Emery and his Shawnee companions came upon the camp and captured two of the men. When the others returned to the base, they discovered their friends, furs, and horses gone. Probably quite insightful as to what was regretted most, one member of the party carved on a tree "2300 dear skins lost, ruination, by God."

Crossing the Line

Combined, the Treaties of Fort Stanwix and Hard Labor had circumvented the Royal Proclamation of 1763, stretching the line farther west on paper at least. But it only took two years for the new boundaries to become obsolete as well. At the Treaty of Lochaber in 1770, Stuart again convinced the Cherokees to shift the boundary westward. A year later, when John Donelson surveyed the new line, Cherokees accompanied him to oversee the work. Recognizing the presence of colonials settled near the Holston River, Cherokee leader Little Carpenter agreed to accommodate this early colonial settlement in what would become Tennessee.

In the meantime, two land company representatives—Thomas Walker of the Loyal Company and Andrew Lewis of the much smaller Greenbrier Company—wanted to draw the Cherokees' northern boundary so as to legitimize their companies' Kentucky claims. Working through Virginia's House of Burgesses, they secured an official request for Stuart to set the boundary as far west as possible in the Treaty of Lochaber, but Stuart refused to offend the Cherokees by demanding even more. Undeterred,

Walker and Lewis promised £500 to the Cherokees upon conceding the Kentucky River as their northern boundary, thereby handing over much of the Great Meadow to the Virginians. The Cherokees accepted (probably with the assistance of a great deal of rum), and Stuart acquiesced. Not surprisingly, the Cherokees were never paid for their additional concession. But the Loyal Company now claimed a tract that stretched across northern Kentucke, almost to the Falls of the Ohio.

Unlike the imperially chartered Ohio Company's original agreement to settle families, the Virginia-chartered Loyal Company had no such condition and could sell directly to speculators. Fearing that the British Privy Council, determined to enforce the Proclamation Line of 1763 and supportive of the Ohio Company, might reverse the Treaty of Lochaber and its alterations, Walker began parceling out the newly acquired lands immediately. By the end of 1773, over 201,000 acres (a quarter of the original land grant) had been sold, most to men who never intended to see the land. The 1770s, then, brought a different tenor to trans-Appalachia. Colonial excursions in the late 1760s had been by groups of like-minded backcountrymen eager to hunt; they were not well planned, nor were they sanctioned by colonial or imperial governments. By 1771, with Donelson's survey, the Long Hunters were no longer the only colonists in Kentucke. They were joined by colonial and imperial agents determined to protect investments. And, resolute to make clear its own authority over the western lands, Virginia's assembly declared Kentucke part of a newly formed Fincastle County in 1772.

By 1773, as land companies, war veterans, backcountry hunters, and Native Americans staked claims to Kentucke, the situation began to spiral out of control. Hoping to bring some order to the chaos, Virginia Governor John Murray, the fourth Earl of Dunmore, authorized a party to survey the "Proclamation Rights" in northern Kentucke. These four-hundred-acre tracts had been promised Virginia's veterans of the French and Indian War. Surveyors James McAfee Jr., George McAfee, Robert McAfee, James McCoun Jr., and Samuel Adams started out in April for Kentucke.

Under the leadership of Thomas Bullitt, an independent party of some thirty men also set off down the Ohio River, where they soon joined with the McAfees. Bullitt made occasional excursions into the Shawnee towns on the north side of the river while others hunted the lands on the south side of the Ohio. In early June, Bullitt and three comrades visited Chillicothe, where he announced to Chief Hokolesqua of the Shawnees, "I am sent with my people to settle the country on the Ohio River as low as the Falls," attributing his right to do so to the Treaties of Fort Stanwix and Lochaber. While Hokolesqua, known to the colonials as Cornstalk, rejected Iroquois and Cherokee abilities to sell the Ohio River valley to Americans, he refrained from denying Bullitt the possibility of settlement. Instead, he firmly warned that the Shawnees would respect white usage of Kentucke as long as the colonials allowed for continued Shawnee hunting in the region. Cornstalk expressed particular concern that Americans keep their "young men" from overhunting, and he promised to advise "our young men to be friendly, kind and peaceable to you." As Robert Butler, a white captive who served as translator at the meeting, explained to Bullitt, "I do assure you that it lies in your power to have good neighbors or bad, as they are a people very capable of discerning between good treatment and ill."

Cornstalk's concession marked a notable shift in Shawnee policy toward colonial infringement on Kentucke. Back in 1767, George Washington, whose personal interests in western land speculation certainly colored his perspective, hoped that the Proclamation Line would be nothing more than "a temporary expedient to quiet the minds of the Indians. It must fall, of course, in a few years, especially when those Indians consent to our occupying those lands." Cornstalk had fulfilled that prophecy, not only authorizing Bullitt to initiate settlement but assuring some security by restraining more radical Shawnees. According to Shawnee tradition, the hereditary chief of the Chillicothe division was nominally the leader of the nation. As that chief, Cornstalk had set new policy for the Shawnees' relationship with the settlers.

With a promise in his pocket, Bullitt continued on. When, in early July, his party reached the mouth of the Kentucky River, the original crews separated: the McAfees headed southward into the Great Meadow while the Bullitt party continued on toward the Falls of the Ohio. The great rush to survey Kentucke was under way. The McAfees measured out claims along the Kentucky River. Bullitt and his men laid out a town near the Falls of the Ohio, each man receiving one lot for his labor. And smaller parties of two or three men, among whom were Isaac Hite and James Harrod, darted into the Kentucke wilderness to make individual claims. At first glance, one might interpret this parceling as evidence of the rugged individualism that underlay the settlement of Kentucke; after all, these men struggled through the wilderness to grab their part of the future. Further reflection, however, demonstrates that few of these surveyors, as agents for wealthier colonials, actually secured anything for themselves. For two decades, investors in the Loyal and Ohio Companies had awaited a return on their investments, and the opening of Kentucke, as fragile and momentary as it might be, promised that return.

Coincidental with the rush to survey Kentucke, then, was a renewed sense of competition between the land companies. Centered upon the Washington and Fitzhugh families, the primary investors in the Ohio Company were men of older, more aristocratic Tidewater lineage. Since the departure of Virginia governor Robert Dinwiddie and the Proclamation of 1763, the Ohio Company had been fairly impotent. The investors attempted to solve their problem by appealing to the crown for a new land company—the Mississippi Company—which would have more than doubled their western claims and held at bay a Pennsylvania land syndicate determined to create a new colony named Vandalia. But without sufficient leverage in London or Williamsburg, the Ohio Company floundered.

The Pennsylvanians, among whom were Benjamin Franklin, his son William, Sir William Johnson, and George Croghan, had the advantage in London, where they had the ear of another investor, Lord Thomas Walpole. Calling themselves the Walpole Company, the investors petitioned Parliament in 1772 for a tract of 30 million acres, including the lands north of the Kentucky River abdicated by Cherokees at the Treaty of Lochaber. To avoid interference by the Ohio and Loyal Companies, they bribed each company's London representative—Arthur Lee and George Mercer, respectively. And with the appointment of the enthusiastic land grabber Lord Dartmouth as secretary of state to the colonies in 1773, the petition was granted, the tract was declared the Vandalia Colony, and the organization took on the name Grand Ohio Company. George Washington and the Ohio Company immediately repudiated the action, denouncing Mercer for failing their interests. When British commander Thomas Gage fretted that settlement so distant from colonial centers would lead to trouble, the Vandalia enterprise bogged down in debate. The Grand Ohio Company investors had to fight another two years to begin selling lands.

Not to be outdone, the Loyal Company had gained the upper hand in Williamsburg. Lord Dunmore had become an investor soon after his arrival in 1771, and the Bullitt party began its Kentucke surveys on his orders. In October 1773, Bullitt returned to Draper's Meadow, where William Preston had relocated, to register the newly surveyed land claims with the official surveyor for Fincastle County. Most likely, Preston was concerned about the legality of veterans' surveys made beyond the Donelson survey line, but his official excuse for refusing Bullitt's requests was that no official county surveyors had accompanied the party. Undeterred, Bullitt alerted Governor Dunmore, who brought the issue before the colonial council. Loyal Company representatives made their case for authorizing the surveys and restricting veterans from settling those lands. Hugh Mercer, a veteran and western lands investor himself, petitioned on behalf of veterans' rights to claim any vacant lands. In mid-December, Dunmore and the council declared the validity of the surveys, giving exception only to veterans' claims preceding Bullitt's registrations in October. More importantly, they validated veterans' rights to claim fifty acres plus another fifty acres for every three acres cleared, laying the foundation for a land rush.

Preston acted quickly to preserve veterans' claims, registering Bullitt's surveys and sending forth a new surveying party under the leadership of John Floyd in early 1774 to produce what became known as the Fincastle surveys. While officially charged with measuring out tracts for military warrants, Floyd had also agreed to survey claims for George Washington, William Byrd III, and Patrick Henry. By the end of May, the men arrived at the Falls of the Ohio, some of the choicest lands in the region, and began surveying their own tracts. The tools of surveying were a compass atop a tripod and a four-pole (sixty-foot) chain. One man would set up the compass, peering through its sights as another walked ahead, cutting through vegetation and establishing a sight line to the next point. The compass would then be moved to the new point and the process begun anew. Two chainmen would follow, laying the chain in the sight path and measuring out the tract. While their directions were fairly accurate, at times the party's measurements were off significantly, particularly those for Floyd's own claim, which was registered at 400 poles square but really measured 485 poles square. Floyd's friends, such as William Christian, received similarly enlarged plots.

When they finished around the Falls of the Ohio, Floyd's surveying crew broke off into smaller parties that wandered the Great Meadow. Floyd led a party along the branches of Elkhorn Creek, where they surveyed over eighty tracts. Others wandered along both banks of the Kentucky River, marking off potential holdings. If the Grand Ohio Company successfully staked claim to the lands north of the river, these men were determined at least to have some lands south of the river, despite the fact that none of that territory had been ceded by the Cherokees.

While Bullitt fought for validation in Virginia and Floyd wandered Kentucke, another surveyor busily established his own claims. James Harrod had been intrigued by trans-Appalachia throughout his life. His initial forays took him into the Illinois Country, where he mastered several Indian languages, and his early life in the Pennsylvania backcountry had taught lessons about the tensions between colonials, Indians, and imperial authorities. In early March 1774, he led nearly fifty men into Kentucke. After a labyrinthine journey along multiple rivers and streams, they arrived at a spot ideal in its beauty and abundance, which they named Big Spring. Harrod proposed laying out Harrodstown, and the men drew up a compact whereby a cabin was built for each person, each cabin was numbered, and upon completion of construction, a lottery determined the owner for each cabin and accompanying lot. Floyd's surveyors made it temporary headquarters as they plied the Kentucky River valley. But the threat of Indian attack remained omnipresent, especially since Harrod and his men had settled on Cherokee lands.

Rumors of Harrodstown inspired other pioneers to enter trans-Appalachia. By early spring, one group under the leadership of Michael Cresap arrived at Middle Island Creek. Ebenezer Zane led another party to settle lands near the mouth of Sandy Creek. A final group, including George Rogers Clark, gathered at the mouth of the Little Kanawha River to await companions before moving downriver to Kentucke.

New pockets of colonials excited Shawnee radicals, who again began to terrorize southwestern Virginia and the backcountries of Maryland and Pennsylvania, and Cherokee radicals, who attacked settlers along the Holston River. The wave of attacks in late 1774 was particularly harrowing. Harrod and his men abandoned Harrodstown. Clark's party retreated to Wheeling for protection, as did Cresap's men and hundreds of colonials from the surrounding countryside. Many pioneers who were poised less than a month earlier to enter Kentucke abandoned their plans and fled to Redstone, but even that would not be secure enough.

Preston, fearful of an alliance between Cherokees and Shawnees that would seal off Kentucke to colonization, pressed Cresap to retaliate. At Pipe Creek in the upper Kanawha River valley, the colonists found their opportunity with a decisive defeat of a Shawnee warring party. The attack incited cries of war from the Shawnees, but their continued inability to draw powerful allies to their cause severely hampered any effort. Cresap, however, found a way to aid the Shawnee cause. Following the Pipe Creek incident, his militia came upon a party of Mingos, killed all save an infant, and left among the dead relatives of Tachnedorus, a moderate Mingo who had proven himself a friend to colonial settlement and was widely known by the colonials as John Logan. The Massacre at Yellow Creek turned Tachnedorus against the American colonials and sparked widespread Mingo demand for retribution. An alliance between Mingos and Shawnees seemed imminent, but Cornstalk refused to abandon his more tolerant stance toward the colonials. Unwilling to wait for the Shawnee leadership, Tachnedorus led two dozen young Shawnees and Mingos to exact revenge on the Pennsylvania backcountry, where they killed thirteen settlers.

The British garrison at Fort Pitt immediately prepared to invade the Ohio River valley, but if the Loyal Company was to secure its claims on the West, Governor Dunmore realized that he could not allow the crown (and the Walpole Company) to establish a presence first. He encouraged the British initiative by offering Virginia militias as backup troops and suggesting that by placing Virginia regiments throughout the Ohio country, the British could take control of the region without great expense. By situating Virginians throughout the region, Dunmore hoped to assert his authority over the lands of the upper Ohio River valley and secure the land claims of the Loyal Company. Central to this scheme was Preston, who, upon organizing the Fincastle County militia, inspired recruits by proclaiming that "the Opportunity we have so long wished for, is now before us."

As Virginia's militias invaded, Cornstalk recognized the clear threat to Shawnee survival bearing down on the Ohio River valley. He sent nearly one thousand Shawnees eastward to intercept the Virginians. On October 10, the antagonists met at Point Pleasant, where the colonials gradually gained the upper hand and chased the Shawnees north of the Ohio River. In the resulting Treaty of Camp Charlotte, the Shawnees agreed to the terms of the Treaty of Fort Stanwix; it was the first time actual inhabitants of the region relinquished lands. Additionally, the Shawnees promised to return captives and abstain from attacking Americans traveling down the Ohio River.

While brief, Lord Dunmore's War exposed deep divisions within Native American populations. Within the multinational villages of the Shawnee nation, residents could not agree on how to deal with the colonial invasion. Tachnedorus's renegade tactics undermined any possibility of diplomatically resolving the situation; Cornstalk's early hesitance weakened a potentially united Indian front. Consequently, the Shawnees lost control of lands south and east of the Ohio River, and the colonials lost strong alliances with Cornstalk and Tachnedorus. Tachnedorus did not attend the negotiations at Camp Charlotte, instead sending a letter agreeing to any concessions that Cornstalk made. His anger over the war, loss of family, and the failure to maintain peaceful relations was very evident in his message:

> In the course of the last year, *Logan* remained in his cabin an advocate for peace. I had such an affection for the white people that I was pointed at by the rest of my Nation. I should have even lived with them had it not been for Colonel *Cresap*, who the last year cut off, in cold blood, all the relations of *Logan*, not sparing women and children. There runs not a drop of my blood in the veins of any human creature. . . . Who is there to mourn for *Logan*? No one.

As more English colonists and then Americans coveted land in the Ohio Country, it would be only a matter of time until thousands of Native Americans discovered that they too would not be mourned.

Lord Dunmore's War had been about more than Shawnee-Virginian tensions. Cornstalk's earlier concession to Bullitt did not escape the notice of the Grand Ohio Company and the planners of Vandalia. Dunmore had outfoxed the Pennsylvanians by pushing for war and situating his own colonists as the guardians of order in the Ohio River valley. The war's conclusion placed the future of Kentucke squarely in the hands of Virginia, or so Dunmore thought.

American Settlements

As James Harrod and his men marched home following the Battle of Point Pleasant, news arrived of a disturbance in Boston, where thousands of pounds of tea had been thrown into the harbor in reaction to the Tea Act. They could identify with the frustration of colonials who felt ignored by British authorities; Lord Dunmore had simply dismissed them from the negotiations at Camp Charlotte with neither supplies nor thanks. By early November, the party arrived at Fort Gower, where, because

> the love of Liberty, and attachment to the real interests and just rights of America outweigh every other consideration, we resolve that we will exert every power within us for the defense of Ameri-

can liberty, and for the support of her just rights and privileges; not in any precipitate, riotous, or tumultuous manner, but when regularly called forth by the unanimous voice of our countrymen.

Lord Dunmore may have won the battle for trans-Appalachia, but he was about to be on the losing side in the war for America.

In mid-March 1775, Harrod and his men returned to Big Spring. When Harrod's party arrived, they found much of the original settlement of Harrodstown destroyed, apparently by marauding Native Americans. The men turned to reinforcing the cabins and constructing a fort on higher ground away from the spring. The cabins were simple structures: most measured twenty feet by thirty feet, with no room divisions save a small loft. Few had windows, and those were mere openings without glass. Many had chimneys constructed from hewn logs and chinked with mud, held up by poles, and semi-detached from the buildings; if the chimney caught fire, the pole could be kicked out and the blaze would fall away. Most had small adjacent plots for gardening. Despite the domestic appearance of Harrodstown, however, the residents were all men. Kentucke was not yet a family frontier. The threat of Indian attack, the trials of the long journey to the Great Meadow—colonial men were unwilling to subject women and children to these perils until defensive structures could provide some security.

The creation of Fort Harrod, then, was the first of many such efforts to enable actual settlement, but as the palisades went up, other events were under way that also made possible the peopling of Kentucke. While the Proclamation Line, the chartering of the Ohio and Loyal Companies, and the general tenor of imperial and colonial actions warned against individual negotiations with Native Americans, Richard Henderson was determined to purchase a large tract for his proposed Transylvania colony. Henderson had been plotting his investment for some years, and Daniel Boone played a central role. Although Boone's western travels between 1769 and 1772 have traditionally been viewed as "long hunts," his interest in the geography of Kentucke suggests that Boone was also considering the potential for settlement and even land speculation. While there is little evidence that Boone was in Henderson's employ before 1774, he had connections to Henderson dating back to 1768. It was not uncommon for wealthier speculators to surreptitiously hire surveyors: George Washington instructed an agent to keep "the operation carried on by you under the guize of hunting game." Whether he was formally serving as Henderson's land agent or not, the stories that Boone related upon his return to the Yadkin River valley in 1771 inspired several prominent North Carolinians to join Henderson's scheme for western development.

In 1775, Henderson was eager to stake his claim to trans-Appalachia. As an associate judge of North Carolina's colonial superior court, Henderson had acted with an arrogance that made him a target of the Regulator movement in 1770. Speculation in other western ventures over the next two years had brought little return. But the Pennsylvanians' Vandalia scheme provided what he considered an ideal model for western development: establish a colony as proprietors, buying the land from the appropriate Indians, and then selling tracts to smaller farmers. The key was to secure the lands. In the late summer of 1774, Henderson organized the Louisa Company to specifically purchase trans-Appalachian lands from the Indians. In January 1775, he offered stakes in the company to several proprietors, and renamed it the Transylvania Company. On March 17, Henderson and eight associates met with Cherokee leaders at Sycamore Shoals on the Watauga River. Carolina Dick (as Henderson was known to the Cherokees) offered two thousand pounds sterling to the Indian leaders, among whom were Little Carpenter, Dragging Canoe, and the old warrior Oconostata. In the end, Henderson had purchased the lands between the Kentucky and Cumberland Rivers, stretching from the Cumberland Mountains to the Ohio River. The tract covered more than half of the future state of Kentucky.

Younger, more militant Cherokees were furious over the transaction, but Dragging Canoe and Oconostata insisted that the Cherokees had no actual claim to Kentucke and therefore in actuality had not transferred ownership. In other words, they had tricked Henderson and actually sold very little to him. "You, Carolina Dick, have deceived your people," Oconostata declared. "We told you that those lands were not ours, that our claim extended not beyond the Cumberland Mountains." Little Carpenter argued otherwise, however, resolute that the sale was valid. In time he convinced most of the attending Cherokees. Henderson also secured a path grant on which to carve a road into Kentucke and immediately sent Boone out to mark what would become the Wilderness Road. As Boone left Sycamore Shoals, Oconostata warned him that "we have given you a fine land, but I believe you will have much trouble in settling it." They were prophetic words indeed.

As news of the negotiations traveled eastward, land speculators and colonial administrators were shocked by Henderson's success. Having circumvented imperial and colonial governments, Henderson and his Transylvania Company were certain to anger the wrong people. Governor Josiah Martin of North Carolina immediately denounced Henderson's treaty, calling the proprietors "land Pyrates" and fearing that if successful the venture would encourage other speculators. Lord Dunmore worried that Transylvania would siphon off potential settlers from the land speculations with which he was involved. George Washington declared that there "is something in that affair which I neither understand, nor like, and wish I may not have cause to dislike it worse as the mystery unfolds." In the months that followed, the Virginia Assembly appointed a committee to investigate the legalities of Henderson's negotiations. Henderson's lone potential ally in Virginia, Patrick Henry, initially defended the Transylvania Company but grew bitter as Henderson rejected his efforts to buy into the venture.

In the meantime, Boone led the road-clearing party—approximately thirty-five colonials, including Boone's daughter Susannah, a couple slaves, and several supply wagons—along a branch of Athiamiowcc toward the Cumberland Gap. While bison and hunters had used these paths regularly, none were sufficiently clear. Athiamiowee itself proved too narrow and cumbersome for the wagons, so the party strayed along buffalo traces, cutting a road that meandered rather than one that was direct. For two weeks, they worked through the Appalachian Mountains.

It must have been a particularly difficult trip for Boone. His last trip into this region, two years earlier, had resulted in the death of two young men, one of whom was his son James. It was as trying this time. On March 25, Indians struck the party as it rested about fifteen miles from its destination. At least three men were killed, including Sam, a slave. Two days later, another attack took two more lives. A few members of the party packed up and turned back to North Carolina. But Boone forged ahead. On April 1, as they descended toward the eastern edge of the Great Meadow, a herd of almost three hundred bison charged away from them. One member of the party recalled the stampede, "some walking, others loping slowly and carelessly, with young calves playing, skipping and bounding through the plain." It was a sight only Boone and a couple others had seen before.

A few weeks behind Boone were Henderson and a larger contingent of settlers, all male and many enslaved. As they breached the Cumberland Gap, they came upon panicked members of Boone's party, fleeing eastward. Some of Henderson's men joined the flight, including John May, who charged his slave with continuing onward to make improvements and a claim. Others refused to scout ahead and leave the meager security of the group. Cowed, the party continued on until it arrived on April 20. Henderson found Boone busily surveying a town to be named Boonesborough. On a small knoll overlooking the proposed town, Henderson and Boone planned a rectangular fort with blockhouses at each corner, eight cabins along each long interior wall and five along the shorter walls. But the other men had scattered along the river to claim their shares of Kentucke. Rough cabins rapidly sprang up across the hills, while construction of Fort Boone took over three years. Frustrated by the party's lack of concern about safety, Henderson privately wished that "the Indians should do us a favor of annoying us, and regularly scalping a man every week."

A few weeks behind was yet another group of Transylvania pioneers led by John Floyd. They followed the Wilderness Road as far as Hazel Path, where they turned westward. Some twenty miles from Harrodstown, they established St. Asaph. As in Boonesborough, however, the men did little to shore up defenses and instead went immediately to the task of land claiming. Fearful of the consequences, Henderson sent word to the small settlements arising in Transylvania to "settle somewhere in a compact body for mutual Defense."

Carolina Dick had no one to blame but himself for his settlers' lack of interest in security. They had, after all, come to Kentucke for land. The Transylvania Company rules dictated that only pioneers who raised a crop of corn in 1775 would be eligible for 500-acre tracts at twenty shillings per hundred acres. Consequently, since it was late spring already, ambitious men had to quickly clear and plant the fields. Over the next few months, failure to establish those fields of corn (and therefore their claims to the future) disheartened most of the original settlement party, which dwindled from over eighty in late April to less than twenty by September.

The result was a crisis that few had anticipated in the abundant lands of Kentucke. Even before the number of settlers had fallen off, supplies of flour were running low, forcing the colonials to turn to nature for sustenance. The bison herds were enticing, but the novelty of stalking the large beasts quickly turned hunting for food into hunting for fun, leaving thousands of pounds of meat rotting under the summer sun. Quickly, the herds disappeared, most having migrated northward and westward to escape the slaughter. Their departure exacerbated the food shortage. Many slaves who accompanied the Henderson party went to work in small vegetable gardens; others fished in the Kentucky River. It was hardly a "starving time," but it was a long and lean summer and fall in Transylvania.

According to Henderson's interpretation of his purchase from the Cherokees, Harrodstown sat within the boundaries of Transylvania. To bring the community into the fold, Henderson invited representatives from throughout Kentucke to a convention in May. Each settlement sent several representatives but among the notables were Henderson, of course, for the Transylvania Company proprietors; Boone, his brother Squire, and Richard Callaway on behalf of Boonesborough; James Harrod from Harrodstown; and John Floyd representing St. Asaph. Floyd also served as proxy for Fincastle County surveyor William Preston. The group convened under a large elm near the unfinished walls of Fort Boone.

Henderson acted quite the sovereign, trying to impose a feudal system over the new settlers of Transylvania. His proposed plan for the colonial government of Transylvania had a lower representative house, an upper house of twelve large property owners, and a council comprised of the colonial proprietors. The proposal also established quit-rents of two shillings per one hundred acres beginning in 1780, and allowed the proprietors to alter the terms of land sales. In other regards, however, it was a quite liberal compact: the lower house would be elected annually, freedom of religion was guaranteed, proprietor-appointed judges were answerable to the people for malfeasance in office, and the power to raise and appropriate funds was reserved for future conventions. Additionally, Henderson raised the issue of overhunting and the need for preserving game, which was delegated to Boone for consideration. While the representatives had no opportunity to approve the government, neither did they reject it. Instead, everyone left seemingly satisfied with the shape of Transylvania Colony.

The only potential hitch in Henderson's plan was William Preston, who had a hand in several land speculations and represented Virginia's (and Dunmore's) interests. During the Boonesborough convention, Henderson bribed Preston's representative, John Floyd, with lands and a surveying job for the Transylvania Company. In return, Floyd was to keep the suspicious Preston at bay, assuring him that Henderson would not interfere with Fincastle County's official claims.

The triangle of Preston, Henderson, and Floyd epitomized the structure of land claiming in Kentucke. Preston represented colonial and, indirectly, imperial authority over the West. Through his own machinations, Henderson had found ways to circumvent that authority and enrich private investors eager to profit from trans-Appalachia. But ultimately, it was Floyd and other men on the ground busily carving up Kentucke who benefited most and suffered the greatest losses in the early westward movement. Their futures depended on negotiating Preston's demands and Henderson's aspirations.

3.

REVOLUTIONS

As the Boonesborough convention met and Henderson consolidated as much power as he could, Lord Dunmore faced the final days of his governorship. In May 1775, the Virginia Convention openly expressed sympathy for the rebellion that had erupted in Massachusetts. In June, George Washington accepted a post as military commander of a new continental rebel army. The security of Virginia's royal government seemed to be unraveling monthly. Seeking military support, Dunmore ordered his troops to abandon the western outposts that secured the Virginia backcountry from Indian attacks and return to Williamsburg, and the governor retreated to a British ship at the mouth of the James River, where he plotted how to retain control of Virginia.

With family names such as Washington, Jefferson, Lee, Henry, and Randolph leading the anti-imperial outcry, Dunmore declared martial law and gathered an army of some three hundred loyalists and soldiers. Among them were a handful of runaway slaves who had shown up at the governor's mansion in April. Their presence inspired Dunmore to take a more drastic measure, and in November, he proclaimed "all indentured Servants, Negroes, or others, (appertaining to Rebels,) free that are able and willing to bear Arms, they joining His MAJESTY's Troops as soon as may be, for the more speedily reducing this Colony to a proper Sense of their Duty, to His MAJESTY's Crown and Dignity." By the end of the month, over eight hundred had joined the "Ethiopian Regiment" and occupied Norfolk, and another thousand sought refuge there. With labels declaring "Liberty to Slaves" attached to their uniforms, the soldiers posed a difficult ideological problem for slave-owning rebels in the Virginia Convention, whose response was to threaten runaways either with being shipped to the West Indies for sale or, if necessary, with death.

By the end of 1775, with weakened western defenses and a Native American threat on the western borders, and an enlarging and increasingly African American army congregating in Norfolk, white Virginians faced a racial context to their rebelliousness against the crown that had not existed a year prior. The peril of slave insurrection joined with the terror of Indian warfare, both armed and encouraged by the British.

Before Dunmore's Ethiopian Regiment, American colonials had actually interpreted the racial divide in quite different terms. Many whites, such as Massachusetts's James Otis in 1764, had imagined the colonies populated by millions of "good, loyal, and useful subjects, White and Black," assuming a loyalty on the part of their slaves as the threat of British-backed Native Americans loomed large. By the time of publication of Thomas Paine's *Common Sense* in January 1776, however, the unholy triumvirate was unmistakable: "There are thousands, and tens of thousands, who would think it glorious to expel from the continent that barbarous and hellish power which hath stirred up the Indians and Negroes to destroy us." Months later, Thomas Jefferson's Declaration of Independence reiterated the theme as one of his complaints against George III: "He has excited domestic insurrections amongst us, and has endeavoured to bring on the inhabitants of our frontiers, the merciless Indian Savages, whose known rule of warfare, is an undistinguished destruction of all ages, sexes and conditions."

Thousands of white Virginians, some living in Kentucke, fully understood what Jefferson meant as they listened to the Declaration being read across the commonwealth. Indians posed an external threat, and blacks posed an internal one. Men, women, and children who crossed into trans-Appalachia in the years of the Revolutionary War carried the anxieties and anger of this racialized fear with them.

The Emergence of George Rogers Clark

Within this heightened racial atmosphere, the peopling of Kentucke proceeded. The expedition to clear the Wilderness Road had ushered Susannah Boone into Kentucke at the beginning of the summer of 1775. By September, Daniel Boone had returned to North Carolina to escort a new party of wives and families westward, including his own family and the McGarys. By the end of the month, another group of family settlers, led by Richard Callaway, reached Boonesborough, followed closely by Squire Boone and his family.

The arrival of women and children in Kentucke marked a significant shift in the settlement process. Previously, men had been free to hunt and survey; if they returned to a settlement that had been destroyed by Indian attack, they merely rebuilt it. Families required a more aggressively defensive posturing. They also forced men to make a commitment to settling. Boone's description of the cabin constructed for his family differed significantly from previous constructions at Boonesborough: it had wooden floors, a door, and glass windows. Likewise at Harrodstown, the arrival of the McGary family and a couple others sparked a period of cabin reconstruction to make settlement more suitable for wives and families.

For every woman and child who arrived in Kentucke in 1775, however, there were another dozen men looking for land. Some sincerely sought the same opportunity for their own families, but most were land jobbers, wanting to make quick wealth by staking a claim and then selling to someone else. To meet the demand, the Transylvania Company relocated its land office to Harrodstown in the fall, but this only encouraged a rush of land claims. By the end of the year, over a half million acres had been registered through some nine hundred claims. In some regards,

Kentucke became less secure, even as the stability of family life began to emerge. With hundreds of men swarming about the landscape—some surveying and registering their claims, others squatting and letting their corn patches mark their territorial claims—anxieties over land acquisition began to peak.

Additionally, news continued to trickle over the mountains about the colonial rebellion around Boston, providing Kentucke pioneers a new understanding of their own western activities. One party entered the Great Meadow in spring 1775, surveying and making improvements along the headwaters of Elkhorn Creek. One evening as they sat around a spring, they received news of Massachusetts Minutemen and their stand against the British Regulars. Subsequently, they named their camp "Lexington," memorializing eastern colonials' rebellion through their own extralegal settlement of Kentucke. Possibly because they expected the British to be distracted by problems in New England and consequently lax in supervising the Proclamation Line, surveyors and potential settlers of 1775 busily established claims in the lands north of the Kentucky River.

Autumn saw conditions degenerate significantly, however, largely attributable to the Transylvania Company. By the end of September, the proprietors had changed the terms of land sales. Men who had cleared and planted fields of corn to lay claim to their five hundred acres were shocked to find that prices had risen from twenty to fifty shillings per hundred acres. Settlers who found salt springs or mineral mines on their claims were to share half of all profits with the proprietors. The company also set aside 200,000 acres of choice land at the Falls of the Ohio for proprietors' use only.

Henderson sent James Hogg to Philadelphia to meet with Virginia's delegates to the Continental Congress, secure Transylvania's sovereignty, and take his seat as the representative for the fourteenth colony. Hogg found little sympathy. Still hopeful for a peaceful solution to the rebellion, John Adams feared that associating with "a body of people who have acted in defiance of the king's proclamation, will be looked on as a confirmation of that independent spirit with which we are daily reproached." Even among those interested in Transylvania's success, there were stern warnings that the proprietors should provide for a free government, avoid charging quit-rents ("a mark of vassalage"), and not become overly ambitious in grabbing the best lands for themselves. Silas Dean suggested he could muster investments from several "speculative gentleman" in Connecticut, but warned that there would be opposition "if we do not act upon liberal principles when we have it so much in our power to make ourselves immortal." The most emphatic rejection of Hogg's overtures came from Patrick Henry, who, despite Hogg's offer of an interest in the company, remained bitter about Henderson's earlier refusal to bring Henry into the fold.

In contrast to an earlier century when proprietary colonies were acceptable to many colonials, by the mid-1770s anything that smacked of corruption and privilege was widely condemned, and not just in Philadelphia. Back in Kentucke, James Harrod and Isaac Hite incited revolt against Henderson and the company. In December, eighty-eight men listed their grievances in a petition to the Virginia Convention. Besides their complaints over the proprietors' land-grabbing and the difficulties of settling Transylvania, the pioneers also questioned the validity of their own land claims under the company's charter, worrying that Henderson's negotiations with the Cherokees would be deemed illegitimate.

The petitioners also did their best to associate Henderson with the larger colonial struggle against imperialism. "And as we are anxious to concur in every respect with our brethren of the United Colonies for our just rights and responsibilities," they concluded the petition,

> we humbly expect and implore to be taken under the protection of the honorable Convention of the Colony of *Virginia*, of which we cannot help thinking ourselves still a part, and request your kind interposition in our behalf, that we may not suffer under the rigorous demands and impositions of the gentlemen styling themselves Proprietors, who, the better to effect their oppressive designs, have given them the colour of a law, enacted by a score of men, artfully picked from the few adventurers who went to see the country last summer, overawed by the presence of Mr. *Henderson*.

The complaint caught the proprietors unaware. They rapidly petitioned the convention themselves, retreating from their desire to create a fourteenth colony and, instead, emphasizing the inalienable right of private property and, given the outbreak of war over individual rights, the utmost necessity to protect private property in the West.

As Harrod and Hite inflamed resentment against the proprietors, on the north side of the Kentucky River, George Rogers Clark took stock of the situation. At twenty-three years of age, Clark was typical of young Virginia gentlemen mesmerized by the mystery of trans-Appalachia. Lord Dunmore's War had forced him into militia duty, established his reputation as a strong military leader, and awakened his curiosity about Kentucke. In the early 1770s, he had made three surveying trips into the region, and he wanted more. Finally, in 1775, the Ohio Company hired Clark to survey part of the Great Meadow, specifically laying out a town for his friend, Hancock Lee, simply named Lee's Town.

Observing the tensions south of the Kentucky River, and well aware of the threat that an unrestrained Transylvania Company posed to his own desires for quality Kentucke lands, Clark planned to undermine the company by assembling colonial settlers, electing deputies to the Virginia Assembly, and in effect transforming Transylvanians into Virginians. General disaffection with the Transylvania Company had rippled outward as more pioneers arrived from Virginia expecting to preempt choice lands, only to find that the best had been assigned through large surveys to absentee speculators. That disaffection with authority spread as well to Virginia's royal government—its land laws, its surveying crews, and its tolerance of the Transylvania Company. "Hundreds of wretches come down the Ohio & build pens or cabins, return to sell them," complained John Floyd to William Preston. "In short they now begin to pay no kind of regard to the officers land more than any other. . . . They make very free with my character, swearing I am engrossing the country and have no warrants for the land, & if I have, they will drive me and the officers to hell."

Virginia's intentions to sacrifice trans-Appalachia had become all too apparent by the end of 1775 as well. Virginia troops had been retracted to a defensive perimeter far to the east. Even as a new government replaced the royal government, Kentucke seemed to be forgotten. Governor Patrick Henry considered forcing an abandonment of the trans-Appalachian settlements, and made clear that even with the arrival of women and children into Kentucke, settlers could not depend on Virginia to allocate resources for their sake. Indian attacks increased, and Native Americans did not hesitate to target sons, daughters, or wives, bringing a new sense of urgency to settlement defense. On Christmas Eve of 1775, Indians ambushed John Campbell and two boys near Boonesborough. Campbell escaped, but the boys did not: one was found scalped in a corn field; the other disappeared forever.

The episode shocked pioneers and strengthened Clark's resolve to secure Kentucke by ending the influence of the Transylvania Company and making Kentucke a part of Virginia, thereby empowering settlers to protect themselves through Virginia's resources. "If valuable conditions was procured, to declare ourselves citizens of the state," Clark explained, "otherwise establish an independent government, and, by giving away a great part of the lands and disposing of the remainder otherwise, we could not only gain numbers of inhabitants, but in good measure protect them." The need for protection became more urgent in early spring 1776. Indians attacked Lee's Town in April, burning cabins and sending residents fleeing to Boonesborough. In June, Andrew McConnell's indentured servant fell victim to a party of Mingos, who also took McConnell's twin sons captive. Through the interference of a Virginian working in lower Shawnee Town, the boys were returned to their family within a few months.

In the meanwhile, Clark joined with Harrod to organize a new meeting of pioneers in Harrodstown. Harrod was less enthused than Clark about moving from the control of the Transylvania proprietors to that of the Virginia Assembly—he had a more independent Kentucke in mind. But Harrod also recognized that the best way to shed Transylvania control was to have Virginia do it, so he agreed to send delegates to the Virginia Assembly. Clark was delayed for the June meeting, and in his absence, settlers follow Harrod's lead, electing Clark and John Gabriel Jones as representatives. Certainly disappointed that the meeting had

Figure 3.1. George Rogers Clark led the Kentucky militia throughout much of the Revolutionary War, becoming well known for his captures of Kaskaskia and Vincennes, which weakened British influence in the trans-Appalachian West. Although he became associated with the settlement of the Northwest Territory, Clark's contribution to Kentucke's settlement was critical to the region's development. Courtesy of the Filson Historical Society, Louisville, Ky.

not been more aggressive in demanding recognition and supplies from Virginia, Clark set off with Jones for Williamsburg, arriving too late in the fall to join the General Assembly.

What the two men left behind was a region in chaos. Henderson desperately grasped to retain control over the lands south of the Kentucky River. Hundreds of potential settlers had also begun slipping into Kentucke, assuming that Virginia colonial veterans' claims would soon be overturned if the rebellion succeeded. Among them were dozens of Loyalists, most members of the Bryan family fleeing the increasingly oppressive atmosphere of North Carolina's Yadkin River valley. "We could hardly get along the road for them," remembered William Clinkenbeard, "and all grand Tories, pretty nigh. All from Carolina Tories. Had been treated so bad there, they had to run off or do worse." As Henderson's British connections became useless in protecting any claims made through the Transylvania Company, the arrival of so many new settlers exacerbated tensions in the West. John Todd fretted, "I am afraid to lose sight of my home lest some invader should take possession"; and John Floyd foresaw "a civil war among the people . . . there'll be bloodshed soon."

Revolutionary tensions combined with land conflict in Kentucke. Years of private and public surveying by Virginians had done little to secure property rights. Whether through the hire of a surveyor or through one's own efforts, Virginians carried their land warrants into Kentucke and marked out their claims (usually by making axe marks on trees). These marks or "metes" were connected by "bounds" that indicated the edges of the property. The claimant then hired a surveyor to legitimize the measurements. It was a system well suited to exaggeration, allowing large landowners to maximize their claims, and making claimant conflict inevitable.

The McConnells, McClellands, McCrackens, and other Scotch-Irish from Pennsylvania's Conestoga region, however, operated under an entirely different set of settlement traditions. The midway points between cabins became the property boundaries, making land claims less individuated and contingent upon actual settlement rather than survey. When John Floyd found John McClelland building a station on Floyd's lands along Elkhorn Creek, he determined to evict the squatters. Upon viewing the meager circumstances of the McClelland family, however, Floyd instead offered to sell the land for £300, which McClelland accepted through credit. From squatting to military claims to Virginia surveys, the increasingly complex land claims infuriated John Todd, a veteran of the Battle of Point Pleasant and a recent member of the Virginia bar. "I'm worried to death almost by this learned ignoramus set," he protested, "and what is worse, there are but two lawyers here, and they can't agree." Well, with John Gabriel Jones's departure for the Virginia assembly, there was only one lawyer to unravel the mess—John Todd.

In the meantime, relations with Indians had also continued to deteriorate. The Shawnees and their allies had been relatively quiet through late 1775 and early 1776, uncertain of the status of the hunting lands and somewhat cowed by the convincing defeat at Point Pleasant. British governor of Detroit Henry Hamilton explained that "the Virginians are haughty Violent and bloody, the savages have a high opinion of them as Warriors, but are jealous of their encroachments and very suspicious of their faith in treaties." There was only one documented Indian attack in the early months of 1776, at Powell's Valley, where a handful of pioneers held off a small warring party.

By late spring, circumstances changed. Incited by the rise of the Watauga settlement on their lands in eastern Tennessee, the Cherokees renewed attacks on the North Carolina and south-western Virginia backcountries. On July 14, one Cherokee joined four Shawnees in attacking three girls, one of whom was Jemima Boone, near Boonesborough. Her father, of course, led the rescue mission, which came across the captives and their captors the fol-lowing evening. "Our study had been more to get the prisoners without giving the Indians time to murder them after they dis-covered us, then to kill them . . . ," described John Floyd; "Boone and myself had each a pretty fair shot just as they began to move off. I am well convinced I shot one through, and the one he shot dropt his gun, mine had none. The place was very thick with cane, and being so much elated on recovering the three poor heartbroken girls, prevented our making any further search." Upon hearing of the kidnapping, Cornstalk sent his apologies to Boone.

The Shawnees who attacked Jemima Boone represented a sig-nificant problem for Cornstalk. Despite his accommodationist stance, Cornstalk failed to rein in the more radical elements of the Shawnee nation. The old divisions that had once secured the Shawnee nation's survival in the face of the Iroquois threat again arose to face a new challenge. The Piqua, Chillicothe, and Kis-poki Shawnees rejected Cornstalk's conciliatory position, deciding instead to send representatives to the Cherokee Overhill Towns in August with a nine-foot war belt, indicating their brotherhood in war against the Americans. Desperate to salvage Shawnee-American relations, Cornstalk blamed Mingo banditti led by Chief Pluggy for misleading Shawnee youth, but there was no doubt that what little unity the Shawnees had enjoyed since their re-turn to the Ohio River valley was splintering.

Rumors of a broader Indian war became ubiquitous among the Kentucke settlements and along the Virginia and Pennsyl-vania backcountries. Faced with the terrifying prospect of a pan-Indian rampage on the frontiers, white colonists who had wa-vered in supporting the revolutionary movement discovered they had little choice if they wanted to protect their homes and families. As David Ramsey wrote a decade later, "Several who called themselves Tories in 1775 became active Whigs in 1776." More importantly, as they took up arms against Indians, backcountry colonists increasingly interpreted their actions as anti-British as well, forcing Loyalists to either become Whigs or, like the Bryans, flee Kentucke.

As tensions mounted, Cornstalk appealed directly to the Continental Congress. In late fall, his petition arrived in Philadelphia, pleading:

> When God created this World he gave this Island to the red people & placed your younger Brethren the Shawnees here in the Center— Now we & they see your people seated on our Lands which all Nations esteem as their & our heart—all our Lands are covered by the white people, & we are jealous that you still intend to make larger strides—We never sold you our Lands which you now possess on the Ohio between the Great Kenhawa & the Cherokee, & which you are settling without ever asking our leave, or obtaining our consent.

Congress, of course, had no power or inclination to withdraw white settlers.

Some relief for white pioneers (and for Cornstalk) arrived in late July when Carolina militias, Continental Army troops, and Catawba allies attacked the Cherokee lower towns, burning villages and fields. As among the Shawnees, the Cherokee leadership had disagreed on how to address the colonial threat. Accommodationists under the leadership of Attakullaculla and Oconostata willingly considered colonials' demands for land; Dragging Canoe refused to concede. Rejecting the terms of surrender, he and his followers fled westward into the Tennessee River valley to establish the Chickamauga Confederacy and continue resistance against American expansion. The splintering of Cherokee resistance left rebellious Shawnees without an alliance.

In the meantime, white pioneers in Kentucke quickly harvested their crops and packed up their belongings. Fearing the threat of attack, especially in the winter months when Shawnee hunting needs clashed so dramatically with white settlement of the

Kentucke hunting grounds, they relocated to more secure settlements, abandoning their small, isolated cabins. As winter set in, the larger forts at Harrodstown and Boonesborough burgeoned with communities of fearful settlers. A smaller defensive home, McClelland's Station in the northern reaches of the Great Meadow, was packed as well with extended families from the surrounding countryside who had abandoned their own cabins. Places like Huston's Station and Lee's Town disappeared from the map as residents fled to shelter. John Floyd reported to Preston the seriousness of the situation: "I think more than 300 men have left the country since I came out, and not one has arrived except a few cabbiners down the Ohio." Kentucke was becoming unsettled at a rapid pace.

Of course, concentrating settlement in fewer places also reduced the number of locations that the Indians had to attack. With white populations crammed into Fort Boone and Fort Harrod, Shawnees and Wyandots discovered that patience and stealth outside these forts could prove rewarding. Settlers could be lulled into complacency: women leaving the fort walls to milk cows, men hoping to sneak in a quick survey, children playing. The capture of the Boone and Callaway girls, for example, should have been an important warning to the colonials: old animosities among the Native Americans had been abandoned to fight a common enemy—the white and black invaders of the hunting lands.

The threat of a pan-Indian force raised concerns over the potential for large-scale Indian assaults. James Harrod had managed good relations with the Lenni Lenapes, who kept him apprised of events north of the Ohio River. In mid-1776, Lenni Lenape messengers brought news of a British alliance with the Kickapoos, a nation located on the Michigan peninsula. While the Kickapoos posed no immediate threat to Kentucke, their influence among younger Lenni Lenapes, Wyandots, and Shawnees was strong. Harrod decided to go himself into the Indian country and assess the situation. What he found was disturbing indeed. British agents had been courting the Shawnees for months, and the Kickapoos seemed determined to lead a new pan-Indian ef-

fort to reclaim the ancient hunting lands of Kentucke. Harrod alerted Clark to the urgency of the situation.

With a heightened threat of Indian attack and determined to make Virginia responsible for Kentucke's security, Clark spent his time soliciting gunpowder first from Governor Henry and then from the Executive Council. Henry fully supported supplying the westerners, largely as a ploy to weaken Richard Henderson's power, but the council, while willing to provide five hundred pounds of gunpowder, seemed reluctant to recognize any responsibility for Kentucke. Clark found his opportunity: he challenged the council that "it was out of my power to convey these stores, at my own expense, such a distance through an enemy's country; that I was sorry to find that we should have to seek protection elsewhere, which I did not doubt of getting; that if a country was not worth protecting, it was not worth claiming." The council reconsidered, guaranteeing delivery of the gunpowder as far as Fort Pitt and implying some responsibility for the trans-Appalachian settlements. Somewhat pleased with his success, Clark headed to Fort Pitt to take charge of his gunpowder.

Having never taken a seat in the Virginia Assembly, Clark nonetheless inspired Virginians to reconsider the organization of the western country. Several of the land companies protested Virginia's further involvement in the West, but it was Henderson and the proprietors who stood to lose the most. The previous June, the Virginia Convention had threatened to reevaluate Henderson's claims, resolving that "the validity of the titles under such *Indian* deeds and purchases, shall have been considered and determined on by the Legislature of this country; and that all persons who are now actually settled on any unlocated or unappropriated Lands in *Virginia*, to which there is no other just claim, shall have the preemption or preference in the grants of such Lands." The collapse of Lord Dunmore's governorship and the schism with the crown left all land companies without significant backing, but Governor Henry seized the moment to undermine the Transylvania Company. Henderson's lobbying fell on deaf ears in the assembly. By the end of 1776, Virginia reorganized Fincastle County, dividing it into Montgomery, Washington, and

Kentucky Counties, effectively ending the reign of the Transylvania proprietors and taking on the responsibility of protecting the Kentucke settlements.

Clark had no news of the decision as he accompanied the gunpowder down the Ohio River on the way to Harrodstown. As he and Jones passed the lower Shawnee Town, mostly abandoned for the winter hunts, a party of more radical Mingos and Shawnees under the leadership of Chief Pluggy caught sight of them. For nearly fifty miles, the Indians chased the two men on the currents of the Ohio. When the colonials gained a bit of an advantage, Clark drifted the flatboat among some small islands, where he and Jones hid the powder. A few miles farther, they came upon the Point, a small jut of land that marked the mouth of Limestone Creek, where they debarked and set the boat adrift.

Meeting John Todd's surveying party, the two men decided to separate: Clark, joined by Simon Kenton, left for Harrodstown to enlist men to help transport and guard the powder; Jones and the others remained at the Point. But Todd convinced Jones that they should retrieve the powder quickly rather than await reinforcements. On December 25, as they approached the Ohio River, the Mingos and Shawnees swept down on Jones, killing him and another man, taking a few captives, and forcing the rest to flee to McClelland's Station, the small fort nearly fifty miles away along the Old Buffalo Trace that connected the Point to the center of the Great Meadow.

New Years Eve was a modest celebration in Kentucke, as throughout the other colonies now at war against Great Britain. Traditionally, small gatherings socialized and toasted each other with eggnog. Among wealthier colonists, the drink was flavored with a little rye whiskey, rum, or sherry. The residents of McClelland's Station had no eggnog and probably only a little corn whiskey with which to toast the new year. But celebration was the last thing on their minds as, on the last day of December 1776, Todd and his partners arrived at the fort, followed closely behind by the Indians. Chief Pluggy's warriors surrounded the station, determined to end white occupation of at least this corner of the hunting lands. During the siege of McClelland's Station, several dozen pioneers and Indians were killed, among them Chief

Pluggy. Unable to breach the station's walls, however, the Indians abandoned their attack and retreated across the Ohio River, not realizing their success. John McClelland suffered for a week before succumbing. The survivors of McClelland's Station abandoned the settlement by the end of January 1777, fleeing south of the Kentucky River or back across the Appalachians.

The Terrible Sevens

Decades later, in reminiscing about the early settlement days with John Dabney Shane, pioneers referred to 1777 as the "terrible sevens." It was not just the coincidence of some three sevens in the year; the figure seven played a dominant role in millennialists' conceptualization of the end times that they claimed were playing out in the late eighteenth century. For many settlers in Kentucke, 1777 seemed apocalyptic, beginning with the demise of McClelland's Station. With the settlement deserted, only Fort Harrod and a nearly completed Fort Boone remained fortified enough to protect pioneers.

Across the Ohio River, 1777 proved equally disastrous for the Shawnees. In late February, concerned over the long-term consequences of their renegade young men and the Mingo influence, Chief Cornstalk and other conciliatory Shawnee leaders appealed to George Morgan, the Continental Congress's new superintendent for Indian affairs. They swore to secede from the Shawnee nation and relocate to a new village. And weeks later, when an invitation arrived from the Lenni Lenapes to join them in a peaceful coexistence with the American colonials, Cornstalk began to make plans.

Cornstalk's sister, Nonhelema, represented a different faction of Shawnees. It was not uncommon for Indian nations to splinter under the pressures of war, and certainly the Shawnees had a difficult choice to make between the Americans who seemed determined to steal their land and the British who appeared desperate to control their trade and their politics. Nonhelema, known among the colonials as Grenadier Squaw, sent warning to officials at Virginia's Fort Randolph that the Shawnees indeed had allied with the British. Morgan knew otherwise, however, reporting to the Continental Congress that while several divisions of the Shawnees had become unmanageable, two others remained loyal to the American cause.

In the meantime, Kentucke's settlers hurriedly completed the fort at Boonesborough, and Benjamin Logan was hard at work on a smaller fort near St. Asaph. When Logan and his family and slaves had arrived less than a year earlier, there were over one thousand settlers in Kentucke. The Indian threat had taken its toll. As he constructed Logan's Station in the early spring of 1777, Logan was one of only 280 remaining colonists.

Logan was also the new sheriff of Kentucky County and one of four militia captains. The others were James Harrod, John Todd, and Daniel Boone, all under the command of Colonel James Bowman and Major George Rogers Clark. As meager as this militia organization may seem, it provided an immediate civil structure to face an increasingly dangerous threat. The British did not hide their interest in reducing the Kentucke settlements, openly encouraging Mingos and Kickapoos to chase colonials from the Great Meadow and to restore the hunting lands. Detroit governor Henry Hamilton keenly understood the loyalty that the British could muster from their Indian allies if trans-Appalachia were wiped clean of its colonial invaders. The Virginia assembly responded by planning an attack upon Pluggy's Town, a stronghold of anti-colonial Mingos and Shawnees. Under pressure from the Continental Congress to avoid inflaming the Mingos, however, the expedition was put on hold. It was a tragic mistake. Nearly seventy Indians under the leadership of Shawnee chief Blackfish marched upon Harrodstown in early March, attacking a party of surveyors but finding the fort itself tightly secured.

By April 24, Blackfish's force appeared outside Boonesborough and laid siege for two days. Defenses remained strong, but the Indians drew settlers out of the fort. The ensuing battle took one pioneer's life and injured several others, including Daniel Boone, who escaped death only through the efforts of Simon Kenton, a settler of the Ohio River valley who had relocated to Boonesborough for safety.

In late May, Blackfish renewed the attack on Boonesborough, using flaming arrows to try to set the fort ablaze. Unsuccessful and certainly frustrated, the Indians turned upon Logan's Fort. Despite two months of attacks in the region, their arrival at St. Asaph took the settlers by surprise. Over the course of a thirteen-day siege, pioneers became increasingly desperate as supplies dwindled. Imagining their attackers had left, Ann Logan, Esther Whitley, and a slave woman snuck out of the fort to milk the dairy cows, but the Indians shot their armed escorts. One wounded man was left outside the fort as the gates closed behind the retreating women. Certain that nightfall would allow Indians to scalp him, Benjamin Logan used a feather mattress to protect himself as he retrieved the injured man.

For the next month, intermittent attacks continued. The Indians waited patiently, allowing settlers to convince themselves that each threat had ended. When Barney Stagner tried to pasture his horse outside Boonesborough, the Indians cut off his head. The tactic was horrifying, reinforcing rumors that Hamilton paid the Indians by the number of scalps they brought into Detroit. On June 26, pioneers found a scalped corpse, this time with a letter from Hamilton offering two hundred acres to any settler willing to fight for the British. Only with the arrival of Colonel Bowman's hundred-man militia did the Indians gradually abandon their attacks. On September 11, a final battle ensued between pioneers and a lingering party of Shawnees.

The escalation of terror in 1777 inspired George Rogers Clark to take a more aggressive stance. With reports from Kaskaskia and Vincennes, Clark concluded that most of the northwestern Indians had joined the British. He devised a plan to surprise the British with an invasion of the Illinois country, specifically targeting the base at Detroit. Clark did not have the resources, however, and decided to again request assistance from Virginia. He left for Williamsburg in October, intending to visit family before revealing his plans to Governor Henry.

Chief Cornstalk also traveled eastward, visiting Virginia's Fort Randolph in November to try to negotiate a solution to the conflict. The last remaining accommodationist Shawnee leader, Cornstalk recognized the fading opportunities to salvage a peace. But the Virginians were in a foul mood after a year of Indian attacks, and Cornstalk, his son, and a companion were slaugh-

tered. Their deaths shocked both Indians and Virginians. Patrick
Henry claimed it was a British conspiracy to incite warfare between the colonists and Indians. Colonel William Fleming apolo-
gized for "a few hot headed rash young Men enraged on seeing
the Body of one of their Officers brought from this Fort," and
then turned to the tactic to which Cornstalk had appealed on so
many previous occasions:

> When you consider how often your hot headed young Men, con-
> trary to your Orders, and without your knowledge have murdered
> and robbed many of our people on the Frontier, in times of pro-
> found Peace, without the least Provocation. There Murders and
> Robberies were overlooked and not revenged; because our great
> Men believed your Chief and Warriors understand that they were
> not committed by the Consent of your Nation.

Which times of profound peace Fleming alluded to went unde-
fined.

Cornstalk's murder infuriated the Shawnees and pushed most
remaining accommodationists fully into the anti-American camp.
Among the most vocal was Cornstalk's successor, Chief Blackfish, who organized a war party to eliminate the white menace in
Kentucke. Realizing the heightened stakes, Clark consulted with
Jefferson, George Mason, and George Wythe about arranging
landed pensions for volunteers to raid the Illinois country. Governor Henry pushed a vaguely defined plan "to march against
and attack any of our western enemies" through the General Assembly, including elevating Clark's rank to lieutenant colonel
and authorizing him to command three hundred volunteers. Privately, Henry encouraged Clark further: "What I have in View is
that your operations should not be confined to the Fort [Kaska-
skia] & the Settlement mention'd in your secret Instructions but
that you proceed to the Enemy's Settlements above or across as
you may find it proper."

As Henry and Clark schemed, Daniel Boone led a couple dozen
men from Fort Boone to the Lower Blue Licks on a salt-making
expedition. In early January 1778 as Boone hunted, the men busily
boiled the briny waters of the springs in order to distill salt. Chief
Blackfish's warring party, 120 men strong, surprised and cap-

tured Boone. Realizing the imminent danger to his companions, Boone negotiated with Blackfish the capture and assimilation of the men into the Shawnee nation. Not surprisingly, the colonials were shocked by his agreement and his assurances to the Shawnees that he would sacrifice Boonesborough as well. His only condition was that surrender of the fort take place in the spring "when the weather will be warm, and the women and children can travel . . . to the Indian towns," where the whites would "all live with you as one people . . . [and] the young men will make you fine warriors, and excellent hunters to kill games for your squaws and children."

Boone had consented to a full assimilation of the Boonesborough settlement into the Shawnee nation. And he had accepted the role of Blackfish's adopted son, replacing a son who had been killed during the attempted kidnapping of Jemima Boone and the Callaway girls. When the captives and captors arrived in Chillicothe, Boone ran the gauntlet, flogged by nearly one hundred Indians, who symbolically vented their grief over the loss of sons and husbands through inflicting physical pain on the captives. Then Boone was cleansed of his whiteness, scrubbed thoroughly, with his hair cut and plucked to mimic the Shawnee style. Finally, he was renamed Sheltowee, or Big Turtle, and adopted into the nation through a great feast. The other captives were not as willing to become Indians. Some ran the gauntlet, but nearly half were deemed unacceptable for adoption and sent on to Detroit for the British to ransom. Others remained at Chillicothe, disgruntled and unsure of the man who had become Kentucke's first legend.

To Excel Them in Barbarity

As Boone's reputation faltered, George Rogers Clark's rose. Clark spent much of the spring of 1778 trying to enlist volunteers for his excursion into the Illinois country. He wanted 500 men, but by May only 150 had joined. Unable to wait any longer, his meager force set off down the Ohio River. When they reached the Falls of the Ohio, they constructed a station, cabins, and stockade fence on a small island, and planted a small patch of corn, ordaining

Figure 3.2. During the Revolutionary War, Corn Island was settled by settlers who remained behind when George Rogers Clark's party departed on its Illinois military campaign in 1779. Its name reflects the importance of sustenance, but it also evidences the urgency in planting corn to lay claim to land. From Z. F. Smith, *The History of Kentucky* (Louisville, Ky.: Courier-Journal Printing, 1886), opp. 160.

the place Corn Island. A few families had followed the force and remained at the island as Clark and his men set off in late June.

By July 4, Clark's men were outside Kaskaskia in the Illinois country, a town of nearly one thousand residents—black and white, and mostly French. The British manned a small fort in Kaskaskia, which was attacked at nightfall and quickly captured. Immediately, Clark scattered half of his men throughout the town to keep anyone from leaving to alert the British or Indians elsewhere. The following day, a contingent of thirty militiamen on horseback under Bowman's leadership left Kaskaskia for Prairie du Rocher, about fifteen miles to the north. Quickly, the village of 350 fell; as did St. Philips, and then Cahokia, where another 400 people lived. Within one week, Clark's troops had secured most of the European settlements in the Illinois country and a great deal of loyalty from the French citizenry, who had merely tolerated British control and eagerly swore allegiance to the Americans upon hearing of France's 1777 alliance with the colonies in their war for independence. When Vincennes fell on July 14, Clark had established an American base in the far West.

It truly was an amazing feat with only 150 men, but more challenging than capturing these villages and forts was holding them. Clark had to present the illusion of overwhelming force and stern intentions. In order to dissuade Indian attack, he invited tribal leaders to Cahokia to negotiate terms of peaceful coexistence. He greeted the leaders with a peace belt and a war belt, and then admonished the leaders to choose carefully, for if they chose the war belt, "this is the last speech you may ever expect from the Big Knives; the next thing will be the tomahawk. And you may expect, in four moons, to see your women and children given to the dogs to eat, while nations that have kept their word with me will flourish and grow like the willow trees on the river banks, under the care and nourishment of their father, the Big Knives."

Almost simultaneous with Clark's June departure into the Illinois country was the return of Daniel Boone to Boonesborough. In the five months since the salt-making party had left the fort, the residents had first heard that Boone and the others had been killed, and then that they had been captured, and finally as a few escapees returned to Boonesborough, they heard of Boone's treason. For his part, Boone insisted his cooperation with the Shawnees had actually saved the other men and Boonesborough. He had escaped Chillicothe under cover of a hunting trip, and he encouraged the men to follow him on a preemptive strike against the Shawnees. In August, the small party crossed the Ohio River and fumbled from one village to the next, failing in all regards save angering Blackfish further. Joined by Wyandots, Lenni Lenapes, Mingos, Miamis, and some British military, Blackfish accumulated a 350-man force and set off toward Boonesborough to fulfill Boone's agreement of full assimilation of the settlement's residents. He arrived on September 6, one day after Boone's embarrassed and discouraged group hobbled back into the fort.

The siege of Fort Boone lasted ten days, during which Boone and other men negotiated with the Indian contingent. Blackfish was sincere in his desire to assimilate the settlers, even bringing forty horses to accommodate women and children on the return trip to Chillicothe. But debate raged inside the fort. If Boone had prevailed, the pioneers would have surrendered the fort and joined the Shawnee nation as adopted sons and daughters. Richard Callaway led the majority of settlers in rejecting Boone's plan, however. Becoming Indian was contrary to ideas of self, of colonial American identity, and of civilization itself. Imposing their will upon Boone, the pioneers determined to fight to the death. Callaway led the defensive effort, positioning shooters along the top of the fort, among which were several women disguised as men to provide the illusion of great manpower. Possibly because Blackfish was intent on assimilating the population rather than killing it, the Indians never attacked the fort and remained content in taking occasional shots at the men atop the fort. Some Shawnees tried to tunnel into the fort, but when their efforts partially collapsed, the Indians' will broke, and they abandoned the siege.

About one hundred Shawnees remained in Kentucke, roaming in small bands and occasionally attacking whites. But this tactic could never recover the hunting lands for the Indians. Instead, a general exodus took place as Shawnees north of the Ohio River recognized the regional war that seemed imminent. They abandoned their villages, some scattering to the Lenni Lenape town of Coshocton in the Allegheny Mountains while others relocated entire villages westward. Reminiscent of a century earlier, the Shawnees again splintered into kinship groups. The Thawekilas, Piquas, and Kispokis, for example, moved en masse down the Ohio River, eventually ending their journey in the Missouri country.

Meanwhile, British governor Henry Hamilton discovered Clark's successes in the Illinois country and, in October 1778, decided to retake the territory with a hodgepodge army of about 240 men. He anticipated picking up numerous Indian allies en route, and gathered about 360 more troops before he arrived outside Vincennes. Hamilton recognized that the town was not well fortified or manned by the Americans, and in mid-December, he easily captured it. Then, he chose to rest. His Indian allies left for the winter; his French troops scattered back to Canada; Hamilton held Vincennes with sixty-nine men.

Upon news of the fall of Vincennes, Clark did not hesitate to begin plans for recapturing it. Warned that Hamilton had stirred up a large contingent of Indian allies, Clark replied that "to excel

them in barbarity was and is the only way to make war upon Indians and gain a name among them." He pushed his men through the
difficult winter conditions to reach Vincennes by mid-February. A
master of psychological warfare, Clark found the perfect opportunity to demonstrate his ruthlessness to Hamilton. A party of
unwary French and Indian marauders was captured by Clark's
men, and four of the Indians were massacred; their mutilated
bodies were tossed in the river. Hamilton remembered how he
met Clark soon after this event: "He had just come from his Indian triumph all bloody and sweating—seated himself on the
edge of one of the bateaus, that had some rainwater in it, & while
he washed his hands and face still reeking from the human sacrifice in which he had acted as chief priest, he told me with great
exultation how he had been employed." Clark capably convinced
Hamilton that he was outnumbered and that the Americans' determination was stronger. Given "honorable" terms to surrender,
Hamilton gave up Vincennes on February 24.

Hamilton's surrender stirred trouble in Virginia. British officers captured at Saratoga in 1777 had been transported to the Old
Dominion, where they lounged as gentlemen prisoners in rented
homes and dined with some of the state's finest families. Hamilton, despite formally surrendering to Clark, received none of
these amenities. Handcuffed, he arrived first in Kentucke and
then was taken on to Virginia, where newly elected Governor
Thomas Jefferson concurred with the council to lock up Hamilton and his fellow officers in the basement of a local jail, deprived
of communication.

Only months before, in defense of the more genteel incarcera-
tion of those captured at Saratoga, Jefferson had asked then governor Patrick Henry:

> Is an enemy so execrable that, though in captivity, his wishes and
> comforts are to be disregarded and even crossed? I think not. It is
> for the benefit of mankind to mitigate the horrors of war as much
> as possible. The practice, therefore, of modern nations, of treat-
> ing captive enemies with politeness and generosity, is not only de-
> lightful in contemplation, but really interesting to all the world,
> friends, foes and neutrals.

But Jefferson refused to apply the same logic to Hamilton. "The indiscriminate murder of men, women and children, with the horrid circumstances of barbarity practised by the Indian savages, was the particular task of Governor Hamilton's employment," he protested. Jefferson believed that formal warfare waged against soldiers justified better treatment of captives, but those who fought in more barbaric, terror-driven manners sacrificed rights to humane treatment. In the first week of October 1779, frustrated by Hamilton's demands for "freedom of speech" and desperate to resolve the issue, he wrote three letters to George Washington, who expressed concerns over the potential treatment of American prisoners and convinced Jefferson to send the captives to New York.

Besides creating difficulties for the new governor of Virginia, Hamilton's capture was possibly the most crucial moment to date in the long struggle between the Ohio River valley Indians and the white pioneers of Kentucke. The British had never formally allied with any of the Native Americans, but before February 1779, Hamilton had successfully spurred Shawnees, Wyandots, Miamis, and others into attacking the American settlements by providing aid and arms. The British had always been more opportunistic than instigative in the trans-Appalachian West. But Hamilton's capture disrupted the British momentum; the Native Americans not only had to muster their own motivation, but also had to inspire the British to reinvest in the effort. It would not prove too difficult to motivate a truly aggressive struggle against the Kentuckians. By the end of February, Shawnees attended a multinational council in Detroit that agreed to wage full war on the "Big Knives." But even as attacks on settlers escalated, with the British in Detroit reporting increased numbers of Indians delivering scalps as evidence of their handiwork and barter for goods, a war did not come.

Much of the reason why a full-scale Indian war did not arise in 1779 must be attributed to a shift in the Kentuckians' approach toward the Indians. Until Clark's invasion of the Illinois country, pioneers had always been on the defensive, anxiously awaiting the next Indian attack. Clark, with his openly aggressive tactics and anti-Indian rhetoric, showed the way to terrorize the enemy. His tomahawking of the four Indians was a message that reverberated across the Ohio River valley. Pennsylvania put a bounty of one thousand dollars on Indian scalps, inspiring Kentucky militiamen to acquire them by any means, including digging up Shawnee graves and scalping the corpses. John Bowman, who had led the raids of Prairie du Rocher and Cahokia, took up Clark's tomahawk and recruited 160 men, including Benjamin Logan and James Harrod, to join him in a May 1779 attack on Chillicothe. They burned houses and stole horses, surprising the Shawnees who had remained in the village. Mortally wounded in the attack was Chief Blackfish. The Kentuckians' only error was in lingering too long and giving the Shawnees time to rally. As the fight escalated, the Kentuckians had to retreat. But the damage had been done: the Shawnees abandoned Chillicothe and moved up the Mad River. With the Indians of the Illinois country sufficiently subdued, the Cherokees cowed, the Shawnees scattered, and the British influence in disarray, the Virginia legislature decided in October 1779 that only one regiment would be needed for its western defenses.

The lone remaining threat—the Chickasaws—had seemed too distant from Virginia to pose a substantial danger. As British allies, the Chickasaws had concentrated most of their efforts on the lower Mississippi River valley, but with British influence waning in the northwest, Clark fully anticipated an assault from the southwest. In September, he appealed to Governor Thomas Jefferson that construction of a fort at the confluence of the Mississippi and Ohio Rivers would awe "our Enemies the Chickasaws and the English posts on the Mississippie, the Strength of the Garison ought not to be less than two Hundred men after built, A Hundred Families that might Easily be got to Settle in a town would be of great advantage in promoting the place." Within six months, Fort Jefferson had arisen, with the small settlement of Clarksville beside it.

Clark's military success (and Boone's blunder in his association with Blackfish) positioned the former as Kentuckians' new hero. In fact, by the spring of 1780, Clark was being called to all reaches of the western country to defend settlers, American and otherwise. He went to St. Louis at the request of its Spanish residents to help them stave off a British siege. After that success, he rushed back to Fort Jefferson to help hold off an assault by one thousand Chickasaws. Then rumor circulated throughout the Kentucke settlements that the British had reorganized in Detroit and prepared to launch an expedition south of the Ohio River. From Williamsburg, Jefferson urged Clark to take on an expedition either against Detroit or against "those tribes of Indians between the Ohio and Illinois rivers who have harassed us with eternal hostilities, and whom experience has shewn to be incapable of reconciliation."

The dual threat of Detroit and the northern Indians became more dangerous in mid-June 1780 when a British force 150 strong, joined by 700 Indians, crossed the Ohio River and captured Ruddle's and Martin's Stations in northern Kentucke quite easily before retreating back across the river. Panicked residents in Boonesborough petitioned Clark: "Destitute of every other hope, the Inhabitants of this Country look to you for Protection." Still, despite the pleas of Boonesborough, as Clark made plans for a northern invasion, he discovered pioneers on the south side of the Kentucky River less concerned. Upon reaching Harrodstown, he found a community almost indifferent to defensive needs. Instead, the land court was overly busy with claimants from across the region. Clark ordered the court closed, and commanded militiamen at Crab Orchard, along the Wilderness Road, to turn back any settlers attempting to flee eastward. He initiated a draft, and when those men combined with the garrison that he recalled from Corn Island, he had over one thousand men prepared to march on New Chillicothe. They arrived in the Shawnee village in July only to find that Chief Black Hoof had ordered residents to retreat to Piqua Town, abandoning New Chillicothe.

Intent on a successful campaign, Clark chose to pursue but ran into a Shawnee and Mingo force led by Simon Girty, a former Indian captive who had turned against the Americans and served as Hamilton's interpreter and scout. Nearly three hundred Shawnees defended Piqua Town, but the Kentuckians fought recklessly, rushing into the midst of the village with a suicidal abandon that startled Girty's men. The Shawnees and Mingos abandoned the village, and Clark burned it down.

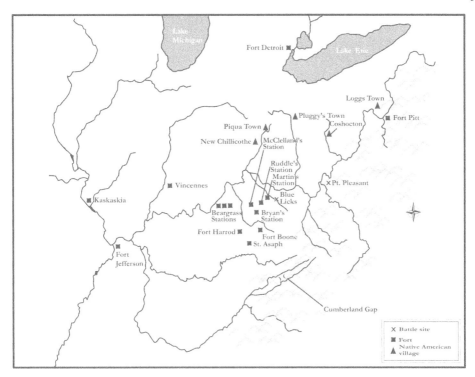

Map 3.1. The Revolutionary War in the Ohio River Valley. Drawn by Sherry Hardin.

In the meanwhile, Kentucke stood exposed. In September 1780, settlers at Squire Boone's station in the western bluegrass fled to the Beargrass stations for defense and right into an ambush at Long Run Creek. In the same month, several Chickasaw attacks and a four-day siege against Fort Jefferson had reduced supplies, and although reinforcements under William Clark had come to the pioneers' aid, nearly half of the population abandoned nearby Clarksville. Early 1781 proved the breaking point. As the winter snows of the upper Midwest melted, the Mississippi River valley flooded, as did Fort Jefferson. By May, there were only eighty-seven colonists remaining, and the decision was made to evacuate the fort and the settlement, and retreat to the Falls of the Ohio. Aided by nature, the Chickasaws had won the fight for control over western Kentucke.

They were the only Native Americans who saw success against the Kentucke colonists. Desperately, in August 1780, the Lenni

Lenapes and Shawnees at Coshocton appealed to warring Shawnees and Lenni Lenapes to join them in pursuing peace. Although traditionally friendly to the Americans, the Lenni Lenapes
sensed the advantage that Clark and the Kentuckians had gained
in taking the fight to the enemy. In spring 1781, General Daniel
Brodhead, who had been charged by Washington with the task
of "reducing Detroit," ambushed Lenni Lenapes headed to Philadelphia to meet with the Continental Congress. His party burned
Coshocton, taking the women and children as prisoners, and
tomahawking the men as per Clark's example.

Brodhead's incursion into the Ohio country disrupted Shawnee activities in Kentucke. John Floyd informed George Rogers
Clark that the "Indians have this year suffered us to plant corn
on Beargrass unmolested; the reason of which I expect, is ow-
ing to the little Expedition you ordered against some of their
Towns early this spring, which has attracted the attention of other
Tribes." While colonial settlers experienced a bit of normalcy, the
Shawnees were in panic. Any pro-American sentiment that had
lingered into the new decade dissipated. Chief Wryneck of the
Shawnee led a multinational delegation to Detroit to solicit British support. "We see ourselves weak and our arms feeble to the
force of the Enemy," he pleaded. Reminding the British that "'tis
now upwards of Twenty years since we have been alone engaged
against the Virginians," Wryneck demanded intercession.

Wryneck, however, grossly misread the situation. The Shawnees held an advantage: their traditional patterns of mobility
made them highly adaptable to the ways in which the Kentuckians chose to take the war to the enemy. In contrast to the American pioneers, who had little choice but to bunker in defensive
structures, hoping to outlast the siege and extinguish the flames,
the Shawnees and their allies who lived among them merely
abandoned villages, as they had done with Chillicothe. American warriors burned down some villages that were never rebuilt.
Others arose from the ashes, testimony to the resilience of the
Native Americans.

And there was a renewed determination under new leadership to eliminate the Kentucke colonists for good. Throughout
the summer of 1781, Shawnee and Mingo warriors led by Simon

Girty struck throughout the region. As George Rogers Clark prepared an expedition to capture Detroit, Iroquois and Loyalists led by Thayendanegea, a Mohawk chief known to the colonists as Joseph Brant, ambushed a Pennsylvania militia company critical to Clark's plans near the mouth of the Miami River. John Floyd warned Clark that the militia in all of Kentucke numbered no more than twelve hundred, "and our numbers seem to decrease." Frustrated, Clark postponed his offensive. A couple months later in October 1781, far to the east of Kentucke, British general Lord Cornwallis surrendered to Generals Benjamin Lincoln and George Washington and their French allies at Yorktown.

Racializing Kentucke

From the colonial perspective, the violence that wracked Kentucke in the 1770s and early 1780s was a contest for land and hunting rights. It had little to do with the Revolutionary War that raged in the East; they fought not for independence but for survival. So too was it a fight for survival by the Indians. While the British eagerly supplied and inspired the Shawnees and others to create chaos on the western frontiers, the Native Americans most certainly would have waged war against the invasion of Kentucke even without British support.

The rapidity with which this struggle began to assume the characteristics of a racial war, therefore, is a bit surprising. But colonial Americans, arriving on the frontier with preconceived notions of race and savagery, quickly reverted to racial categorization to define their enemies. Most often, they employed various shades of yellow to describe the Indians. "Shawnees were almost gold-yellow and small," Sarah Graham recalled decades later. In fact, color became a primary identifier in the midst of battle. James McMullen shot and killed "a sort of yellow man," only to discover that it was Peter Harper, the son of a former Indian captive. In his version of the capture of Jemima Boone and the Callaway girls, Nathaniel Hart rationalized the girls' initial lack of caution because they confused one of the Indians for Simon, "a yellow man, who staid at the Fort."

The term "copper" also became common, merely requiring a little red be added to the yellow skin tones. In 1782, an unidentified settler on the upper Ohio River related a premonition she had about an Indian attack: in her dream, "a 'copper' snake struck, fastening its fangs in the palm of her husband's hand, and that all her efforts to detach the venomous reptile were unavailing." A decade later, David Meade was alarmed by boats on the Ohio River "rowed by naked Copper colored men—of very savage appearance." Daniel Drake remembered how "nearly all my troubled or vivid dreams included either Indians or snakes—the copper colored man & the copper headed snake." The connection of skin color to nature was particularly poignant for colonials. After all, the settlement of Kentucke required the conquest and reconfiguration of nature, and as extensions of the natural world, Indians too needed to be conquered and either assimilated or destroyed.

Intimately incorporated into colonials' conceptualizations of skin color was a conventional wisdom about savagery. Yellow and copper were not just colors, they were categories: colonials portrayed Indians with more reddish hues as more vicious, more poisonous—like snakes. As when used to describe mulattos, yellow suggested mixture not only of race but of civilized state. Red meant purely savage; yellow meant mutability—it was an important distinction since it allowed for the opportunity of converting "yellow" Indians to whiteness. In 1772, Baptist missionary David Jones puzzled about whites who adapted to Indian culture: "It seemed strange to me to see the captives have the exact gestures of Indians. Might we not infer from hence, that if Indians were educated as we are, they would be like us?" Of course, the answer was "yes," but in the 1770s, the possibility was more theoretical than actual.

In the midst of war, colonials had little use for theory. In the most practical way, skin color was a quick and easy indicator of foes and friends. But as in the case of the Boone and Callaway girls or that of Peter Harper, it was not always a reliable marker. In fact, *despite* skin color, identity was rather fluid on the Kentucke frontiers. On several occasions, Daniel Boone lived as an Indian among his Shawnee family, so successfully in fact that he could not convince the settlers at Fort Boone of his "whiteness"—and therefore his trustworthiness—upon his return.

Some white captives preferred to remain among Native American peoples, adopting similar identities to their captors. Captain Riddle lost his sons to Indians in 1780, only to be reunited fifteen years later. As Daniel Trabue related the meeting:

> Emedeately Old Reddle cryed out aloud and fell Down on the floore, Crying and bewailing his condition. Said he, "My cheldrin is Indians!"
>
> Stephen took hold of his father and said, "Holt your heart, fatter. Holt your heart, fater."
>
> . . . The Old Capt. Riddle continued some time crying. When ever he would look at his children he would renew his crying. This was after night. The next morning O Capt. Riddle gave his sons clean Cloathing and got them to wash of the paint and put on these clean cloaths.

In Riddle's view, appearance—clothing and painted skin—signified the young men as Indians. While difficult for the old man, however, the moment was probably far more traumatic for the sons. Despite their father's effort to convert the young men back to whiteness, within two hours, they had donned their Indian clothing again. As individuals with a sense of familial connection, they recognized Riddle as father, but they clung to their Indian-ness, an identity shaped by a decade and a half of communal reinforcement. Riddle's fear that his "Cheldrin is Indians" evidences a fear among frontier whites that Indians were much more successful in refashioning individuals and their identities.

Indeed, Shawnees and other Native Americans expected to conquer and assimilate (as Blackfish's intentions with the Boonesborough colonists indicates), and since the Seven Years' War, they had been somewhat successful at both. Perhaps Simon Girty epitomized the advantage that Native Americans had in this contest for bodies and souls. In 1750, Indians murdered his father over a land dispute. A few years later, in the midst of the Seven Years' War, the entire Girty family became Seneca captives, and his stepfather was burned at the stake. For over a decade, Girty lived among the Senecas, learning as many as eleven native lan-

guages and adopting the Seneca culture as his own. Even upon
returning to the colonial side of the frontier in the early 1770s, he
continued to dress and live as an Indian, moving between whites
and natives with ease. During Lord Dunmore's War and again in
the early years of the Revolutionary War, he fought on the colonial side. But then, in 1778, he joined an American militia sent to
engage an Indian force in the Ohio County. The enemy could not
be found, and Girty watched as militiamen turned their frustration on four Indian women and a boy; only one woman survived.
The moment catalyzed Girty's Indian identity. He abandoned the
colonials and enlisted with the British Indian Department in Detroit. For the next decade and a half, he joined with Shawnees
and Mingos in raiding the Kentucke settlements, leaving a trail
of destruction behind that earned him the title "white savage."

Girty's identity contrasts dramatically with that of Daniel
Boone, who for a brief time was also a "white savage." While
both men underwent initiation into native society, Boone abandoned (at least publicly) any fondness he may have developed for
his adopted father Blackfish or for Indian life. Girty, in contrast,
fully embraced the opportunity to become an Indian and understood the stakes for his adopted community. In 1782, as he led a
large war party into Kentucke, he inspired his warriors: "Brothers, the Long Knives have overrun your country and usurped
your hunting grounds. They have destroyed the cane, trodden
down the clover, killed the deer and the buffalo, the bear and the
raccoon. The beaver has been chased from his dam and forced to
leave the country. . . . Were there a voice in the trees of the forest, or articulate sounds in the gurgling waters, every part of this
country would call on you to chase away these ruthless invaders,
who are laying it to waste." For Native Americans, reclamation
of Kentucke required a quick conquest and preservation of nature. Delay would result in loss of the game that made the hunting grounds worth war and the ultimate destruction of Girty's
adopted culture.

With a racial war emerging, the racial distinction often ignored
was that between blacks and whites. In *Notes on the State of Virginia*, published in 1781, Jefferson recognized the "first difference" among people as "colour." When comparing blacks to In-

dians, he seemed dumbfounded how these two "inferior" peoples could be so different:

> Some [blacks] have been liberally educated, and all have lived in countries where the arts and sciences are cultivated to a considerable degree, and have had before their eyes samples of the best works from abroad. The Indians, with no advantages of this kind, will often carve figures on their pipes not destitute of design and merit. They will crayon out an animal, a plant, or a country, so as to prove the existence of a germ in their minds which only wants cultivation. They astonish you with strokes of the most sublime oratory; such as prove their reason and sentiment strong, their imagination glowing and elevated. But never yet could I find that a black had uttered a thought above the level of plain narration; never see even an elementary trait of painting or sculpture.

Jefferson's formulation of race credited Native Americans with intellectual potential while denying any for blacks.

On the Kentucke frontiers, whites most certainly shared Jefferson's view of black inferiority, but the common goal of survival mediated divisive racism. In the stories of the era, African Americans played important if not occasionally central roles. In 1773, Adam escaped an Indian attack that killed his fellow slave Charles and several whites, including Daniel Boone's son James. In 1775, Sam died at the hands of Indians as the Boone party cleared the Wilderness Road for Richard Henderson. Three years later, as Shawnees laid siege to Fort Boone, Nathaniel Henderson's slave London shot at the enemy throughout the night until the flash of the gun revealed his position to Indian marksmen. At the siege of Estill's Station in 1782, Wyandots captured a slave named Monk, who yelled from the woods that there were only about twenty-five Indians, inspiring the settlers to keep fighting. When he effected his escape and returned to the station after the Indians abandoned their efforts, his master freed him. That same year, "Black Sam" heard the Indians whooping as they attacked his owner's family and, approaching the cabin, discovered an Indian placing a white baby in the grass. He stealthily retrieved the child and raced to a nearby station. Later, he found his master and related that at least a daughter had survived. Near

Crab Orchard, Indians attacked a cabin inhabited by a woman, her daughter, and their lame slave. When one Indian breached the doorway, the slave held him as the daughter hacked him with an ax. As individuals just trying to stay alive, black pioneers were identical to their white neighbors.

Some, like Ben, found opportunity in the fluidity of racial identity on the Kentucke frontiers. As related by Lewis Collins, whose 1848 publication of *Historical Sketches of Kentucky* reflected his own interviewing of pioneers and access to the stories they related to their children, the slave Ben had a reputation for hating Indians and relishing opportunities to chase the "yaller varmints." One day, he joined a vigilante crowd intent on retrieving stolen horses from a party of Shawnees, but as they breached a hilltop, the pioneers discovered that the thieves were part of a much larger force. A retreat was called, but Ben determined to engage the enemy and bounded down the hillside. He shot an Indian, the rifle crack shocking all of the Indians and creating chaos in the camp. He then ran back up the hill to join his retreating party, chastising the Indians to "take dat to 'member Ben—de 'black white man.'"

Within the liminal space of the trans-Appalachian West, a "black white man" was conceivable. The shared dangers of frontier life drew the two races closer together. In Powell's Valley, en route to Kentucke, John Redd met a "dark mulatto" who "notwithstanding his coller he was treated with as much respect as any white man." Henry Parvin's recollection of seeing a party of Indians as a child is most revealing: "We saw them, a parcel of swarthy, yellow looking things, with shining pieces of silver on, and we thought they had killed a snake, and thought of going to see what kind of one it was they were gathered around, taking them to be a parcel of mulattoes." Some Indians looked like mulattos but, of course, they *were not* mulattos because they were actual threats. Blacks, light-skinned or dark-skinned, were safer and more reliable as fellow victims of the terror.

Where the possibility existed for a "black white man," so too were opportunities for black Indians. When captured in 1778, Boone met a man who lived among the Shawnees and served as Blackfish's interpreter. How Pompey became Shawnee is unknown, but by 1778, he leveraged important diplomatic power. It was Pompey who negotiated with Boone for the surrender of Boonesborough, and it was through the African American's translations that Boone convinced the Shawnees to delay their attack. When Boone escaped to warn the settlers, Pompey followed, advancing ahead of the Shawnees and initiating negotiations between Blackfish and Boone. In the colonial mind, however, Pompey was no longer black: he was Indian and therefore dangerous. As the siege continued, he climbed a tree to aim at pioneers. In a flurry of gunshot from the fort, Pompey fell dead. It was impossible to discern who actually shot Pompey, but Boone, his fellow settlers, and early historians quickly attributed it to the great frontiersman, restoring whiteness to one whose ethnicity had been questioned hours before. In fact, when Richard Callaway and Benjamin Logan charged Boone with treason, the jury of militia officers not only cleared him but promoted him to major.

In Kentucke, most whites bunkered down with black slaves on the trans-Appalachian frontier in a desperate struggle for survival against the Native Americans. As participants in the white side of the war, blacks seemed reliable and safe companions in the face of terror. But Lord Dunmore's War had exposed heightened racial tensions as British-supported Indians menaced Virginia's western frontier and as a British-sponsored Ethiopian Regiment threatened its coastal counties. Black Indians such as Pompey represented the potential for a most dangerous identity in the West's fluid matrix of racial and ethnic identities.

Still, because the frontier continued to moderate racism, Indians remained the only immediate and real threat. Only Indians became identified as Others, those who were culturally different and outside civilized settlement. In 1776, citizens of Fort Harrod petitioned Virginia's assembly to supply arms and ammunition to prevent "the inroads of the Savages and the effusion of innocent blood." In using adjectives such as "savage" to describe Indians and "innocent" to portray whites *and* blacks, white colonials drew sharp cultural distinctions between themselves and those they sought to replace. "We Virginians had for some time been waging a war of intrusion on them,"

Daniel Boone readily acknowledged, "and I, amongst the rest, rambled through the woods in pursuit of their race, as I now would follow the tracks of ravenous animals." As with the association of copper-skinned Indians with copper-skinned snakes, the identification of native peoples with the desperation of starving animals muted their humanity and justified the invasion of Kentucke. Indians were terrifying, but episodes when captives elected to remain with Indians rather than return to white society also demonstrated that Indians were alluring, making them all the more dangerous.

4.

PEOPLING KENTUCKE

Below Kentucke's topsoils lay fissures and fault lines, hidden scars of the earth's primordial continental collisions. From the Point, the small jut of land pushing into the Ohio River where George Rogers Clark and John Gabriel Jones had debarked as they fled from the Shawnees, a minor fault line stretches southward across the region. Over millennia, as the two plates met and pushed downward, shale pushed upward onto the surface, creating a natural barren trace for bison and humans. The Shawnees called it Alanantowamiowee.

In mid-August 1782, a force of some three hundred Indians—Wyandots, Shawnees, Mingos, and Lenni Lenapes—joined by some members of Colonel John Butler's Loyalist "Rangers" moved southward along Alanantowamiowee. Simon Girty addressed the warriors on the eve of their advance on Bryan's Station, a small fort in the center of the Great Meadow. The following morning, the force laid siege to Bryan's Station with little effect before retreating northward along the trace. Less than a day behind them raged a hodgepodge of determined militiamen from Boonesborough, Lexington, and Harrodstown who had gathered as news of the siege spread across the countryside, determined to strike a fatal blow to the northwestern Indians' incessant attacks on Kentucke's pioneers.

After the Indians crossed the Licking River, they camped atop a wooded hill overlooking the U-shaped river bend and the bottom-lands known as the Lower Blue Licks. On August 19, two days after the siege on Bryan's Station, the militias finally caught up to their enemies. Initially, the men hesitated, hoping reinforce-ments under Kentucke sheriff Benjamin Logan would catch up. Hugh McGary, however, insisted that no further time be lost and taunted his own militia troops: "Them that ain't cowards follow me, and I'll show you where the yellow dogs are." As McGary's men charged across the river, the rest could not abandon them to death. Daniel Boone led the Fayette County militia up the west-ern slope of the hill; Stephen Trigg led a Lincoln County regi-ment up the eastern slope; and McGary's Lincoln County militia marched directly from the south: all were under the leadership of John Todd. But the pioneers lost the Battle of Blue Licks in minutes. The Indians rained gunshot down on the regiments as they climbed the hill. With Wyandots and Shawnees crashing into the flank of Trigg's regiment, his men broke into full re-treat, colliding with McGary's militia. Unaware of the collapse, Boone's troops kept fighting until McGary rode by in retreat, warning his comrades to abandon the battlefield. As they turned to run, Boone's men had to fight through the Indians who had surrounded them. Most of Boone's militia made it to the river, where they swam to safety; his son, Israel, did not.

Israel Boone was among the seventy-seven pioneers who died at Blue Licks, as were John Todd, Stephen Trigg, and Andrew McConnell, whose twin sons had been captured and returned seven years earlier. The Native Americans celebrated their vic-tory by torturing the few prisoners they had taken. Jesse Yocum, who escaped, "did not know how many they burned but the smell of a human was the awfullest smell he ever in his life." Over the course of the next few days, stragglers like Yocum, some severely injured, returned to Bryan's Station. In the meantime, Benjamin Logan had busily gathered reinforcements, and four days after the battle, when he had nearly 470 ready at Bryan's Station, Logan led them to the battleground. The Indians, however, had already retreated north of the Ohio River.

Just as Americans had begun to move into Kentucke in larger numbers, the embarrassing and overwhelming defeat at Blue Licks made a significant statement about the lack of security that all pioneers faced. Blame was spread widely, from the militia leaders on the ground to George Rogers Clark. As early as 1780, Clark had been pushed by Governor Jefferson to oversee construction of six forts along the Ohio River, which, when joined with the posts already established at Pittsburgh, the mouth of the Wheeling River, the Falls of the Ohio, and Fort Jefferson, would have formed a defensive chain. Yet, Jefferson had no money to fund the constructions, and seemed to expect Kentucke's settlers to invest: "We have nothing to depend on for the present but the virtue of the people," complained Captain Benjamin Harrison. Clark, never convinced that defense was a better option than aggression against the enemy, did nothing to support Jefferson's plan. The forts might have been handy over the next two weeks, as smaller Indian parties slipped into Kentucke and attacked settlements, including Kinchloe's Station, where they murdered or captured its thirty-seven settlers.

Determined to save face and Kentucke, Clark called up over eleven hundred men to invade the Indian country north of the Ohio River. Their first target was New Chillicothe, which the Kentuckians reached in early November. Yet, the inhabitants fled rather than fight, and in frustration, Clark's men laid waste to the village. After four days, with no enemy engaged, the militias became restless, and Clark had to release them back to their Kentucke homes.

Frenzies of Mean Fear

The Battle of Blue Licks was another milestone in the long war that raged in the West between the 1750s and 1790s. The Revolutionary War had ended in the East, but in Kentucke, hostilities remained, a frustrating situation for many Americans, who believed Indians' claims to the hunting grounds to be futile without

British support. While the violent tenor of Indian attacks remained constant, pioneers increasingly portrayed Shawnees and their allies as unreasonable, desperate, and indiscriminate in their attacks, rationalizing their own actions—defensive and offensive—as justified. "I can with truth say, that . . . the Indians have always been the aggressors," explained Harry Innes; "any incursions made into their country have been from reiterated injuries committed by them."

Like most Americans, Innes accepted without evaluation the notion that Indians were belligerent and barbaric and their actions unprovoked. A Virginian, Innes received appointment as Kentucke's first federal judge in 1782 and was planning to move westward even as militiamen fell at Blue Licks. When considering the war that continued to rage in the West, he refused to acknowledge Kentuckians' role in the racial animosities that had exploded in the Ohio River valley. The Native Americans, and particularly their aggressive nature, he argued, forced white and black Americans to cower in cabins, stations, and forts until given the opportunity to strike out against the barbarous savages.

Barbarity is not an ethnic characteristic, however; it is a conscious act, and the Indians employed it as a military tactic in their continued fight with western pioneers. When Logan's troops arrived at Blue Licks days after the battle, they found about forty bodies, most scalped and mutilated beyond recognition, strewn across the bottomlands along the river. Stephen Trigg's corpse had been chopped into several pieces and scattered. Native Americans purposefully created such scenes, leaving disfigured bodies on the battlefield and alongside roads to inspire horror. Because Alanantowamiowee, the main route from the Ohio River to the Great Meadow, crossed directly through the battleground, it would have been impossible for new settlers and other travelers to avoid the scene, reminding all that any path through Kentucke could be staged likewise. Unable to identify most, Logan's men buried all in a mass grave atop the hill.

The mutilation of bodies served important ritual purposes, in both Indian and American societies. From the Native American perspective, scalps carried ceremonial value, not to mention the financial rewards offered by British officials for those evidences of military success. Scalping and other bodily mutilations implied social and spiritual death for the victims by transferring power and identity into the victors' hands. Recall, for example, Ottawas' and Chippewas' consumption of Memeskia's body in 1752. Even when considering those who survived scalping, Indians believed they had appropriated some degree of spiritual identity from the victim. As Moravian missionary John Heckewelder noted, "when the Indians relate their victories, they don't say that they have taken so many 'scalps,' but so many 'heads.'" The scalp was not a small piece of dead flesh that Indians carried back to their villages: it was a symbol of human identity.

While whites did not believe a victim's identity could be appropriated, they did accept bodily mutilation as a form of social death, one that deprived the individual of relevance. Those convicted of capital crimes, for instance, often became cadavers for medical dissection after death because their corpses were considered insignificant. There was no need for bodily wholeness for murderers because there was no hope of bodily resurrection into a heavenly afterlife. Certainly, pioneers conceived of native warriors similarly. After Indians raided the Montgomery home in early 1781, for example, they left behind an injured warrior, whom the whites "fineshed . . . and let him lie their for the wolves and fowls of the air to eat." Hugh McGary killed an Indian who wore a shirt similar to that of his dead stepson, and then "cut him up and fed him to the dogs." David Morgan, after a fatal "scuffle" with an Indian, flayed the corpse and tanned the hide, earning himself the nickname "savage Morgan." In these moments of frenzied fear, settlers gave little conscious thought to their treatment of native corpses. Yet, unlike the Indians, their barbaric acts were not staged to instill fear into their enemies. They were moments of uninhibited blood lust in which desecration of a body destroyed physical, spiritual, and social identity.

As they acted out on their rage, frustrations, and fear, whites confirmed to Native Americans that their terroristic tactics were successful. The term "terrorism" was not yet in use, although it would become a very common word by the end of the century as French Jacobins proudly appropriated it to describe their own revolutionary activities. Still, even without the specific word,

Europeans, Americans, and Native Americans understood what it meant "to terror"—the tactic of inspiring excessive fear and dread to solicit specific political reactions.

In fact, Americans such as Benjamin Franklin had employed the specter of frontier terror during the Revolutionary War to push fellow colonists into action, although most were quite safe, given their distance from the frontiers. The Confederation Congress charged Franklin with creating a "school book" of British atrocities, and so in May 1779, he drew up a list of potential illustrative prints, including "Savages killing and scalping the Frontier Farmers and their Families, Women and Children, English Officers mix'd with the Savages, & giving them Orders & encouraging them" and "Prisonners kill'd and Roasted for a great festival where the Canadian indians are eating American flesh, Colonel Buttler an english officer Setting at table."

Three years later, Franklin published a hoax supplement to Boston's *Independent Chronicle and Universal Advertiser* in which he fabricated the story of a New England militia officer who intercepted correspondence and goods sent by the Senecas to the Canadian governor. Upon opening the goods, "we were struck with Horror to find among the Packages, 8 large ones containing SCALPS of our unhappy Country-folks, taken in the three last Years by the Sennka Indians from the Inhabitants of the Frontiers of New-York, New-Jersey, Pennsylvania, and Virginia." An accompanying fictional letter detailed the contents: package one contained the scalps of congressional soldiers; two, farmers killed in their houses; three, farmers killed in fields; four, farmers burned alive; and

> No. 5. Containing 88 Scalps of Women; Hair long, braided in the Indian Fasion, to shew they were Mothers; Hoops blue; Skin yellow Ground, with little red Tadpoles to represent, by way of Triumph, the Tears or Grief occasioned to their Relations; a black scalping Knife or Hatchet at the Bottom to mark their being killed with those instruments. 17 others, Hair very grey; black Hoops; plain brown colour; no Mark by the short Club or Casstete, to shew they were knocked down dead, or had their Brains beat out.

No. 6. Containing 193 Boys' Scalps, of various Ages; small green Hoops; whitish Ground on the Skin, with red Tears in the Middle, and black Bullet-marks, Knife, Hatchet, or Club as their Deaths happened.

No. 7. 211 Girls' Scalps, big and little; small yellow Hoops; white Ground; Tears; Hatchet, Club, scalping Knife, &c.

No. 8. This Package is a Mixture of all the Varieties above-mention'd, to the Number of 122; with a Box of Birch Bark, containing 29 little Infants' Scalps of various Sizes; small white Hoops; white Ground; no Tears; and only a little black Knife in the Middle, to shew they were ript out of their Mothers' Bellies.

The shocking descriptions tapped into the horrific dark side of romantic literary traditions that had begun to creep into European and American literature. Yet, while easterners read Franklin's fictions with a mix of horror and fascination, such depictions were all too real to Kentucke settlers. As when militia men found a dead white baby near the Ohio River, "lying tomahawked and scalped with its mother's apron spread over it, she not being able to carry it any further and keep up with them. Perhaps she might have thought, that by spreading her apron over it, the wolves would not devour it, that they would be pursued, and that probably her child would be found, carried to the fort, and buried." Fear, or more specifically, the production of fear, was the purpose behind terror.

In deciding how to respond, Kentucke's pioneers appropriated terror as well. On an Indian-hunting expedition along the Ohio River in early 1778, Daniel Trabue described a bloodthirsty companion who "wishd he could come up with the Indians. He wanted so bad to have the chance of killing them. He said he knew he could kill 5 him self. He Could shoot. He could Tomerhack and make use of his butcher knife and slay them." Later that year, George Rogers Clark excelled his enemies in barbarity: by massacring four Indians outside Vincennes, he wanted to terrify Henry Hamilton and the small British and Indian force inside the fort into submission; and he was successful. Hamilton later remembered his encounter with Clark "yet reeking with the blood of those unhappy victims with rapture of his late achievement while he washed of the blood from his hands stain'd in this inhuman sacrifice." The Detroit governor, who paid northern Indians for the numbers of scalps they accumulated, had more difficulty accepting the idea that a white leader could act so similarly and with such "rapture."

Clark's successful employment of terror inspired Pennsylvania governor Joseph Reed to mimic the Kentuckian's tactics. By 1780, Reed was distributing broadsides throughout the backcountry encouraging settlers to turn the tables, scalp Indians for profit, and instill fear in their enemies. "The savages are not to be gained or preserved," he explained, "on any other Principle than Fear." The profit to be made from terror was $2,500 per scalp, a handsome sum that Reed expected would inspire "that Spirit which is so necessary in an Indian War, a Spirit of Hostility & Enterprize which will carry our young Men to their Towns." Americans, having learned the techniques of terror and intimate violence from years of frontier interaction, turned to the same tactics to exact their revenge.

The convenience of revenge was that whites did not need to discriminate between Indian peoples. Kentuckians would invade the Indian country, Harry Innes warned Henry Knox, "upon the principle of *revenge, protection, and self-preservation*, and Government will not be able to counteract them; the consequences will be, that the volunteers who may thus embody will not discriminate between the Indians who are hostile and those who have treated." Americans were inclined to lump all native peoples together, as did Jefferson in 1779 when he empowered Clark to decide whether the Indians of the Ohio River valley should be exterminated or removed, arguing that the "same world will scarcely do for them and us." That was the philosophy of most settlers as well, so that any Indian was suspicious and potentially dangerous. Jefferson's perspective was not so simple, however, and neither was the reality of frontier life. Two years later, Governor Jefferson hosted Jean Baptiste du Coigne, a mixed-blood Kaskaskia chief allied to George Rogers Clark. Du Coigne offered continued friendship as the colonials fought the British. Jefferson replied, "We wish to learn you all our arts and to make you wise and wealthy." Du Coigne clearly was a "good" Indian in Jefferson's eyes. (That the chief had named his son Thomas Jefferson du Coigne certainly affected the governor's opinion as well.) Jefferson found common ground with du Coigne, proclaiming, "We, like you, are Americans, born in the same land, and having the same interests."

Kentucke pioneers found it far more difficult to identify "good" Indians or conceive that they shared any interests with Indians beyond their mutual desires to control Kentucke. As Harry Innes explained, "the depredatory mode of war and plundering carried on by them, renders it difficult, and almost impossible, to discriminate what tribes are the offenders." Whites' inclination to employ fixed cultural identities became particularly critical in the 1780s as war with the Indians ground on, and frenzies of mean fear often overwhelmed combatants. George Rogers Clark made little effort in his battles against northwestern Indians to differentiate, although following his meeting with du Coigne, Jefferson had asked Clark to distinguish between friend and foe: "against those who are our enemies let loose the friendly tribes." "Indian" as a cultural identifier had become firmly—and negatively—lodged in western whites' collective imagination as the source of terror.

Plenty of examples evidence how Indians and settlers employed terror against each other, but as the stories of Daniel Boone's many escapes demonstrate, when Kentucke was an all-male world, the dynamics had been different. Before the late 1770s, Shawnees, Cherokees, and other Indians were less intent on terrifying those colonials they found wandering Kentucke. A reprimand and confiscation of the interlopers' supplies often sufficed, although capture or death was not unusual. If the Indians were accommodationists, they often allowed white men to retain some sense of masculine identity as well. By the early 1780s, as the accommodationists lost influence among native peoples and as trans-Appalachia became peopled with American families, terror as a military tactic took on new meanings, becoming increasingly popular among native warriors and, as a form of revenge, among their American counterparts. As their British allies abandoned them, northwestern Indians found new friends among the Chickasaws and Chickamauga Cherokees. In late 1782, Wyandots and other Great Lakes Indians met with the Chickamaugas to coordinate attacks in Kentucke and the Illinois territory. Their goal was to scare Americans out of the hunting grounds, and if that did not work, exterminate them.

For Americans, the Indian terror directly threatened identity. Racial identity could be fluid, as evidenced by "white savages," "civilized Indians," and "black white men." Among the men captured with Boone at the salt licks, several chose not to return to Boonesborough: Micajiah Callaway became an interpreter, and Joseph Jackson accepted adoption into the community and even fought against the residents of Fort Boone. Such "go-betweens" made Americans very uncomfortable. When they raided a Miami village in 1782, George Rogers Clark's men were disconcerted to find a white woman who "looked as much like an Indian for color and for dress as an Indian herself," and they could not understand why she "didn't know her name, or her people's." In white pioneers' minds, her adoption into a Native American community had erased the woman's whiteness, separating her from her people's name, the patriarchy of white America, and most importantly, the American civilization that it represented.

Significantly, the need to establish patriarchy in Kentucke during the years when more and more women, children, and slaves came into the region coincided with the escalation of Indian terror during the very late 1770s and early 1780s. Men—as husbands and fathers—had great difficulty proving that they could protect their families. Asa Farrar remembered a man near the Falls of the Ohio who, with his son, spotted two Indians in the fields: "He left his plough, ran and picked up the boy, the Indians pursuing till he got over the fence, *safe*, toward his cabin. They then shot without hurting him. He found one of his children at the woodpile, with his brains dashed against a stick; some yet sticking on. His wife tomahawked and scalped, and laying in his house on the floor, and her child knocked in the head and laying beside her." Truly, there was nothing safe about his homestead: had they chosen to pursue, the Indians would have overtaken the undefended settler and his boy as well. But leaving behind a scene of terror for his consumption, they did not need to physically destroy him. "Hardly one wek pass without someone being scalped between this [place] and the Falls," explained John Floyd in 1780, "and I almost got too cowardly to travel about the woods without company."

Adding to the atmosphere of terror were the new waves of pioneers arriving as families who—single-mindedly determined to establish their land claims or unbelieving of the severity of the Indian threat or both—avoided fort life altogether. In 1779, the Jefferson County Court recommended that settlers "keep themselves as united and compact as possible one other year, settling themselves in towns and Forts." But they did not. Rosanna Wallace wrote her sister that "the Terror it had on me about the Indians after the Nine People were killed 15 miles within us was past discribeing, and it was nothing but the great Mercy of God that preserved us for the Indians were both behind us and before us." New arrivals' proclivity to settle on their small claims rather than congregate in forts led Boonesborough settlers to complain to George Rogers Clark:

> Nothing less than the preservation of these settlements and to insure from utter ruin the many Families in this Country could have induced us to trouble you with an address of this kind.
>
> The few among us who have long experienced the intolerable hardships of maintaining our Post against the Barbarous savages, Derive very little consolation from the vast addition of Numbers now scattered through the various Parts of this Country. The almost incredible number of Distressed and defenceless Families settled through our woods for the sake of substinance instead of adding to our strength are in fact, so many allurements, and must become a daily sacrifice to the savage brutality of our inhuman enemies; who from the unavoidable success will be encouraged to reiterate their attemps and Render this Country a Mere scene of Carnage and Desolation.

Not only did new pioneers neglect their own defense by shunning life in the forts, but their actions invited Indian attacks, making all of Kentucke more dangerous, a situation that made white men increasingly incapable of providing for and protecting their dependents. With each attack, then, the Indians chipped away at white manhood and patriarchy.

The Family Frontier

Patriarchy was necessary because families symbolized stability. The years in which men hunted bison and land without concern for permanent defenses were ending. Familial households were the foundation of neighborhoods, communities, and the civilization that Americans projected onto the trans-Appalachian wilds, and as such, they required vigilance. Each woman who disappeared forever into the wilderness, each child who cried for a lost mother or sibling, and each scalped victim found along a trail testified to the failure of Kentucke's patriarchs, both as fathers and as founders.

It is difficult to imagine family life within the context of this violence, but beginning with the arrival of Rebecca Boone and her children in 1775, Kentucke had become a family frontier. In the East, sustenance was a husband-wife-children activity, largely provided through gardening and hunting. Children watched the livestock; women tended gardens and created some domestic productions like butter; and men hunted and defended and helped with everything. As the Indian threat intensified in 1776 and 1777, any semblance of normalcy that colonists had sought in Kentucke dissipated. Farming, herding, and hunting all became problematic. Abandoning their rudimentary farms and unfinished stations, settlers huddled in only three centralized settlements by 1778: Fort Harrod, Fort Boone, and Logan's Fort at St. Asaph.

Consequently, defensive structures became highly gendered spaces. The men—fathers, husbands, older boys—ventured beyond the confines of forts and stations to survey and fight Indians. Women and younger children lived inside the walls, cut off and secured from Kentucke. "A woman dare not go 40 yards to pick beans without a guard," remembered one pioneer. Children who did wander, like the Boone and Callaway girls, learned the lessons of terror in the most direct way. As an eleven-year-old, Keturah Leitch Taylor witnessed the horrors of western life— mangled bodies, a scalp with beautiful blonde ringlets hanging from a tree limb—as her uncle brought her and her sisters to live in Kentucke in 1784. She spent the next eleven years living behind

Figure 4.1. Kentucke's frontier defenses consisted of a series of stations interspersed among larger forts. Stations were defensible, single-household residences to which neighbors and other surrounding settlers fled for safety. The station at Lexington architecturally typified many stations, stockaded and with a second floor that overhung the first to thwart Indian attempts to climb onto the roof. From Z. F. Smith, *The History of Kentucky* (Louisville, Ky.: Courier-Journal Printing, 1886), 149.

the walls of Bryan's Station and Leitch's Station, and during heightened threats of Indian attack, at Fort Washington. Many settlers such as Taylor lived for years on the defensive behind the walls. They called it being "forted," the psychological consequences of which were summed up by Daniel Trabue: "They was a couragus people but yet I will say they all looked very wild. You might frequently see the women a walking around the fort looking and peeping about seeming that they did not know what they was about but would try to incourage one another and hopt for the best."

Less difficult to envision were the potential costs of leaving the walls. When Rachel McCutchens wandered, Shawnees killed her young son and took her captive to a village north of the Ohio River. Months later, McCutchens escaped, but by the time she returned to her settlement, she was clearly insane, roving "about with a rake, turning over the leaves in the fence corners, looking for her son." Despite the defensive role of the forts and stations, children *did* sneak out to fish or pick berries or just play, and women *did* leave the defensive walls to get water, tend gardens, and retrieve children. It was up to the men to protect them.

Defensive structures may have been the first attempts at providing security, but they were insufficient without constant vigi-

Figure 4.2. Like other larger defensive structures, Fort
Boone was a neighborhood of individual cabins that shared
a common defensive wall. Fort life was dull and dirty, and
the persistent threat of Indian attack disrupted normal
planting cycles, occasionally leading to food shortages.
From George W. Ranck, *Boonesborough: Its Founding, Pioneer
Struggles, Indian Experiences, Transylvania Days, and Revolutionary Annals* (Louisville, Ky.: Filson Club, 1901), opp. 78.

lance, and apparently men needed to be reminded of that responsibility. During the siege of Boonesborough, Elizabeth Callaway
had to forcefully coax Tice Brock from his hiding place to go
fight: "I was not made for a fighter—I was not made for a fighter,"
he appealed. Women often chastised men for their cowardice or
even indifference toward the possibility of danger. Jane Sprowl
sternly reprimanded her brothers: "It is easy to fight Indians sitting in the chimney corner, with your bellies' full of mush and
milk." Maybe it was an underestimation of the Indian threat or
a belief that their forts and stations would withstand direct assaults, or maybe white men just assumed that they could relax,
imagining that they had done enough. Yet, with every attack

came the reminder that white men could do only so much to preserve their families' lives.

Indian sieges exposed the frailty of frontier patriarchy, making some men cower with fear and, ironically, turning some
women into soldiers. During a Shawnee attack on McConnell's
Station, an Indian crawled under the cabin and "was trying to
lift the slabs, and one of these, a very heavy woman, would always jump upon it, and he hadn't purchase enough to throw
her off." A couple women then poured boiling water through the
floor planks: "Twas said he made a dreadful howling." During
the siege of Fort Boone, Richard Callaway put hats and hunting shirts on the women and made them "man" the walls to project the appearance of many defenders. When Shawnees attacked
her family's cabin near St. Asaph, Hannah Woods took up an ax
and severed the arm of an Indian attempting to push open the
door. In 1777, Esther Whitley bested all the men at a sharpshoot-
ing contest at St. Asaph. A decade later, she performed before a
company of Cherokees who were visiting her husband. Amazed
at her skill, the Cherokees asked how she had learned to shoot
so well. Whitley replied that she "had learned on purpose in
order to kill them should occasion ever make it necessary." Years
later, in conversation with an elder Cherokee chief, Cephas Washburn remembered a woman who "moulded bullets and loaded
the rifles for her husband" as he held off the attacking Indians.
His Cherokee friend concluded, "*She* was a *man*, and worthy to
sit at the council fire with the wisest chiefs."

Not surprisingly, then, when occasion did make it necessary,
white men ferociously and sometimes incomprehensibly reacted
to Indian attacks. Because women could display courage and
combativeness in the crucible of the Indian wars, men exaggerated masculinity through overhunting, oversurveying, and as
happened at Blue Licks, overestimating their own martial abilities. Whites interpreted the Indian threat—and specifically, successful Indian attacks—as affronts to manly honor. Following a
1781 attack against his "Horse Militia," John Floyd complained to
George Rogers Clark: "My party, 27 in number are all dispersed
& cut to pieces except 9 who came off the field. . . . *I want satis-*

faction." Indeed, anything less than satisfaction would have been interpreted as unmanly.

Contributing to the strains on frontier patriarchy was a population boom precipitated by Virginia's Land Law of 1779. The act officially opened Kentucke to settlement, except in the lands south of the Green River, where settlers could potentially agitate the Chickasaws. French and Indian War veterans' claims, which had been surveyed under John Floyd's supervision in the mid-1770s, were formally recognized; so too were preemptions made before 1779, as well as thousands of acres claimed by Virginia's finest men: George Washington, Patrick Henry, and William Preston among them. To decide the anticipated flood of claims, the state established four land courts.

The land law opened the floodgates on Kentucke, but only a trickle initially flowed westward. Leading the way was John May, a Virginia merchant and land speculator who, with the financial assistance of his partner Samuel Beall, became Kentucke's largest trader in preemption and settlement warrants. "The Country has been very little explored since the passing of the Land Law," May wrote Beall in early 1780; "the Indian War, the Business before the Commissioners and the Severity of the Winter having prevented it." Even as May wrote his letter, however, around three hundred flatboats populated with new pioneers arrived at the Falls of the Ohio.

Men who had tried to preempt lands in the 1770s rushed back into the region hoping to establish their claims in one of the new land courts. A land office opened in Harrodstown, facilitating settlers' submissions of claim surveys. Reverend David Rice, on a visit to Kentucke, declared that the "spirit of speculation was flowing in such a torrent that it would wear down every weak obstacle that stood in its way. I looked forward to fifty or sixty years and saw the inhabitants engaged in very expensive and demoralizing litigations about their landed property." In May, the Virginia legislature had established Louisville. It was an immediate draw for migrants and a center for economic activity. "You would be surprised to see ten or fifteen wagons at a time going to and from the Falls every day with families and corn," recalled John Floyd. When, in late 1781, the legislature set up a system to distribute lands south of the Green River to Virginia's Revolutionary War veterans, the peopling of Kentucke was well under way. In 1777, almost all of Kentucke's colonial population of 280 people had bunkered in Fort Boone and Fort Harrod; by the end of the 1780s, over 73,000 would claim Kentucke as home, seemingly aware but determined to overcome the terror of the Indian threat. Within two years of the land law's passage, the surveyor's office approved 557 settlement certificates, 699 French and Indian War veterans' military warrants, 2,847 treasure warrants, and 700 preemption claims. Most of the claimed 3.5 million acres lay in the Great Meadow, stretching from the eastern hills of the Appalachian Mountains to the Falls of the Ohio, and from the Ohio River to the Green River. Only 9,400 acres were claimed in the Big Sandy River valley of eastern Kentucke, and the south side of the Green River remained off-limits.

Importantly, nearly 65 percent of claimants already had two or more entries in the books. Some were land jobbers, men hired to establish and record a claim for an absentee purchaser. Others were outliers who did the work of building a shack, clearing and planting a field, and then selling the "claim" as preempted land to a desperate newcomer. Like many investors, John May schemed to attach his name to as many claims as possible, hoping to secure some through legal machinations. He "desired my Brother to search out all the Land which belongs to british Subjects, and make himself well acquainted with its Quality Situation and other Advantages; and also to endeavor to get one of my Brothers appointed Escheator in Order to make sure of our Assumpsits being received in Paiment." Anything was possible: "I think the Success of the Scheme will in great Measure depend upon the Secrecy with which the Business is conducted." Even the land commissioners were rumored to be devious: "some of them having entered largely into the Land Business by purchasing Claims & then sitting in Judt upon them; and granting Certificates to themselves; and in order to procure Land have admitted hundreds of Claims entirely out of the Letter & meaning of the Law."

None of these people or the officials who recorded their claims worried that each survey may have overlapped others' lands. The

pattern of shingled land claims that made Kentucke so litigious
and unappealing to national planners such as Jefferson and James
Madison arose from the shoddy bureaucracy that oversaw its
distribution. For less-than-sincere claimants, however, shingling
was also a tactic. Confusion created an atmosphere in which it
became easier to win land through court cases than actually to
secure them on the ground. And Virginia just kept selling the
land, anticipating that the courts or circumstance would sort it
all out. The scenario lent an air of uncertainty to any claim and,
indeed, the entire settlement process.

In the 1770s, station and fort life had provided at least some
stability within this mad rush of land. When settlers had grouped
together behind defensive walls, they found comfort and com-
monality with others. Following the harrowing winter of 1777,
settlers constructed several larger forts and stations for community defenses, including Fort Lexington in 1779, John Todd's Fort
in 1780, and Fort Nelson at the Falls of the Ohio in 1782. Several hundred such defensive structures persisted over the 1780s
and 1790s, but increasingly, many families employed them as
community centers—places where economic, governmental, and
communal business occurred. Fort life itself was a disgusting experience, as William Fleming described of Fort Harrod:

> The whole dirt and filth of the Fort, putrified flesh, dead dogs,
> horse, cow, hog excrements and human odour all wash into the
> spring which with the Ashes and sweepings of filthy Cabbins, the
> dirtiness of the People, steeping skins to dress and washing ev-
> ery sort of dirty rags and cloths in the spring makes the most
> filthy nauseous potation of the water imaginable and will cer-
> tainly contribute to render the inhabitants of this place sickly.

Additionally, "continually Harrased" and "confin'd to stations,"
pioneers saw themselves as "debarr'd from applying the necessary means for the support of their Families," consequently
equating defensive living with weak families. With insufficient
and unhealthy space to accommodate settlers, no new forts under
construction, and men yearning to establish their families, Kentucke's defensive network of stations and forts lost favor.

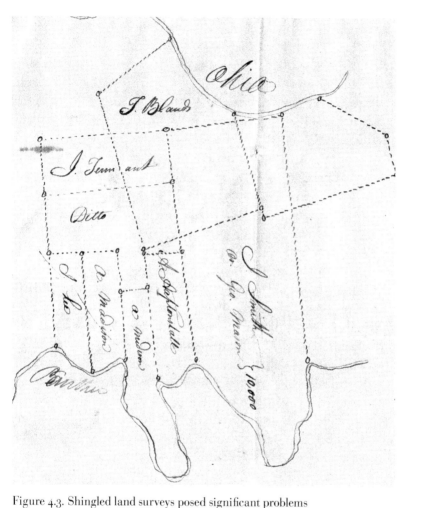

Figure 4.3. Shingled land surveys posed significant problems
for Kentucke's land courts, initiating law suits that lasted for generations.
This 1798 plat from the Jefferson County surveyor's office illustrates the
overlapping survey boundaries of several land claims. Courtesy of the Reuben
T. Durrett Collection on Kentucky and the Ohio River Valley, Miscellaneous Manuscripts, Special Collections Research Center, University of Chicago Library.

As the land law made it possible for families to escape the stations and forts, settlers of the early 1780s came to believe that there was as much security in a cluster of houses or a small town. For some, it was a cultural preference. When the Shotwells and Drakes began building their cabins in Mayslick, they agreed to "live so near each other that no house . . . would be unsupported by some other." Others did so purely for protection, constructing cabins within running distance of the nearest station or fort. By 1786, it was conventional wisdom that "any land that sells now at Kentucky is Places within the Settlements where Familys will be safe. . . . This keeps up the Land [prices] in the thick settlements." An incidental but very effective wartime tactic, the peopling of Kentucke and their congregation in the "thick settlements" of the Great Meadow made it increasingly difficult for Native Americans to strike without warning. When the Indian threat against the Beargrass Creek settlement escalated in 1785, for example, William Christian recognized that "as we are very near the frontier we cant think of staying here much longer we intend to move off to Danville and continue there until some better prospect here."

Whether they built cabins in eyesight of other cabins or secluded from the world, with or without proper title to the lands, pioneers tried to establish homes for their families. Most brought very few material belongings with them to Kentucke. Under the constraints of the difficulty of transportation, houses were stocked meagerly. The Abraham Van Metre family was among the more fortunate, bringing one rifle, a frying pan and several pots, fire tongs, a tea kettle, dishes, a lamp, a hand mill, a spinning wheel, a ten-gallon kettle, a pitchfork, an auger, a hammer, a whipsaw, several lengths of chain, and two plow irons. They had to supply furniture, bedding, clothes, and other "amenities" after arriving, largely through barter, purchase, or their own skills.

The most valuable belonging in the Van Metre household was the rifle, not just in monetary value but in its symbolizing hunting and security. The more common weapon had been the British Brown Bess, a musket with poor accuracy and slow rate of fire. Coinciding with the settlement of Kentucke and the Revolutionary War, however, the Pennsylvania rifle had been gaining admirers with its accuracy and swift velocity. Boone carried a Pennsylvania rifle, making it the more fashionable weapon for young Kentucke frontiersmen eager to emulate the legend. More importantly, the rifle and its accessories symbolized security, as engraved on William Whitley's powder horn:

Wm Whitley I am your Horn
The truth I love, a Lie I scorn,
Fill me with best of powder
I'll make your Rifle crack the louder.
See how the dread terrific Ball
Make Indians bleed and Tories fall
You with Powder I'll supply
For to defend your Liberty.

The powder-horn poet's focus on defense suggests the shifting mentality of Kentucke's settlers as the peopling of Kentucke revised the significance of the rifle. Hunting became less important and less necessary in family households. "When I got me a family," explained James Wade, "I found hunting was no way to make a living." As men left the rifle hanging above their fireplaces awaiting an Indian attack, they stepped away from the type of frontier masculinity epitomized by Boone, the Long Hunter.

Men consequently confronted the insecurity of frontier patriarchy. As husbands and fathers, they were responsible for the provisions, survival, and perpetuation of the family. But the persistent Indian threat and the scramble for land made fulfilling those responsibilities difficult. "I have suffered much in this Country," lamented a settler in early 1780 who had "nothing left to chare my drooping spirits but the pleasing prospect I have of acquireing a Computant Fortune for my Children that they may never expereance the fatiege & hard ships of Acquireing it themselves." Not that this farmer was a failure: in the first few lines of his letter, he described a recent purchase of 2,800 acres along Beargrass Creek. Yet, he did not feel successful as a patriarch. He fretted over the legitimacy of the title, the new crowds of land-lusty pioneers who might preempt his lands, and the warrants issued to Virginia's war veterans that could invalidate his claim. As he watched thousands of Americans join him in the parceling of Kentucke, he determined "to shear it with them or die in the cause. I will have more rich land or I will cease to be."

In contrast to the 1760s and 1770s when hunting made the man, by the 1780s, land gave meaning to manhood. Hunting, particularly the long hunt, had relieved men of many responsibilities associated with yeoman farming. While still living in North Carolina, Daniel Boone, for example, abandoned Rebecca and their children on several occasions for his Kentucke long hunts, making sustenance and survival his wife's responsibility. After one prolonged absence, Daniel returned home to find Rebecca nursing a new child—Jemima. Frontier rumors flew that the child was not his, and according to one version, Rebecca responded to her husband: "You had better have staid at home and got it yourself." Hunting was a poor foundation on which to fulfill the responsibilities and prerogatives of patriarchy, and those men who neglected the former often did not enjoy the latter. Farming, in contrast, bound a man to his household.

The fluidity of identity in Kentucke made for interesting households. Women acting as soldiers, the weakening and reactive exaggeration of masculinity, even the blurring of racial identities exacerbated the chaos spawned by the land rush. For example, in a less-disordered place like tidewater Virginia or even the North Carolina backcountry, a woman legally forfeited her identity and property upon marriage; her husband assumed control over the household economy, their children and slaves, and her behavior and reputation. Legal constraints, however, were only as strong as the reach of the law, and in Kentucke, where Virginia law was unfamiliar to some and disregarded by others, women found opportunities to push back against conventional patriarchal restraints. It was not uncommon in the 1780s to see a woman filing a warrant at the land office or attending court as an administrator of her husband's estate. The judicial system was designed for a stable, patriarchal society in Virginia, but in Kentucke, patriarchy was not yet strong enough.

Still, women needed men. When husbands decided to move westward, they separated wives, children, and slaves from support networks of family and friends. Men had to assume more responsibility in bolstering women's spirits. When husbands died, then, widows sometimes found themselves in particularly desperate circumstances, trapped without a man to provide for them physically or emotionally. "Oh what troubles has the death of that ever dear & beloved husband of mine brought on my poor helpless Family," worried Ann Christian. The community did not abandon such women, but they certainly became secondary concerns to men defending their own families and lives. Hugh Wilson's widow waited less than two months to remarry when the Indians killed him in spring 1777. The thought of a wedding in Harrodstown in the midst of war seems strange, but in the most challenging of times, settlers sought stability.

As adults, husbands and wives experienced the frontier as another home, another way of life. But children approached the frontier far differently. For many, it was the only way of life they knew, and the Indian threat occupied a central role in their psyches. They had been taught to always be on edge and to always distrust Indians. At Scott's Station, Daniel Scott and several other boys snuck off to fish so that "old aunt Sarah would cook them, and pa wouldn't know it." They set their fishing lines and returned to the station for the day. That evening, as they checked their lines, they heard an owl and, having been warned that Indians often mimicked owls, the boys fled back to the station to face their parents' anger. After being told of her capture and rescue, Betsy Callaway's son never wandered again, fearful that "the yard was full of Indians and I was afraid to go outdoors." Even the youngest children could not escape the terror that circumscribed pioneers' lives. Daniel Drake remembered how his mother put him and his younger siblings to bed with the admonition to "lie still and go to sleep, or the Shawnees will catch you." For years, he had dreams of "either Indians or snakes. . . . Happily, I never suffered from either, except in dread."

Kentucke's children of the 1780s not only inherited the revolution, they inherited the terror of frontier life. Drake, whose family lived adjacent to Alanantowamiowee in northern Kentucke, remembered when he was four years old how

the axe and scythe . . . were kept at night under the bed as weapons of defense, in case the Indians should make an attack. On the morning the first duty was to ascend a ladder which always stood, leaning behind the door, to the loft and look through the cracks for Indians lest they might have planted themselves near the door, to rush in when the strong crossbar should be removed, and the heavy latch raised from its resting place.

Because children were easy to overtake, Indians often targeted them first. Hannah Woods's daughter barely escaped capture, running into the family cabin, where her mother and a slave fought off six attackers. When one breached the door and fell to the floor, she joined her mother in "finishing" him with a "Broad Ax & Bar of Iron."

While parents tried to shield their children from the physical dangers of frontier living, they did not—and probably could not—protect them from the psychological scars of terror. Some sons responded by appropriating the hypermasculine posturing of their fathers. After an attack on Masterson's Station, the boys "taunted each other with the imputation that their fathers had refused to go in pursuit [of the Indians], or had fled to Lexington." The lesson for boys was that bravery in the face of terror evidenced manliness. Others were obviously traumatized by their childhoods on the frontier. Nearly sixty years after the event, William Niblick still remembered how, as a child, "I stood at the little gate, having hold of my mother's apron, and heard the women crying; and directly I saw them bring in Wymore in a sheet that was all bloody, hanging on a pole."

The Shapelessness of Slavery

In 1787, Virginia's George Mason advocated the end of the slave trade before the Constitutional Convention in Philadelphia and declared that "the western people are already calling for slaves for their new lands; and will fill that country with slaves, if they can be got through South Carolina and Georgia." Certainly, many frontier families (particularly those from Virginia) counted slaves among their household members. Mason anticipated that Kentucke's development would mimic Virginia's, embracing a staple crop economy and its requisite labor. Still, in the 1770s and 1780s, nothing yet was written in stone.

Slavery did meet an immediate need on Kentucke's frontiers: providing bodies. As we have seen, slaves often played important roles in fighting against Indians. Men such as Ben the "black white man" received recognition for their furious warfare—and the loyalty to whites that it implied. Joe Gray, a white pioneer, armed his slaves as they cleared lands and built a station: "They made good soldiers." When captured by Wyandots outside Estill's Station, another slave named Monk convinced his captors that the structure was well defended and could not be breached, even though the men were absent and only women and children remained. Informed of Monk's sacrifice when they returned, the men tracked down the Wyandot party and saved him. When the Indian breached Hannah Woods's cabin door, her slave wrestled him to the floor and, lying underneath, held on while she and her daughter hacked away. Certainly, while they would not have intended to injure or even kill the slave in the process, his position put him in harm's way.

Since slaves were more expendable in such circumstances, whites frequently placed slaves in dangerous positions during Indian attacks. When their station came under siege, one family sent Moses to find help, but he got lost in the woods and returned. They "let him in and put out Bob," who found his way to a nearby station. Some slave-owners sent slaves westward (supervised by one or two of the farmer's younger male relatives) to prepare the way for the family. Recall John May's decision to send his slave on to Kentucke as he and other members of the Henderson migration party turned back to North Carolina under threat of an Indian attack. Others put slaves in charge of tending claims while they returned eastward to gather families or supplies. John Bruce left two slaves behind to work his claim while he gathered supplies: the man was scalped and the woman was taken captive. Four slaves—two men, a woman, and a girl—accompanied Nathaniel and William Ewing to their new Kentucke claim. When the Ewing brothers returned to Maryland for supplies, one of the slaves panicked about a potential Indian attack. Unable to convince the others to join him, he went to a nearby station for help, returning a few days later to find the others slaughtered: "It was believed from the sign, that the Negro man had fought, and that with an axe. The wall was seen bloody . . . off a little piece from where the Negro lay." Like so many other settlers, when faced with the decision to "send a parcel of poor slaves where I dare not go myself," Thomas Hart decided that slaves offered a better way to secure and sustain a claim without risking his life or that of his family.

Slaves were also needed for clearing land. Of course, there was always the possibility of hiring landless white pioneers to do the work. Indeed, some landowners, such as John Floyd, opted to negotiate with squatters rather than run them off. Floyd found eleven white families on his Beargrass Creek lands in 1779 and allowed them to stay in return for clearing the lands on which they lived. But tenants, always looking for other opportunities and unrestricted in their mobility, recognized their own advantages in these arrangements. When William Christian's tenants on his Beargrass claims refused to pay their rents, the absentee landowner needed Robert Daniel to intercede. "You will not be displeased," promised Daniel, "with any of our proceedings relitive to recovering the rent as I believe they are as grand Villians as live on Earth." Furthermore, those whites willing to work were in a position to negotiate higher pay. Daniel was disappointed, for example, that he could not secure slaves before the summer of 1784 because "I am oblige to give such enormous wages for work men."

In 1787, two early salt-licks entrepreneurs faced a similar situation in coming to terms with one of their workers: "Time desires me to apply to you to give him every other Saturday for himself . . . his hire will not amount to quite as much per year." That the correspondents were both women and the worker was a slave relates how, as with patriarchy, the institutional structure of slavery was compromised by the chaos of settlement and the fluidity of identities. As a "hired-out," the slave negotiating his contract enjoyed certain liberties banned by Virginia law. While slave-owners could rent their slaves to whomever they pleased, a 1782 act forbade slaves from the advantages of hiring themselves out, including negotiating terms of employment. On the east side of the Appalachians, a slave's breach of the law would have resulted in his seizure by the county court and his eventual sale— a punishment both for the slave and for the negligent master. In

Kentucke, however, the reach of the law was not quite as long. County courts inundated with land disputes and militias on alert against Indian raids had little incentive to interfere with a slave activity that, while illegal, provided much-needed labor. Additionally, those who brought multiple slaves found hiring out— legal and illegal—to be profitable. Hired-outs shared their earnings with their masters. Consequently, slave-owners tolerated the practice even as they expressed anxiety over the potential for slaves running away.

As the Revolutionary War ended and the trickle of westward settlers began to swell, the wartime fear of conspiracy between slaves and Indians became part of the cultural baggage carried into Kentucke. John May brought a slave westward who "fell in with some worthless Negroes who persuaded him to run away & attempted to get with the Indians." The natural collusion between Indians and blacks (with British support, of course) was assumed by many white Americans. In fact, Benjamin Franklin's list of prints that had so demonized Native Americans included one of slaves rising up against their white masters:

A large House
Blacks arm'd with Guns & Hangers
Master & his Sons on the Ground dead,
Wife & Daughters lifted up in the Arms of the Negroes as they are carrying off

Whites could ignore neither black complicity in Lord Dunmore's War nor the potential for disaster implicit in the opportunities that existed for Kentucke's slaves: that is, to hire themselves out and thereby find occasion to talk to other slaves and conspire insurrection against whites; to enjoy some leverage in negotiating the terms of work and thereby exert economic influence against whites; and to hide away among the Indians and join in the massacre of white pioneers. Despite the fact that within ten days his slave had returned, May conceded that "I fear this will be a bad place to bring slaves to."

Because slave-owners could not be assured that Kentucke was a good place for slaves, their suspicions may have contributed to another way in which they used slaves—as money. Since slaves were expendable, and since the possibility always loomed that they might run away, many settlers opted to sell their slaves to acquire land and supplies. One land claimant sent his brother with several slaves to secure the preemption warrants on his claim and clear the lands. If his brother ran into any financial difficulties, "he must make use of the only one then remainding which is to sell a Negro immediately. This I am unwilling to do but it must be done in case he cannot get money to clear out my lands no other way." William Christian advised his mother that "unless you can sell in Botetourt to get some good working Negroes & money to bring with you you had better remain where you are." In 1780, a trader made known his intentions in Williamsburg to "purchase young Negroes for the Gent men whos going to Cantuckey." A decade later, Samuel McDowell anticipated his neighbor bringing "7 or 8 Negroes amongst whome would be Some young fellows or which I might have my Choice and I might depend that Some of them would be very valuable and likely." In Kentucke's cash-poor economy, slaves' monetary value was second only to land.

In October 1785, Virginia's assembly required immigrating slave-owners to swear that their "removal to the state of Virginia, was with no intent of evading the laws for preventing the further importation of slaves, not have I brought with me any slaves with an intention of selling them, . . . since the first day of November 1778. So help me God." Kentucke's slave-owning pioneers ignored the law, however, transporting slaves into trans-Appalachia from all reaches of the nation and regularly planning to sell them. Less than three years later, the assembly specifically targeted them with "An Act concerning the importation of slaves, into the district of Kentucky," demanding that the "many persons who have removed from other parts of the United States, into the district of Kentucky" take the oath within six months and giving future settlers sixty days to comply. As Benjamin Stevenson discovered, "by neglecting to take the Oath prescribed by law his Negroes were entitled to freedom, and himself liable to heavy penalties." While an ad hoc slave trade had emerged by the mid-1780s, no one could predict the shape of slavery that would emerge. Virginia's legal structures—from trying to slow the slave trade to restricting slaves' economic activities—had little effect in Kentucke.

Virginia's Kentucke Problem

When Thomas Jefferson stepped down as governor of Virginia in 1781, he retired to Monticello, where he began to piece together a series of notes that he had gathered over the years. In November 1782, as he revised the materials, he wrote George Rogers Clark: "Any observations of your own on the subject of the big bones or their history, or on any thing else in the Western country, will come acceptably to me." Jefferson's *Notes on the State of Virginia* was published two years later, a response to French curiosities about the character of the American people and the nature of the American continent. One line in Jefferson's *Notes* hints of a political problem brewing in the Old Dominion: "suppose our country [Virginia] to be bounded, at some future day, by the meridian of the mouth of the Great Kanhaway." By 1784, Jefferson had accepted the inevitability of Kentucke's separation from Virginia, preferably with the Kanawha River as the boundary.

The debate over separation began as soon as there was a federal government to petition. Kentuckians appealed to the Confederation Congress twice in 1780. The first, signed by nearly 700 westerners, including signatures from the Illinois country, demanded a separation from Virginia. The second, signed by 350 Kentuckians, argued that their need for self-governance was so great (and Virginia's help with the Indian threat so lacking) that rather than remain Virginians, they would consider leaving the United States to have Spain protect their interests or, as they sarcastically threatened, move across the Ohio River and live among the Indians. Both petitions were troublesome messages to the Confederation. Indian attacks were a persistent problem in trans-Appalachia: in 1782, one Fayette County militiaman complained how 860 settlers had been killed in that county alone over the previous six years. Still, from Congress's perspective, a large and immediate migration into the Ohio territory could inflame a broader Indian war, dragging the new nation into a conflict it could not afford. Additionally, Kentucke did not stand alone: the possibility that a wider western alliance might break away from the United States was even more worrisome.

By 1780, Congress was embroiled as well in debate over forcing Virginia to cede its western claims. In New York City, Thomas Paine published *Public Good*, a widely influential pamphlet on the emerging fight. Citing a 1770 letter by British secretary of state Lord Hillsborough, Paine explained how the Crown had expected to create a *"new colony* on the *back* of Virginia," an indication in his opinion that those lands were never part of Virginia's original charter. Specifically referencing the transmontane lands between the Ohio River and the "North Carolina line"—a "colony" where settlers were already "fighting the enemy at their own weapons"—Paine proposed that Virginia would not suffer by conceding its claim to Kentucke. The new state would export down the Mississippi River but import through Virginia because, "tho' there is a navigation from it, there is none into it, on account of the rapidity of the Missisippi." Despite the Appalachian Mountains, Kentucke and indeed the entire Ohio River valley naturally would be dependent on Virginia for commerce.

Paine's argument was less convincing to Virginia's political leaders. The flow of westward migration was increasing and, although Virginia had been selling and overseeing distribution of the Kentucke lands since 1779, Jefferson and others were unsure that westerners would remain loyal. John Floyd chided the governor that the Indians "have absolutely been hitherto kept off your back settlements by the Inhabitants of Kentucky," but Kentuckians had not seen Virginia's gratitude for the sacrifices of its western citizens. Others, frustrated over their difficulties acquiring land, signed a petition asking the Confederation to annul Virginia's land titles and redistribute Kentucke. Some petitioners from Kentucke indicated not only a desire to separate from the Old Dominion but a hostility toward it: "almost the whole of the lands . . . are Engrossed into the hands of a few Interested men, the greater part of which live at ease in the internal parts of Virginia." Rumors in the East were that Kentucke was on the verge of revolution: "Without the interposition of some power to quiet the minds of the Virginians in that quarter, it is probable there will be bloodshed among them." By 1783, when Virginia finally ceded its western claims to Congress, talk of Kentucke statehood was already in the wind.

In response to what seemed to be Virginia's neglect of its western counties, Governor Benjamin Harrison reassured George Rogers Clark that the Old Dominion's lack of action had been only because, following the close of the war, the "British had call'd in all their scalping parties, and intended no more to carry on that type of war against our back settlements, whether they really mean as they say, Time will discover." Some Indian nations such as the Shawnees had in fact relaxed their attacks on the Kentucke settlements in 1781 and 1782 as they tried to shore up alliances and restore some semblance of normalcy to their own lives north of the Ohio River. Kentuckians persisted, however, in their own occasional attacks on the Shawnee villages, leaving fields scorched and food supplies destroyed. The Shawnees and their allies faced a subsistence crisis, forcing more residents to migrate westward. Many abandoned the Ohio River valley altogether, moving into the lower Missouri River region. "They [Americans] treat us as their cruelest enemies are treated," explained Shawnee chiefs to the Spanish governor at New Orleans in 1782, "so that today hunger and the impetuous torrent of war . . . have brought our villages to a struggle with death." Still, remaining behind in the northwest were dozens of villages packed with families hoping to keep their ancestral lands and hundreds of younger Shawnee men determined to sustain war against the Americans.

The lull in Indian attacks, albeit a short one, gave Virginia's political leaders an opportunity to talk about something other than defense. The topic turned to Kentucke's independence. For Virginians, however, Kentucke's probable separation was always about what was best for Virginia. James Monroe expected that separation "will enable [Virginia] to economize affairs . . . and give greater strength in the federal councils." Jefferson, concerned over retaining the valley of the Kanawha River for Virginia's commercial development, believed "It is for the interest of Virginia to cede so far immediately; because the people beyond that will separate themselves, because they will be joined by all our settlements beyond the Alleghaney if they are the first movers." Anxious over his own western investments as well as Virginia's political influence, Washington appealed to Confederation president and fellow Virginian Richard Henry Lee: "The spirit of emigration is great, people have got impatient, and tho' you cannot stop the road, it is yet in your power to mark the way; a little while and you will not be able to do either. It is easier to prevent, than to remedy an evil."

The flurry of correspondence peaked in 1784, reacting to a confluence of events that forced Virginia to face its Kentucke problem. Kentucke's population nearly doubled by some twelve thousand migrants, bringing with it a change in political leadership. The men who had overseen the early stages of settlement—Boone, Clark, and Harrod—began to fade from the scene as more recent arrivals took up the separation cause. The 1779 land law had required surveys, and because primogeniture remained the law of Virginia, second and third sons of the state's planter class saw an opportunity to make their futures as surveyors (and speculators) in Kentucke. Among them were Thomas Marshall, who became surveyor of Fayette County in 1781, appointing his nephew Humphrey as his deputy surveyor; John Todd, who joined them as a deputy surveyor in 1782; and Alexander Breckinridge and his brother Robert, surveyor and deputy surveyor of Jefferson County, respectively, in 1784. Together, this crowd imagined themselves an entitled and articulate leadership—men who understood their identities in Kentucke to be as Virginians. Younger Virginia lawyers similarly imagined personal and political opportunity in Kentucke. In 1782 and 1783, Caleb Wallace, George Muter, Samuel McDowell, and Harry Innes arrived in a region overflowing with land disputes—many involving recently arrived surveyors—and insufficient courts, even though a district court was established in the new village of Danville, in the center of the Great Meadow.

These men brought local and state politics westward with them, introducing into Kentucke a new level of political intrigue. "That you have enemies you must not doubt, when you reflect that you have made yourself eminent," Thomas Jefferson warned George Rogers Clark of the impending migration of George Nicholas in the late 1780s; "I was not a little surprized however to find one person hostile to you as far as he has personal courage to shew hostility to any man. Who he is you will probably have heard, or may know him by this description as being all tongue without either head or heart." Nicholas, a friend to James Madison, obviously was less favored by Jefferson.

Joining these self-appointed men of distinction were thousands of nameless pioneers who distrusted any agents of Virginia. While the 1779 land law brought greater order to Kentucke's land distribution, it eliminated any real possibility for squatters to succeed in claiming land. Hundreds of families became landless and disgruntled. Additionally, many were not from Virginia. Drawn to trans-Appalachia by the call of opportunity, thousands of backcountry North Carolinians and Pennsylvanians relocated westward in the early 1780s, only to find their chances at land acquisition blocked by surveyors/speculators and the legal system that seemed to support them.

Not surprisingly, then, when two agitators arrived from the East with Paine's *Public Good* in hand, an eager audience welcomed them. Predicting the inevitable assumption of Virginia's western lands by the Confederation Congress, the two men— Pomperoy and Galloway—promised the dispossessed that Congress would invalidate Virginia's land claims and redistribute land more equitably. Some listeners built cabins and planted corn on claimed lands, anticipating recognition of homestead rights, but angering the justices charged with straightening out the already confused land claims. Both agents were quickly jailed and convicted under a colonial Virginia law of being "propogators of false news, to the disturbance of the good people of the colony." After paying their hefty fines, both were chased out of Kentucke.

Pomperoy and Galloway, however, had sufficiently stirred the mass of lately arrived settlers who were struggling to acquire lands against what appeared to be a conspiracy of county surveyors and judicial officials. When Congress passed the Ordinance of 1784, laying out a policy for state creation in the lands north of the Ohio River that it had acquired from Virginia, then, some pioneers interpreted it as an invitation to form their own state south of the river. "Many of the inhabitants of this place are not natives of Virginia, nor well affected to its government," one loyal Virginian warned Governor Harrison in mid-1784; "I fear the Faction will increase, and ere long we shall revolt from government in order to try if we can govern ourselves, which, in my opinion, will be jumping out of the frying pan into the fire." Daniel Boone worried: "I hope our petitioning for a new State will be no barrier against any assistance government might give us as it is entirely against the voice of the people at large. A few individuals who expect to be statesmen have put this afoot. Some petitions will be sent down [to Richmond] in opposition to the new State this assembly." Virginia could not afford to ignore the problem. Without political order, "a Revolution in this Country will ensue, and then no man can say that he is sure of this property an hour." Walker Daniel, Kentucke's attorney general, similarly cautioned Harrison that "no two thinking men in the District, of honest disinterested Intentions, at present, wish a separation from the Eastern part of the State, I am at a loss to say how long they will continue in their present sentiments." By the end of year, however, even "thinking men" were reconsidering their loyalty to Virginia.

Directly influencing their ideas about Virginia was a rejuvenated Indian threat. In the Old Northwest, the Wabash Indians declared war against the United States, initiating a wave of terror throughout Kentucke. A loose confederacy of Weas, Piankashaws, and other Ohio valley peoples, the Wabash had remained neutral during the Revolutionary War, even refraining from interfering when Clark invaded the Illinois country in the late 1770s. Yet, in 1783, Governor Harrison had given license to Clark to attack "them in their Country [as] the only way to keep them quiet and save expense," inspiring the Wabash to react in kind.

To the south, the Chickamaugas similarly appeared poised to renew their attacks on travelers along the Wilderness Trail. One Kentuckian fretted that "There is much Reason to expect a War with the Cherokees, who it is to be feared, have before this time made an attack on the Kanetuck Settlements." Benjamin Logan wanted to go on the offensive and invade the Chickamauga towns, but in November 1784, when district court opened in Danville, some of Kentucke's most prominent lawyers and justices convinced Logan that he could not act without Virginia's authority. State law constrained militias from offensive action.

Only the governor could sanction preemptive strikes against native peoples.

Logan might have appealed to George Rogers Clark to intercede. After all, since the mid-1770s, Kentucke's settlers had looked to Clark as their protector. Needing someone to blame for the disaster at Blue Licks, the failure to erect more defensive structures, and the Shawnees' continued hostilities, however, Governor Harrison had accepted Clark's resignation some ten months earlier. "I feel myself called, in the most forcible manner," Harrison wrote Clark, "to return you my thanks and those of my Council, for the very great and singular services you have rendered your country in wresting so great and valuable a territory out of the hands of the British enemy, repelling the attacks of their savage allies, and carrying on a successful war in the heart of their country." The Confederation Congress, recognizing his value, immediately recruited Clark as an Indian commissioner.

By the mid-1780s, Kentucke was on edge. Although his "family is quite safe," William Christian wrote, "we release the Cows with caution. I see nothing here at present desirable for Farmers who have Improvements elsewhere." Virginia seemed willing to do nothing to relieve the situation. In fact, the assembly appeared determined to make life difficult in the West: Levi Todd complained that "the Legislative Body have tied the Hands of the Kentucky people in such a manner as to prevent our lifting Arms against those who daily invade us." Daniel Boone, the Kentuckian who may have sensed most keenly the rising tensions, warned Patrick Henry: "The injries done to the Indens are terrible. An Inden war is exspcted."

5.

SEEKING SECURITY
AND STABILITY

In May 1785, many of Kentucke's self-selected leadership followed up their November 1784 gathering that had dissuaded Benjamin Logan from invading the Chickamauga towns with a meeting in Danville to discuss their options when addressing the Indian threat. The conversation turned to grievances against Virginia and concluded with a petition for separation and a "declaration of independence," written by the recently arrived James Wilkinson:

> We hold it as a self evident truth that the government is ordered for the ease and protection of the governed: and whatever ends are not attained, by one form of government, it is the right, it is the duty, of the people to seek such other mode, as will be likely to insure to themselves and to their posterity those blessings to which, by nature they are entitled.

In the accompanying list of "benefits of government which every citizen had a right to expect," the foremost complaint was that "we have no power to call out the militia, our sure and only defence, to oppose the wicked machinations of the savages, unless in case of actual invasion."

Neither the petition nor the declaration was sent to Virginia, but news quickly carried over the Appalachians. Frustrated and angered by the state's apparent inattention to its western citizens, Caleb Wallace complained to James Madison, "We conceive the people of this District do not at present enjoy a greater portion of Liberty than an American Colony might have done a few years ago had she been allowed a Representation in the British Parliament." For Virginians, the handwriting was on the wall. Jefferson hoped that the Old Dominion would "not leave to the Western country to withdraw themselves by force and become our worst enemies instead of our best friends." Madison accepted that "no interval whatever should be suffered between the release of our hold on that Country, and its taking on itself the obligations of a member of the Federal body." Washington wanted to "meet them upon their own ground, draw the best line, and best terms we can of separation and part good friends."

An amicable separation depended upon how Virginia would handle the growing confederation of Indian peoples. Wyandots, Shawnees, Chippewas, Odawas, Potawatomis, Lenni Lenapes, Miamis, Kickapoos, Weas, Piankashaws, and Chickamaugas found a common enemy in the white and black pioneers of Kentucke. By 1785, having resigned themselves to American settlement in the trans-Appalachian West, native peoples had formed a Western Confederacy, initiating a new and more intense series of attacks in Kentucke and along the eastern backcountries in order to dissuade Americans from crossing the Ohio River. Even moderate Indians who were willing to accommodate American settlement found it increasingly difficult to make their cases to their peoples.

The Confederation Congress was fortunate in January 1786, then, to draw some of the more moderate Shawnees, Lenni Lenapes, and Wyandots into a conference with its commissioners George Rogers Clark, Samuel Parsons, and Richard Butler at Fort Finney, at the confluence of the Miami and Ohio Rivers. Two years earlier, in the fall of 1784, the Confederation had met at Fort Stanwix with the Iroquois. Mohawk chief Thayendanegea—known to the Americans as Joseph Brant—had attended the 1768 Fort Stanwix negotiations with the British. This time, he led the Iroquois delegation, and as they had some eighteen years earlier, they ceded all claims to the Ohio River valley. Several months later, commissioners had convinced Lenni Lenape, Chippewa, Wyandot, and Ottawa representatives at Fort McIntosh to abandon claims to lands in southern and eastern Ohio territory. Again, the Shawnees watched as other nations sacrificed their lands.

When the Confederation approached the Shawnees to meet at Fort Finney, then, more radical elements led by Simon Girty discouraged Shawnee leaders from attending. Moderate elements, however, saw this as an opportunity to acquire what they could from an increasingly hopeless situation. Several hundred arrived at Fort Finney with great fanfare: Moluntha, the oldest civil chief and a veteran of the siege of Fort Boone, beat a small drum and sang as he led the contingent into the camp. Immediately behind him were several dancers—as commissioner Butler described, "the whole of the party painted and dressed in the most elegant manner, in their way, which is truly fantastic, but elegant though savage." Then followed the warriors, led by war chief Kekewepellethe, known to the Americans as Captain Johnny; and finally, Ca-we-chile, the head Shawnee woman, led the women and children into camp. Upon meeting the commissioners, Moluntha shook hands because "the heads of the people should be on an easy and familiar footing," but the warriors and women remained aloof: as "the strength of the nation, [they continued] more distant till peace is certain."

The Native Americans had undertaken quite a journey from Maquachake on the upper Great Miami River to reach Fort Finney. Delayed by frozen rivers and inclement winter weather, they arrived several weeks later than the commissioners had anticipated. Clark, Parsons, and Butler had remained patient, however, because the mission was a critical one. They expected that success would establish the Confederation's authority in the Old Northwest and offer a sign of friendship toward both the Shawnees and Kentucke's settlers by emptying the lands between the Great Miami and Ohio Rivers, essentially creating a middle ground in which Confederation troops would keep the peace. The commissioners had arrived in the Ohio River valley with one hundred infantry who had already begun the process, warning off squatters to return to Kentucke.

The arrival of an American army in the northwest, however, was not received warmly by the region's native peoples. The warriors in attendance at Fort Finney mocked the American soldiers for cooking their own meals, even as they demanded more alcohol and food: "They conceived us all old women clad in uniform," complained one soldier. Contrasting Moluntha's seemingly good and sincere intentions with those of the warriors, Butler wrote, "I find that many of these young fellows which have grown up through the course of the war, and *trained like young hounds to blood*, have a great attachment to the British." And his suspicions were soon verified when, during one conversation, Kekewepellethe rejected the commissioners' overtures of a land cession and threw a string of black wampum on the table, threatening continued war. "God gave us this country," he declared; "we do not understand measuring out the lands, it is all ours." Butler responded, smashing the wampum and threatening Kekewepellethe that unless the Indians abandoned the lands south and east of the Great Miami River, "the U.S. will take the most effectual measures to . . . distress your obstinate nation." He placed a black and white wampum string before the warrior chief, demanding that he choose between war and peace.

Despite Kekewepellethe's stance against granting lands to the Americans, Moluntha and other civil leaders overruled the warriors and relinquished the Shawnee lands south and east of the Great Miami River. By early February, after two weeks of negotiations, Moluntha and his people returned home to inform nearby villages that their lands had been sacrificed for the security of their peoples. Many Shawnees, frustrated by moderates like Moluntha who had sold them out and by Americans who were cunning with their manipulations, joined in the Western Confederacy's renewed campaign of violence, escalating attacks along the Ohio River and into Kentucke. When the Confederation Congress demanded to know why Moluntha could not control his people, he cowardly blamed the attacks on the "disorderly mischievous" Cherokees.

Impetuous Spirity of Kentucke

As the Fort Finney conference ended, rumors circulated throughout Kentucke that Confederation commissioner Parsons had written friends back east that Kentuckians were "a banditti of refugees, not worthy of Congress's notice," and the Confederation seemed to concur. As the Indian attacks increased, Patrick Henry solicited the Confederation to help defend Kentucke, but Congress persisted in directing its troops to remain neutral in the escalating war. "I don't think this country, even in its infant state, bore so gloomy an aspect as it does at present," George Rogers Clark cautioned Governor Henry. Still unable to attack without permission of the governor, Kentucke's pioneers remained exposed more than ever. "Great part of these beautiful Settlements will be laid waste, without protected by volunteers penetrating into the Hart of the Enemy's County," complained Clark; "nothing else will do, Scouts and Forts on the Frontiers, answer but little purpose."

Desperate for relief, in the spring of 1786, Kentucke militias planned raids into the Ohio country without their governor's consent. Over twelve hundred men gathered on the north side of the Falls of the Ohio, where Clark, reluctantly coming out of military retirement, strategized a two-prong invasion. He would lead a larger contingent against the Wabash Indians, and, suspecting that many Shawnee warriors would then join the Wabash in staving off Clark's troops, he directed Benjamin Logan to take a smaller force of eight hundred into the Shawnee villages of central Ohio.

When Clark's troops reached Vincennes, however, hundreds of militia men abandoned the effort, returning to Kentucke and stifling Clark's ability to attack. Wabash Indians had posed a constant menace to the Jefferson County settlers along Beargrass Creek and around the Falls of the Ohio, but pioneers to the south in Lincoln County had greater complaint against the Chickamaugas and refused to risk their lives against Indians who did not directly threaten them. Without the regiments from Lincoln County, Clark bunkered down in Vincennes and attempted to negotiate with the Wabash, returning to his old ploy of pretending he had far more troops that he actually did. When Spanish traders arrived to supply local residents, Clark's men seized the goods, infuriating the French population and risking war with Spain. Enraged over Clark's carelessness, the Confederation ordered him and his men to vacate Vincennes in early 1787.

In the meantime, Logan's forces found their way to the upper Great Miami River and were within fifty miles of Maquachake when Logan instructed his officers that "in case any person, under any description or any color, attempts to come to the army, all persons are forewarned to receive them in a friendly manner." He clearly anticipated the Kentuckians' eagerness to avenge years of Indian menace, and his qualification of "any description or any color" lays bare the racial undercurrent of violence on the frontier. Living in Maquachake, Chief Moluntha flew an American flag as a symbol of his alliance with the Confederation following the Fort Finney treaty. As Kentucke militias stormed into the village, Moluntha surrendered peacefully and was taken before Hugh McGary, the militia leader who had recklessly charged into battle at Blue Licks. Still stung over the accusations of his poor leadership, McGary mistakenly accused Moluntha of having had a hand in the Kentuckians' defeat at Blue Licks, withdrew his hatchet, and hacked the old man to death. When a fellow militia officer tried to intercede, the frenzied Kentuckian threatened to chop him down, as well as anyone else who kept him from killing Indians. McGary's spontaneous fury evidenced a growing attitude among many Kentuckians that they were forgotten Americans, struggling against Indians and an indifferent Confederation to secure the West.

In June 1786, soon after McGary's rage destroyed the Americans' last true Shawnee ally, George Washington considered how "it may require some management to quiet the restless and impetuous spirit of Kentucke, of whose conduct I am more apprehensive about this business, than I am of all the opposition that will be given by the Spaniards." The "business" was not Indian affairs but open commerce along the Mississippi River. The issue of western commerce was worrisome to state and national leaders. If economically tied to Spain, Kentuckians would be drawn away from the Confederation. Washington continued:

> In my judgment it is a matter of very serious concern to the well being of the former [eastern states], to make it the interest of the latter [western states] to trade with them, without which, the ties of consanguinity which are weakening every day will soon be no bond, and we shall be no more a few years hence to the inhabitants of that country, than the British and Spaniards are at this day.

As if to verify Washington's suspicions, the Kentuckians, having met for a third time to discuss separation, petitioned Virginia to pass "an act declaring and acknowledging the Sovereignty & Independence of this district," mentioning not once a desire to be attached to the Confederation. Jefferson related his "fear that the people of Kentucky think of separating, not only from Virginia (in which they are right), but also from the confederacy. . . . I should think this a most calamitous event, and such a one as every good citizen should set himself against." James Wilkinson and Harry Innes were among the most radical separatist voices in Kentucke and had proven their influence at the third convention. A new convention with such men in charge, then, could certainly take Kentucke toward Spanish control. But in September 1786, when a fourth convention was to meet, many of its elected representatives were with Clark in Vincennes or Logan in the Ohio country. The meeting languished for months without a quorum, forcing the attendees to appeal to Virginia for an extension on the deadline for statehood. The legislature took the occasion to insert a new requirement in its second Enabling Act: "and to the end that no interval of anarchy may happen to the good people of the proposed state," the statehood convention was to write a constitution and transmit it to Virginia's federal representatives, "who are hereby instructed to use their endeavors to obtain from congress a speedy concurrence." Kentucky would be pushed into the union if need be.

Yet, even as Virginia tried to tether Kentucke to the Confederation, circumstances were working against those plans. Through trade, George Washington had hoped to strengthen "the ties of consanguinity," but Kentucke's settlers were little interested in schemes to facilitate trade eastward. Maybe too many remembered the trials of their westward journeys: the ruggedness of the narrow and rocky trail known as the Wilderness Road; the Indian attacks along the Ohio River; and the pricey and unreliable "guides" who often offered their services on both routes. Even with Washington's dream of transforming the Potomac River into an inland gateway to the West, few Kentuckians looked back over the Appalachians for economic opportunity.

Instead, the future of Kentucke lay westward, down the Mississippi River to Spain's vibrant trading center of New Orleans. Land speculator John May said so in 1780—"the value of Land here will much depend on the Convenience of Navigation"—and Congress was well aware of it by 1785, having sent John Jay to Madrid specifically to negotiate access to the Mississippi River. But Jay returned with a document that sacrificed western trade for eastern merchants' and traders' access to Spain's markets in Europe and the West Indies. Although ratification of the Jay-Gardoqui Treaty failed in Congress, its very existence created a tempest in Kentucke. "There are many ambitious and turbulent spirits among its inhabitants," Washington explained, "who from the present difficulties in their intercourse with the Atlantic States, have turned their eyes to New Orleans, and may become riotous and ungovernable, if the hope of traffick with it is cut off by treaty."

Washington expected the problem would remedy itself: "Whenever the new States become so populous and so extended to the westward, as really to need it, there will be no power which can deprive them of the use of the Mississippi. Why then should we prematurely urge a matter, which is displeasing and may produce disagreeable consequences, if it is our interest to let it sleep?" But Kentuckians were livid. Rumors circulated that Jay had dismissed westerners' needs because he believed "the Western people had nothing to export, & therefore the cession of the Mississippi would be no injury to them." When they met for their fifth separation convention, delegates concluded that only by entering the Confederation could they exert enough pressure to gain trading rights on the Mississippi River. They quickly and unanimously voted for independence along the terms of the second Enabling

Act. Still, Kentucke's future would not necessarily play out as Washington hoped. Elaborating on the frame of mind of his fellow pioneers, Isaac Dunn concluded that "the direction of the current of the rivers which run in front of their dwellings points clearly to the power to which they ought to ally themselves."

Inability to trade on the Mississippi River was part of a much larger economic problem facing Kentucke. As William Christian explained, "Money there is none & everybody is waiting to get a little from new Emigrants. . . . This country is not at present possessed of any Money. The stores get what little the Lawyers leave & I guess both are often disappointed." Almost every migrant who had money (or something that could be sold for money) put it into land, hoping that legal disputes would not undermine the investment. Land, slaves, food, taxes, surveys, guides, household goods, lawyers—the list of expenses was endless for new arrivals. "There has gone such a Train of Surveyors, Collectors & Tax-gatherers before me," complained John Breckinridge of Virginia, "that they have drained, I believe, every farthing the poor people had." Kentuckians' capital was invested: "Kentucky is the greatest field for Speculation, I believe, in the World," continued Breckinridge. But speculation and investment made the region cash-poor and slowed economic development. By the 1780s, saltworks and saltpeter productions were the only significant manufacturing, both heavily consumed domestically. Hoping to put their investments to use, farmers produced surplus foodstuffs, filling warehouses at the Falls of the Ohio with corn, flour, pork, and tobacco.

James Wilkinson, facing his own desperate financial situation, decided to challenge the Spanish restriction on trade and take several flatboats of agricultural productions to New Orleans. Risking confiscation of his goods, he finally arrived in early July 1787 and met with Governor Esteban Rodríguez Miró to negotiate river access. In later years, Wilkinson would be vilified by contemporaries and historians for his "treasonous" actions, but in his meetings with Rodríguez, Wilkinson demonstrated that neither Kentucke nor Spain was his primary concern: he was determined to advance his own fortunes. He laid before Rodríguez six "facts and natural inferences":

First: That the American Settlements, whose rivers flow in the Mississippi are already powerful and on account of their nature, irresistable, and should daily increase in strength.

Second: That the navigation of the Mississippi is the fountain from which they must hope for future relief and comfort, in consequence of which each individual is of himself always attentive to this object, and through the powerful incentive of self-preservation will employ any means, no matter how desperate, to attain it.

Third: That in order to promote his much desired end, they are working to separate themselves from the American Union, and that Congress has neither the power nor inclination to prevent this measure.

Fourth: That the Notables of these new Settlements are considering two projects, either of which they believe can be conducive to the success of this, their favorite object: i.e. *an amicable arrangement with Spain, or hostilities with the help of Great Britain.*

Fifth: That this Power is courting those Settlements and will endeavor to insiduously bind them to attack Louisiana.

Sixth: That the above mentioned Settlements have determined to make the first propositions to Spain and in case these are not accepted, to embrace the policies of Great Britain.

Wilkinson truly was a master manipulator, arguing that Kentucke, as the most mature of the western states, was positioned to lead all western Americans against those who impeded Mississippi River trade, and essentially offering to Rodríguez the choice to seize control of the American West or have it ripped from him by England. He then swore "that my principles and the motives which prompted my conduct are the good of the country in which I live and the interest and aggrandizement of the Spanish Monarchy." Having left Kentucke before the fifth convention, he was unaware that his colleagues had already accepted Virginia's second Enabling Act and statehood in the federal union.

In the meantime, the Confederation Congress, still in session, refused to accept Kentucke's application for statehood. Kentucke's representative, John Brown, had argued for admission since January 1788, but not until early August—one month following the deadline established in the second Enabling Act—did Congress appear ready to approve. Then news arrived that New Hampshire had joined eight other states in ratifying the new federal constitution, essentially making the Confederation Congress obsolete and leaving the issue of Kentucke statehood and the problem of western trade for a new federal government.

Wilkinson offered Kentuckians an alternative to the new federal government. Even before his return to Kentucke, his agents began to promote commerce along the Mississippi River. To ensure continued trade and goodwill with the Spanish, Wilkinson advertised in the *Kentucky Gazette* for tobacco, tallow, butter, bacon, hams, lard, and smoked beef briskets, insisting that "these articles being intended for a foreign market it is necessary that they be handled in the manner not only to do the seller credit but to recommend our commodities to foreign merchants and make them desirous of engaging in a commercial intercourse with the Western Country." Anticipating Wilkinson's sale of their produce in New Orleans, Kentucke settlers filled warehouses along the region's waterways, and as one pioneer observed, "for some time all the trade from the Ohio was carried on in his name, a line from him sufficing to ensure to the owner of the boat every privilege and protection he could desire."

Easterners seemed oblivious to the economic and potential political consequences of Wilkinson's negotiations with the Spanish. The *New York Journal and Weekly Register* championed Wilkinson's second fleet of boats headed down the Mississippi River as an American success story: "This is the first Armada that ever floated on the Western waters, and I assure you, the sight of this little squadron, under the Kentucke colours opens a field of contemplation, what this country may expect from commerce at a future day." Despite the fifth convention's decision to bind itself to the American republic, the Confederation's delay in admitting Kentucke to the union frustrated many, and over the course of 1788, several events unfolded that resurrected concerns over whether the United States could expect western commerce "at a future day."

First, the new federal constitution went before Virginia for ratification. Harry Innes feared that "if the Constitution is adopted by us that we shall be the mere vassals of the Congress and the consequences to me are horrible and dreadful." In June 1788, the Virginia ratifying convention convened, and while Innes did not attend, fourteen Kentucke pioneers took part in the debates and voted. James Madison led the proponents of the new government, joined by his friend George Nicholas. Among his Kentucke allies, Madison counted Humphrey Marshall. Arguing against ratification were Patrick Henry and other anti-federalists, including the majority of Kentucke delegates, led by the reactionary Henry Lee of Bourbon County, who foresaw the enlargement of a national government as detrimental to personal independence. With comparable numbers on both sides of the debate, Madison, Henry, and other more vocal debaters dedicated considerable time to trying to sway the votes of the Kentucke delegation. Nearly a fifth of the debates centered upon commercial access to the Mississippi River. "The only danger I apprehend is from the Kentucky members," Madison confided to Washington, "and one consideration only has any weight with them: a fear that if the new government should take place, that their navigation would be given up."

Hoping to counter those concerns, Nicholas argued before the convention: "Are not the United States as much interested as the people of Kentucky to retain that navigation? Congress will have as much interest in it as any inhabitant of that country, and must exert themselves for it." In response to counterarguments that under a new federal government, Kentuckians would have to pay an import tariff, Nicholas retorted that "under the present system, and without the navigation of that river, [it will] be furnished with the articles of her consumption through the medium of the importing states. She will, therefore, be taxed by every importing state." At least with a new constitution, "Kentucky will participate on equal advantage with the importing states."

Anti-federalist William Grayson responded that the votes on the Jay-Gardoqui Treaty revealed an eastern indifference toward Kentucke's economic needs. Those who supported the treaty had fallen short by two votes, and under the new structure, only nine states would be needed to approve treaties: "If nine states give it away, what will the Kentucky people do?" Patrick Henry concurred: "the people of Kentucky, though weak now, will not let the President and Senate take away this right." But it was Nicholas who won the day by claiming that only through union would Kentucke exert any strength:

> I think that Kentucky has nothing to expect from any one state alone in America. She can expect support and succor alone from a strong, efficient government, which can command the resources of the Union when necessary. She can receive no support from the old Confederation. Consider the present state of that country. Declared independent of Virginia, to whom is she to look up for succor? No sister state can help her. She may call on the present general government; but, whatever may be the wish of Congress, they can give them no relief. That country contains all my wishes and prospects. There is my property, and there I intend to reside. I should be averse to the establishment of any system which would be injurious to it. I flatter myself that this government will secure their happiness and liberty.

His arguments convinced a sufficient number of delegates, and Virginia ratified the constitution by a count of eighty-nine ayes and seventy-nine nays. Still, the meeting had proven to Madison that "the impression of Kentucky, like that on the rest of the State was at first answerable to our wishes; but, as elsewhere, the torch of discord has been thrown in and has found the materials but too inflamable." It was a fire that could be easily extinguished with the waters of the Mississippi.

The second event of 1788 to complicate Kentucke's joining the union was a sixth statehood convention that convened to draft a constitution. Following the Confederation's inaction, Spanish ambassador Don Diego de Gardoqui approached John Brown in Philadelphia, promising that "if Kentucky will declare her independence and empower some proper person to negotiate with him, that he has authority and will engage to open the navigation of the Mississippi." Wilkinson, too, saw an opening to nudge his fellow westerners toward Spain. Having been made a similar offer by Rodríguez, and joined by Harry Innes and other allies, he argued to the statehood convention that they should proceed with their constitution-making, and since the current government would not accept Kentucke and since Virginia's timetable for statehood had elapsed, Kentucke would be independent of both. More cautious voices prevailed, however, forcing the convention to postpone any actions for another four months, to meet again in November 1788.

One month before the November meeting, one of Wilkinson's closest allies, George Muter, changed sides. As Kentucke settlers prepared to elect delegates to their seventh convention, Muter warned them through a letter in the *Kentucky Gazette* that they would be alarmed at schemes being bantered about to separate Kentucke from the United States. He argued that, under the conditions of the new national constitution, only through statehood and an appeal to the federal government could the Mississippi River *legally* be opened. If Kentucke elected another option— independence or alliance with Spain—it would be in constant conflict with the Northwest Territory and the United States over access to the Ohio and Mississippi Rivers.

Wilkinson saw Muter's defection as more of an opportunity than a problem. With the Spanish intrigue out in the open, he brought it quickly to the floor when the convention met, pointing out both the federal government's and Virginia's unwillingness to resolve western problems and encouraging the delegates to frame a constitution and plan for independence. While Wilkinson did not reveal his own negotiations with Rodríguez, he did intimate that Ambassador Gardoqui had proposed a Spanish alliance to another delegate in the room. John Brown, however, sat quietly, reluctant to acknowledge Gardoqui's overtures or any complicity in a "Spanish conspiracy." Wilkinson's moment slipped away. Thomas Marshall related how, later, Brown "told us that he did not think himself at liberty to mention what pass'd in private conversation between himself and Don Gardoqui respecting us: but this much in general he would venture to inform us, that provided we were united in our councils every thing we could wish for was within our reach." With the delegates unaware of the full possibilities during the convention, their most important decision was to petition Virginia yet again for a new enabling act.

As the convention deliberated its petitions, John Connolly arrived in Louisville. A British citizen and apparent envoy from the Canadian governor, Connolly met with several of Kentucke's political leaders to offer yet another option: as Harry Innes explained to George Washington, Connolly "touched the key to Fomentation and offered assistance to enable the Inhabitants of the Western Country to seize on the City of New Orleans, and secure the navigation of the Mississippi." A "British conspiracy," however, was even less likely than the Spanish one. "The people of this country were so strongly prejudiced against the British, not only from circumstances attending the late war, but from a persuasion that the Indians were at this time stimulated by them against us," Thomas Marshall assured Washington,

> and that so long as those Savages continued to commit such horrid cruelties on our defenceless frontiers & were recieved as friends and allies by the British at Detroit it would be impossible for them to be convinced of the sincerity of Lord Dorchesters offers let his professions be ever so strong; and that if his Lordship would have us believe him really dispos'd to be our friend he must begin by shewing his disapprobation of the ravages of the Indians.

Rumors of Connolly's gambit as well as Wilkinson's intrigues spread eastward. Additionally, word was that George Rogers Clark had become involved with the Spanish. In early 1788, he proposed to Gardoqui that he lead a colony of pioneers to Spanish territory (what would become southern Missouri). A year later, John Brown also broached the topic, offering to organize and settle a colony near Natchez. All of this news weighed heavily on the Virginia legislature. So, less than a month after Kentucke's seventh convention, the state assembly passed a third Enabling Act, calling for an eighth convention the following July and encouraging Congress to confer statehood within a year thereafter. When the eighth meeting convened, the delegates nitpicked at the details of the Enabling Act, requesting that the assembly revise it, which it did quickly in December 1788. Finally, in July 1789, Kentucke's leaders congregated in a ninth convention, accepting the full terms laid down by the Virginia assembly, setting April 1792 for a constitutional convention, and petitioning President Washington for admission to the United States.

The Sword of the Republic

Even as delegates debated the advantages and disadvantages of allying with either Spain or England, striking out on their own as an independent state, or joining the federal union, most of the people they represented paid little attention to the proceedings. In the late 1780s, as a decade earlier, many Kentucke settlers returned to the security of forts and stations, "so that it is entirely out of their Power to Raise any thing for the support of their families." The Western Confederacy, particularly the Wabash and Shawnees, had appropriated George Rogers Clark's tactic of creating a subsistence crisis in the enemy's lands. While a murder or two provoked confusion and terror, warriors knew that just their presence psychologically immobilized settlers, impeding the growing and harvesting of crops, milking of cows, and retrieval of spring waters. Indians killed wandering cattle and pigs by the hundreds and stole horses regularly. One resident, discouraged by the federal army's refusal to impede the Indians' excursions into Kentucke, alerted Governor Henry that the Beargrass settlements would "be entirely Destroyed, without the most prompt and Decided Exertions on the Part of the Government."

In the aftermath of the Fort Finney conference and the murder of Moluntha, the Western Confederacy of Indians was enraged and ready to engage full war against Kentucke's pioneers. In 1786, William Christian fell in battle against the Wabash; and in 1789, a Shawnee attack on the Ohio River ended John May's life. The deaths of more prominent men confirmed that no one was immune, although geographically the majority of killings now took place in or near the Ohio River, deceptively relaxing settlers in Lexington and the Bluegrass villages. Raiding parties continued to haunt the Great Meadow. William Fleming warned his wife, "In Fayette there are parties of Indians but I will not dwell on these disagreeable things."

Within the context of a heightened threat, the settlement of Kentucke's eastern mountains began. For years, land investors such as George Washington and the Breckinridge brothers had purchased large holdings in the Big Sandy River valley, expecting that, once the Revolutionary War concluded, Appalachian lands would increase in value. While the lands were claimed, therefore, they remained unsettled. Over those same years, migrants along the Wilderness Road had viewed the Appalachians as a barrier rather than a destination. The length of road from the Cumberland Gap to the southern rim of the Great Meadow was labeled "The Wilderness," specifically because the lands were less choice, the travel rugged, and the Indian threat magnified.

For nearly thirty years, Matthias Harman had wandered the lands around the headwaters of the Big Sandy River, and on many occasions, he had confronted Indians determined to chase him back to Virginia. Once, he and his companions chased and killed three bison along the branches of Buffalo Creek, memorializing their kill in the names of three tributaries—Bull Creek, Cow Creek, and Calf Creek. Like the Great Meadow to the west, the valley of the Big Sandy seemed a blank slate to American pioneers, who believed they could hunt, name, and in 1788 when Harman led two dozen settlers into the region, settle the landscape.

Running adjacent to the Big Sandy River was a branch of Athiamiowee, which Shawnees and other northwestern Indians still employed to visit with and fight against the Cherokees and Catawbas. It was a party of Shawnees, Wyandots, and Cherokees who wandered the trail in October 1789, hoping to run across their longtime nemesis Matthias Harman. Instead, they came upon the cabin of Thomas and Virginia Wiley. With her husband away, "Jenny" Wiley was preparing her four children and brother to board with a neighbor for protection when the Indians attacked. Within moments, four were dead and scalped, and Wiley held tight to her toddler as a Shawnee and Cherokee argued over what to do with her. The former wanted her as a captive to replace a daughter who had recently died; the latter preferred to kill her and her baby.

Like Mary Draper Ingles some thirty years earlier, Jenny Wiley found herself hiking through the rugged mountains of Appalachia on her way to the lower Shawnee Town. Unlike Ingles, however, there was no uncertainty in Wiley's predicament. She knew her husband was alive and the rest of her family was dead, and she depended completely on the grace of a Shawnee to save her from the tomahawk of a Cherokee. In one panicked moment, Wiley bolted into the woods. When she was caught, the Cherokee grabbed her baby, dashing its head against a tree before scalping the child. The party then forged on. Wiley, certainly sickened by the losses of her children and strained by the demands of hiking, became increasingly weak. By the second week of their journey, as the party reached the banks of the Ohio River, she was too ill to continue. Frustrated by the Shawnee chief's determination to keep Wiley alive, the Cherokee and a few others left the party as it reached the Ohio River. There, in a rock shelter, Wiley prematurely gave birth to a son. Patiently, her captors set up camp for the winter, and the party remained for three months. In time, they decided to test the infant by placing him in the cold waters of an adjacent creek, but when the baby cried, a Wyandot scalped this child as well.

Wiley's story is an incredible captivity narrative. The Indians never took her to the lower Shawnee Town, choosing instead to move from hunting camp to hunting camp, teaching her skills like hide tanning and lead smelting. Over a year passed, and while she remained frail, Wiley acted as the sole domestic worker for her captors. One evening, a large party of Cherokees arrived with a young white man as their captive, tortured him, and burned him alive within earshot of Wiley. In what was most likely a ritual of adoption, they then bound her hands, tied her to a tree, and told her they intended to burn her as well. Whether they pitied her or were impressed by the stoicism of a woman who had nothing left to lose, the fire was never lit. But her Shawnee "father" did sell her to a Cherokee who promised to take her to one of the Overhill Towns, where she would teach his wives to write and weave cloth.

Soon thereafter, Wiley escaped and tried to navigate back along the Big Sandy and its tributaries to her home. Nearly three weeks passed before she came upon Harman's Station. Her Cherokee "owner" was close behind, however, and his party lingered in the vicinity for days. Months later, Indians laid siege to Harman's Station, frightening its inhabitants enough so that as soon as the siege ended, they abandoned the Big Sandy valley.

The demise of Harman's Station—as part of the larger Indian war in which Kentuckians found themselves—incited Kentucke settlers to action. Since raiding parties frequently stole food, the *Kentucky Gazette* encouraged residents to spike foods with arsenic and other poisons. John Hardin led angry pioneers across the Ohio River on retaliatory strikes. The new governor of the Northwest Territory, Arthur St. Clair, warned Washington of Hardin's "habit of retaliation . . . without attending precisely to the nations from which the injuries are received"—a point emphatically made by Hardin when, in early 1789, he led his militia against Wea villages along the Wabash River, killing twelve men, women, and children and then parading the scalps around Vincennes. Secretary of War Henry Knox furiously wrote Washington that "some of the inhabitants of Kentucky, during the year past, roused by recent injuries, made an incursion into the Wabash country, and, possessing an equal aversion to all bearing the name of Indians, they destroyed a number of peaceable Piankeshaws, who prided themselves in their attachment to the United States."

To the federal government, at least, Hardin's raid was a disaster. John Hamtramck, an officer in the federal army posted in the Northwest Territory, heatedly declared that "this Kentuck affair will undo everything." The vicious cycle of vengeance that had characterized the later years of the Revolutionary War in Kentucke reappeared. "The angry passions of the frontier Indians and whites," Knox insisted, "are too easily inflamed by reciprocal injuries, and are too violent to be controlled by the feeble authority of the civil power." As dramatic as Indian murders had been on the Kentucke frontier, Knox suspected that "the injuries and murders have been so reciprocal, that it would be a point of critical investigation to know on which side they have been the greatest."

As Kentucke settlers continued to raid lands that had not been ceded at Fort Finney, the situation spiraled out of control and the Western Confederacy of Indians found new allies. St. Clair anticipated that neutral Indians "will unite with the hostile nations, prudently preferring open war to a delusive and uncertain peace." To thwart the enlarging war, Knox insisted that "the sword of the republic only, is adequate to guard a due administration of justice, and the preservation of the peace," and sent more federal troops to the Northwest Territory and funded construction of five federal outposts north of the Ohio River. Still, the Indians continued to infiltrate Kentucke, and Kentuckians continued to invade the Indian villages. Early in 1789, the president considered the veracity of "what the Officers on the NW side of the River assert—viz.—that hostilities are always commenced by the People of the Kentucky District." "The people of Kentucky," declared one officer, "will carry on private expeditions against the Indians and kill them whenever they meet them . . . the thirst of war is the dearest inheritance an Indian receives from his parents, and vengeance that of the Kentuckians, hostility must then be the result on both sides." The only way to end the violence was through decisive federal actions against the Indians, expeditions in which the Kentucke militias would be invited to join and would be controlled.

The first such attempt was in April when Kentucke's General Charles Scott led two hundred militia to join General Joseph Harmar's federal troops on an excursion to track down raiding Indians parties. Only a few were discovered. Twelve miles west of Limestone, the small village that had arisen on the Point along the Ohio River, "four moccasin tracks were discovered. General Scott detached a small party of horsemen, who fell in with the savages, killed them, and brought the four scalps into Limestone." While Scott was busy chasing Indians, other Indians attacked Low Dutch Station in the western reaches of the Great Meadow and "killed a girl of twelve years old, and boy of eight years old, cutting them in a cruel manner, with tomahawks supposed; cut an ancient lady of both respectable family and character, in her right arm, head and back, in a cruel manner, with a scimitar, and after having scalped her alive, left her, and his scimitar with her, and carried off the daughter of this deponent, a girl near eleven years old, into captivity."

In October, Harmar again called militias to join his troops, this time against the villages of Kekionga and New Chillicothe.

It was a disaster. As one federal soldier described, "the Kentucky militia appeared raw and unused to the woods . . . half of the men did not have weapons and the other half possessed weapons of poor quality. General Harmar was much disheartened by the Kentuckians." Nearly sixty men were killed in the initial battle, and when a detachment returned to the villages to recover the injured, over 180 were ambushed and killed by a Miami force. The Americans retreated in disgrace, and Knox transferred Harmar out of the Northwest Territory. The victory empowered the Western Confederacy Indians, who now spurned any American efforts to negotiate.

In January 1791, Knox informed Congress that he planned to have a larger campaign against the Western Confederacy, requesting an expansion in the numbers of federal troops so that Kentucke's militias would not be needed. Governor St. Clair was to lead the expedition. Jefferson, frustrated by the federal army's incompetence, the Indians' defiance, and the Kentuckians' complicity in exacerbating the situation, hoped that "we shall give them [the Indians] a *thorough* drubbing this summer, and then change our tomahawk into a golden chain of friendship."

In October 1791, St. Clair began his march on the Miami villages with nearly two thousand men. Congress had not expanded federal troops, so alongside his regular soldiers were over one thousand Kentucke militiamen. At Fort Washington, where hundreds of Kentuckians had gathered for protection, Keturah Leitch Taylor led the women in making knapsacks and preparing coffee for the soldiers. Also among the troops were fifty Chickasaw guides, volunteered by Chief Piomingo to try to gain some favor with the United States government. The Chickasaws wisely segregated themselves from the militias, however, knowing the Kentuckians' unwillingness to differentiate between friendly and enemy Indians. When the army blundered into an ambush led by Miami war chief Little Turtle, over 630 men fell and another 270 were wounded. Abandoning their injured comrades to fate, the others fled back to Kentucke, ironically protected under the fire of the Chickasaws. On the battlefield fell Richard Butler, the aggressive negotiator at Fort Finney who had smashed the black wampum of war. Shot off his horse, Butler laid on the ground until a Shawnee bashed his skull in with a tomahawk. Other dead Americans had soil stuffed into their mouths: the Indians used the stage of battle to mock the Americans' land lust.

Harmar's and St. Clair's failures were catastrophic not only for the federal government's efforts at negotiation but for Kentucke pioneers, who now faced an agitated Western Confederacy empowered by success against federal military efforts. Several Indian parties raided Kentucke in the fall of 1791, sending fear even into the supposedly secure Bluegrass. Angry with the Chickasaws, the Western Confederacy also sent Kickapoos to exact revenge on a Chickasaw hunting party in western Kentucke. With the Indians to the north energized, Kentuckians went on the defensive again. In late November 1790, Virginia had passed a law requiring militiamen to patrol the Wilderness—the stretch of country between Cumberland Gap and the Great Meadow through which thousands of migrants passed but where few settled. Each county's militia officer was to call up thirty men to scout for Indian threats. A year later, in the wake of St. Clair's defeat, Indian patrols moved beyond the Wilderness, becoming common throughout Kentucke as militiamen stood guard against the "depredations and murders committed by the hostile tribes of Indians."

A Good Poor Man's Country

In the early 1780s, John Filson took up surveying and consequently acquired some thirteen thousand acres in Kentucky, becoming a speculator in the process. He moved by 1783 to Lexington, where he wrote *The Discovery, Settlement and Present State of Kentucke* (1784) and produced the accompanying "Map of Kentucke." Fifteen hundred copies of the book and map sold at $1.50 each.

The Discovery, Settlement and Present State of Kentucke has rightfully been described as foremost a promotional tract. Still, the watermark on Filson's map advanced the economic philosophy of "Work & Be Rich." As a land speculator, Filson was hardly the type to use the word "rich" in any metaphorical sense. He did not see attainment of self-sufficiency or embrace of republicanism as being "rich." Filson meant money and material acquisition, and because he prefaced the words with a call to labor, we may be certain that he was not speaking to the wealthy slave-holding planters or urban folk who would eventually dominate Kentucke's economic landscape. "Work & Be Rich," he called to the yeoman farmers, and they responded by the thousands.

Kentucke could be anything and many things: James Wilkin-son imagined it as opportunity for self-aggrandizement, George Washington saw it as a profitable extension of the early republic, and Daniel Boone enjoyed it as personal liberty. Filson's expectations mixed the biblical ideal of a promised land with a more democratic message:

> The recital of your happiness will call to your country all the un-fortunate of the earth, who, having experienced oppression, political or religious, will there find a deliverance from their chains. . . . Let the memory of Lycurgus, the Spartan legislator, who ban-ished covetousness, and the love of gold from his country; the excellent Locke, who first taught the doctrine of toleration; the venerable Penn, the first who founded a city of brethren; and Washington, the defender and protector of persecuted liberty, be ever the illustrious examples of your political conduct. . . .
>
> Like the land of promise, flowing with milk and honey, a land of brooks of water, of fountains and depths, that spring out of val-leys and hills, a land of wheat and barley, and all kinds of fruits, you shall eat with scarceness, and not lack any thing in it. . . . Thus, your country, favoured with the smiles of heaven, will probably be inhabited by the first people the world ever knew.

Kentucky as a political and religious asylum? Filson was not dreaming. Living in Lexington, he witnessed a vanguard of re-cently arrived, religiously and politically disaffected settlers as they stocked up on supplies before moving on into the Great Meadow.

In the East, young men faced the challenges of depleted soils, escalating land prices, and in North Carolina and Virginia where primogeniture remained on the books until 1784 and 1785 respec-tively, inheritance patterns that left many sons looking across the Appalachians to replicate their fathers' estates and lives. Politically, Kentucke was a blank slate. Migrants with more democratic leanings wanted to shape it in a manner that offered the most liberal political and economic possibilities. Those committed to republicanism sought to extend the hierarchical society of Virginia, rewarding men with status, offering hope to those below them, and creating bonds of dependence and obligation between the two groups.

The nine statehood conventions evidenced the struggle between the two visions. When James Wilkinson wrote the petition to Virginia's legislature during the third convention, for example, his employment of familial metaphors and florid prose was frowned upon by some men. Caleb Wallace was "not pleased with the Splendid Dress in which they are clothed," although Wilkinson believed he had "discarded the complimentary style of adulation and insincerity" for "the plain, manly, and unadorned language of independence." So what had Wilkinson written?

> Your Memorialists thro' the Paternal Tenderness they have for their Infant Families, the obligation which Nature binds to provide for them, Removed from the Interior parts of the Country through a Wilderness infested with the most Savage and cruel Enemies, combating with the greatest Difficulties, and yet continue to be Invaded by the Merciless Banditty, continually Harrased, confin'd to stations, and even debarr's from applying the necessary means for the support of their Families, and have thought proper first to have recourse to redress through your Honourable Body, as Duty calls us to pay all Imagenable Deference to your Paternal Authority and Guardianship over us which your Memorialists are bound to observe while you Act for their safety and defence.

Before he became immersed in the Spanish intrigue, Wilkinson and many of his colleagues viewed themselves as a court party, a political faction that included the majority of Kentucke's lawyers and district court judges. They also imagined themselves as the requisite leadership for expanding the American republic westward. In *Federalist No. 10*, Madison had defined what "the two great points of difference between a democracy and a republic are: first, the delegation of the government, in the latter, to a small number of citizens elected by the rest; secondly, the greater number of citizens, and greater sphere of country, over which the latter may be extended." Kentucke's court party envisioned themselves as the "small number of citizens" who would be looked to for leadership.

It was the vision of republicanism that drove the court party. Many of its more influential members, including Harry Innes and John Brown, were related through familial connections to William Preston, Virginia's original surveyor in Kentucke. Through Preston, they had inherited both land and political stature, and they little hesitated to demonstrate status through opulence: handsome brick houses, china, and tea services. They and their colleagues were also regular correspondents with Jefferson, Madison, and other prominent republicans. Wilkinson requested "Ideas of that System of Government, which is best suited to the genius of our Country and Times" from Dr. James Hutchinson, a Philadelphia republican. Jefferson and Madison were both requested to draw up constitutions for Kentucke. Whatever form the state's government might take, the court party wanted an organized separation from Virginia that would preserve their land holdings and protect the political strength that emanated from their patriarchal status. But in Kentucke, "Paternal Tenderness" struggled to protect and sustain "Infant Families," making it difficult for "Paternal Authority and Guardianship," as modeled by Virginia, to take root.

The constant theme in court party petitions was a complaint against Virginia's tyranny, a suggestion that the Old Dominion purposefully sought to retard Kentucke's growth through levying taxes, controlling judges' salaries, and monopolizing imports. The members of the court party demanded access to the Mississippi River, pushed consistently against the Confederation Congress, flirted with Spain, and even considered British overtures because they believed that Virginia's "Paternal Authority and Guardianship," while needed to enable separation, was also stifling Kentucke's economic growth. As Wilkinson explained, "A Free Trade out of the Mississippi and we are a blessed People indeed. It would push Kentucky most rapidly to Individual opulence and Public wealth. . . . 'Tis an inestimable prize and we are all unanimously ready to wade to it through Blood."

In 1789, Madison's friend George Nicholas moved to Kentucke and joined the court party. A political veteran at thirty-six years old, Nicholas believed a western republic was well within reach, but its success depended upon turning the region into the economic center of trans-Appalachia. He lived and worked in Lexington as a lawyer, but also owned a plantation on the south side of the Kentucky River, invested in a cotton factory and iron furnace, speculated in land, and became the leading voice for access to the Mississippi River as Wilkinson's star began to fade.

By 1790, Nicholas was Kentucke's attorney general as well, appointed by President Washington in a calculated move to bind Kentucke to the new nation. In fact, most members of the court party received federal appointments through the Washington administration because they had been the most vocal against federal inaction and in favor of Kentucke independence. Innes became a justice in Kentucke's district court, and Peyton Short accepted a position as collector at the port of Louisville. John Brown had been elected a congressman. In early 1792, deeply in debt, ignored by Washington, who suspected his Spanish connections, and frustrated by his own failures, Wilkinson joined the U.S. Army and left Kentucke. Returning to the "plain, manly, and unadorned language of independence," he wrote Innes that "I am unfortunate and distressed but I have ever deserved the Character of a Man of honor."

While Washington believed the court party needed to be reined in, George Muter and fellow members of a country party were assumed to be loyal to the United States. As land surveyors and large land holders, Muter, Thomas Marshall and his nephew Humphrey, Robert Breckinridge, Alexander Bullitt, and others held similar views to the court party, although they had no intention of abandoning the United States. They were less interested in securing the Mississippi River than they were in enhancing trans-Appalachian commerce, and they very much saw themselves as the men who could successfully extend the republic westward. Washington trusted these men far more than their court party peers, so he offered only Thomas Marshall a federal appointment, as chief revenue officer for Kentucke in 1791.

Despite their political differences, the court and country parties did share in a republican vision for Kentucke. In the weeks and months following the fourth statehood convention of September 1786, members of both groups, anticipating a quick reply from the Virginia legislature, decided to stay in Danville. Thirty men—including Innes, John Brown, Muter, Short, Christopher Greenup, and Samuel McDowell—gathered at a local home each Saturday evening to discuss the pressing political issues of the day, formulating principles of government that would shape their own state constitution in 1792. The Danville Political Club was born.

The club's deliberations offer an interesting window into republicans' expectations for Kentucke. At each meeting, the group debated a question and produced a resolution that reflected their consensus. On citizenship: "In a free government ought there to be any other qualification required to entitle a right of suffrage than that of freedom?" The club concluded that freedom was not enough to support citizenship, although they did not decide what the other qualification should be. On whether "Indian tribes have an exclusive right to the territory claimed by them by virtue of the law of nature and nations," club members resolved that "Indian tribes can not, consistent with the laws of nature and nations, be deprived without their own consent of the exclusive right to the territory claimed by them." The club also decided that "encouragement of intermarriages between the inhabitants of this District and the neighboring Indian tribes would not be consistent with the policy of the District" and that as a staple crop, tobacco would not be beneficial to Kentucke. Quite possibly, their most interesting decision was one of silence on slavery. They never took it up as an issue, although they did resolve not only that the clause in the U.S. Constitution permitting the slave trade until 1808 should be expunged, but that Congress should move to end the trade "as soon as it saw fit to do so."

As the final decade of the eighteenth century opened, the republican members of the Danville Political Club offered a vision of Kentucke less elastic than the fluid social climate that had dominated the 1770s and 1780s: racial lines were not to be crossed, property ownership (even by Indians) was sacrosanct, race (whiteness) and gender (masculinity) were insufficient to citizenship, and slavery as a philosophical and moral topic was not to be touched. Kentucke was to be Virginia anew, possibly even Virginia perfected. Impulses toward individualism let loose by the Great Awakening and the Revolutionary War had transformed the Old Dominion: the rising religious and political influence of New Lights, the emergence of sensibilities and humanitarianism, the moral questioning of slavery, even the emigration to Kentucke that epitomized the pursuit of individual gain. Conceivably, those influences could be held at bay by the Appalachian Mountains, and the hierarchy of ruling "fathers" could be reestablished. The debaters in the Danville Political Club—as delegates to the statehood conventions—had been selected by less wealthy and influential Kentuckians, but they were never truly representative of their constituents. Country and court party members were men who had benefited most from Kentucke's settlement.

Some men of status, however, had become convinced by democratic impulses back east that a strict republican form of government was not ideal for the new American West. Far more radical, these democrats did not want to extend Virginian republicanism westward. Instead, they sought to democratize Kentucke politics and land holdings, some even arguing for redistribution of both for the benefit of the majority, including the landless. The leaders—men such as James Brown (John Brown's brother), John Campbell, Ebenezer Brooks, and Henry Lee—were typically better off than the masses, but they embraced majoritarian leanings that differentiated them from the republicans of the court and country parties. They supported pursuit of trade on the Mississippi River to expand economic opportunity to all of Kentucke's settlers. They also opposed slavery—some for moral reasons, others because its development and use would mean less land and political power for them and their constituents.

They had an immediate and eager audience. Caleb Wallace had expected Kentucke to draw many pioneers of lesser circumstances: "the fertility of the soils makes it a good poor man's Country." But excluded from land acquisition by large speculators and expensive court arbitrations, many people found little promise in Kentucke, complaining as early as 1779 that their only recourse was to go "Down the Mississippi, to the Spanish protection, or becoming tenants to private gentlemen who have men employed at this junction in this country at one hundred pounds per Thousand." Virginia statute allotted citizenship only to white men "possessed of twenty-five acres of land, with a house . . . and a plantation thereon," or fifty acres of unimproved lands, or a town lot. Additionally, Virginia had required as a condition of Kentucke's separation that all land rights "remain valid and secure," thereby protecting the speculative interests of absentee Virginia landowners. For men without land, only by turning Kentucke into a democracy could they end the tight grip of Virginia's hierarchical republicanism.

Still, in a good poor man's country like Kentucke, the persisting fluidity of identities gave hope to disaffected settlers. There was the potential for a truly democratic suffrage for all white men regardless of property ownership. Following the ninth convention, as Kentuckians anticipated statehood, public debates that played out in the *Kentucky Gazette* centered upon not only the shape of state government but the extent of suffrage. In 1791, one anonymous author known only as A.B.C. argued that "every cast and denomination of men amongst us," having faced and suffered the same dangers of clearing the frontier, "are entitled to a representation in forming a constitution by which they will be equally bound."

"Politically Mad the whole District of Kentuckey has become by the Approach of our Convention," remarked one observer. This was unfortunate, at least according to the court party's Harry Innes. As the April 1792 convention approached, he considered how the "Peasantry are perfectly mad—extraordinary prejudices and without foundation have arisen against the present Officers of Government—the Lawyers and Men of Fortune. They say *plain honest Farmers* are the only men who ought to be elected to form our Constitution." Innes keenly understood the problem facing him and others who had assumed their rightful place as the political and economic leaders of the western republic: if the masses gained too much influence, anarchy would reign, and all those who had invested in western settlement, absentee and resident, could lose everything. "There is a wide difference between power being derived from the people, and being seated in the people," wrote one editorialist. "Disorder and tyranny must ensue from all power being seated in the bulk of the people." As Kentuckians prepared to select delegates to the constitutional convention, one commentator warned against electing "novices who will only be able to establish under the name of a constitution, a collection of absurdities expressed in unintelligible languages, which will bring misery at home and disgrace abroad." Not only did the people express too much of their political will, but they also seemed to want a share of the political leadership. "We have a great clamor respecting our Separation from Virginia," explained one Kentuckian; "our different Candidates for different posts are as numerous as Stud Horses at a Court House on Election Day." As Innes concluded, "They have given a very serious alarm to every thinking man."

The Promised Land

In 1775, Anglican minister John Brown wondered of his Virginia neighbors, "What a Buzzel is this amongst People about Kentuck? To hear people speak of it one would think it was a new Paradise." Ten years later, Judge Harry Innes was amazed by migrants "absolutely infatuated by something like the old crusading spirit to the holy land." After the War of 1812, Congregationalist minister Timothy Flint imagined "Heaven is a Kaintuck of a place." And in his old age, Methodist elder Samuel Rogers remembered Kentucke as the "Canaan of the West." It is easy to dismiss such Edenic metaphors as the laudations of men with a vested interest in promoting land sales, but that was not the case. These men had given much thought to crusades and paradise and the promise of Heaven. Even Innes, the son of an Anglican minister, had his fill of theology.

Just as it offered a blank political slate, Kentucke offered opportunity to create religious utopias where social structures were unfixed and identity still malleable. Failure to trade along the Mississippi River may have retarded economic and social development, but for many settlers, that was not necessarily a bad thing. Debates over the shape of a new state constitution may have been intensifying, but none of the discussions had raised issues of religious freedom. As long as commercial and political structures remained in flux, there was room for religious people who were not quite comfortable or secure in the East.

In 1780, Hendrick Banta led one such group of northwestern New Jersey Dutch Reformists. After a few years living in western Pennsylvania, the group had grown impatient with the increasing numbers of English, Scotch-Irish, and German pioneers migrating into the region. Hoping to preserve their Dutch language and religion, they traveled down the Ohio River and found lands along Beargrass Creek on which they built Low Dutch Station. Of course, as with most peoples arriving in Kentucke in the 1780s, they soon discovered that they were squatters. "With a view and expectation to procure a Tract of Land to enable them to settle together in a body for the conveniency of civil society and propogating the Gospel in their known language," they unsuccessfully petitioned the Confederation Congress for help.

Despite John Floyd's willingness to let them remain on his lands, as the Indian threat among the Beargrass settlements increased in 1783, the colony relocated southeastward into the Great Meadow, where they officially formed the Low Dutch Company, purchased several hundred acres of land, and formed a written "constitution" called the Articles of Agreement. Over the next few years, more settlers arrived from New Jersey, eager to join the colony. Each family received a farm of approximately two hundred acres, but the company retained legal title to the land. The community agreed to "subscribe to and support the Low Dutch Reformed Church Society by giving a Call and Invitation to a Regular Instituted Low Dutch minister . . . and that we will indeavouer to have our children Taught and instructed in the Low Dutch Tongue so that they may Read the word of God and understand the Gospel when Preached unto them."

Another congregation crossed into Kentucke around the same time, hoping that distance from eastern societies would free them from religious discrimination. The religious climate in wartime Virginia, particularly in counties such as Orange, Caroline, and Spotsylvania, was not particularly friendly to Baptists. In 1776, the state assembly had passed a bill repealing penal laws against religious dissenters and exempting them from supporting the state-established Anglican Church. But verbal condemnations and physical abuse of Baptists were widespread, and while Thomas Jefferson had drafted an act for establishing religious freedom by 1779, it would not be approved for another seven years. Regular Baptists faced less discrimination, having traditionally abided by Virginia's laws governing dissenters, specifically requirements to obtain licenses for their churches. Separate Baptists, in contrast, had demonstrated a suspicious independent streak: they had never applied for such licenses, and their liturgical dismissal of creeds and confessions of faith clashed with the Regular Baptists' more complex theology. Joseph Craig remembered one night in Caroline County when "in one minute a gang of men, some on horseback, and a gang of dogs, of different sizes, were after me" for refusing to register for a preaching license. Without the commonwealth's protection, Separate Baptists and other evangelical radicals found themselves resolutely resisted by many Virginians.

So, in 1781, Craig, his brother Lewis, and William Ellis led at least five hundred Separate Baptists through the Cumberland Gap, settling on the southern rim of the Great Meadow at Craig's Station. One Spotsylvania County preacher composed a hymn for the party leaving for Kentucke, including the verse:

> Great sorrows of late have fill'd my poor heart
> To think the dearest of friends soon must part;
> A few left behind, while many will go
> To settle the desert down the Ohio.

The "Travelling Church," as the congregation became known, found Kentucke to be far from a desert. They established several congregations, and over the next two years, three more migrant groups connected to the Craigs and Ellis arrived in Kentucke, constructing more meetinghouses throughout the Great Meadow.

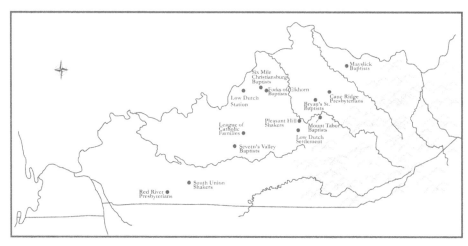

Map 5.1. The Religious Frontier. Drawn by Sherry Hardin.

During those years, Regular Baptists arrived in the region as well, settling among the Separate Baptists. The two shared some theological positions, but the Regular Baptists employed the Philadelphia Confession of Faith as their creed and preferred ecclesiastical structure within their religion. In 1785, they formed the Elkhorn Association to organize their multiple congregations, inviting the Separate Baptists to join them. Instead, the Separate Baptists, many of whom lived south of the Kentucky River, created their own South Kentucky Association in 1787.

In the same year that Elkhorn Association took shape, the League of Catholic Families began its migration to Kentucke. A loose compact for mutual support, the league consisted of nearly eighty-five families eager to escape St. Mary's County, Maryland. Their decision to migrate emanated not from religious intolerance, although during the war they did face increased harassment from revolutionaries and incessant confiscations by British troops. Instead, they were originally motivated by the declining soils and weakening tobacco markets of the Tidewater region. Purchasing tracts of Kentucke land from some Baltimore speculators, in 1785 the families settled in the western parts of the Great Meadow around Pottingers Creek.

Two more significant migrations of Maryland Catholics soon followed, one group preferring the central Bluegrass. While St. Mary's migrants were not driven westward by religious motivations, their faith quickly became their primary identification. They petitioned for a priest, finally receiving one in 1787. Two years later, however, the league still had considerable undistributed acreage. Advertising a "land lottery" in the *Maryland Journal and Baltimore Advertiser*, the organization offered some 40,000 acres in 150-acre-minimum plots for fifteen dollars a ticket, spurring three more waves of emigration from St. Mary's County into Kentucke.

In the 1780s, then, three significant groups initiated religious migration into Kentucke, bringing with them practices of faith that had been marginalized in eastern societies. Each faced difficulties in the promised land. Land title conflicts impeded the Low Dutch Company's efforts and frustrated Baptist and Catholic pioneers as well. Never confident of and usually without a minister, members of the Dutch Reformed and Catholic populations trickled back to the East seeking stability. Quite amazingly, despite the challenges, these communities sustained their religious identities.

Yet, for many settlers who did not migrate for religious reasons, the early arrival and collective strength of large religious communities posed obstacles. When the Drake and Shotwell families arrived in 1786, they settled about twelve miles south of the Point, in a hamlet called Mayslick. As Regular Baptists from New Jersey, the families found themselves among large numbers of Separate Baptists who dominated not only the religious community but the local culture as well. "Their camp-meetings in the woods," remembered Daniel Drake, "presented scenes of fanatical raving among the worshipers, and of levity and vice among the young men who hung about the camp." The Separate Baptists were far more emotional and frenetic in their worship, a liturgical form rejected by Drake's parents.

With Presbyterians and Methodists also in the neighborhood, Drake found the atmosphere rife with opportunity to learn and think: "In a despotic country, such a country boy as I was, could never have heard any of the discussions in religion and politics to which I had so many opportunities of listening." Yet, his parents and most of their relatives were Emancipationist Baptists as well, believing that slavery was immoral and rejecting their Virginia Baptist neighbors who held slaves. What young Drake interpreted as opportunity his parents viewed as interdenominational and intradenominational conflict. While Kentucke was a promised land, religiously, it was to be a segregated one, as William Scott learned in 1788 upon his suspension by the Mount Pisgah Presbyterian congregation for "inviting the Baptists frequently and permitting a Methodist to preach in his house." The Transylvania Presbytery, the ruling authority over Kentucke's Presbyterian churches, founded in 1786, overturned Scott's exclusion one year later for insufficient evidence, but the principle remained: in Kentucke's religious marketplace, denominations were competing for souls.

As republicans and democrats bickered over the character of white male suffrage, some churches recognized opportunities to draw upon those people who would not be included in the citizenry regardless of which side won the political debates. In the 1780s, the Baptists were the first to people their congregations by appealing to white women and slaves. Given the weakness of frontier patriarchy and the shapelessness of slavery, many churches used these groups to create social order, albeit an order that contrasted dramatically with the patriarchal structure that republicans and democrats imagined. White patriarchy had emerged from the revolutionary era empowered by the ideal that "all men are created equal." The gendered and racial privileges of being a white man were daily demonstrated by acts of assertive independence, relegating white women and slaves to more submissive and dependent roles. The Baptists, however, exhorted both groups to think and act independently as well, replacing the order of patriarchy with the egalitarianism of Christianity.

Economically, Kentucke's demographic character made an egalitarian vision quite viable. Although the 1790 census counted 73,677 residents of Kentucke, white women and enslaved blacks comprised 56 percent of the population, and when white boys under sixteen years of age are excluded from the count, only 20 percent of Kentucke's population was white men. In order to establish economic stability, white women and slaves *had* to be integrated into the regional economy on very liberal terms. Stores,

particularly in Lexington, Limestone, and Louisville, granted
significant latitude to female and black—both free and slave—
customers, specifically in extending credit and accepting barter
for purchases.

Slaves gained mobility and a sense of autonomy through the
illegal but unregulated practice of hiring out. Ironically, when
slave-owners advertised for runaways, they assumed that their
slaves would "pass for free men," an identity that made sense in
the structured slave systems of the East but made little sense in
Kentucke, where the differences between actual slave activity
and passing for free were minimal. How could an observer tell if
any given black person was enslaved, free, hired-out, or passing
for free?

White women too, both as widows and as wives acting in their
husbands' absences, enjoyed some economic independence, exerting authority over salt manufactories, artisan shops, slaves,
and farms. In John Hunt's store in Lexington, one of every seven
customers was a woman. A 1794 poem in the *Kentucky Gazette*
joked about "Susan the Breeches Maker," a spinster yearning for
a husband.

> Beside a lamp besmeared with oil,
> Sue toiling sat for riches.
> Her aching heart, a husband fill'd,
> Her lap, a pair of breeches.
>
> "Ah me!" with feeble voice she cry'd
> While sighs oft rose the stitches;
> "Ah me, and must I live a maid
> And only MAKE these BREECHES?"
>
> "Ye Gods!" then raised to heav'n her eyes—
> "O grant my wish soon, which is
> A husband young, a kind good man,
> And let me WEAR the BREECHES."

Some Kentucke women, of course, had metaphorically been wearing the breeches for over a decade, exerting economic influence
in local stores, shooting rifles and wielding axes in combat, and
representing their families' legal interests in the courts.

Baptists worked to conserve that frontier order: allowing white women and black slaves to enjoy some personal independence. They were very aware of how their evangelicalism to slaves and white women could be perceived as threats to patriarchal order and result in public condemnation. "Disorder cannot be countenanced," warned members of the Bryan's Station Church. Yet, frontier families had never been stable. Fathers, mothers, and children were often killed or captured during Indian attacks, turning what had been potential nuclear families into weakened and sometimes dysfunctional families. Consequently, Baptists promoted a stable, if less traditional, definition of family. "How do you do sister Taylor," queried one recent Baptist convert; "I am born again, I can now call you all brothers and sisters." In a "church home," individuals became families, although the ideal was far more elastic than allowed in the stable societies of the East. Baptist and later Methodist "families" flourished in the fluid atmosphere of the West. Kinship need not be formed through marriage and bloodlines. Indeed, the Shawnees and other native peoples demonstrated regularly an ability to adopt non-native peoples into their own families and villages, creating such strong emotional bonds that captives did not want to return to their biological kin. Similarly, Kentucke's Baptists and Methodists employed emotion to form families; and when a brother or sister was lost, evangelicalism and conversion provided replacements.

Requisite to membership in these families was acceptance of Protestant Christian values. When Baptists drew slaves and white women into their congregations, they simultaneously imposed on their converts a requirement to act morally, as defined by those values. Theirs was a practical solution to a real problem: in the unstable family atmosphere of Kentucke, how could stability be created? Churches that reached out to white women and black slaves sought to extend orderly moral community into both farmhouses and slave quarters. While white men were most likely to enjoy suffrage and the access to justice and politics that accompanied it, white women and black slaves were to become the models by which white men could secure eternal life.

By the early 1790s, then, Kentucke was filled with competing visions, some emanating from political ideologies, others from religious creeds, and the majority from individual dreams and expectations. The fluidity that characterized racial and gender identities throughout the 1780s also typified the political and religious development of Kentucke. For those men who would join together in 1792 to create the first state constitution, the challenge was to negotiate the multitude of expectations.

6.

FROM KENTUCKE TO KENTUCKY

In 1789, George Nicholas complained to James Madison about "the management of Indian affairs" in the West. Kentuckians had lost a voice in dealing with Indians, replaced by "persons, living on, and interested in the welfare of, the other side of the Ohio . . . men who have a contrary one [interest] to pursue and who have already given sufficient proofs that they will follow their own interests when they clash with our's." Nicholas was particularly angry over rumors that "their policy is to hold out to the Indians that we were a separate and distinct people from them and that they might be at peace with them and at war with us." Federal troops had been deployed to the Northwest Territory less to protect Kentucke's settlers than to act as "a check upon us. I can only say if we are treated as fellow citizens any check will be unnecessary, but that if it is intended to withhold from us all the benefits of good government, a little time will shew that as heretofore we have found the troops useless and faithless as friends, hereafter, we shall despise them as enemies." But as the federal government attempted to assert its military authority, Nicholas and other Kentuckians continued to watch their agency in Indian affairs slipping away. During both the 1791 Harmar campaign and the 1792 St. Clair campaign, Kentucke's militias imposed themselves on the federal officers, insisting on a military role despite the reluctance and occasional antagonism of the federal army. Consequently, in both defeats, the Kentuckians received significant blame in reports back to President Washington.

Despite the federal government's seemingly halfhearted efforts, Kentucke was no more secure in the early 1790s than it had been throughout the 1780s. "Must we suffer our Inhabitants to be murdered daily or taken Prisoners when about their necessary business, and perhaps massacred or tortured in the most excruciating manner, and tamely submit to it?" pleaded one pioneer. For years, westerners had looked to first the Confederation and then the Washington administration to provide simple defense. "Is the united States unable to do themselves Justice; or are they afraid?" the settler continued. "Does Congress consider the lives of their People of more value than money?" The federal government must "assert its own power," insisted the editors of the *Kentucky Gazette*, "convince the feeble enemy of his impotence, and we lay him at our feet."

Indeed, the only success against the Western Confederacy had been when Charles Scott led Kentucke mounted volunteers against the Shawnee towns in the summer of 1791. The expedition was joined by federal troops under James Wilkinson's command. Nicholas celebrated "the taking of so many prisoners, the undeniable proof that the Indians have received that they may be attacked at any time without their having any previous notice of the design, the appearance of such a body of men on horseback, the return of the army without the loss of a single man, and the knowledge that the whole army came from a country which ten years before was their hunting ground, must all tend to strike a great terror into the Indians." Unlike the chorus of condemnations that followed the Harmar and St. Clair defeats, Kentuckians praised President Washington for supporting the Scott expedition to avenge the Indian threat. Determined to sustain the momentum, Nicholas encouraged giving the Cherokees "a blow immediately: Seven hundred men had prepared to pay them a visit at the time the other expedition was on hand, but were prevented by an account that they were then treating."

Only a few months later, however, following St. Clair's defeat— an excursion in which many of Scott's men participated but Scott himself refused to assist—the military prowess of the Kentuckians was forgotten, and the responsibility for addressing the Indian problem was again on the federal government. George Rogers Clark complained that federal agents in the Northwest Territory were indifferent to Kentucke's situation. "The Indians are spreading Fire and Tomahawk through the frontiers, without much resistance," he argued; "I am as well as many others led to believe that those at the Helm of affairs on your side of the Mountains either know nothing about the business or wish to prolong the war; except they are deceived by their servants." By 1792, as Kentucky began to enjoy statehood, Governor Isaac Shelby authorized Scott to organize and call up militias for thirty-day Indian patrols to protect the state. Small but successful Kentucky militia excursions in 1792 and 1793, however, exacerbated the deteriorating relations between the Kentuckians and the federal government, and excited responses by the Western Confederacy.

When Washington decided to undertake yet another expedition against the Western Confederacy in 1793, then, he decided to do so without Kentucky. Passing up both Charles Scott and James Wilkinson, Washington enlisted General Anthony Wayne to form the Legion of the United States in western Pennsylvania, rather than in Ohio Territory. Secretary of War Knox instructed Wayne to enlist "mounted Volunteers of Kentucky . . . [who] shall make your real force superior to the highest force of the Enemy," but Wayne only reluctantly contacted Scott and refused to acquiesce to Scott's demand that the Kentucky troops act as an independent force. Wayne responded to Knox:

> Nothing shall induce me to commit the honor & dignity of Government nor to expose the Legion (unnecessarily) to the whole Combined force of the enemy, whilst *two thousand* mounted Volunteers . . . of the State of Kentucky (in pay of the United States) were stealing a March very wide from the Army—in order to burn a few Wigwams & capture a few women & Children & in which . . . they cou'd not meet with any Opposition, until they returned *triumphantly* & *safe* to their respective homes—leaving the Legion to contend with the difficulty and danger.

Scott, apparently recognizing that his refusal to place the Kentuckians under Wayne's command jeopardized their participation in the expedition, conceded leadership of the mounted volunteers. But in late 1793, as the army set out toward the Shawnee villages, the Kentuckians quit marching and demanded to be released from service. When Wayne and Scott refused, nearly half decamped and returned home. Furiously, Wayne dismissed the remaining mounted volunteers and warned Scott to prepare a larger and more dedicated force for service in the spring. Privately, however, he did not want the Kentuckians involved: "Let the Legion be completed," Wayne disgustedly wrote Knox, "& I wish no *further other force.*"

Circumstances changed both the Kentuckians' attitude and Wayne's willingness to incorporate them into his military campaign. By late 1793, Kentucky was in a panic: one petition decried how Kentuckians were "surrounded by a rugged desart . . . surrounded by a tractless desart, which is infested by savages dispersed over an extensive country whose stream we durst not navigate." A month later, Shelby informed Knox, "We have every reason to expect that we shall be Vigorously attacked by the Indians early in the spring and the present defenceless condition of our citizens who live in that exposed situation must render them an easy prey whenever they are attacked." Even if the federal government would engage the Indians of the Northwest Territory, Kentucky was not safe.

"I fully expect that we shall be attacked by the Creek and Chickamaggy Indians as soon as the winter breaks," Shelby warned, accurately. The Chickamauga had been harassing settlers in the Wilderness for several years. In the spring of 1794, they swept down on a party of settlers, tomahawking and scalping fifteen of the nineteen travelers. In response, William Whitley, a settler at a strongly fortified station named Sportsman's Hall, organized a company of rangers under the 1790 Indian patrol law to discourage future attacks. When the Chickamaugas escalated their attacks in mid-1794, Whitley—who had seen three children scalped at the hands of Chickamaugas and his wife and another child taken captive—determined to take the war to the Chickamauga villages. He and the rangers invaded the villages of Nickajack and Running Water, killing dozens of warriors, taking women and children captive, and destroying the crops.

Whitley's independent and impromptu actions evinced exactly what Secretary of War Knox did not want to see from the Kentuckians. He remained resolute that Wayne employ the Kentuckians in an organized plan, and reluctantly Wayne complied. Scott was in Philadelphia, however, and months passed without the mounted volunteers forming. "Wou'd to God that early & proper means had been adopted by Congress for the Completion of the Legion," Wayne complained, "I wou'd not at this late hour have to call for Militia . . . from Kentucky who may not have a relish to meet this Hydra now preparing to attack us." Not until late July, three months after Wayne's initial call for the militia, did the Kentucky troops arrive and the Legion of the United States begin its march against the Western Confederacy.

In August, Wayne's army attacked fifteen hundred warriors of the Western Confederacy under the leadership of Shawnee chief Blue Jacket at Fallen Timbers. It was a quick battle: outnumbered, the Indians fled to Fort Miami, but the British who manned the fort refused to open the gates. Forced into surrender, Blue Jacket agreed to negotiations at Greenville a year later. Over the next months, further excursions against villages aligned with the Western Confederacy cowed the Native Americans. In early August 1795, Little Turtle—the Shawnee chief who had commanded the Western Confederacy's defeats of Harmar and St. Clair—led a delegation to Greenville and conceded Shawnee claims to much of the Ohio Territory, a concession that Wayne interpreted as acknowledgment of the federal government's sovereignty north of the Ohio River.

From Kentuckians' perspective, federal victory at Fallen Timbers was a mixed blessing. In conjunction with Jay's Treaty of 1794, in which the British agreed to abandon all forts in the Northwest Territory, the victory at Fallen Timbers appeared to relieve Kentucky of the Indian threat. Yet, the United States had situated itself as the final arbiter of all western affairs, meaning that the military and diplomatic victories had come at the expense of Kentuckians' belief that they directed not only the course of their futures but all of western development. As new Indian problems arose and as the Mississippi River remained closed to Americans, Kentucky would have to acquiesce to federal authority.

In making Kentucky more secure, the Treaty of Greenville opened the floodgates on migration. Between 1790 and 1800, Kentucky's population nearly tripled to 220,955. Economically, the Legion's presence in the Northwest infused Kentucky with something desperately needed: "Kentuckey is more full of Mony arising from the Circumstances of the Army North of the Ohio than any other Part of America," explained William Blount, "and land will sell for as good a Price at this as at any Time for seven years to come." Merchants and artisans took full advantage of the economic boom created by the infusion of cash, and throughout the 1790s, commercially vibrant villages and towns popped up across Kentucky. Ironically, the federal army that stole the Kentuckians' thunder became critical to Kentucky's development:

> Our existence almost depends on it in a toofold point of view, first as to defence, secondly as to the circulating money amongst us— which is much less than wd have been had the main Army come down the last fall. Nothing else could have keep us from distress until the trade of the Mississippi shall be opened the prospect of which we are flattered brighten very day, but a confirmation of it would be greatfull tidings Indeed.

Decades later, John Bradford, the founder and editor of the *Kentucky Gazette*, remembered the 1795 Treaty of Greenville as "Ending Kentucky's Indian Menace." After twenty years of an unrelenting Indian threat and with the federal government assuming responsibility for dealing with the Western Confederacy, Kentuckians threw off the restraints of constant defense. They were at liberty to build upon the nascent economic, social, and cultural institutions that had languished in the midst of terror. They were free to transform Kentucke into Kentucky, a process formally initiated with the Constitution of 1792.

Defining Citizenship

At the heart of this transformation was a belief that fluidity of identities, the shapelessness of slavery, and the weakness of patriarchy could not be tolerated in a mature, civilized American society. Republicanism demanded white male citizenship as the foundation of society. As they did east of the Appalachians, slaves and women would serve as the mirrors in which white males would recognize their own citizenship and patriarchal roles. Strengthening patriarchy required a political structure that would elevate white men and make them relevant both in Kentucke and in the new nation.

When, in the fall of 1790, the U.S. Congress considered Kentucke's request for statehood, President Washington had encouraged quick approval: "the sentiments of warm attachment to the Union and its present government, expressed by our fellow citizens of Kentucky, cannot fail to add an affectionate concern for their particular welfare." Other Americans were more cautious. Some northern newspapers circulated the ditty:

> Kentucky to the Union given
> Vermont will make the balance even.
> Still Pennsylvania holds the scales,
> And neither South nor North prevails.

When Vermont entered the union a year later, it became the first state to provide universal manhood suffrage regardless of property ownership. But Vermonters also decided to officially end slavery, determining that "all persons are born equally free and independent, and have certain natural, inherent, and unalienable rights, amongst which are the enjoying and defending life and liberty, acquiring, possessing and protecting property, and pursuing and obtaining happiness and safety." The newspaper poet assumed that Kentucke, born out of Virginia's western counties, would follow its mother state as a slave society. Free and slave, North and South—already national politics had begun its march toward the Civil War.

While probable, however, slavery was not certain in early 1790s Kentucke. Throughout the 1770s and 1780s, Virginia's legislators had worked to institutionalize slavery in its western counties. But several factors worked against it: the fluidity of identities available in a frontier region, an undeveloped staple crop economy, and despite Virginia's 1785 slave code, little resolve or effort to enforce it in trans-Appalachia. Kentucke slave-owners regularly broke the law by hiring out their slaves, allowing slaves social and geographic mobility, and selling slaves in a nascent slave trade. Without a strong institutional structure, slavery was hardly inevitable. When delegates gathered to write their state constitution in the spring of 1792, therefore, there was a possibility, however slim, that slavery could fade in Kentucke.

Early that spring, Kentuckians began to select delegates to their constitutional convention. More democratically minded men tried to usurp the delegate selection process by having the choices made in county committees. Each county militia would select a committee that would then elect delegates and instruct them how to vote. For republicans, the county-level committees were suspicious in themselves. Harry Innes complained that "the People of Kentucky are mere Fanatics in Politics. Constitutions are forming in every Neighborhood." One editorialist to the *Kentucky Gazette* warned, "Let no man, or set of men, endeavor to impose a chimney corner constitution upon us: for literally speaking, instructions generally originate in some chimney corner; they are drawn up by some demagogue to suit his own inclinations." Committees, the author concluded, "obstruct the free suffrage of the people in making the elections by presuming to guide their choice."

Only in a few counties did the committee system take root. In Bourbon County, a community that prided itself on its more egalitarian and radical citizenry, William Henry proclaimed that "we know of no distinctions among men. The farmer, the mechanic, and even the common labouring man have a voice in this, equal to the lawyer, the colonel or the general." Among the directives designed by Henry's committee were orders to oppose the practice of oral voting, push for a popularly elected single-chambered legislature, and reject a code of laws that resembled any in Europe, "but that a simple, and concise code of laws be framed, adopted to the weakest capacity."

On April 2, 1792, the constitutional convention met in Danville. Quickly, one man emerged as Kentucke's constitutional leader: George Nicholas, widely known for his epistolary conversations with James Madison and his political moderation, spoke early and often at the convention. "Government must be strong enough to compel confidence and respect in the people," Nicholas inspired his colleagues, "or they will resort to expedients that will destroy it." One way in which to assure confidence and respect was to allow for universal manhood suffrage. Nicholas had discussed the idea with Madison, who insisted on property ownership as the foundation of citizenship. Nicholas retorted that "the most serious reflection has convinced me that all such qualifications are inadmissible in a free state; . . . Exclude any particular class of citizens and sooner or later they will certainly be oppressed," the natural consequence of which was civil unrest and even rebellion. "If a man is poor treat him as a freeman his ambition will make him rich," Nicholas debated, "but if the laws consider him as a slave his dejection will sink him below their *general* level." Yet, as if to reassure himself, Nicholas added, "Notwithstanding *all* have a right to vote and to be elected, the wealthy will nineteen times out of twenty be chosen. . . . I will give up my opinion as soon as I see a man in rags chosen to that body."

While universal manhood suffrage had been a hot topic of debate prior to the convention, it passed easily, as did most of Nicholas's proposals. He advocated an indirectly elected senate and a powerful and independent governor to check and balance the popularly elected house of representatives, which might be swayed by the whims of the people. Still, the people had to be heard and addressed. One commentator described the county committees' demands for "exclusion not from the Legislature only, but from the barr. of Lawyers, the abolition of Slavery, and low Salaries to the Officers of Government, and that to be paid in produce"— all meant to keep farmers, mechanics, and laboring men equal to lawyers, colonels, and generals. While the commentator mockingly concluded that "It will be a new scene to see a Chief Judge at the end of term, riding upon a bag of Corn, & driving home the Cows & Calves, he has receiv'd for his quarters Salary, And the Governor trudging home with a basket of Eggs on his Arm," Nicholas grasped the essence of the county committees' complaints. Although unwilling to grant majoritarian control over state officials, he did agree that sheriffs and other local officials should be elected rather than appointed by county courts or the governor. Finally, in order to more speedily resolve land issues and facilitate migration and settlement, Nicholas proposed that land-title cases be decided in an independent court of appeals.

Nicholas's proposals went almost without debate, until the issue of slavery came to the floor. Antislavery proponents raised the topic, and leading the delegation was Presbyterian minister David Rice, who pushed the convention to "resolve UNCONDITION-ALLY to put an end to slavery in this state." Rice's argument centered upon the idea that slavery undermined the natural law that all men are created equal, forcing humans who are accountable only to God to feel obligated to obey men. "Slavery is the national vice of Virginia," Rice argued. "As a separate State, we are just now come to the birth, and it depends upon our free choice, whether we shall be born in this sin, or innocent of it."

Rice's sentiments reflected the opinions of a fairly large minority of Kentuckians. As the possibility of statehood grew greater, readers of the *Kentucky Gazette* had heatedly debated the pros and cons of slavery in the paper's pages, sometimes lyrically:

> O come the time, and haste the day,
> When man shall man no longer crush!
> When reason shall enforce her sway,
> Nor these fair regions raise our blush;
> Where still the African complains,
> And mourns his, yet unshaken chains.

Like this poet and Rice, nearly all Kentuckians recognized the immorality of slavery. For the proponents of slavery, however, economics trumped morality. Nicholas proposed that the elimination of slavery would result in a poorer state: "Excluding slaves . . . from this country, amounts to a prohibition of all the inhabitants of states, except those who are among the poorest of their inhabitants." Another delegate argued that blacks and whites could not coexist without slavery. If the institution were dismantled, blacks would have to leave Kentucky or else whites would need to "just get all the Negroes asleep, knock them in the head, and kill every one of them." In the end, Rice's effort to expunge slavery from Kentucke failed.

As a result, Kentucke's constitution of 1792 was a milestone in American history. It was the first to guarantee universal manhood suffrage regardless of property ownership while also endorsing slavery. Indeed, the implications of Nicholas's vision and the convention's actions were that whiteness defined citizenship

Figure 6.1. A Revolutionary War veteran, George Nicholas was a vocal proponent of Virginia's ratification of the federal constitution in 1789. He arrived in Kentucke just in time to take a leading role in the constitutional debates over Kentucky statehood in 1792. Courtesy of the Filson Historical Society, Louisville, Ky.

and blackness defined slavery. One Kentuckian argued the absurdity of so racial a constitution, claiming that any bill of rights that Nicholas may want to attach to the constitution would invalidate such definitive distinctions between the races: "I view the blacks as part of the human species, and therefore I think that they are included in every bill of rights." In penning the bill of rights, Nicholas seemed to concur with the critics, leaving open political opportunity for black men by insisting that, contrary to the Declaration of Independence, "all men, when they form a social compact, are equal." By not indicating which men, Nicholas theoretically left room for any person who joined in common defense, common economic interest, and common political discourse to claim his (or her) role in the social compact and, consequently, claim citizenship. But the racial construct would hold. As positively as Nicholas may have imagined the expansion of white male suffrage, in the end, he and his peers created it in a negative way by forcing independent and semi-independent peoples to become more dependent upon the free white men at the heart of society.

Institutionalizing slavery was not Nicholas's intent. In his opinion, Kentucke need not have been defined as a slave state in 1792. Anticipating the possibility that slavery might die out, he argued that in the meantime, Kentucke might as well benefit from the economic opportunities that slavery provided: importation of slaves into Kentucke "will not add one to the number of slaves in the world; the only difference being that they will be slaves in Kentucky instead of Virga. or Maryland." Without constitutional protections, he expected that slavery would not bloom, but "the friends to emancipation . . . [had] been so clamorous on that subject, as well in the convention as out of it, as to make it necessary either to give up that property or secure it. And the measure wh[ich] has been adopted was only substituted to a proposition introduced by them declaring that the legislature should provide for a gradual emancipation without saying anything about an equivalent to the slave holders." In other words, by insisting on debating slavery, Rice and other antislavery proponents had forced the convention's hand.

Ironically, Kentucke's institutionalization of slavery coincided with federal passage of the Militia Act of 1792, consequently sharpening the racial constructions of Kentucke society. The law required "each and every free able-bodied white male citizen" eighteen through forty-five years of age to serve in local militias, with some exceptions such as civic officers, postal carriers, and ferrymen. The law also sanctioned executive use of state militias in two specific circumstances: first, "whenever the United States shall be invaded, or be in imminent danger of invasion from any foreign nation or Indian tribe." In the Northwest Territory, of course, President Washington had already employed Kentucke's militias on several occasions, but the Militia Act codified his right to anticipate "imminent danger" and respond preemptively. For many westerners, the Indian threat—real or not—was always imminent. "America has fixed in the minds of the Indians," Nicholas warned James Madison, "such an inveterate hatred of her citizens that nothing will keep them quiet but the operations of their fears."

In relationship to the new constitution, the timing of the Militia Act carried special significance, however, for the second circumstance under which the president could draw upon state militias was "in case of an insurrection in any state." In slave societies such as Virginia and potential slave societies such as Kentucke, slaves embodied the most obvious and immediate threat of violence. Since 1738, the Old Dominion had empowered its militias (and Kentucke had adopted the model) to preempt slave rebellions by patrolling "all negro quarters, and other places suspected of entertaining unlawful assemblies of Slaves, Servants or other disorderly persons." In Kentucke, the relationship between Indian threat and black insurrection—one propagandized in the heat of the Revolutionary War—was resurrected by the confluence of the Militia Act of 1792 with the methods in which Kentuckians already employed their militias as Indian patrols and as slave patrols, and was reinforced by the constitutional convention's effort to define citizenship in black and white. Thus, race became part of the new state's political structure.

In November 1792, the U.S. House of Representatives applauded President Washington for his facilitation of Kentucky statehood: "The adoption of the constitution for the State of Kentucky . . . is another conspicuous demonstration of the facility & success with which an enlightened people is capable of providing, by free & deliberate plans of Govt for their own safety & happiness." Even Nicholas, however, was not confident that Kentuckians had provided for their own safety and happiness. By allowing for democratic participation, Nicholas and his fellow conventioneers relieved the bottom-up political pressure of poor whites while legitimizing the political leadership of the well-to-do. But the issue of slavery had not truly been resolved, and Nicholas anticipated that statehood would inspire waves of new pioneers and dramatic changes. He included a clause in the constitution allowing for a new convention as early as 1797 to revise Kentucky.

Strengthening Patriarchy

Not even a year had passed when George Nicholas wrote to James Madison: "The fact is that there seems to be a foundation laid here for a great degree of unhappiness":

> This is in part owing to the constitution, in part to the uncommon mixture of extra-ordinary character which we have amongst

us. The constitution is I think defective and bad consequences have already arisen from, the same men being permitted to be members of the legislature and also of the body of electors. . . . The peculiar character which belongs to our citizens in general will contribute for a time at least to our unhappiness. They were formerly citizens of other countries, and a great proportion of them have been induced to come here by a spirit of discontent or adventure: citizens generally consisting of such men must make a very different mass from one which is composed of men born and raised on the same spot. Our people are all wise, and *ought to be great* men; they see none about them to whom or to whose families they been accustomed to think themselves inferior; ambitious themselves and desirous of office, they suppose all others to be equally so, and that all have self interest in view more than the public good.

Despite the republican successes of the constitutional convention of 1792, Nicholas may have begun second-guessing his universal white male suffrage almost immediately. It was not that the masses were to be distrusted; after all, he imagined them "all wise" and potentially "great men." Nicholas worried instead about a specific group of men, ideologues "desirous of office" whose ambitions and self-interest would undermine the common weal.

When one looked about Kentucky in 1792, some of those ambitious men sat on the benches of county courts. Before statehood, when Virginia's government and laws seemed to be far to the east, county courts were the principal agents of local development and order, not only trying criminal and civil cases but implementing Virginia's laws, overseeing militia activities, setting tavern prices and the terms of agricultural inspections, and facilitating community affairs as well. While county court justices were not yet "great men," their economic and social clout was considerably greater than that of their neighbors. In 1792, justices in the Bourbon, Fayette, Lincoln, and Madison county courts owned nine times as much land, seven times as many slaves, and over twice as much taxable chattel property as the average Kentuckian. As communal patriarchs, these men dictated the terms of local social order.

Most certainly, then, in 1789 when the federal government passed the Judiciary Act, the creation of a higher court system was not particularly welcomed by county court justices and their constituents, who suspiciously eyed the new level of judicial authority as a usurpation of power. The new chief justice of the United States Court for the District of Kentucky, Harry Innes, desired specifically to remove judicial decisions from the capriciousness of local justices by introducing English common law tradition, with its layers of precedence and codification, to trans-Appalachia.

Three years later, when the new state constitution established a Kentucky Court of Appeals, yet another layer of judiciary was formed. Innes turned down the position of chief justice, but he insisted that the court strictly adhere to English common law. In his stead, George Muter accepted the chief justiceship. Although Muter had broken political ranks with Innes over the Spanish conspiracy, the two shared an interest in standardizing Kentucky's judicial decision making. In 1794, along with his two associate justices—Caleb Wallace and Benjamin Sebastian—Muter heard *Kenton v. McConnell*, a case that challenged the legitimacy of a land title and thereby questioned the authority of the land commissioners under the Land Act of 1779. Representing the defendant, George Nicholas so handily employed the rhetoric and reason of English common law and precedence that Muter and Sebastian agreed that, while there was no reason to overturn the lower court ruling, land titles certified by the 1779 land commissioners could be ruled invalid. The decision sent Kentucky into a panic. If the state court could claim authority over land titles, all claims verified by the land commissioners would be susceptible. County-level petitioners angrily appealed to the legislature to replace all three appellate justices (despite Wallace's dissenting opinion) with men who would decide cases "with as little formality and legal criticisms as possible."

Sentiment against the common law orientation of the state and federal judiciaries grew quickly. Even Nicholas was tainted by the ordeal: critics interpreted his insistence in 1792 on constitutionally codifying the court's original and final jurisdiction in land title cases as a scheme to increase litigation and redistribute lands to those who could afford the time and expenses of the law. Petitioners deemed only the county courts as responsive to Kentuckians' reality; the court of appeals and the U.S. district court were too rooted in formality. With the force of universal white male suffrage behind them, the "people"—led, of course, by "ambitious" and "desirous" local county militia officers and county court justices—refused to watch lawyers redistribute their lands and successfully forced the legislature, governor, and court of appeals to secure their properties. Within the year the court reversed its opinion, declaring valid all land titles resulting from the 1779 land act.

Then, in 1795, the state legislature created a new headrights system that opened up much of southern Kentucky to settlement. Elisha J. Hall had allied with investors in Lexington and Philadelphia to form the Hall Land Company, intent on settling five hundred families in the region south of the Green River by the turn of the century. The state legislature rejected Hall's overtures, however, and instead passed a settlement and preemption bill requiring potential claimants to physically locate and settle on no more than two hundred acres before January 1, 1796. For every two acres cleared, settlers were allotted up to two hundred acres at thirty cents per acre. Given its passage in December 1795, the small window of opportunity relates how the law was intended for current residents of Kentucky, releasing some of the frustration exhibited in reactions to *Kenton v. McConnell*. Potential and, in some cases, desperate pioneers swarmed onto the lands south of the Green River, a region characterized by gently rolling hills, dense forests, and occasional barrens that were advertised as good for little more than pasturage.

The furor surrounding *Kenton v. McConnell* signaled class divisions among white men, and despite the sudden availability of new lands, class suspicions lingered as the legitimacy of land titles continued to be challenged in the courts, including new conflicts created by the Green River country land rush. Contributing to deteriorating relations among white men was the rise of a village West. Because stations and forts had served not only as defensive structures but as nodes of emerging communities, they became logical locations for recently arrived merchants and

lawyers—more of Nicholas's "ambitious" men—to set up shop.
During the 1790s, Fort Boone evolved into Boonesborough, Huston's Station became Paris, Crossthwaite's Station became Winchester, McConnell's Station became Lexington, Kenton's Station
became Limestone before the town changed its name to Maysville, Mefford Station became Washington, Spring Station became Louisville, several stations including Cowan's Station and
Clark Station became Danville, Bardstown Station became Bardstown, Fort Harrod became Harrodstown, and three stations became Elizabethtown. In 1792, commissioners selected a station
community—Blanton's Fort—to become the new state capital of
Frankfort. Fort Jefferson, on the far western end of the state, had
become the foundation of Clarksville. And in the 1790s, other stations arose along the western Chickasaw boundary and in the
eastern Appalachian region that would soon follow suit: Stock-
ton's Station for Flemingsburg, Paint Lick Station for Paints-
ville, Landford's Station for Mt. Vernon, and Cook's Station for
Russellville.

This village West was not quite an urban frontier, for none of
these places preceded more rural settlement and none developed
distinctly from the more rural environs that surrounded them.
But, because they became hubs of economic and legal activity,
Kentucky's towns—in particular, Lexington, Paris, Maysville,
and Louisville—filled with younger men who, having failed to
secure land or land titles, found work in stores, artisans' shops,
liveries, construction, and, in the two latter towns, on the docks.
Yet, the village West provided little of a safety valve to these
men. Frustrated by their inabilities to acquire land, they now
faced restrictive political rights. In Maysville, Paris, and Louisville, only residents owning in-town real estate could vote for or
serve as town trustees; and in Lexington, that property had to
have a value of at least £25. Although Nicholas had granted them
Kentucky citizenship, many white men were disfranchised from
town politics. Instead, merchants, artisans, and lawyers voted on
and peopled the boards of trustees in the little kingdoms that became the village West.

Additionally, outside the village West, younger and poorer white
men faced disfranchisement despite the universal male suffrage

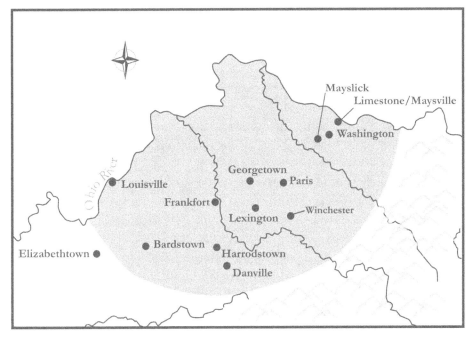

Map 6.1. The Bluegrass. Drawn by Sherry Hardin.

promised in the 1792 constitution. George Nicholas had been hopeful that Kentucky would offer democratic opportunity and majoritarian political participation, but a clause in the constitution required residency "in the state 2 years, or the county they offer to vote one year next before the election." In other words, poorer and younger Kentuckians in search of land and labor were denied political participation regularly because they were too mobile. Many wandered Kentucky, surviving hand to mouth: "How many poor unfortunate fellow creatures weakly appear before you demanding . . . the crumbs which fall from your tables of plenty?" questioned one observer. "They are looked down upon as beings of an inferior class; they are viewed as objects fit only to be the slaves of their fellow creatures of affluence." And that was indeed how they were employed: many poor whites became tenants on the lands of wealthier landowners as useful alternatives to slave labor. No wonder that landed men worried about *Kenton v. McConnell* and that John Breckinridge denounced the legislature's power to end slavery as a prelude to extinguishing land titles. They witnessed daily the hardscrabble life of the economically and politically disfranchised. When, in 1803, Fayette County's land title office burned down, some propertied men immediately suspected that "the office was set on fire to destroy land claims."

Like poorer white men, blacks and white women watched as opportunities that had existed for them in Kentucke withered as Kentucky took shape. As we have seen, during the 1770s and 1780s, some members of both groups tasted social, economic, and religious independence. In the 1790s, however, both blacks and white women faced greater legal restrictions on their social and economic activities.

First came the tightening of marriage laws. In 1780, the Virginia legislature passed a law requiring all marriages to be performed by licensed preachers. In Kentucke, a dearth of clergy made the requirement nearly impossible, forcing a revision in the law allowing county court justices to perform marriage ceremonies. It was the first legislative recognition that the institution of marriage was not stable west of the Appalachians and needed to be strengthened quickly. In fact, like gender roles, marriage was fluid in Kentucke. Throughout the 1780s, the Virginia legislature heard Kentucke divorce cases in which marriages had not been formally sanctioned by church or state, or one or both spouses were adulterous, or in some cases, a spouse was bigamous or even trigamous. Given the difficulty of pursuing legal divorces, many Kentuckians informally and unofficially divorced as well.

Many complaints about the weakness of Kentucky marriages focused on how, for too long, the fluidity of identities and the chaos of Kentucke had allowed women to operate beyond the bounds of American womanhood, men to avoid their patriarchal responsibilities, and the matrimonial narrative to exist outside of the law. As Kentuckians developed their state's legal canon in the early 1790s, they rewrote that narrative and reordered marriage. With statehood, divorce cases moved to the Kentucky assembly, where each case decision became codified. Throughout the 1790s, lawmakers forced patriarchal obligations onto white men, and in the process relegated women to subservient roles.

For example, in 1793, John and Rebecca Green petitioned for divorce "mutually and by our own consent" because they "had been unhappily joined in a state of Wedlock." The petition went before the legislature's Committee on Religion, where it was revised to promote a particular idea of marital relations. The "Act concerning the marriage of Rebecca Green" concluded that her husband had "treated her inhumanely, deserted her for five years . . . refused to live with her, or to contribute any thing towards her support"—none of which was true. This practice of rewriting the content of divorce petitions pervaded the legislature's divorce hearings throughout the 1790s. While several men petitioned for divorce based upon their wives' abandonments, only one successfully maneuvered the state legislature, and that most likely was because he had five children, who legislators determined needed a new mother as soon as possible. Mutual agreement that the marriage had failed, as in the case of Rebecca and John Green, was insufficient reason to grant divorce because it suggested an equal status between husband and wife. In other words, regardless of the reasons for any given petition, the Committee on Religion consistently wrote (and the legislature consistently approved) acts for divorce based upon the premise of male authority and female dependence—men could abandon their marriages; women could only be the victims of abandonment.

By rejecting women's capacity to abandon the marriage contract, Kentucky's political patriarchs simultaneously empowered men as the masters of their small worlds. The English legal tradition championed by Harry Innes fully supported this vision of marriage. The foundation of the American legal system (and Innes's vision for Kentucky's legal structure) was Sir William Blackstone's *Commentaries on the Laws of England*, in which Blackstone explained, "By marriage, the husband and wife are one person in law: that is, the very being or legal existence of the woman is suspended during the marriage, or at least is incorporated and consolidated into that of the husband; under whose wing, protection, and cover, she performs everything."

Accompanying the empowerment of patriarchy was the responsibility of being a patriarch; the husband had to be "wing, protection, and cover" for his wife, responsibilities that extended to children as well. In 1795, the assembly gave women the right to identify the paternity of their children to local justices of the peace. Negligent fathers—some who had abandoned their families, others who had never married the mothers, and still others who lived with the family but were neglectful in their fatherhood— went before county courts that, upon determining defendants' guilt, "may at their discretion make such order for the keeping and maintaining of such child, as they may think proper, by charging the father of the child with such sum or money as they may think necessary for its annual support."

In 1798, the state assembly followed up its earlier marriage laws with what may be labeled a "marriage code," consolidating into one act several laws that dictated the terms of marriage (and gender relations) in Kentucky. Satisfied that enough clergy now inhabited the region, the assembly returned marriage to local church authority, requiring licensed Christian ministers to perform ceremonies. Ministers from some Christian sects—the Quakers and Mennonites, for example—were restricted to their own communities; and in western Kentucky, where the threat of Chickasaw and Chickamaugua attacks remained constant, the allowance for civil magistrates remained. Still, marriage was to be a formal institution, one certified by licensed ministers on behalf of the state.

Much of the code attended to husbands' and wives' rights within marriage, especially concerning the woman's dower. While men assumed the usage of their wives' property during marriages, the 1798 marriage code protected that dower as the only means by which women could provide for themselves in the event of divorce or abandonment. This was particularly necessary in the case of minors who married. The law required that "if either of the parties intending to marry shall be under the age of twenty-one years, and not therefore married, the consent of the father or guardian of such infant, shall be personally given before." But young people often ignored their fathers' wishes, so the law protected paternal interests, even if the father was absent:

> If any *feme sole*, of the age of twelve or under sixteen years, shall marry any person whatsoever, contrary of the will and consent of her father, or guardian, then the next of kin to such *feme* to

whom the inheritance shall come, shall have right to enter upon and take possession, of all lands, tenements, hereditaments and other real estate whatsoever, which such *feme* at the time of her marriage had in possession, remainder or reversion.

In other words, when an underage *feme sole*—a woman lacking the "wing, protection, and cover" of a husband—married without her father's permission, he remained her protector nonetheless, and his interests were to be safeguarded by a relative. Not until she turned twenty-one and became a legally recognized *feme covert*—a woman covered by her husband—did the estate "revest, be and remain in the said *feme*, and her heirs, other than her husband, and she and they, and every of them, may re enter and take possession thereof, as if this act had never been made."

While a woman could marry without her father's permission, she could not own property, sign legal documents or enter into a contract, make binding economic decisions, or even employ herself without her husband's permission. If she did work, coverture required she relinquish her wages to her husband. The legal restrictions of the 1790s represented a dramatic shift away from the less restrictive culture of the 1780s, when women could act as legal representatives and economic agents. Some women, such as Rebecca Green, recognized the personal advantages of remaining *feme sole*. Upon her divorce from John, she transformed her Lexington home into a cape manufactory, where she and her slave Mary produced mantuas and other outer garments. Her craftsmanship was part of a larger artisanal tradition emerging in Kentucky's booming village West, but her work also evidenced a reaction to the more rigid marital patterns of the 1790s that increasingly limited women's opportunities.

Simultaneous with the constriction of white women's opportunities, black Kentuckians found their activities dramatically restricted. On the heels of the constitutional convention of 1792, proponents of slavery eagerly promoted the institution. "Negros hire very well in this country," Samuel Meredith bragged to John Breckinridge in Virginia. A young Daniel Drake watched "great wagons, laden with merchandise for the interior; the caravans of travelers, mounted on horseback; and the gangs of negroes on foot—all moving south" from the Ohio River. To secure and benefit from their slave properties, slave-owners needed state-sanctioned mechanisms: the institutionalization of slavery found in the 1792 constitution was the first such instrument. Slave patrols, already active throughout the Bluegrass region, were another such apparatus. At least once each month, patrollers were to monitor slave activities, and slaves deemed suspicious could be punished with up to twenty lashes. Both the existence of the patrols and their overly violent measures evidenced for Kentuckians that a slave threat existed and needed controlling.

Yet, another device was "An Act concerning the Importation and Emancipation of Slaves," passed in late 1794. The law repealed all former laws that prohibited importation of slaves, essentially opening Kentucky up as a slave society. The few restrictions that remained—no direct importations via an international slave trade and no importation for purposes of sale—sought stability by assuring that the slaves brought into Kentucky were culturally assimilated and under the control of a specific planter. The law also included directions for personal emancipation of slaves: "under last will and testament, or by writing witnessed by two. Slave must have a certificate of freedom with county seal affixed; emancipator pays 5 shillings." County courts oversaw the process by recording the means of emancipation, issuing certificates, and collecting fees intended to "bond" the freeperson, keeping her or him from becoming a charge of the county.

Like the marriage code, however, the most important legal ordering of slavery (and race relations) came in 1798. The state assembly passed a slave code detailing every aspect of the institution, beginning with reaffirming slaves as "real property" defined by their own enslavement prior to 1785 or as descendents of females enslaved prior to that year. Restrictions were placed on slaves' legal access (they could not sue and were prohibited from witnessing against whites in court trials), mobility (they had to carry a pass signed by their owners to move about and could not visit other plantations for longer than four hours without their owner's consent), and economic participation (they could not sell or buy anything without express written notice that they were doing so on their owner's behalf). The act forbade slave-owners from arming their slaves with "any gun, powder, shot, club, or other weapon, whatsoever, offensive or defensive," although it did allow that "every free negro, mulatto or Indian, being a house-keeper, may be permitted to keep one gun, powder, and shot; and all negroes, mulattos and Indians, bond or free, living at any frontier plantation, may be permitted to keep and use guns, powder, shot and weapons, offensive or defensive, by license from a justice of the peace of the county." As the threat of Indian attack persisted, the presumption that heads of household needed to protect their families ideologically trumped racial fears. Still, slave patrols, empowered to interfere in free black life as well, stood ready to counter black discontent and rebellion if necessary. Only on the frontiers of western Kentucky and Appalachia, where slaves remained crucial for protection against Indian attacks, could the rigid new code be relaxed.

The slave code foremost delineated slavery, but it also codified whiteness, if indirectly. By grouping "negroes, mulattos and Indians," the law situated those groups as different from whites, and as with the constitution of 1792, classified whiteness and citizenship by restricting non-whites' activities. Even where non-whites could wield weapons on frontier plantations, the state served as the final arbiter for this allowance through county court licensure. So, while the slave code may be seen as further institutionalizing slavery, it also served to draw finer lines between whites and blacks (and the Indians who remained symbolically associated with blacks). This was most evident in a contemporary law defining master/servant relations, which prohibited blacks from purchasing servants "other than of their own complexion." If a free person of color "shall nevertheless presume to purchase a white servant, such servant shall immediately become free." Although whites could be "owned" through indentured servitude or apprenticeship, they could still sue in court over "injurious demeanor" of their masters. Even in servitude, whites had legal rights. The negation of rights—to assembly and speech, to sue, to fair trials and serving as witnesses, from search and seizure, and to enter into contracts—differentiated Kentucky's blacks from the whites who lived around them.

Neither did whites—indentured or free—have to fear constant invasion of their daily lives. Blacks viewed the slave patrols as

Figure 6.2. The slave code provided for slaves on the frontier to carry rifles and other weapons. James Estill's slave, Monk, was a veteran of the terror, having escaped captivity by Wyandots, fought alongside a white settler to stave off another attack, and then carried his injured companion over twenty-five miles to safety. From Z. F. Smith, *The History of Kentucky* (Louisville, Ky.: Courier-Journal Printing, 1886), 194.

an iniquitous threat to their privacy and personhoods. Patrollers employed a variety of terror tactics to cow all blacks into subservience: they broke up church meetings where evangelicals taught slaves to read and write; they stormed black homes on the pretense of searching for weapons or runaways, verbally and physically abusing men, women, and children; and when they came upon blacks assembled, even for the revelry of frolics, they fired indiscriminately into the crowds. While whites found greater security as Indians faded from Kentucky's countryside in the 1790s, blacks found more immediate dangers in the white slave patrols. As Baptist preacher David Barrow noted in 1795, there was a clear bond between the two: "If the Indians whip and cruelly treat the whites; it is no more than the whites serve the blacks." Terror remained.

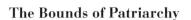

The Bounds of Patriarchy

The 1790s were good years for proponents of republican patriarchal order in Kentucky as they sought to rein in Kentucke's majoritarian ethos and fluidity of identities. Still, without full trade along the Mississippi River, the region's economy was not strong enough to support the new republican order. Without sufficient markets, dreams of staple agriculture—and the institution of slavery designed for it—were folly. With the regional economy still struggling, merchants willingly engaged white women and blacks in local economies despite the laws that forbade such actions. Kentuckians found ways to blur the lines between white women's and blacks' acceptable and unacceptable behaviors.

When women entered local stores, they took the legal categories of *feme sole* and *feme covert* with them. As *femes sole*, they established their own accounts and exerted their own purchasing power; as *femes covert*—wives, daughters, sisters, mothers, or slaves—they relied on patriarchs' accounts to purchase goods. Widowed and single women most often acted as independents, and in John W. Hunt's Lexington mercantile in the mid-1790s, they comprised more than a third of women purchasers. They established accounts in their own names and were directly responsible for eventually paying for items purchased on store credit. Merchants such as Hunt extended credit to nine out of ten independent women, including Rebecca Green, who purchased from Hunt twice in 1796: she personally bought tea, broadcloth, and imported cloth on credit on one visit; her slave Mary visited the store in late summer to buy trimmings for clothing on Green's account. While legally still married (although actually separated from her husband), Green nonetheless acted as a *feme sole* in her economic relations with Hunt. Her outwork—the capes that she and Mary made and sold—facilitated her participation in the market, and merchants gladly transformed those domestic productions into buying power. The role of economic decision maker had increasingly belonged to husbands, so Rebecca Green's ability not only to shop but to negotiate and contract the terms of a transaction represented a dramatic exception to the trend.

Like Green, many other women shopped in local stores, exerting their own economic influence in the marketplace, but the majority of women who visited stores in the 1790s were married and purchasing on their husbands' accounts. Still, even *femes covert* acted semi-independently when shopping, demanding the attentions of merchants as they made their selections but having little voice in the terms of payment. Over a third of John Hunt's customers were such women. Whether dependent or independent, they evidenced lingering patterns of economic decision making that had been openly permitted in Kentucke when survival was paramount.

African Americans, as independents or dependents, also shopped in local stores in the 1790s. Blacks, surprisingly, do not show up in store ledgers before 1792, but that may be a result of little need to racially distinguish them before the 1792 constitution. By the mid-1790s, however, they appeared regularly in Hunt's mercantile and Daniel Halstead's store just up the street. In Hunt's store, most were slaves purchasing on behalf of an owner and on his credit. Still, occasionally, slaves purchased goods for themselves, and Hunt permitted it. In 1795, Rebecca Hite's slave, Jack, bought bohea tea, a hat, shoes, thread, and buckles, paying in raccoon skins on one occasion and with cash on another occasion. In Halstead's store, alongside the few slaves who represented their owners' interests were free blacks acting to their own independent benefit. David and Sam, for example, were regular shoppers who paid with either barter or cash whenever they shopped.

Statehood and legislative ordering may have brought about Kentucky, but the patterns of Kentucke's economic life lingered. White women and blacks enjoyed similar consumer roles in local stores as did white men, purchasing the same types of items, paying with similar means, and exerting comparable economic authority. Not until the marriage and slave codes of 1798 did a gradual shift away from white women's and blacks' mercantile participation accelerate.

As in the marketplace, religion actively sought to reduce patriarchal influences and indulgences through church tribunals and willingly encouraged white women's and blacks' participation in the 1790s. Separate Baptists held night meetings for the instruction of slaves, and some slaves became religious leaders. Among the many preachers of the Travelling Church migration was Peter Durrett, one of Lewis Craig's slaves affectionately known as "Old Captain." (Importantly, while rhetorically anti-slavery, many Baptists such as Craig continued to hold slaves.) With Craig's consent, Old Captain hired out in Lexington, where he routinely preached to black and white Baptists and Methodists. In the mid-1790s, he applied to the South Kentucky Baptist Association for ordination. To ordain Durrett meant to challenge the racial structure and the recent institutionalization of slavery in the 1792 constitution. To deny him the right to preach, however, could spark anger and possibly revolt among the fifty enthusiastic converts whom Durrett had brought into his fold. In the end, the association "gave him the right hand of Christian affection, and directed him to go in the name of their common Master," without ordination.

Despite Old Captain's visibility, he was still a slave and subject to the incrementally restrictive laws passed by the state legislature in the 1790s. In response, some churches dictated their own rules. In October 1794, Paint Lick Presbyterian Meeting House ordered its slave-owning members to "teach every slave not above the age of fifteen years to read the word of God & give them such good education as may prepare them for the enjoyment of freedom." At Bethel Presbyterian Church in 1797, congregants spent an afternoon debating "Is slavery a moral evil?" and "Are all persons who hold slaves guilty of a moral evil?" While they decided simply "yes" and "no," respectively, the exercise heightened awareness about moral responsibility among its slave-owning congregants. The following year, New Providence Presbyterian Church chastised its own minister, Rev. William Mahon, for whipping a slave woman unmercifully and demanded he "temper his intercourse with all men & particularly with his slaves."

Equally important was the role of church tribunals. As new laws and judicial decisions tilted toward white patriarchy, the dispossessed found some recourse in Baptist, Methodist, and Presbyterian arbitrations that offered more equitable access to justice. Of course, churches had little legal force, but for congregants, the weight of a tribunal decision carried enough moral suasion to change actions and attitudes.

Church tribunals reinforced the sacred and proper roles they ascribed to wives and husbands. Just as the state legislature rewrote the circumstances of divorce cases to reflect a more orthodox and patriarchal view of marriage, church tribunals reinterpreted the marriage laws to provide greater latitude to women and promote more equality in marriage. White women were just as likely to bring marital complaints—bigamy, spousal abuse, adultery—before church tribunals as were white men, and further, white women found such tribunals willing to consider their complaints concerning slander, wills, and control over domestic productions.

The church early and often criticized the patriarchal ideal. Caleb Wallace, writing under the pseudonym "Abigail Trueheart," condemned his fellow white men's "passions for domination . . . groveling selfishness, aspiring ambition, and daring profanity." Baptist minister David Barrow denounced "republicans, patriots, friends to the American revolution &c. &c." who "were absolute monarchs, despots, and aristocrats at home." Church tribunals had already begun to curtail that unrestrained patriarchalism in the 1790s. Every man who joined a Baptist, Methodist, or Presbyterian church made himself a target of the tribunals as they sought to curb his manly independence. Men were to be patriarchs, but in a Christian manner so that their families would act "under the same order and Disciplin as they themselves are bound to observe in their Walk & Conversation." Men stood before tribunals on accusations of adultery, intoxication, mistreating wives, and swearing. Additionally, tribunals took up cases that rightfully belonged in a county court: stealing, destroying trees and other property boundary markers, and land purchase disputes. In 1790, for example, the Severn's Valley Baptist Church resolved Brother Johnson's complaint against Brothers Dodge and Dye over five hundred acres, instructing Brother Philips to "Make the Deed in the Space of one year." For men, then, church tribunals became both overseers of their personal conduct and alternatives to official courts in resolving public disputes.

Churches expected women to meet the same standards of moral discipline. In 1793, Betty McCluer went before the Severn's Valley Baptist Church charged with "fornication viz of being with child by the person whom she married at the same time she was married to him [her first husband]." One of the many who viewed their marriage vows far more liberally than the Kentucky legislature desired, McCluer had left her husband without official divorce, married another man, and become pregnant by him. The church stripped her of membership, a punishment that so traumatized McCluer that she "shewed so much tokens of repentance both to the Church and the world" that the church subsequently restored her membership.

Throughout the 1790s, Presbyterian, Methodist, and Baptist tribunals worked to stabilize families by reining in patriarchy: its sense of honor, its tolerance of spousal and child abuse, and the institution that ultimately empowered it—slavery. As Barrow argued, God so liberally blessed Kentucky "with his bounties, in respect to soil &c." that a patriarch could sustain family "without falling into the line of speculation, or that of holding slaves." In 1796, Severn's Valley Baptist Church decided that its slave-owning congregants were obligated to let slaves purchase their freedom. In many Baptist, Methodist, and Presbyterian churches, "slaves were received by the congregation, in the spirit of religious equality, partaking of all the privileges of full membership."

Along with privileges came responsibility: although it was illegal for slaves to marry, churches and slaves acted as if they could and did. The Elkhorn Baptist Association considered in 1787 "whether it is lawful for a slave being an orderly member and compelled to leave his wife and move with his master about five hundred mile then to take another wife?" Grave Creek Baptist Church developed a dual conception of slave marriage. The congregation recognized marriage between slaves and actively excommunicated adulterous slaves. Yet, the church refused to question slave-owners' decisions to separate their "married" slaves.

For enslaved blacks, this dual conceptualization of slave marriage left gender and family roles as ill-defined as they had been a decade earlier. Even as the Indian threat declined and white families found greater stability, black families struggled. Decades later, William Hayden remembered his separation from his family: "No mother's smiles were decreed to welcome me—

no maternal words to soothe my pains, no kind and long known home to yield me sustenance and repose—naught but the clanking chains of slavery—the roof of a stranger, and my own sad reflections were meted out to me."

The Bounds of Patriotism

Kentucky's relationship to the new nation in the 1790s was as contentious as its domestic reordering. As Hubbard Taylor wrote in 1793, Kentucky held great promise "if the Indians was at peace, the Mississippi open, & the titles to our Lands adjusted; if I live to see all those take place, I shall behold the happiest & richest Country in the world." But in 1793, none of those things had come to pass. Instead, George Rogers Clark contacted the French, promising that he could raise fifteen hundred militiamen to invade the Mississippi River valley and "take the whole of Louisiana for France." In return, he expected the river to be opened to Kentucky commerce. His offer was accepted by Citizen Genêt, France's representative to the United States, who arrived a few months later and commissioned Clark as commander in chief of the French Revolutionary Legion of the Mississippi. Hoping to excite anger against Spain, John Breckinridge proposed that "Louisiana groaning under tyranny, is imploring you with uplifted hands," and Kentuckians should work to bring democracy to their western neighbors. "Our all is at stake," declared George Nicholas, "for we can never be a flourishing people until we have what we demand and we had better lose what we possess in attempting to get what is necessary to it's free enjoyment than hold it in the terms we now do."

In the summer, Genêt visited secretary of state Thomas Jefferson, informing him of Clark's plans and France's support. The scheme was dangerous, Jefferson responded; "enticing officers and soldiers of Kentucky to go against Spain, was really putting a halter around their necks, for . . . they would assuredly be hung, if they commenced hostilities against a nation at peace with the U.S." Clark began recruiting regardless, and James Brown encouraged Governor Isaac Shelby to use the news to inspire Congress: "Such information might call their attention to our situation, and give our interests a place in their political deliberations." When Jefferson conveyed the news to Washington, the president responded in early 1794 with a proclamation against "invading and plundering the territories of a nation at peace with the United States."

Clark's plans fizzled, but unlike Wilkinson's Spanish intrigues in the 1780s, this "French conspiracy" had significant consequences. Statehood had shifted the political context of Kentuckians' complaints about access to the Mississippi River. Threats of independence and alliance with Spain subsided. In their place, disgruntled Kentuckians believed they either had to push the United States to solve the problem or act extra-legally, as Clark had threatened. Breckinridge's argument for spreading republicanism added ideological gravitas to the Mississippi River trade issue. "If the General Government will not procure it for us," Breckinridge argued, "we shall hold ourselves not answerable for any consequences that may result from our own procurement of it. . . . Patriotism, like every other thing, has its bounds." While Indian attacks continued and occasionally were referenced in petitions throughout the 1790s, the Mississippi River dominated Breckinridge's and other Kentuckians' complaints against the federal government.

Alongside their petitions demanding an open Mississippi River, Kentuckians also protested the excise tax on whiskey that riled much of the western backcountries. Commenting on Congress's passage of secretary of the treasury Alexander Hamilton's tax in 1791, Nicholas warned Madison:

> The spirit of it must be that it shall be uniform in fact as well as name: An excise established on tobacco or indigo would be uniform in name but as those articles are made only in a few states, it would not be uniform in fact, and therefore would be unconstitutional. So it is as to distilled spirits from home materials. They are not made from those materials, at least from grain, any where but in the Western country where from their situation they cannot carry their grain to market.

Unlike the backcountries east of the Appalachians, Kentucky's inability to get domestic productions to market made their compliance with the tax nearly impossible. Frustrated, John Brecken-ridge complained, "Nature has done everything for us; Government everything against us."

In order to enforce the whiskey tax in Kentucky, President Washington appointed Thomas Marshall as chief revenue officer, but without a federal attorney to bring charges against those who refused to pay, the law was impotent. Partially out of protest against what he perceived as an unjust tax, John Breckinridge rejected Washington's invitation to serve as the federal attorney to Kentucky, as did George Nicholas. As Marshall's list of trans-gressors grew between 1791 and 1794, Hamilton became more de-termined to collect the revenue. Occasionally, distillers attacked collectors, destroyed their records, "rescued" confiscated whis-key, and, in Fayette County, pulled a collector from his horse, tarred him, and rolled him in leaves.

Combined with the Kentuckians' obsession with opening the Mississippi River, their refusal to abide by the whiskey excise tax sent an ominous message to the Washington administration. While Jefferson never expressed concern that Kentuckians would actually act on their threats, his successor as secretary of state, Edmund Randolph, was far less confident: "What if the Gov-ernment of Kentucky should force us either to support them in their hostilities against Spain or disavow and renounce them?" Kentuckians seemed determined to embarrass the federal gov-ernment. When news arrived of John Jay's mission to England, hundreds gathered in Lexington for a speech filled with "most inflammatory & invective language" that denounced Jay's failure to secure the Mississippi River in 1786 and questioned his moti-vations in the current trip. As difficult as the Kentucky situation became, however, when like-minded distillers in western Penn-sylvania decided to burn down the tax collector's home, they pro-vided the Washington administration the opportunity to make a statement by sending armed troops to extinguish the insur-rection.

Kentuckians avoided direct confrontation with the federal army, although as late as August 1794, President Washington consid-ered using the military against Kentucky. "Do you think it is un-just to subject us to the excise until you give us the use of our rivers," Nicholas had asked in 1791; "is it not requiring us to make brick without straw?" Secretary of State Randolph agreed. If the Mississippi River was opened, enforcement of the whiskey tax in Kentucky could be justified. Washington sent a diplomat—Thomas Pinckney—to Spain to negotiate access to the Mississippi River, and within fourteen months, Pinckney had secured what Jay could not: rights to navigate the Mississippi River and to trade in New Orleans. In the meantime, Anthony Wayne had signed the Treaty of Greenville, providing greater physical security for Kentucky. Through diplomatic and military ventures, the United States had granted Kentuckians all they had desired.

By 1796, then, Kentuckians seemingly had little reason to continue avoiding the excise tax, and yet they did. Even when President Washington finally appointed William Clark as federal attorney to Kentucky in 1796 and grand juries began issuing presentments, whiskey tax evaders continued to escape prosecution. Trial jurors refused time and again to indict their neighbors. When John Adams became president in 1796, some Kentuckians feared the worst. Caleb Wallace related how "it was apprehended by several of the most respectable & intelligent of my acquaintances, that the Federal government wished for a pretext to send an army into this country to awe the people, and enable it to punish those, who by speaking, writing, or otherwise, should oppose such of its measures as were thought to be unconstitutional or rigorous." When, in 1798, the Federalists pushed through the Alien and Sedition Acts, many Kentuckians expected an invasion.

While many valid reasons underlay Kentucky's contentious relationship with the federal government in the 1790s, the perception that the Federalists had little interest in Kentucky's development lay at the heart of Kentuckians' discontent. John Breckinridge played a large role in energizing those animosities and constructing some of the most striking anti-Federalist episodes of the 1790s. Having received five hundred acres from his uncle William Preston in the mid-1780s, Breckinridge and his family migrated to Kentucky in 1793. Almost immediately upon arrival, he organized the Democratic Society of Kentucky, a political activist group that regularly petitioned the federal government on many topics but remained true to one theme: "attachments to governments cease to be natural, when they cease to be mutual." The Indian threat, opening of the Mississippi, the whiskey excise tax—each garnered significant attention from the Democratic Society, which impressed upon the federal government its responsibility to westerners.

In 1798, Breckinridge spearheaded Kentucky's opposition to the Alien and Sedition Acts, encouraging statewide citizen meetings to petition for repeal of the laws. In the Frankfort *Palladium*, one commentator declared that had the Federalist-controlled Congress "continued much longer, we had every reason to expect, in a post of two, to have heard of a bill interdicting the liberty of *thinking*." The Alien and Sedition Acts infuriated Breckinridge, who wrote James Monroe that "I have at present not a doubt, from the apparent temper of the people, that any, & every attempt, to enforce the two first mentioned laws, will be publickly resisted & repelled." Crowds of angered Kentuckians gathered at rallies: "There was a Barbacue in the vicinity & great excitement against the Alien & Sedition law." In Lexington, a young Henry Clay arose before a crowd to denounce the Federalists, so exciting the people that they refused to allow any Federalists to speak and eventually hoisted Clay upon their shoulders and paraded away.

In the meanwhile, Breckinridge traveled to Virginia to meet with Jefferson and Madison on the topic. Along with George Nicholas, the men conspired to undermine the Alien and Sedition Acts through state legislation. Jefferson wrote resolutions that he expected Breckinridge and Nicholas to shepherd through the Kentucky Assembly. It would not be difficult. Even in Breckinridge's absence, Kentuckians agitated for "resolutions praying for a repeal of every obnoxious and unconstitutional act." So when Breckinridge delivered the document in October 1798, the assembly debated and overwhelmingly approved the resolutions. Less than a month later, Madison's set of resolutions passed Virginia's legislature.

Both Kentucky's and Virginia's resolutions characterized the relationship between the states as a compact in which "each party has an equal right to judge for itself, as well of infractions as of the mode and measure of redress." More so than Madison, Jef-

ferson willingly employed the word "nullify," but he did not em-
phasize it, hoping the weight of the argument would sway public
opinion. When Kentucky sent out its resolutions in hopes of drawing an alliance, however, the other states were less receptive than
its own citizens had been. A flurry of condemnations arrived in
Frankfort, most from the New England states. In Philadelphia,
the Federalist newspaper *Porcupine's Gazette* mocked the Kentuckians:

> If these sagacious and learned citizens had assembled in any
> place, where there had been a single magistrate of spirit and
> good sense, he would have dispersed them by his constables and
> thereby spared his country the disgrace, which their barbarous
> resolves are calculated to reflect on it. If this Kentucky newspaper
> were to fall into the hands of a person totally unacquainted with
> the rest of America, he would take us all for a sort of savages; and,
> in fact, the Kentuckians do appear to be just civilized enough to
> be the tools of faction, and that's all.

Furious, several members of the assembly appealed to Jefferson to write a new document, but he refused, yielding to "a
mass of talents in Kentucky sufficient to every purpose." Certainly, Jefferson had in mind Breckinridge, who took the pen
and wrote another set of resolutions that denounced federal efforts to repress freedoms of speech and the press, and proposed
congressional repeal of the Alien and Sedition Acts. Breckinridge
abandoned Jefferson's nullification argument, largely to restore
Kentucky's reputation among the states. Beyond the condemnations arising from New England, old rumors of western disaffection and possible secession had begun circulating throughout the
East. Breckinridge left no doubt that, angry as they were, Kentuckians were foremost Americans.

Simultaneous with the considerations and passage of Breckinridge's resolutions, many Kentuckians also pushed for a new constitutional convention. Since 1792, criticisms of the state government had become increasingly louder and persistent, so that by
late 1798, the movement for revision could not be ignored and the
state assembly agreed to a May 1799 election to select convention
delegates. For months, aspiring conventioneers—including many

of George Nicholas's "ambitious men"—jockeyed in the pages of the *Kentucky Gazette* as well as on the ground. Nicholas labeled the move for a new constitution "mad and wicked schemes," even as he and John Breckinridge worked county by county to encourage certain "good men, but such of that class as are most popular" to run. At a Fayette County meeting, he presented five "principles" by which his county's selection of delegates should proceed: select men who supported representation by population rather than county, an independent judiciary, loyalty to the Union, and a two-house legislature, and who opposed legislative emancipation of slaves. The crowd fully approved and then elected Breckinridge as one of their representatives.

Not surprisingly, it was the last of Nicholas's principles that became the center of controversy as the convention approached. Unlike Nicholas, who had always assumed that the people would acquiesce to their patriarchal leaders willingly, Breckinridge saw a more sinister force at work: the people were not beyond overturning society in order to gain a bit of an advantage for themselves. Emancipationists sought not only to end slavery but, in so doing, to resurrect the challenges to land titles that had panicked Kentuckians years earlier. "Where is the difference," Breckinridge asked, "whether I am robbed of my horse by a highwayman, or of my slave by a set of people called a Convention? . . . If they can by one experiment emancipate our slaves; the same principle pursued, will enable them at a second experiment to extinguish our land titles; both are held by rights equally sound." Nicholas denounced emancipators as "Thieves, Robbers and beardless boys"!

Debate over slavery and emancipation became ferocious and widespread, sparking imagery and language reminiscent of Kentucke. One citizen complained of the "Ignorant Savage Heathens" who waited, poised to strike. If slavery ended, "our wives and daughters will be besieged in our own houses, for fear of violence and abuse from these strolling heathenish, ugly creatures." Philemon Thomas, a pro-slavery Mason County conventioneer, declared that he "would wade to his knees in blood before it [emancipation] should take place." But enough doubt about the security of slavery remained that one planter warned a friend, "I would not advise Slaveholders to come here immediately."

Emancipators aggressively struck back. One accused Nicholas of failing to live up to the ideals of personal freedom and limited government that he had espoused with the 1792 constitution, eliciting Nicholas's response that "if there is an inconsistency in these speeches, all the patriots in the southern states, who were slave holders, have been guilty of the same inconsistency, from '76 to this day." The young and popular Henry Clay appealed through the *Kentucky Gazette*, "All America acknowledges the existence of slavery to be an evil which, while it deprives the slaves of the best gifts of Heaven, in the end injures the master, too, by laying waste his lands, enabling him to live indolently, and thus contracting all the vices generated by a state of idleness." Turning Breckinridge's equation of emancipation with land redistribution on its head, one emancipationist jokingly proposed that the new constitution deny suffrage to a citizen "unless he has either a tract of land or a slave," hinting that Breckinridge and his ilk might insist upon property requirements for citizenship. Ironically, the rhetoric played into Breckinridge's plan to fill the convention with landed delegates. By acknowledging Breckinridge's equation of slavery to land ownership, the jokester reinforced the slavery debate as central to questions of citizenship. Fearing the possibility of losing slaves and land, Kentuckians selected delegates who promised to protect the propertied interests. Of the fifty-eight men who arrived in Frankfort in late July as convention delegates, fifty-seven owned slaves and fifty held substantial property.

Unlike the 1792 convention, which, like the frontier context in which it occurred, seemed open to possibilities, the 1799 convention delegates left little room for negotiations or compromise. Only a handful of men—most notably Harry Innes, Caleb Wallace, and George Nicholas—had experienced the trials of Kentucke. Nicholas, along with Breckenridge and Wallace, had planned a series of resolutions to guide the convention (just as he had done seven years earlier), but he died suddenly on the third day of the convention, creating a leadership vacuum. Eager to step into it were dozens of aspiring politicians such as John Breckinridge, William Bledsoe, Felix Grundy, Green Clay, and Humphrey Marshall, all men who would use their convention experiences to jump into nineteenth-century state and national politics. Despite the delegates' jostling for position, however, there was just not significant difference among these men on most topics. Debate became heated over the power of the lower house and the independence of the judiciary, but most energy went into the slavery issue.

Of course, slavery was more entrenched in Kentucky than it had been in Kentucke. While public debate could be stirred by the emancipationists, there was very little emancipationist fervor among the delegates. Quickly, the convention revised the state bill of rights, creating greater political opportunity for white men and ensuring that citizenship remained exclusively white by insisting that "all *free* men, when they form a social compact, are equal." While the absence of "free" in the 1792 constitution had not really swung open doors for free black political participation, its specific inclusion in the 1799 constitution signaled a determination to draw the racial lines clearly and definitively, expressly excluding "negroes, mulattoes, and Indians" from citizenship.

By a thirty-seven to fourteen vote, the convention also voted down a provision that would have empowered the legislature to prohibit importation of slaves. The minority included the handful of emancipationists and some of the wealthiest and most established Bluegrass planters. The majority comprised more recently arrived young men and a block of large slaveholders who truly believed Breckenridge's rhetoric that the power to end slavery or even the importation of slaves could translate into the power to redistribute land.

With that vote, Nicholas's expectation that Kentucky would one day shed slavery died, ironically less than a week after Nicholas. On the eve of a new century, Kentucky had moved from a society with slaves to a society economically, intellectually, and socially invested in slavery. The patterns set by the 1799 constitution ushered Kentucky into the nineteenth century and into the Old South. In fact, Kentucky's model of slave exclusion from the social compact and prohibition of legislative emancipation was so impressive that future slave states incorporated both in their own constitutions.

7.

AN OLD SOUTH FRONTIER

In late December 1798, a "war party" moved along the Wilderness Road, murdering a peddler, two immigrating Marylanders, and a Virginia gentleman. The latter's body was so mutilated that he was beyond recognition, requiring a local tavern owner to identify the clothing of the young man who had boarded with him the previous night. Within a week, a Lincoln County militia tracked down and captured the killers: brothers Micajah and Wiley Harpe and their consorts, Susan Roberts and her sister Betsy, and Sarah Rice. As they awaited trial, the brothers escaped, abandoning their "wives."

The separation did not last long. The Danville court acquitted one of the women. Another went free on mistrial. Although the third was convicted originally, a judge decided to grant a new trial, and the state's attorney general opted not to re-try the case. Each woman had borne a baby while in jail, and the community gathered clothes, money, and a horse to relocate the three to Tennessee. The women, instead, traveled westward along the Green River until they eventually met the Harpe brothers again at Cave-in-Rock.

A limestone bluff overlooking the Ohio River, Cave-in-Rock had harbored outlaws for many years. Its strategic position in a river bend afforded significant protection and good vision, allowing robbers to easily attack southbound boats. When the Harpes arrived, however, they were too savage even for the outlaws of Cave-in-Rock. One evening, as other criminals celebrated their cache from a passing flatboat, the Harpe brothers took the survivor of the attack to the top of the bluffs, blindfolded the horse onto which he had been tied, and ran both over the edge. Shocked by the brutality, the other outlaws forced the Harpes and their wives to leave.

Throughout the summer of 1799, the brothers and their family wandered the Kentucky-Tennessee borderlands, randomly killing at least a dozen people and striking terror throughout the region. At some point, Micajah Harpe, irritated by the incessant crying of Sarah's baby, smashed the child's head against a tree and tossed its body into the woods. The spree ended in late August when the two brothers, posing as Methodist ministers, boarded at the home of Moses Stegall. After bashing another boarder's head in with an axe handle for snoring too loudly, the Harpes slit the throat of the owner's infant child and then turned on Mrs. Stegall. To cover their crimes, they set fire to the house and, hoping to overtake the local justice of the peace when he came to investigate, hid in nearby bushes, killing two other men whom they mistook for the magistrate.

Residents of Henderson County demanded something be done. The county militia quickly formed and took off in chase, eventually capturing Micajah. After Micajah confessed to twenty murders, Moses Stegall vengefully beheaded him, placing the decapitated head atop a stake to warn other would-be murderers. Wiley Harpe escaped to the Mississippi Territory, to meet a similar fate along the Natchez Trace some five years later. In late October, the three wives again went on trial and again escaped prosecution. Sarah Rice Harpe fled to Tennessee, where she married into a respectable family. Susan Roberts Harpe remained in the Green River country, living out her life in Russellville. Betsy Roberts married and migrated to Illinois. The surviving Harpe children disappeared into history, in many ways freed from their fathers' legacy.

At the turn of the nineteenth century, neither Chickamaugas nor Creeks terrorized the southern reaches of Kentucky. Instead, two brothers born in North Carolina had appropriated and twisted the promise of trans-Appalachia revealed by their fellow North Carolinian Daniel Boone: to get ahead in Kentucky, one need only use excessive violence and an atmosphere of terror to deprive others of the promise.

In contrast to the developing Bluegrass region, the Green River country of southern Kentucky retained the reputation of a frontier. In 1796, John Breckinridge asked a friend determined to move south of the Green River, "You are in a genteel, agreeable neighborhood. . . . And what are you about to exchange all this for? A country you have never seen: a country when you do see— you will see filled with nothing but hunters, horse-thieves & savages. And a country where wretchedness, poverty & sickness will always reign." While the landscape had changed very little by 1799, however, a shift in attitude had occurred. The state legislature and the courts had worked throughout the 1790s to recast Kentucky in a patriarchal mode, and as the south side of the Green River evolved, it did so in a less-fluid atmosphere than had existed when the Bluegrass took shape. Gone were the days when women shot Indians or hacked their arms off with axes. Judges, juries, and even James Blair—the state attorney general who, in 1801, would undertake *A Review of the Criminal Law of the Commonwealth of Kentucky* (1804–1805) to make the laws more accessible to the public—were unwilling to accept that the Harpe women, or any women, were capable of such savagery.

While there was evidence to convict at least one of the women for complicity in multiple murders and all of the women for involvement in the Stegall murders, officials thought it more useful to rehabilitate these unruly women. Theirs had not been normal marriages or a normal family. Micajah Harpe had officially married Susan Roberts, and Wiley had wed Sarah Rice. But both men apparently copulated with all three women, complicating the paternity of their children. Indeed, when Micajah confessed to his murders, he included among them "his" baby daughter, although she was also the child of his sister-in-law, Sarah. As they sat on trial, the Harpe women—representative of frontier chaos, the disorderliness of extramarital sex, and poorly defined marriages—were vestiges of a less-than-venerable past, even in the "wretched" and "savage" lands south of the Green River.

Becoming Southern: Slavery and Agriculture

In 1798, "Aristedes" celebrated "the Western people—ready to support the government of their choice, and determined not to survive it." For a decade, Kentuckians had wrestled with loyalty to a federal government that seemed, at best, indifferent to their circumstances. With the election of 1800, however, they found an administration in office that was responsive to their western situation. During Thomas Jefferson's presidency, Kentucky would become more stable, secure, and southern. As one Kentuckian proclaimed in 1802, "Times are greatly changed, and I am really happy to see it."

Westward migration exploded following the Treaty of Greenville, as potential pioneers believed that the Indian threat had been sufficiently mitigated. But the migration of the late 1790s and early 1800s was different in character from that of the previous two decades. Only about half of Kentucke's earliest settlers had migrated from Virginia, with the next-largest migration populations from Pennsylvania and Maryland. More New Jerseyites than North Carolinians had moved to Kentucke by the mid-1790s, and communities such as Washington had notable pockets of New Englanders. The two primary routes into Kentucke had accommodated very different migration groups, partially contributing to the emerging settlement patterns. Those coming through the Cumberland Gap tended to be poorer Virginians and Carolinians, as well as slaves sent westward in advance of their masters. Like the Travelling Church, these pioneers moved into the central and southern portions of the Bluegrass. Some ventured as well south of the Green River. Migrants traveling down the Ohio River were just as likely to be poor, although they were largely from Maryland, Pennsylvania, and New Jersey. Occasionally, they found wealthier men traveling alongside them: Philadelphia and Baltimore merchants headed to Lexington, Danville, Frankfort, and Louisville; and Virginia planters transporting possessions and sometimes entire households. The debarking points at the Point and the Falls of the Ohio ensured large populations of northerners in places such as Maysville, Louisville, and outlying villages and hamlets. Alanantowamiowee, the old buffalo trace that coursed southward from the Point into the central Bluegrass, became an economic and migratory corridor that drew most arrivals into Lexington, where they sold possessions, bought goods, and set out for their new homes.

By the late 1790s, however, the "southernization" of Kentucky had begun. The Treaty of Greenville opened up southern Ohio to settlement, not only creating a territorial buffer between Kentucky and the northwestern Indians but providing an outlet for Kentuckians—many northern-born—disgruntled by the slave society forming around them. Daniel Drake remembered his father, an antislavery New Jerseyite who settled at Mayslick, exploring Chillicothe, Ohio, in anticipation of relocating his family, motivated by "the existence of slavery in Kentucky . . . the uncertainty of land titles . . . the want of good water." In 1798, James Smith and his brother-in-law Philip Gatch relocated their families north of Cincinnati specifically to manumit their slaves. After 1799, the new state constitution verified Kentucky as a slave state and provided the final impetus for outmigration. By the turn of the nineteenth century, thousands of Kentuckians, including hundreds of manumitted blacks, crossed the Ohio River for new homes in the Old Northwest. Among them were poorer whites originally from Virginia and Maryland, many of whom had been former tenant farmers who lost access to Kentucky lands as large farms converted into plantations or owners sold off their properties. Joining them was George Rogers Clark, who, having acquired thousands of acres in the Indiana territory, found it easier to leave Kentucky than to face public rumors of alcoholism and treason over his acceptance of the position of commander in chief of the French Revolutionary Legion years earlier. Also fleeing Kentucky was Daniel Boone, bled dry by taxes levied on contested lands and the legal fees he had to pay to secure ownership. In 1799, he left for Missouri.

As antislavery proponents and poorer whites abandoned Kentucky, "portable planters"—an agrarian and mostly Virginian elite dedicated to slavery and willing to transport it anywhere—found new opportunities to create large estates and pursue staple crop agriculture. In order to justify slave labor, John Breckinridge, David Meade, Thomas Jones, and other portable planters initially dabbled with tobacco as a cash crop: as early as 1790, over 250,000 pounds of Kentucke tobacco sold on the New Orleans market. But tobacco was difficult to grow and market. It depleted soils, an acute problem in a state with limited and confused land titles, and it was pricey to ship down the Mississippi River, a trip that took nearly a month. Still, the expectation that Kentucky could mimic Virginia's plantation-based economy drew hundreds of ambitious moneyed men and tens of thousands of new settlers.

Most pioneers arriving in the late 1790s and early 1800s were typically younger, poorer, and more desperate than many abandoning Kentucky for the Old Northwest. Some held land claim certificates from their fathers' service in the Revolutionary War; many discovered land was impossible to come by regardless. "New comers can be at no loss (if they have Cash) to secure an estate to their taste," explained the wealthy and genteel David Meade, but thousands had little or no cash. Compared to lands in the Old Northwest selling at $2 an acre, even the most remote lands south of the Green River were at $3.50 by the mid-1790s. In the northern Bluegrass, $8 an acre was common; and improved properties around Lexington and Louisville were well beyond the reach of most new arrivals. "In various parts of the state," noted one visitor, "land has risen 100 percent . . . and in some cases it has risen 3, 4, and even 500 percent."

Even upon finding land, only the wealthiest and best-connected could provide the necessary labor. While many poor whites took up tenant farming, slavery became the increasingly common labor source. Between 1790 and 1800, Kentucky's slave population outpaced the growth of its white population, booming from 11,830 to 41,084 slaves. Kentucky physically appeared more southern as plantations sprung up across the state, dozens of tobacco warehouses arose along navigable streams and rivers to ensure quality productions, the docks at Louisville filled with shipments headed down the Mississippi, and black slaves became more visible. By 1800, nearly one of every five Kentuckians was a slave.

White Kentuckians became more southern as they replaced the Indian terror with a fear of blacks. Since the Treaty of Greenville, hardly a word about Indians circulated around Kentucky, particularly in the Bluegrass, where most settlers lived. Occasionally, the *Kentucky Gazette* acknowledged a Creek, Chickamauga, or Chickasaw attack along the Cumberland or Green River, but such episodes were dismissed as remnants of frontier Kentucke. Instead, blacks—specifically slaves—became the dangerous Others. During the eighteenth century, slavery had never been central to the story of Kentucke, but by the turn of the nineteenth century, as Kentucky was realized, slavery was *the* story. In the past, the laxity of frontier slavery had created patterns in which slaves could hire out and negotiate terms of service, shop at some stores, and appeal to church tribunals for recourse against abusive masters. Although he probably was not thinking of blacks, George Nicholas understood back in 1792 that if the constitutional convention excluded "any particular class of citizens . . . sooner or later they will certainly be oppressed," the natural consequence of which was civil unrest and even rebellion. With the Slave Code of 1798 and the constitution of 1799, white Kentuckians specifically excluded blacks from the modicum of economic and political freedoms they had enjoyed just years earlier. To imagine that blacks would reject oppression was not too great a leap, and neither was the probability that they would do it violently.

Rumors of slave rebellion circulated as early as the mid-1790s, drawing upon the terror of racialized violence that had characterized Kentucke. In the summer of 1800, Lexington was abuzz with rumors of recent attacks by two blacks on travelers northwest of town. The town trustees issued restrictions on Saturday and Sunday slave gatherings. When, two months later, the *Kentucky Gazette* reported Gabriel Prosser's slave revolt in Virginia, the news compounded already tense relations between black and white Kentuckians. In 1801, a Clark County slave killed his overseer. The following year, the "Easter rebellion" in Richmond and Petersburg not only threw white Virginia into panic but sparked fears in Kentucky as well. When the Kentucky legislature approved continuing the slave trade in 1802, several towns, including Lexington, passed ordinances prohibiting slave importation because "the Slaves in the South are strongly bent on insurrection" and began constructing watch houses where militiamen could observe black Kentuckians at work and leisure. The structures most certainly reminded whites that a menace was out there, waiting for the opportunity to bring chaos to their world.

The psychological terror was so powerful that even a planter and politician dedicated to the institution considered sacrificing it for the sake of security. Reflecting upon the Haitian Revolution in 1804, John Breckinridge hoped "the time is not far distant when not a slave will exist in the Union. I fear our slaves in the south will produce another St. Domingo." Just as militia leaders had informed the secretary of war of imminent Indian threats a decade prior, former Indian fighter Charles Scott warned the same office in 1804 that "I can assure you that ther is Strong reasons to believe that we Shall have Some trouble ere long with the Blacks." By 1807, in response to Virginia's decision a year earlier to require manumitted blacks to leave the Old Dominion, Kentucky's legislature restricted free black migration into the state.

The Indian threat was not gone: it had been transformed and attributed to different yet still racialized Others living among white Kentuckians. In 1801, the *Kentucky Gazette* reported what might as well have been a parable of terror. A man, his two sons, and thirteen slaves traveled aboard an Ohio River flatboat on their way to Kentucky. The sons killed their father, only in turn to be slaughtered by their slaves, who then attempted to flee to the Creeks before being caught by the federal army. Unbound and uncontrolled, unpropertied white youth and enslaved blacks replaced Native Americans as the newest threats in trans-Appalachia. Rumors of the Harpes and of potential slave uprisings only confirmed the danger. Of course, as the narrative had played out time and again since the mid-eighteenth century, Indians stood ready to harbor those threats, possibly even join with them at some future date. Surprisingly (or possibly not so with the Treaty of Greenville and then Jefferson's ascendancy to the presidency), the hero of this morality tale is the American government.

Kentuckians placed great weight on Jefferson's election, anticipating that his vision for agrarian republicanism was one that recognized the West's importance and would bring stability. Jeffersonian agrarianism was not monolithic, however. The Bluegrass, filled with large planters and elite politicians, embraced a political economy that celebrated all things agrarian while also championing gentility, unbridled consumerism, and conspicuous display of wealth. The networks of planters, merchants, and law-yers in the Bluegrass sought greater political and economic roles in the nation. By the early 1800s, Henry Clay was finding his voice as the spokesman for the "Bluegrass System"—a political economy bolstering commercial, agricultural, and industrial entre-preneurialism that would one day become the foundation of his "American System."

In sharp contrast stood the region south of the Green River, where cotton early became the staple crop of choice even as a more localistic but no less economically vibrant strain of Jef-fersonian agrarianism flourished. Part of a larger geographical basin with a southern border along the Cumberland River in Tennessee, the lands south of the Green were settled by fewer large-scale planters. The mechanisms by which the lands had been distributed—via Revolutionary War pensions or the land act of 1795—created a landscape upon which thousands of pio-neers worked much smaller farms than those in the Bluegrass. By 1800, nearly two-thirds of heads of household owned land, and a large majority owned the maximum two hundred acres allo-cated by the state. In land distribution alone, south of the Green looked dramatically more egalitarian than the Bluegrass.

Additionally, the earliest of settlers discovered quickly that cotton would grow well. One Bluegrass farmer noted in 1789 that "our climate is not favorable to [cotton], and we shall always be obliged to get it from Cumberland." In the 1800s, while Bluegrass planters dominated the political realm and demanded the state's attention to their economic needs, therefore, Kentucky south of the Green quietly epitomized Jefferson's agrarian republic: thou-sands of settlers tilling their two-hundred-acre tracts and tap-ping into the cotton market—and four of five households did so without slaves. That would not last. Within ten years, slaves com-prised more than 10 percent, and in some cases as much as 30 percent, of the inhabitants in most counties south of the Green.

Among the Green River pioneers was George McWhorter, a small South Carolina planter who purchased fifty-seven acres through the 1795 land act and sent his slave, Frank, to settle the

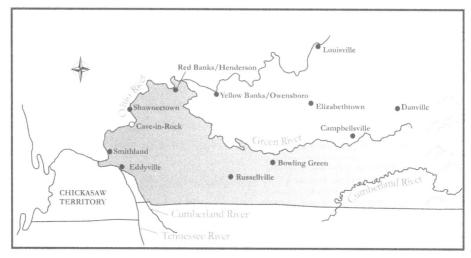

Map 7.1. The Green River Country. Drawn by Sherry Hardin.

tract to secure ownership. Four years later, Frank met Lucy, a slave on a distant plantation, whom he "married" without legal recognition and with whom he did not live for twenty years. In 1800, Frank and Lucy had the first of twelve children. Despite the challenges of settling the Green River country as a slave, the greater challenge was to sustain family and improve his quality of life. The slave code of 1798 allowed Frank to wield a gun to protect himself and his master's property from Indian attack, but it did not empower him to safeguard his own family from Indian threats or from the tenuous financial situation faced by slave-owners who could sell a child or wife at any moment. That insecurity underlay Frank's determination to eventually buy his freedom and that of his family. Having saved money from hiring out and from a saltpeter business that he established during the War of 1812, in the 1830s Frank moved his family to Illinois, where they established New Philadelphia.

Also headed for the Green River country was Matthew Lyon, a Vermont congressman and champion of Jeffersonianism. Lyon had been imprisoned under the Sedition Act and, as a congressman, had cast the deciding vote for Jefferson's election to the presidency when an electoral tie threw the election into the House of Representatives. In 1799, he encouraged some fifty fellow Vermonters—

including his daughters and their families—to relocate to western Kentucky, where they designed and populated Eddyville. The next year, Kentucky relaxed its prices, selling one-hundred-acre tracts south of the Green for as little as $20. Taking advantage of the changing terms, Lyon left Vermont in 1801, leading another settlement party of seventy Vermonters to join the original party. While hundreds of antislavery settlers fled Kentucky because of slavery, Lyon demonstrated how many newer pioneers overcame reservations about slavery. In 1803, Congressman Lyon pronounced that "the blacks who are slaves are much more useful and beneficial to the community and to the nation, according to their number, than those that are free."

Late to the migration were Thomas Jefferson's nephews, Randolph and Lilburne Lewis. By 1806, lands in the Green River country were no longer cheap, particularly when purchased through a Richmond, Virginia, land speculator. Neither brother was wealthy. Lilburne settled for paying $2.38 per acre for unimproved lands, but Randolph preferred better-quality lands and eventually paid $5.50 per acre, having to sell off slaves and Virginia properties to do so. In 1807, the brothers transported entire households down the Ohio River to Louisville (something that a decade earlier would have been prohibitive to all but the wealthiest) and then another three hundred miles past Shawneetown and Cave-in-Rock before debarking into Kentucky's most western reaches to join others in the new cotton kingdom. Five years later, Lilburne and another brother, Isham, killed a seventeen-year-old slave named George for breaking a pitcher. Assembling their other slaves in the kitchen cabin, the Lewises bound George on the floor and with an axe decapitated him as a lesson to the others. As Lilburne lectured his slaves on obedience, the brothers dismembered George and threw him in the fireplace to cremate. Shortly after two o'clock in the morning, as George's body burned, the New Madrid earthquake struck, changing the course of the Mississippi River, altering western Kentucky's landscape, and collapsing the kitchen chimney. When his slaves rebuilt the chimney, burying George inside it, they overlooked the decapitated head, which was found by a neighbor's dog and eventually the neighbor.

Only four days earlier, the state legislature had recognized that "certain citizens of this Commonwealth possessing slaves, do treat them with inhumanity and cruelty" and was considering a law forbidding beatings, abuse, and torture. Although defeated two months later, the law would have directed justices of the peace to arrest anyone suspected of such treatment and potentially would have stripped ownership of abused slaves from their masters. One of the law's supporters was attorney general John Gray, and despite the 1798 slave code that forbade slaves from testifying against whites, he determined to indict the Lewis brothers for murder as an example of the need for such a law. Unwilling to face justice, Lilburne committed suicide and Isham fled Kentucky. Even though the number of slaves south of the Green remained low compared to the number of slaves in the Bluegrass, slavery had already begun to define life in Kentucky's cotton kingdom.

In contrast, the Bluegrass had plenty of slaves but no true staple crop. Some were employed in Danville's new cotton manufactories. When he traveled Kentucky in 1799, François Michaux recognized how the Green River country and the Bluegrass were "united by commercial interests, of which cotton is the basis, and the Ohio the tie of communication." In 1789, the Kentucky Society for Promoting Manufactures had formed, importing machinery from Philadelphia and acquiring raw cotton from the Green River region to produce cloth and stockings. They set up shop in Danville: each of several stone buildings housed a carding machine, two spinning machines, and several looms.

The agricultural breakthrough in the Bluegrass was hemp. By the early 1800s, Bluegrass planters experimented with hemp production as a complementary crop to cotton. Used to make ropes, bagging, and slave clothing, hemp quickly bound the Bluegrass not only to southern Kentucky but to the lower South as well. By 1803, Bluegrass planters exported over forty thousand pounds of raw hemp fiber southward. On the eve of the War of 1812, the state supplied hemp to the entire South. Ropewalks in Fayette and Bourbon Counties accounted for over 94 percent of the nation's bagging. Both in the fields and in the manufactories, hemp

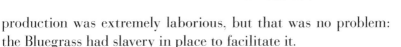

production was extremely laborious, but that was no problem: the Bluegrass had slavery in place to facilitate it.

A consequence of the development of the Bluegrass and Green River country was the opening of eastern Kentucky. The reasons to avoid Appalachia had been considerable: cheap and available lands could be had south of the Green River; even as the Shawnees disappeared from the region, Cherokees, Catawbas, Chickamaugas, and Creeks continued to move along branches of Athiamiowee; and in the late 1760s, much of the mountains had been parceled among absentee landowners, so establishing land claims was as great a challenge in Appalachia as in the Bluegrass. Since the abandonment of Harman's Station and two other settlements—the Leslie settlement and Vancouver's Fort—in 1790, few settlers had wandered into the Appalachians.

Thwarted by steep land prices in the Bluegrass and the crowds flocking to the south side of the Green River, however, some migrants decided that eastern Kentucky offered the best opportunity to secure land. John Spurlock, who led his family and slaves from southwestern Virginia in 1791, brought another seventy-five residents into the Johns Creek region by the mid-1790s. Although these early pioneers of Appalachia had no staple crop to grow and minimal market access, that Spurlock and other men imported slaves into the region demonstrated their commitment to a southern "way of life," one that bound them to the Bluegrass and Green River regions.

Spurlock settled directly along Athiamiowee and for six years had no difficulty with Indians. Instead, he was undone by John Preston, son of William Preston, who had overseen much of the early surveying of Kentucke. Preston held a land grant in eastern Kentucky, most likely inherited upon his father's death in 1783, that numbered 100,000 acres and was formally entered at the Virginia land office in 1787. But he dawdled for over a decade in having the tract surveyed. Preston himself never came to the region, satisfied to be an absentee landowner.

Preston was not alone: absentee landowners claimed nearly three-fourths of Appalachia. Several, however, had already begun to solidify their claims. Alexander Wolcott, an investor in

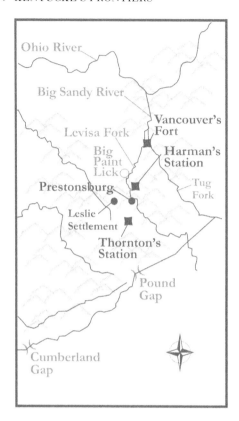

Map 7.2. Appalachian Ken-
tucky. Drawn by Sherry Hardin.

the old Louisa Land Company, acquired one of the company's
old surveys, which overlapped parts of Preston's grant. Because
the Virginia/Kentucky border was ill-defined, the boundaries of
Wolcott's 650,000-acre claim were uncertain. Hoping to secure
the lands, he gained a patent from Virginia. In the meantime,
Charles Salmons, a small farmer who had built a cabin and cleared
some land for farming, received a patent from Kentucky for a
small tract that sat on Wolcott's claim. The courts found in Salmons's favor, and a minor rush of homesteaders quickly grabbed
up what remained of Wolcott's mountain property.

Wolcott's loss was certainly a warning to Preston, who, in the
summer of 1797, hired several "old hunters" such as Matthias
Harman to survey several pieces of his grant, including the site
for Prestonsburg. His timing was perfect. In 1798, the first Treaty
of Tellico was signed with the Cherokees, securing lands in north-

eastern Tennessee. In 1804 and 1805, two more treaties of Tellico followed, negotiated by Indian commissioner Return J. Meigs
(who would play a notable role in the Cherokees' removal from
Appalachia in the 1830s). The final treaty ceded lands in the Big
Sandy valley that would form Kentucky's final four southeastern
counties. Preston's lands were secure not only from homesteaders but from Indian claims as well. Combined with the Treaty of
Greenville, the founding of Prestonsburg and the three treaties of
Tellico made Appalachian Kentucky safe for settlement, although
like Spurlock and Salmons, many settlers would see their claims
challenged in courts by absentee landowners.

While the Indian threat was greatly diminished, fear and danger
continued to shape life in Appalachia. Around 1801, three-year-
old Elijah Auxier followed his older brother Daniel into the woods
to gather firewood. At some point, the boys were separated, and
Elijah disappeared forever. Alarms went out, and men from several settlements arrived to search for Elijah. Still, to demonstrate
how distant the Indian threat had become by 1801, the prevail-
ing theory as to Elijah's disappearance was that a bear or wildcat
had attacked him and carried him away. Not even a decade had
passed since the Treaty of Greenville, and Kentuckians even in
the most remote reaches of Appalachia or on the western boundary with the Chickasaw territory seemed to have forgotten the
Indian threat that had dominated life only a generation earlier.

The growth of Kentucky's agriculture in the Bluegrass and
Green River country, as well as the opening of Appalachia, were
made possible by continued access to the Spanish port at New
Orleans. But in 1802, superintendent Don Juan Ventura Morales
closed the port. News reached Kentucky in early 1803, infuriating
farmers who found the wheat market cut off at the height of harvest. "No price has yet been talked of for wheat, and the quan-
tity at hand is immense," complained one Kentucky farmer. Outraged, Kentuckians demanded the federal government intercede,
as it had in 1796. "Most people calculate on war," one resident
wrote newly elected Senator John Breckinridge. President Jefferson sent James Monroe to visit Napoleon Bonaparte, who, rumor
had it, had forced Spain to cede all of Louisiana to France. When
Napoleon offered to sell Louisiana to the United States, Jefferson

quickly accepted the offer. The Spanish insisted the sale was illegitimate, but Jefferson determined to take Louisiana, by force if necessary.

Unlike a decade earlier, when Kentuckians found themselves shunned by the American Legion in its invasion of the Western Confederacy villages, Jefferson called upon Kentuckians and other westerners to stand ready for military duty. Four thousand westerners signed up to descend on New Orleans should the Spanish authorities refuse to leave. "Armies, Sieges, and Storms, completely engross the public mind," noted Henry Clay, "and the first interrogatory put on every occasion is Do you go to New Orleans?" Outmaneuvered by the French and Americans, however, Morales and his peers abandoned New Orleans, disappointing (or maybe sparing) Kentucky's militias. In August 1803, Lexingtonians celebrated at a grand feast where they toasted "our present administration" and "The People of Kentucky—whom no injuries nor inflammatory addresses could excite to insurrection." The *National Intelligencer*, a newspaper based in the nation's capital, applauded the "patriotism, republicanism, and steadfast adherence of our western friends to those principles and measures on which the welfare of all America depends."

As certain as he was that Louisiana must be purchased, Jefferson was less sure of the nation's destiny as a result. He wrote to Breckinridge:

> The future inhabitants of the Atlantic & Missipi States will be our sons. . . . We think we see their happiness in their union, & we wish it. Events may prove otherwise; and if they see their interest in separation, why should we take side with our Atlantic rather than our Missipi descendants? It is the elder and the younger son differing. God bless them both, & keep them in union, if it be for their good, but separate them, if it be better.

But Kentuckians were elated, finally seeing the federal government not only addressing their needs but rising above all expectations. The Kentucky Resolutions, only four years past, seemed decades away. As James Brown declared, "We who have long been from our very hearts *Western men*, who have seen our country

grow, and have grown with our country, can now view its unfore-
seen and unparalleled prosperity with pleasure and with pride."

If ever there was a time when Kentuckians would not be ame-
nable to ideas of secession, the years following the Louisiana
Purchase were it. While Kentucky had joined the union in 1792,
their contentious relationship with the Federalists had kept Kentuckians thinking of themselves as distinct "Western men." Jefferson's attention to the West, however, incorporated Kentuckians into the national dialogue, winning over their loyalty to the
Democratic-Republican Party for the next two decades. Consequently, anyone who questioned Jefferson likewise challenged
Kentucky. When Federalist Francis Flourney critiqued the president's purchase of Louisiana in Frankfort's *Guardian of Freedom*,
his effigy was tarred and burned by a mob chanting "perpetuity
to the union, confidence in the government, and the free navigation of the Mississippi."

Indifferent to Kentuckians' newfound and widespread nationalism, Aaron Burr arrived in Kentucky in May 1805, fleeing arrest for the killing of Alexander Hamilton and hoping to draw
disaffected westerners into a secessionist scheme. In the final
months of his vice presidency, Burr had convinced Jefferson to
elevate an old acquaintance, James Wilkinson, to the governorship of Upper Louisiana. Upon arriving in Kentucky, he met with
land office registrar John Adair and former senator John Brown,
and even ventured into Tennessee to call on Andrew Jackson.
Burr intended to do exactly what Wilkinson could not only a decade earlier: draw the inhabitants of the Mississippi states away
from those of the Atlantic states, and maybe even conquer parts
of Mexico to supplement the new western union.

Burr's meetings, however, became open secrets. Rumors circulated that he intended to lead Kentucky into secession, inspiring
the *Kentucky Gazette* to respond, "If he calculated on withdrawing the affections of the people of the Western States from their
Government, he will find himself deceived, if he has not already
made that discovery." In early January 1806, Jefferson received a
warning from Joseph Hamilton Daviess, the federal district attorney for Kentucky: "The plot is laid wider than you imagine.

Mention the subject to no man from the western country how-ever high in office he may be. Some of them are deeply tainted with this treason." The president suspected the warning might be a partisan trick and demanded specific names. After all, Da-viess was a Federalist, had been a close friend to Hamilton, and was related through marriage to Kentucky's most famous and outspoken Federalist family (and Jefferson's distant cousins)—the Marshalls. Daviess replied with a list of conspirators, some of whom were rumored to have intrigued with Spain a decade earlier. Among them were Wilkinson, Adair, federal judge Harry Innes, Governor William Henry Harrison of Indiana Territory, Congressman John Fowler, Henry Clay, and Senator Breckin-ridge. Unconvinced but sufficiently alarmed, Jefferson sent his own man to Louisiana to investigate.

Daviess did not wait for Jefferson and demanded that Innes re-quire Burr to appear before a grand jury. With Clay as his law-yer, Burr used charm and Daviess's inability to secure witnesses to sway the grand jury. By early December 1806, when Innes dis-missed the case, the entire episode had devolved into partisan-ship. Burr's guilt or innocence did not matter, and neither did his schism with Jefferson. Public outrage turned on Daviess's obsession with disparaging Burr's name and by association the Democratic-Republican Party. A decade before the Federalists undermined their own national viability through the Hartford Convention, Daviess brought to an end what little influence Ken-tucky Federalists wielded. He resigned as federal attorney. His close friend Humphrey Marshall became the loudest, most antag-onistic, and increasingly impotent Federalist voice in Kentucky's political arena.

In contrast, those men whom Daviess had suggested would lead Kentucky to disunion grew in popularity. Adair, despite his arrest in New Orleans as a conspirator, recovered his reputa-tion and became governor in 1820. Breckinridge became Jeffer-son's attorney general in 1806. Clay was overwhelmingly elected to serve out Adair's senatorial term, a precursor to his 1810 elec-tion to the House of Representatives as a War Hawk. Burr did go on trial for treason in federal court with Humphrey Mar-shall's uncle, Chief Justice John Marshall, sitting on the bench.

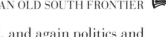

Clay again served as Burr's legal counsel, and again politics and poor prosecution set Burr free. The victory was bittersweet for Clay: writing to a Kentucky friend soon after the acquittal, he admitted, "Having left Kentucky under a belief that he was innocent, it was with no little surprise upon my arrival here that I found that I had been deceived."

Becoming Southern: Faith and Family

Burr was not the only person trying to draw converts in 1805. In January, three Shakers arrived in Kentucky to establish a new religious colony. Within a year, they convinced forty-four people to covenant in mutual support and common property ownership, and Pleasant Hill Shaker community was born. Begun on Elisha Thomas's farm, Pleasant Hill quickly swelled to three communal "families" on an estate well over four thousand acres. Converts agreed to dismantle their traditional family relationships, emotionally disconnecting from parents, children, and spouses to concentrate on new "family" relations with Shaker "brothers" and "sisters." While the Kentucky legislature had spent much of the 1790s codifying marriage, the Shakers rejected such definitions, prohibiting sex even among legally married husbands and wives and removing child-raising from parental responsibilities. According to the Shakers, it took a village to raise a child.

Not unexpectedly, the Shakers drew suspicion and animosity from other denominations. They were unwelcomed competitors in a religious marketplace already occupied by Episcopalians, Roman Catholics, Presbyterians, Methodists, and Baptists. By 1805, as well, six years of revivalism had made the latter three denominations more aggressive in their pursuit of souls. It was from the pulpits of those churches that the greatest condemnations of Shakerism echoed, and when a second Shaker community formed at South Union, the denunciations amplified. One Methodist hymn, written by Kentucky minister Samuel Hoosier, warned that "I often heard of Shakers while in my native land / That they were a deluded, a blind bewitched band."

The Shakers' form of family seemed most disconcerting to more mainstream Christians. In the 1790s, Baptist, Methodist,

and Presbyterian congregations had offered tribunals in which
women and slaves could find some justice, and they had embraced enslaved and free blacks as part of their church families.
As these churches appropriated familial models more in line with
the legislature's model of patriarchal and nuclear families, however, their tribunals became less accessible to women and slaves,
and Christians such as the Shakers who continued to cling to the
more egalitarian definition of family were condemned as threats
to social stability. "Let Shakerism predominate," warned state
legislator James Smith, "and it will extripate Christianity, destroy Marriage, and also our present free government, and finally
depopulate America."

In the early 1800s, Shakers became the religious Other, and
critics likened them to other Others. They were comparable to
Indians in their animalism: "Several times while dancing they
hallow much like Indians in their corn dances, and sometimes
you would see after done dancing a man in one end of the house
& a woman in the other turning round for at least a half hour."
Like slaves, they modeled the negation of acceptable values: "We
humbly conceive they ought to be reckoned among the foes of liberty and the constitution." Shakers provided a countercurrent to
the strengthening of patriarchy. They claimed a right to define
family in the broadest sense, supervising gendered and household
behaviors publicly. In the early 1800s, as privacy, patriarchal
authority, and the nuclear model increasingly defined southern
families, there was no room for Shakerism.

Ironically, Shakerism in Kentucky would not have been possible without the flurry of revivals that energized religion, beginning on the south side of the Green River in 1798. Among the recent wave of Green River migrants was James McGready, a North
Carolina Presbyterian who took over three struggling congregations in western Kentucky. Concerned with what he perceived as
religious indifference among his new neighbors, McGready decided to host several four-day communion services that required
participants to travel, camp, and become immersed in religious
conversation and fellowship. The communion had long been a
critical component of Presbyterian theology, but it had fallen out
of favor in trans-Appalachia because there just had not been suf-

ficient clusters of people to form religious communities. Rotating the revivals to each of the three congregations, however, generated greater numbers of participants and created a spiritual momentum from one event to the next.

At McGready's Red River communion in 1800, Kentucky revivalism began to assume a more ecumenical character. After the Presbyterian ministers preached, Methodist preacher John McGee exhorted a crowd numbering as many as a thousand people drawn from Kentucky and Tennessee. His spirited and extemporaneous sermons stirred attendees to cry, swoon, shout, and faint. As revivals continued south of the Green, the mourner's bench emerged as a new ritualistic space where revival attendees who felt moved toward conversion could solicit special prayers and focused attention. Rumors began to spread of the spiritual power of these revivals and the strange physical exercises inspired by them.

The success of communions south of the Green encouraged Presbyterians north of the Green to follow suit. In 1801, at least fifty Kentucky congregations scheduled four-day communions, including the Cane Ridge Presbyterian Meeting House, where Barton W. Stone, another pioneer who arrived in the late 1790s, hoped to revitalize the religious community. He planned for a communion at the peak of the revival season in early August, and he invited Presbyterian, Methodist, and Baptist preachers to attend. Between August 6th and 8th, approximately ten thousand people wandered the meetinghouse grounds, listening to one stump preacher and then moving on to another. Cane Ridge's proximity to Lexington, some twenty miles distant, certainly drew many spectators and itinerant merchants, but most attendees were seeking a spiritual connection.

Prior to revivalism, faith was acted out in churches where pulpits were elevated for visibility; congregations, seated in gradations of racial hierarchy, were separated by railings and balconies. At the Great Revival, those patterns shattered. As preachers pontificated from stumps, their words became background noise for the real revival experience of inner conversion. Faith was an issue of the heart, supernaturally activated within the soul, where artificial hierarchies could not be enforced. Revival preachers communicated a new worldview, one in which greater individualism and egalitarianism restored participants' hopes. Rather than uphold white paternal authority, revivalists affirmed female virtue, questioned racial slavery, contested the idea that youth should always defer to age, and prized communal fellowship over family ties. More-traditional Christians who came to Cane Ridge out of curiosity were horrified to find slaves, free blacks, women, and children occasionally exhorting as equals to the ordained preachers.

They were also appalled by the mystical experiences they witnessed. As an ecstatic state of consciousness overtook participants, they "fell down," testifying to the power of the Spirit as it overwhelmed the fragile earthly bodies of humans. Some who fell remained conscious, relating to onlookers the conversion experience under way. Others lay in a coma-like condition. God reportedly revealed himself to the fallen, triggering a conversion unmatched by other faith manifestations. "I have brought forward the falling down as a certain test of true religion," explained a visitor, "and that I have expressed no doubt respecting the real conversion of those who thus fell down."

For some participants, the fellowship and *communitas* of revivals reminded individuals of the collectivity of frontier life. Physical manifestations at Cane Ridge—falling down, rhythmic dancing, hymn singing, and shouting during sermons—appeared not that different from the rambunctious dances at taverns, quilting bees, and barn raisings; and bodily writhings and convulsions hinted of the sexual pleasures at corn huskings and log rollings. Indeed, the passion of revivalism often led to indiscreet intimacies. One preacher recorded his shock at certain women who participated in the revival: "Becca Bell—who often fell, is now big with child to a wicked trifling school master. . . . Raglin's daughter seems careless. . . . Kitty Cummings got careless. . . . Peggy Moffitt was with child to Petty and died miserably in child bed."

For others, revivalism was the birth of new theologies and rituals. Among Old Lights, communion held a central role in evidencing and reinforcing conversion. Hence, James McGready imagined the communion as a means to draw and recruit to his small churches. As the revivals progressed, however, the conversion experience became more ritually important. The traditional sacraments of communion and baptism were de-emphasized, joining group prayer, love feasts, baptisms, healing services, foot washing, new hymns and new singing styles, lay exhortation, and mourning benches among the variety of techniques to reinforce the primary ritual of conversion.

Conversion required believers to develop a heightened sense of moral uprightness, bringing public attention to new expectations on morality. In the early 1800s, church tribunals undertook greater regulation of worldly vices, partially because churches did not want their congregants' problems aired publicly. As the Six Mile Christiansburg Baptist Church instructed, "church members [should] carefully avoid going to Law with each other on any pretence whatever without liberty from the church," particularly when morality was concerned. Instead, morality would be regulated by churches. "Is it not a matter worthy of Exclusion for parents to suffer their Children (that are under their Jurisdiction) to attend Barbacues, Balls &c.," questioned the Forks of Elkhorn Baptist Church in 1807. Yes, the church concluded, "it is a duty of parents to prohibit their Children from all licentious practices as far as possible." Two years later, at Mount Tabor Baptist Church, Judith Rogers charged Benjamin Crenshaw for failing to complete payment on hogs he had purchased from her father, refusing to pay interest on a loan he had taken, and neglecting to meet her father at court to resolve the situation. Although the case was meant to address Crenshaw's economic dishonesty, one judge asked if "Sister Rogers hath been guilty of sin in the above case, saving in her suffering her passion to rise too high." The tribunal cases of the early 1800s concerned themselves with the moral worthiness of their members as much as they sought to resolve disputes.

For some revivalists, the explosion of religious enthusiasm evinced a reaction to the political disfranchisement, declining opportunities to purchase land, shifting gendered and racial patterns, and entrenchment of slavery in the 1790s. The revivals and their immediate aftermath demonstrated that not all was stable in Kentucky, even in the Bluegrass. While the 1790s had seen white men's notable efforts to order society through government and court, after the turn of the century, individuals and groups empowered by the Spirit contested the boundaries and authority of government—secular and ecclesiastical, legislative and judicial, state and local.

In some cases, they turned to county courts to use civic authority against moral turpitude, specifically profanity, which they associated with white male honor and entitlement. Evangelical discourse recognized law as the protector of moral society, and the constitution of 1799 had increased the power of county courts, making them a perfect venue through which revivalist morality could be impressed on less-than-virtuous neighbors. In the 1800s, grand juries repeatedly indicted and reproved county officials for profanity, including a Henderson County grand jury that indicted the circuit court judge. Nearly every person charged for profanity by county court grand juries was a white man. Between 1799 and 1806, Livingston County jurors indicted an average of 0.45 percent of the county's white males; in 1807 and 1808, they came close to 1 percent. Another peak in religious enthusiasm from 1811 to 1813 provoked another spike in indictments. In most cases, the juries reproved men for swearing in order to enhance their reputations, particularly when confronted with challenges to their honor. Specifically, the use of "God damn" was targeted. In Caldwell County, upon indicting one defendant, the jurors were shocked by his outburst: "I'll be Goddamned if I don't swear when I please!"

Prior to the revivals, Baptist, Methodist, and Presbyterian tribunal interventions had chastised white men for failing to meet husbandly and patriarchal responsibilities. During and after the revivals, however, attention turned to white men's moral failings as citizens of a community. Where they could control grand juries, revivalists used them to curtail the public manifestations of those moral failings—profanity. Where their influence over county courts waned, revivalists employed church tribunals to set standards of moral responsibility and neighborly interaction.

Alongside revivalists' desires to eliminate moral vices coursed a heightened sense of social inequalities. Among the crowds at Cane Ridge and elsewhere were African Americans who preached, fell down, testified, and joined in the Christian fellowship. Since

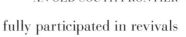

blacks, most of whom were slaves, fully participated in revivals presumably with equal opportunity for salvation, white revivalists acknowledged them as individuals.

Presbyterians and Baptists had provided the core of antislavery activism during the 1792 and 1799 constitutional conventions. Following their failure in the last convention, antislavery Baptists, Methodists, and Presbyterians turned to their churches to exact change—but they had to change their churches first. With the exception of the Shakers, there were congregants in every church in Kentucky who owned slaves. Hoping to influence their denominations, antislavery members severed ties with their churches and formed dozens of new emancipationist congregations in the early 1800s. From their pulpits, emancipationist preachers such as David Barrow attacked both the secular state and their fellow, slaveholding churchgoers.

Proslavery Christians, however, rejected the idea that slavery was sinful. They tried to moderate charges of immorality by converting and instructing slaves, converting and reforming masters, and justifying slavery through Scripture. One particular argument, based upon Paul's letter to Philemon, claimed that slaveowners should view converted slaves "no longer as a slave, but more than a slave, a beloved brother . . . both in the flesh and in the Lord."

As emancipationists grew more boisterous, denominational governing bodies began to purge churches of emancipationists, who were deemed threats to denominational security. The Elkhorn Association rebuked emancipationist Baptists in 1805, judging it "improper for ministers, churches, or associations to meddle with emancipation from slavery or any other political subject, and as such, we advise ministers and churches to have nothing to do therewith in their religious capacities." The following year, the North-District Association of Baptists expelled David Barrow from their association for "preaching the doctrine of emancipation, to the hurt and injury of the feelings of the brotherhood." Then the association sent an investigative committee to Barrow's church, unleashing proslavery Baptists' anger against their emancipationist brothers. Antislavery preachers were dismissed from churches, and some emancipationists were excommunicated for their views. Nearly a dozen churches split in 1806 and 1807 as a result. Not to be quieted, Barrow joined other anti-slavery Baptists in creating the "Baptized Licking-Locust Association, Friends of Humanity" to counteract proslavery's influence: "We are now distinguished from *our former brethren*, by reason of our professed abhorrence to unmerited, hereditary, perpetual, absolute unconditional Slavery."

Proslavery churchgoers recognized slavery's immorality, but over the early 1800s, they were dedicated to separation of political and religious spheres: "Let it not be supposed that we are now discussing the subject of slavery. To do so in our religious assemblies would be an interference with the concerns of civil government for which we have neither precept nor example." Emancipation, even for individuals committed to greater social equality, was a frightening prospect. So, in May 1806 when a member of the Forks of Elkhorn Baptist Church chose to leave the congregation, it was a sign of Kentucky's evolution into an Old South state. Winney, the slave of a white congregant, stood before the church and testified that she had "once thought it her duty to serve her Mister & Mistress but since the lord converted her, she had never believed that any Christian kept Negroes or Slaves." The church expelled her after she speculated that there were "thousands of white people Wallowing in Hell for their treatment of Negroes and she did not care if there was as many more." In less than a decade, the spiritual equality proclaimed by revivalist preachers and embraced by slaves such as Winney dissipated as a proslavery majority forced emancipationists out of pulpits and pews.

Despite the rhetoric of spiritual egalitarianism, white church members remained vigilant, especially as larger numbers of blacks joined their congregations. Around 20 percent of new members in 1801 and 1802 were black, although some churches that had welcomed blacks prior to the revivals, such as Bryan's Station Baptist Church, doubled that percentage. But African Americans received different treatment within revivalist churches, where whites expected blacks, even enslaved blacks, to uphold the same moral standards as themselves. On some level, this acknowledgment of the equal station of all before God empowered black congregants. Hence, Winney had a voice in her congregation and did not fear using it.

Winney's departure from Forks of Elkhorn highlighted what had become so very "southern" about revivalism's aftermath. Her speech before the congregation was one woman's defiant rebellion against slavery and white society—and it scared her fellow white congregants into expelling the racialized Other. There was little uniquely "southern" about the revivals until the emancipationists were chased from revivalist churches in 1806 and 1807. With the emancipationists marginalized, revivalists stepped back from the notion of social equality.

Tribunals had been used throughout the 1790s and the early years of revivalism to rein in patriarchy, its sense of honor, its celebration of profanity, its tolerance of spousal and child abuse, and the institution that ultimately empowered it—slavery. By 1805 or so, revivalist tribunals began to retract from their dedication to full social equality as men used them to rebuild patriarchy and control over slaves. For example, William Brown successfully had his slave Sarah expelled from the church for theft and lying. Another slave woman, Hannah, was dismissed for swearing and keeping another man besides her husband. Forks of Elkhorn Baptist Church excluded a slave named Robin for lying and disobeying his master. Despite Kentucky's refusal to acknowledge slave "marriages," when Condorus took a second "wife," his church chastised and expelled him. When Nancy brought charges against her master and mistress for whipping her, keeping her in chains, and denying her food and water, the church excluded Nancy for slander.

Even when white men were tried, they were increasingly found innocent. The Synod of Kentucky restored John Moore to church privilege after being suspended for "exposing to sale by public Auction a Negro boy at Nicholas Court house." John Snodgrass, accused of fathering two illegitimate children by two different women, was acquitted despite his refusal to participate in the hearing. Patriarchy had capitulated to revivalist equality long enough, as Polly Rice discovered. She led family worship in their home "with his [her husband's] consent . . . this was yielded to for awhile, and perhaps would have been more sufferable, if company did not come." The appearance of white manly control mattered.

While revivalist churches continued to celebrate a sense of spiritual "family," their intentions were significantly different from the use of such rhetoric at the revivals. At Cane Ridge, men and women, black and white, old and young, joined in a community of like-minded believers. Within five years, such inclusion had eroded dramatically. Only those who agreed that slavery was acceptable, that women should defer to men, and that youth should defer to age remained members of progressively more exclusionist churches. When the Shaker family at Pleasant Hill formed, then, it was much more than another competitor for souls. The Shakers' commitment to Christian equality, communal ownership, lay ministry, full equality of blacks, and equal status of women ran counter to Kentucky's emerging "southern" religious structure.

Becoming Southern: The Refinement of Kentucky

In 1787, "Abigail Truehart" (also known as Caleb Wallace) asked fellow Kentuckians, "Shall we not be as comfortable and lovely clothed in homespun as in foreign lace and brocade? And shall we not in this way effectually secure the independence of our families and our country?" Twenty years earlier, homespun had become a popular symbol of colonials' genuine disgust at British luxury. When anger over the Stamp Act erupted in 1765, demands for homespun spiked as Americans boycotted British cloth and clothing. Throughout the 1770s and 1780s, homespun represented a simple patriotism. The Jeffersonians relished pointing out the Federalists' fine clothing and attention to European fashions as indicative of being out of touch with regular Americans. When he became president, Jefferson (who spared little in filling Monticello with fine art and French wallpaper) purposefully underdressed in homespun as a political statement about the values and simplicity of America. His vision for America articulated the importance of domestic productions, making women's production of homespun symbolic of the progress (and appropriately modest scale) of American manufacturing.

Despite the patriotic meanings attributed to homespun, however, the reality was that Jefferson *chose* to wear it. As eighteenth-century gentlemen, he and other members of the Virginia gentry had the luxury of wearing whatever they wished, a luxury that distinguished them from the rest of society. One need only to have visited their estates to see that genteel people had finer sensibilities, or to have read their correspondence to understand that they had more delicate reactions, or viewed the portraits hanging in their homes and the clothes hanging in their wardrobes to recognize they had a more compelling taste for beauty. Gentility meant one did not *have* to wear homespun or sit on American-crafted chairs or go without tea.

The earliest gentry to arrive in Kentucky in the early to mid-1790s could not fully share in that luxury. John and Mary Breckinridge lived at Cabell's Dale, a log house with a carpeted reception hall, polished pine floors, and tinted wallpapers. David Meade and his wife lived at La Chaumière des Prairies, originally a log house but quickly expanded with an entrance hall, a formal dining room with black walnut wainscoting, and cabinets displaying Chinese porcelain and printed ceramics. Constrained by the lack of refined building materials, Meade tried to distinguish the log cabins of the "uncultivated" from log houses in which "many opulent and some Genteel people [live] . . . & I am told that they are by the latter made more than barely comfortable."

Determined to demonstrate gentility, the gentry demanded local merchants import what was needed to make a statement. Ornamental gardens, glass for windows, brass knobs and locks, more refined cloth and clothing, tea and coffees: luxuries defined gentility. So too did brick. Although Levi Todd had the first two-story, Tidewater-style brick mansion in Kentucky, not until he expanded it in 1794 did the house announce the presence of Virginia planter culture. In the Bluegrass, a flurry of brick construction followed, particularly around Lexington and Louisville. David Meade's house exemplified the gentrification of the material landscape, moving from log to frame to brick as the 1790s progressed. Gentility—a most "southern" brand of it—arrived in Kentucke with a flourish in the 1790s.

Stamping a genteel architectural imprint on the landscape was necessary as the gentry observed around them the persisting markers of pioneer culture. There were neighborhoods of rustic log houses, crude frame shanties, and hundreds of log cabins in varying stages of deterioration that evidenced how the lower sorts were not simply poorer or less well educated, but stood lower on the scale of civilization. Planters acquired an expansive array of consumer amenities by 1803. Imported consumer goods created distinctions in dress and equipage that mocked the rhetoric of egalitarianism and democracy that so frustrated and disappointed many people of wealth. "This *equality*, my Love, is a mighty *pretty* thing upon *paper*," the recently arrived Margaretta Brown wrote her husband John, but "where none are *beaux*, 'tis vain to be a Belle."

By the turn of the nineteenth century, a growing availability of refined goods foretold the beau society that Brown desired, transforming the material lives of middling sorts who realized that they could aspire to greater respectability by acquiring more genteel goods. A "consumer frontier" emerged in Kentucky, incorporating westerners into a market revolution well under way in the East. By the early 1790s, enough artisans had moved into Lexington, Maysville, and Louisville to supply crafted tea services to such aspirants to refinement. "God must be prospering you if you can have a Silver Teapott & Shugar Dish," a relative wrote Thomas Davis; "I did not think Lexington was big enough to have a silversmith." Like Mary Walker Holloway, who carried a Chinese punchbowl from Virginia to her new Kentucke home, thousands of people with little cash on hand brought one or two pieces of china, teacups, and silver spoons westward to evidence their modicum of gentility and serve as a foundation upon which their refinement would eventually be demonstrated. In 1806, Priscilla Heale Calmes's gentility manifested through her fine clothing, samples from her tea service, and the portrait in which she displayed both. The desire was there; only the availability had been lacking.

As refined goods became more accessible in the late 1790s and early 1800s, then, the demand was already high, and Kentuckians spent money as if "dollars at any time might be gathered

Figure 7.1. Priscilla Heale Calmes and her husband, Marquis Calmes, settled in the southern Bluegrass in 1782. Twenty-four years later, Priscilla posed for an itinerant limner, Jacob Frymire, with her tea cup and saucer—symbols, along with her dress and the portrait itself, of her acquired gentility. Courtesy of the Chicago History Museum.

from the tops of their Hickorys and Buck-eyes, and their only anxiety seemed to be, but what means to get rid of them fast enough." A sophisticated pattern of consumption arose, driven by the tastes of the gentry. By 1802, François Michaux estimated that "seven-tenths of the manufactured articles in Kentucky . . . are imported from England," among which were jewelry, cutlery, drapery, fine earthenware, muslins, teas, and coffee. Merchant importers benefited from the crazed spending, and their own ownership of refined material goods expanded significantly. One editorialist noted how "the merchant's *dwelling*, his *equipage*, his *apparent amount of his stock in trade*, the *improvements* that surround him, and his *domestic conveniences* bear the aspect of a flourishing opulence."

As the nineteenth century proceeded, many Kentuckians would denounce gentility as effeminizing, turning once proud men into dandies. But early in the century, refinement itself was a masculating process. Homespun and other domestic productions empowered and evidenced women's economic significance. As male artisans produced refined goods and male merchants imported them, however, women found the social as well as economic value of their productions diminished. Additionally, as we have seen,

laws in the late 1790s limited women's legal and economic opportunities. Women watched their economic roles evolve from contributing producers in local economies to primarily consumers.
But even that role was framed by male consumer power. By 1810,
femes sole such as Rebecca Green saw prospects to purchase on
book credit in stores in Lexington and Maysville reduced nearly
50 percent from fifteen years earlier. Over the same period, merchants extended greater credit opportunities to *femes covert*, primarily because their husbands' capital backed the purchases.

Although some *femes sole* such as Green sustained crafts shops,
the economic boom was a white man's world as investment capital became critical to economic success. By 1809, Henry Clay and
other investors had given rise to fifteen cotton manufactories,
thirteen bagging manufactories, thirty-eight ropewalks, thirty-
three fulling mills, eleven naileries, nine flaxseed oil mills, six
paper mills, sixty-three gunpowder mills, and thirty-six saltworks.
By the War of 1812, Charles Wilkins's Mammoth Cave saltpeter
business became the main supplier for the Du Pont Gunpowder Manufactory in Wilmington, Delaware, joining other Kentucky saltpeter industries in providing three-fourths of the ni-
trate needed for gunpowder during the war. Alongside these
new industries were hundreds of artisans—including cabinet-
makers, silversmiths, whitesmiths, carriage makers, tailors, and
watchmakers—who migrated into Kentucky in the early 1800s to
tap into the demand for refinement and the availability of money.
The most successful assumed master craftsman roles, taking on
apprentices through contracts allotted by the county courts. In
1805 and 1806, for example, Fayette County Court approved ap-
prenticeships for a printer, weaver, chairmaker, locksmith, stone-
cutter, tanner, bricklayer, saw miller, cartwright, fuller, silversmith, and several inn and tavern keepers. Hence, the county
courts promoted not only the production of refinement but the
vitality of village and town economies.

Kentucky's towns and villages thrived in the early 1800s. By
the War of 1812, a village West was fully formed. In the 1810 census, enumerators in Kentucky, Georgia, and Indiana identified
citizens by place, and although the percentage of Kentuckians
living in towns and villages was much smaller than in Georgia

and Indiana, fifty-three hamlets, towns, and villages dotted Kentucky's landscape, compared to Georgia's twenty-seven and Indiana's four. The Deep South and the Old Northwest frontiers were both overwhelmingly rural, generating large expanses of lightly populated countryside and occasional centralized populations, just as Kentucke had been. In comparison, Kentucky was composed of moderately populated towns and villages offering commercial services to a moderately populated countryside.

While hamlets and villages offered social and economic rendezvous, larger and more complex places provided the sources of refinement. Louisville assumed its place as one of the state's leading towns in the early 1800s, establishing the *Louisville Gazette* in 1807, its first theater in 1808, and its first dedicated church in 1809. In 1800, the town had 359 residents; ten years later, with a 400 percent growth rate, Louisville had become the fastest-growing town in Kentucky. Frankfort experienced comparable growth. Not even considered a village in 1790, the state capital had become the second-largest town behind Lexington by 1800 and continued to boom after the turn of the century. Danville and Washington not only housed significant populations but served as regional centers as well: Washington was the primary town along the old buffalo trace connecting Lexington to the Ohio River, and Danville was the most important town in the southern Bluegrass.

By 1810, Lexington had earned the title "city" as census officials defined it. With most of its 4,279 residents concentrated in the original in-lots, population density had reached over 6,000 persons per square mile. It continued to resemble other Kentucky towns, maintaining strong rural ties by providing market outlets for the productions of its hinterlands and serving as a distribution center. Lexington also rapidly developed the unique qualities of early national urbanism: an expanding and dense population, a large artisan sector, increasing numbers of free blacks, and the segregation of neighborhoods by economic status. As early as 1796, and with good reason, the town had been crowned "the Philadelphia of Kentucky."

What set Lexington and the other larger towns apart was that merchants, along with artisans and manufacturers, served as the lynchpins connecting the countryside with the larger national and international economy. They traded Kentucky's domestic manufactures for goods in New York, Philadelphia, Annapolis, and Alexandria, then wholesaled the goods for country productions to the stores of the surrounding villages and hamlets. They also developed the financial networks to sustain their trade. The Kentucky Insurance Company was chartered in 1803 as an insurer of river exports. Two years later, the Bank of Kentucky opened branches in Lexington and Louisville, enhancing merchants' access to capital. By 1811, merchants such as George and Samuel Trotter created extensive western commercial networks centered in Lexington. The brothers had stores in towns such as Danville and Louisville and villages such as Maysville, Springfield, and Russellville—all of which they placed under the management of associates. They also sponsored stores in Ohio, Indiana, Tennessee, and the Missouri Territory. In return for cash, cotton, or hemp, the Trotters sent linens, queens ware, books, paper, and other finished goods (some produced by Lexington artisans) to their satellite stores for sale. Cash was sent to eastern suppliers for more imported goods. Cotton was sold to factories in Lexington, Maysville, and Cincinnati. Hemp, after being converted to hemp yarn, was delivered to their New Orleans exporting firm as payment for shipping. Merchants such as the Trotters provided the connection between agriculture, domestic productions, industrial manufactories, artisans' goods, and refined imports.

Merchants penetrated every part of Kentucky, although their stock-in-trade varied. Established entrepreneurs such as the Trotters offered goods of significant retail value. Aspiring merchants, such as the young John James Audubon who arrived in Red Banks in 1811 with seven slaves and stock goods for a store, had invested far less. Having failed to establish a store in Louisville where the competition was fierce, Audubon celebrated his good fortunes a year later: "in less than twelve months I had again risen in the world." Whether in the emerging city of Lexington or the far western village of Red Banks, merchants drove Kentucky's expanding economy and refinement.

Not surprisingly, then, few merchants spoke out against slavery, for the institution not only underlay Kentucky's growing hemp

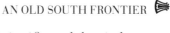

and cotton agriculture but also provided significant labor in bagging manufactories, ropewalks, artisan shops, and mercantile stores. Prices for slaves were highest in the towns and villages, where investors paid between $350 and $450 for a female slave and between $400 and $700 for a male. With slave prices in mind, Humphrey Marshall cautioned that

> the strap, gentlemen, you are probably aware, is an instrument of refined modern torture, ordinarily used in whipping slaves. By the old system, the cow-hide—a severe punishment—cut and lacerated them so badly as to almost spoil their sale when brought to the lower markets. But this strap, I am told, is a vast improvement in the art of whipping negroes; and, it is said, that one of them may be punished by it within one inch of his life, and yet he will come out with no visible injury, and his skin will be as smooth and polished as a peeled onion!

Slavery, like all other aspects of Kentucky culture, also needed to be more refined, at least in presentation.

The Last Indian War

Coming of age in the 1790s and early 1800s, the first generation of white Americans—thousands of whom had joined the great migration into Kentucky—had been molded to patriotic service. They had followed their parents in mourning processions upon George Washington's death, they had been taught the mythic grandeur of the Founding Fathers, and they had come to know Kentucky as the vanguard of the nation's western destiny.

Kentuckians, however, had also learned that they were not quite as "American" as citizens of the eastern states who had actually fought the Revolutionary War. Over the previous two decades, eastern newspapers and politicians had dismissed the Battle of Blue Licks and other struggles between American settlers and Native Americans as a prolonged "Indian War," distinct and separate from the American Revolution. Even some older Kentuckians such as Charles Scott, who had not only fought the northwestern Indians but served under Washington in the Revolutionary War, laid claim to a revolutionary legacy that younger generations of Kentuckians could not. Whenever the older generation sought a political advantage, they turned to the Revolutionary moment to promote their position, as when Scott responded to opponents of war veterans' pensions: "These men who were dirtying their little clothes when I was fighting for my country ought to have more grace, than to spit lies in my face, because I have purchased the privilege of their doing so."

The War of 1812 offered an opportunity for Kentuckians young and old to participate in an event comparable to the Revolutionary moment. Upon Congress's declaration of war against Great Britain, Kentuckians seemed perfectly mad with unrestrained nationalism. Nearly 3,800 enlisted as United States Regulars, and another 21,900 joined volunteer units that fought in specific campaigns. Beyond the fighting, however, Kentuckians were determined to get full credit for their participation in this war. When the state legislature resolved in 1809 that members should wear only homespun (with Humphrey Marshall loudly dissenting), observers applauded the appropriation of Revolutionary imagery to bind their patriotism to that of the Founding Fathers: "It gave us pleasure on this occasion to observe a considerable number of our citizens clad in domestic manufactures." Determined to engage the crisis as fully appreciated Americans, Kentuckians repelled suggestions that the western theater would again be less important, less a conflict against Britain than against Native Americans. In late 1811, the *Kentucky Reporter* complained against an eastern newspaper's dismissal of Kentuckians' role in the conflict: "You may as well call the revolutionary war, a Hession war because the Hessions were hired by the British, as to term this an Indian war."

In reality, however, Kentuckians were still fighting an Indian war. While bellicose language spewed from Congress against British interference with American trade, the rhetoric in Kentucky focused on the Indians and only indirectly upon their British backers. Even though northwestern Indians no longer occupied the lands on the northern banks of the Ohio River from whence they could launch attacks, Kentucky was recast as a threatened "frontier." The *Kentucky Gazette* warned that "the hour is at hand; we are not yet prepared to kiss the hand that wields the tomahawk and scalping knife against the heads of our old men, our women and infants." When Samuel Hopkins urged the state legislature in 1811 to acquire some 2,500 acres that the Chickasaws claimed in the most remote western part of Kentucky, he chose to cast the Indians as a continuing threat, even though his own language indicated that the threat fell far short of Kentucke's terror and death: "The Indians have not, for a very long time past, used the land within this boundary, for any of the purposes of cultivation or hunting; and only retain their title to apologize for the many vexatious insults, and marauding incursions with which they are in the constant habit of alarming and injuring our citizens on the frontiers."

In many ways, then, Kentuckians framed this new war as the last Indian war, a conclusion to the Indian-inspired terror they and their parents had faced for three decades. Employing the language of the Revolutionary generation to frame their desires for war, the state legislature declared Great Britain guilty of "inciting the savages to murder the inhabitants of our defenseless frontiers; furnishing them with arms and ammunition lately, to attack our forces." Reminiscent of Jefferson's condemnation in the Declaration of Independence that the King "hath endeavoured to bring on the inhabitants of our frontier, the merciless Indian Savages," the language bound Kentucky to the Revolutionary moment. Periodically after the Treaty of Greenville, newspapers and orators reminded audiences of Britain's role in the Indian atrocities of the 1780s and 1790s, and of their friends and families who had died under the tomahawk.

And just as during the Revolutionary War, Kentuckians drew upon the imagery of a dual threat of Indian attacks and slave revolts that had been previously successful in reinforcing the racial constructions of war. While no one directly argued that African Americans were again involved with the Indian and British enemies, simultaneous with the run-up to war was heightened suspicion of black activities. "The eternal dread that is on the mind, of their mutinizing, or joining an invading foe. . . . The Africans . . . are always ready to join our enemies. . . . The Africans that are among us do not make our interest theirs." Years of slave rebellion rumors seemed verified by November 1810 when Lexington's slave patrol arrested thirty blacks suspected in an insurrection conspiracy extending from Maysville on the Ohio River to Henderson in far western Kentucky. In early 1811, the state legislature passed a conspiracy law that made such actions capital offenses, and over the next fourteen months, suspicious fires in Lexington, Louisville, and Frankfort resulted in three public executions. One hanging was admittedly meant as "a Lesson for Negroes for setting fire to, and burning, the rope walk of Mr. WELCH."

The great irony was that many Kentucky volunteers and most Kentuckians had never experienced slave uprisings or Indian attacks, or even seen an Indian. The closest they had come to witnessing an Indian scalping was the frontispiece of Humphrey Marshall's newly published *History of Kentucky* (1812), which depicted an Indian scalping a white settler as his friends ran away. While many older Indian fighters remained in Kentucky, the bombastic rhetoric of war overwhelmingly came from men who had only imagined the terror of racial war on a defenseless frontier. But Kentucky was neither defenseless nor a frontier, at least not in the sense it had been as Kentucke. Refinement, a proliferation of towns, staple agriculture and emerging industries, revivalist religion, and the federal government's diplomatic maneuverings that had pushed native peoples farther westward had all transformed what had been a western frontier into a region comfortable as both southern and American. Without a real immediate threat to their lives and those of their families, Kentucky's fighting men might have used the rhetoric of an earlier generation, but they were fighting for very different reasons. As a meeting of Millersburg men put it, "We must prove to the Union at large that we have the Good will, the courage & the power to defend our rights, our property our families our Country."

Manhood—that was the cause of Kentuckians' enthusiasm for war. A second war with Britain and a concluding war with the northwestern Indians would bring glory and recognition to Kentucky's white men, capping off the shift to patriarchy that had been under way for the previous two decades. Surrounded by effeminate revivalism and softening commercialism, many hoped that the conflict would revitalize white masculinity and restore moral virtue. The *Kentucky Reporter* described the war's objec-

Figure 7.2. The only illustration in Humphrey Marshall's *History of Kentucky* (1812) was the frontispiece, an image of white men attacked in the wilderness by a party of Indians. One white settler has been captured and is being scalped as his companions flee. From Humphrey Marshall, *The History of Kentucky* (1812; reprint, Frankfort, Ky.: George S. Robinson, 1824), frontispiece.

tives as "something ten thousand times more valuable" than importation rights and diplomatic honor: "The *lives of the women and children on the frontier* are at stake, and the settlement of the western territories is deeply involved." The same motives that had inspired westerners' participation in the Revolutionary War were revived to justify Kentuckians' involvement in a new war. At a moment when traditional means of demonstrating manhood—as warriors and as hunters—became less available in Kentucky, the war provided an alternative way. Richard Mentor Johnson, a Kentucky congressman, related to President Madison how Kentuckians "are a spirited people and nothing can satisfy them but some military enterprise to engage at least a part of our men." The war offered an arena in which manhood could be demonstrated and celebrated. Thomas Bedford, a volunteer from Bourbon County, probably put it more bluntly and honestly: "hearing of the girls getting married so much, I must confess disturbs me a great deal, however, I expect there will be some left for me yet."

Itchy to engage the enemy, Kentuckians and other westerners joined William Henry Harrison's military excursion in the first battle of the new conflict months before Congress officially declared war. The Shawnees and other northwestern Indians living in the Wabash River valley had formed an Indian confederation under the leadership of the Shawnee brothers Tenskwatawa (the Prophet) and Tecumseh. Having recently concluded with other Native Americans a land cession treaty that the confederation refused to acknowledge, Harrison was determined to make the Shawnees yield. In early November 1811, as Harrison's men encamped near Tippecanoe Creek, Tenskwatawa's followers attacked. Although Harrison declared victory, over 180 Americans died, including many Kentuckians, including Joseph Hamilton Daviess, Aaron Burr's prosecutor. In Frankfort, the state legislature claimed for the deceased "a country's gratitude that compensates the soldier for his scars, perpetuates grateful recollections of his services, and induces the living to emulate the heroic deeds of the dead—that it is a country's gratitude that softens the rugged pangs of those left to mourn husbands, fathers and friends lost in avenging a country's wrongs."

As men died on the battlefields, the war provided an opportunity to reinforce the "proper" roles for women. "Let the spinning wheel, the loom, knitting needles all be busily plied with your fair hands," proclaimed the *Kentucky Gazette.* "Warm linsey clothes, socks, blankets, linen shirts, added to shoes, to be furnished by your fathers and brethren, will enable our brave militia who have marched to think only of the enemy, of revenge and of victory." Speeches and editorials called on women to support their men by producing clothing and maintaining the home front. In Washington, at the Fourth of July festivities of 1813, participants toasted *"The Kentucky fair—They clothed our Republican army. Their patriotism ought to put to shame the non-combatant states."* Once a means to economic empowerment, women's domestic productions were redefined as military support. There were no unruly women in wartime Kentucky: "The American Fair," proclaimed a celebrant a year later in Lexington, "Patriotism with them is inherent—they despise the tory, coward and traitor." Far from the arena of war, Kentucky's women need no longer brandish the axe or wield the rifle. They could serve the appropriate role for women in wartime, supporting the soldiers and reinforcing their bravery and masculinity: "Rouse, fair patriots, it is with you to mitigate their sufferings."

Even as Kentucky's home front celebrated its soldiers and their families, however, the enthusiasm for war began to wane. By January 1813, thousands of volunteers marching upon Canada were poorly clothed and fed. They had not fought any Indians or British, and their enlistments were about to run out. Harrison faced the possibility of losing nearly four thousand tired and frustrated Kentucky troops. Hearing of an army of some four hundred Canadian and Indian troops at Frenchtown, the Kentuckians essentially forced their commanding officer—James Winchester—to let them attack. They chased the enemy from the village and took control of Frenchtown, earning Harrison's praise.

Four days later, two thousand British and Indian troops arrived outside Frenchtown to take it back. While the Kentuckians in the garrison successfully withstood the assault, other detachments were quickly killed or captured, including Winchester. The British negotiated with the garrisoned troops, promising protection from Indian massacre if they would surrender. As the captured marched to nearby Fort Malden, about eighty wounded remained behind at Frenchtown. The following morning, nearly two hundred Indians attacked the injured, scalping and killing most and taking a handful into captivity.

In Kentucky, the response was one of determined revenge. Calls went out for more volunteers. Militia leaders found little difficulty in raising new regiments, including Richard Mentor Johnson's mounted volunteers. The state legislature issued a call for service:

> The spirit of your fathers aroused you from the slumber of indolence to undertake the turmoils and surmount the labor and hardships of camps, to shew our ancient enemy that you knew how to value and maintain the independence we held as the gift of Heaven only, to wipe off the foul stain which had been cast upon the American name by the base surrender of one of our armies—to avenge the shades of slaughtered brethren, of helpless women and infants.

Even Governor Isaac Shelby, aged sixty-six and veteran of both the Revolutionary War and the Indian war of the 1780s, volunteered and led four thousand troops northward.

In September 1813, Harrison led a larger and very determined army of some 6,500 men, most from Kentucky. They crossed Lake Erie into Canada as the British retreated, despite Tecumseh's insistence that the British engage the Americans. Finally, at the Thames River, the British and Indians decided to hold ground. Johnson's mounted volunteers crashed through the Indian contingent and British lines, nearly capturing the British general. Demoralized, the British surrendered. Their Indian allies scattered.

The Battle of the Thames was decisive and significant. Ten days later, the Kentuckians were mustered out and en route home, leaving only two brigades of United States regulars to hold the region. Most important, however, was that Tecumseh died in the fighting, and with him died the Indian confederation. Although the war would continue in other theaters for another sixteen months, Kentuckians had proven their mettle, and the majority returned as heroes to their farms, artisan shops, and families.

No longer the frontier, Kentucky fully arrived as an American state in the War of 1812. In early January 1815, American forces under Andrew Jackson defended the port city of New Orleans from British invasion, unaware that the Treaty of Ghent had been signed a month earlier. Officially, Jackson's report to the secretary of war criticized one Kentucky regiment that he claimed gave way to the British. His account touched off years of anger, mostly within Kentucky, over Jackson's disparagement of the state's honor. Yet, despite the report, Kentuckians became national symbols of patriotism, masculinity, and the war effort, championed by "The Hunters of Kentucky; or, Half Horse and Half Alligator," a popular song written circa 1820 by Samuel Woodworth.

> We are a hardy free-born race,
> Each man to fear a stranger;
> Whate'er the game, we join in chase,
> Despising toil and danger;
> And if a daring foe annoys,
> Whate'er his strength and forces,
> We'll show him that Kentucky boys
> Are alligator-horses . . .

[Chorus] Oh, Kentucky, the Hunters of Kentucky,
Oh, Kentucky, the Hunters of Kentucky.

. . . But Jackson, he was wide awake,
And wasn't scared at trifles;
He knew what deadly aim we take
With our Kentucky rifles.
He led us down to Cypress Swamp,
The ground was low and mucky;
There stood John Bull in martial pomp,
But here stood Old Kentucky.

Kentuckians had demonstrated to the nation their patriotism and military valor. "You have done your duty," lauded the *Kentucky Gazette*, "and future generations will say, *you were worthy of your sires, and the sacred legacy which they bequeathed.*"

The men who had led Kentucky into war found their political futures bright. Henry Clay became one the greatest orators of his generation, the Great Compromiser, a founder of the Whig Party, and a leading advocate for modernizing the American economy. Isaac Shelby received the Congressional Medal of Honor for his service. Despite encouragements to run for national office, he completed his term as governor and retired. Richard Mentor Johnson returned to his plantation west of Georgetown and to Julia Chinn, a light-skinned slave whom he could not legally marry and with whom he would have two daughters. He continued to serve Kentucky as a congressman and senator until 1836, when he ran for the vice presidency, only to face ridicule for his interracial "marriage," although his wife had died three years earlier. But as Daniel Boone had done a half-century earlier, Johnson countered his association with one racial Other by claiming to have killed another racial Other. It was impossible to discern who actually ended Tecumseh's life, but Johnson, his supporters, and early historians quickly attributed it to the mounted volunteer, restoring a semblance of whiteness to one whose racial loyalties had been questioned for decades. As the campaign ditty championed, "rumpsey-dumpsey, rumpsey-dumpsey, Colonel Johnson killed Tecumseh."

8.

REMEMBERING

In mid-October 1824, a Choctaw delegation en route to Washington, D.C., stopped in Maysville to dine at Langhorne's Inn. Among them was an eighty-year-old chief, Puckshunubbe, a veteran of the Indian resistance against American settlement between the 1760s and 1790s. As he leaned forward to look down the Ohio River, the old man stumbled and fell off a twenty-foot abutment. He died two days later.

Residents of Maysville and other Kentuckians gathered by the hundreds to memorialize Puckshunubbe. The ceremony and funeral were, as a 1930s historian depicted, "military to the nth degree . . . [and] the largest concourse ever assembled in the little Kentucky town. Came from all parts of Kentucky those who had warred against him, to pay a just tribute to his great military powers." Then, in an understandable moment of exasperation, the historian concluded, "Pioneers!" Nearly three decades of war against Indians in the late eighteenth century had ushered terror into the homes of Kentucke's settlers, but here in the streets of Maysville were their children and grandchildren celebrating the enemy, praising his martial acumen, and interring him with full military honors in the town graveyard alongside men who had lost their lives trying to exterminate him and his people. How they could so easily forgive and forget gave rise to the historian's frustration.

The following year, a more joyous festivity for the Marquis de Lafayette eclipsed the pomp of Puckshunubbe's memorial. A large assembly crowded to watch the Revolutionary icon step ashore in Maysville and traverse a path of expensive Turkish carpets to a ceremonial feast hosted by the town's most prominent merchant, John Armstrong. Afterward, Lafayette inspected the local militia before being escorted back to his steamboat. Kentuckians watched and waved from the wharf as the boat labored up the Ohio River. The Frenchman's western tour through Maysville and other Kentucky towns inspired new fashion among the younger generation: "Evry thing was *Lafayette*," murmured a laborer with little appreciation for refined dress; "All the new Fashions were *Lafayette*. It Ran to such Extrems that you Could not By a Hat nor anny thing out of A Store But it was *Lafayette*."

Curiosity may have drawn Kentuckians into the crowded little river town to reach out and touch Lafayette's coat or Puckshunubbe's casket, but the eloquence of public speakers and the opportunities to reminisce contributed to a broader sense of historical significance for their lives. Collective memory is constructed in moments like these, when populations pause to reflect on their shared past and its meaning for their individual and communal lives. Yet, collective memory also evolves with each successive generation. Children and grandchildren do not attach the same meaning and worth to symbolic representations as did those who witnessed actual events. For example, older Kentuckians viewed Lafayette as a Revolutionary hero who had helped to secure American life, liberty, and pursuit of happiness. A younger generation of Kentuckians, while acknowledging him as a participant in the birth of an American nation, reinterpreted him as a symbol of refined European gentility, justifying their own rampant commercialism and rush to respectability in the process. Only Maysville's wealthiest and most powerful citizens attended the banquet with Lafayette. The teleological meaning of the Kentucke frontiers and their revolutionary context had been appropriated by the middle class.

Likewise, Puckshunubbe had been transformed from a warrior who terrorized western settlers into a symbol of the Vanishing Indian. In 1819, Henry Clay summed up the conventional wisdom:

> We are powerful and they are weak: . . . to use a figure drawn from their own sublime eloquence, the poor children of the forest have been driven by the great wave which has flowed from the Atlantic ocean to almost the base of the Rocky Mountains, and, overwhelming them in its terrible progress, has left no other remains of hundreds of tribes, now extinct, than those which indicate the remote existence of their former companion, the mammoth of the New World!

Like the great mammoths of Big Bone Lick whose remains had once drawn American imaginations westward, native peoples faced extinction, if not physically at least culturally. As Thomas Jefferson asserted in 1824, "barbarism has . . . been receding before the steady step of amelioration; and will in time, I trust, disappear from the earth."

Few Kentuckians in the 1820s appreciated the irony in celebrating Indians who had sought to kill their parents and grandparents, or in commercializing the image of the Revolutionaries who had sacrificed their lives, their fortunes, and their sacred honor. They venerated their elders, but the trials of frontier settlement had become lore. Still, both elder and younger participated in the larger event under way in the post–War of 1812 era—the construction of a frontier mythology that celebrated the struggle, initiative, and success of white Americans in displacing Indians and conquering the hunting grounds of Kentucke. Residents old and young gawked at Puckshunubbe and Lafayette and recalled their exploits, transforming victims of historical circumstance into the villains and heroes of bedtime stories. "Lie still and go to sleep, or the Shawnees will catch you": now, in 1824, Puckshunubbe was dead, and Kentucky's children could sleep soundly at night.

The Vanished Indian

After the War of 1812, when Native Americans such as Puckshunubbe re-entered the Kentucky story, they had been replaced as the dark Other against which white Kentuckians measured self-identity. Instead, the savage warrior had devolved into the Vanishing Indian, a nostalgic image of Indians as harmless shells of their former selves, impotent to ever again be the antagonists. Even before the war, Matthew Lyon wrote from western Kentucky about the inability of the Chickasaws to employ terror against settlers moving onto the lands framed by the Tennessee, Ohio, and Mississippi Rivers: "This land comes within 7 miles of my door and is a part of it within this Country. It is with difficulty the people can be persuaded to keep off from it. Fear of the Indians by no means restrains them, and for my own part I do not think fear of any kind can restrain them long." The Indians had lost their ability to terrify.

Western leaders such as former Kentucky governor Isaac Shelby and Tennessean Andrew Jackson furthered the fiction by revising the historical narrative of Indian-white relations. To "perpetuate that peace and harmony which has long happily subsisted between the United States and Chickasaw nation" was their stated purpose in September 1816, when Jackson led negotiators in procuring the Chickasaw lands that Lyons's neighbors coveted. The longstanding animosities that had led to the construction of Fort Jefferson and inspired Chickasaw attacks against Clarksville, Red Banks, and other western Kentucke settlements were seemingly forgotten. In their place, the Americans imagined a "peace and harmony" that allowed Chinnubbe and other accommodationist chiefs to preserve their lands in northeastern Mississippi by ceding to Jackson and Shelby two thousand acres that became the last part of Kentucky, the lands where Fort Jefferson had once stood, henceforth to be known as the "Jackson Purchase."

Not that white Kentuckians had waited for the Chickasaws or the American negotiators. Claiming that his fellow westerners were entitled by their "valour and patriotism," state senator Samuel Hopkins had declared half a decade earlier that hundreds of "deserving citizens hold titles to the greater part of the soil [in the future Jackson Purchase], as the reward of their revolutionary labors." Throughout Kentucky's history, however, land titles had proven unreliable, and so too with the Jackson Purchase. Anticipating a land rush with Jackson and Shelby's official acquisition, the state legislature proclaimed all previous warrants and surveys null and void and appropriated the grid system of the Old Northwest to structure an orderly distribution of the lands.

Determined to protect his claims, Thomas Randolph argued to Governor Gabriel Slaughter that the state's decision to nullify land claims was based on a faulty belief that the territory had been off limits. Back in 1785, Virginia governor Patrick Henry had forbade surveying and land claims in the region as a "necessary measure of precaution to save the lives of the many Citizens engaged therein whom the state was then unable to defend against the irritated Savages." But, Randolph continued, Henry had not wished to inhibit surveys and claims per se. Disputing that the Chickasaws had ever legitimately owned the lands, Randolph argued that, at the Treaty of Lancaster in 1744, "Virginia acquired the right to the soil as fully as it had ever been possessed by that [Iroquois] Confederacy." Suspecting that he might be challenged on whether the Iroquois had original right to cede those lands, Randolph devised a convoluted argument that included Iroquoian diplomacy, linguistic comparisons of Nottaway and Tuscarora languages, and Chickasaw aggressions, concluding that "it would very probably be found that a tribe of the six nations [at] some [time] have been dispossessed by the Chickasaws; and *then* a very short chain would form the connexion between the aboriginal title to the soil in question; and that of the persons whom Kentucky threatens now to dispossess." From Jackson and Shelby's revision of Chickasaw-American relations to Randolph's fantastic narrative of Native American land possession, whites took great liberties in remaking history. But who was to dispute them? No Indians remained to challenge the narrative: such was the essence of the Vanishing Indian.

The ideal of the Vanishing Indian was becoming popular just as English tourist Thomas Ashe visited Kentucky in 1806. Lexington, he described, "stands nearly on the site of an old Indian town, which must have been of great extent and magnificence." The story related to him was that in the 1780s, early settlers had come upon a cave entrance that, once entered, opened up into catacombs where they found "nitches and compartments . . . occupied by figures representing men!" The Indian mummies, "preserved by the art of embalming to great preservation and perfection of state," were as unfortunate as their living progeny, however. "Filled with terror and a spirit of revenge" against the Indians they were fighting, settlers "dragged the mummies to the day, tore the bandages open, kicked the bodies into dust, and made a general bonfire of the most ancient remains antiquity could boast." Eager to find some evidence for the story, Ashe was told only that "they burned up and destroyed hundreds" and that "they were well lapped up, appeared sound and *red*, and consumed in the fire with a rapidity that baffled all observation and description." Kentuckians' narrative of discovery and destruction of dead Indians was probably more apocryphal than it was historical. By 1806, the Indian menace was over a decade removed, and although it would be resurrected in the jingoistic rhetoric of the War of 1812, the Indian threat had become more symbolic than literal. Had not three decades of war eliminated the Indians who stood in the way of "civilization"?

Even when living Indians interacted with white Kentuckians, they were treated as if they no longer mattered. In 1807, residents of Russellville were visited by a small group of Lenni Lenapes and Shawnees wanting to harvest salt from the local salt licks, now a private business. Among the visitors was Kekewepellethe, who at the treaty conference at Fort Finney in 1786 had rejected American overtures for land concessions by throwing a string of black wampum at Richard Butler. Twenty years later, he faced down a group of whites barring him from access to the salt licks, and when a quarrel erupted, he threatened to organize a party of "Shawnees, Delawares, Mingoes, Peankeshaws, Muscogas, Kickapoos; and the White River tribe" to "kill all the white people, and give the Indians all their country"—the futile ranting of a frustrated old man. The settlers neither conceded access nor shrank in terror. In the Kentucky mind, like the Indian mummies of Lexington, Kekewepellethe represented the Vanishing Indian. Even if his personhood persisted, Kekewepellethe's cultural identity, his power to threaten, and his ability to use the land

and resources now appropriated by white settlers were stripped from him. Settlers had not found Kentucke a virgin land: they had known all along that the Indians considered it their hunting lands, and the Americans had to take it, conquer it, and claim it as their own. But conquest required more than the physical mastering of trans-Appalachia; it also demanded the erasure of Indians from the western narrative. Commemorations like that for Puckshunubbe legitimized the American civilization that pioneers constructed atop a vanishing Indian landscape.

The Vanishing Indian instead became a curiosity. Around 1813, slave laborers at Charles Wilkins's Mammoth Cave saltpeter business uncovered something shocking in nearby Short Cave—a mummified woman. She was the second mummy discovered in two months. The first, "an infant, of nine or twelve months old, was discovered . . . in a perfect state of preservation," but before Wilkins arrived from Lexington, his slaves had destroyed the corpse in the furnace; only the skull survived. The promise of a reward for future finds ensured that the next discovery would be delivered to Wilkins, and when the woman was unearthed, he moved her to Mammoth Cave. As the price of saltpeter fell in the aftermath of the War of 1812, Wilkins discovered a new source of income: rather than destroy the mummy or dismiss her presence, he decided to showcase her for sight-seers. Among the tourists was Nahum Ward, who, in 1816, purchased the mummy and shipped her eastward, where, eventually put on display at the American Antiquarian Society, she joined a larger national celebration of all-things-Kentucke, evidencing the region's antiquity and the inevitable demise of Native America.

The Vanishing Indian was a constant in late-eighteenth- and nineteenth-century American thought, but not all Indians needed to die. Educated in Lockean ideals of the transformative power of environment, the men who oversaw the creation of the United States believed that Indians could become civilized through education and Christianity. President Washington's secretary of war, Henry Knox, rejected military conquest of Native Americans for a more pacifist approach that included formal recognition of Indians' right to the land and a "civilization" program. But animosities between American settlers and Native Americans had grown too fierce on the frontiers, forcing Washington to postpone implementing an assimilation policy and leading Knox to plan a defensive chain of forts garrisoned by the regular army to bring order to the chaos.

The forts were insufficient for many pioneers, who, with little appreciation for assimilation, preferred instead a quick eradication of the Indians. In 1791, the *Kentucky Gazette* had championed a view of Indian peoples as "a race of beings, who acknowledge no laws, human or divine," deserving destruction by the United States, which would "assert its own power, convince the feeble enemy of his impotence, and we lay him at our feet." A year later Hugh Henry Brackenridge's "Thoughts on the present Indian War" declared that Indians may claim Kentucke, "but supposing these natives to have had an absolute and exclusive right, is it not destroyed by a supervenient right on our part"? Given that the Shawnees and other northwestern Indians had allied with the British, had not American victory in the Revolutionary War undercut their claim to Kentucke? "Were they not in his [King George's] hand, as the tomahawk and scalping knife was in theirs?" Despite the catastrophe at Blue Licks, military victory had secured Kentucke for Americans and required the Indians to abdicate their hunting grounds.

Still, while Kentuckians interpreted the Vanishing Indian as physically disappearing from the landscape, by 1803, President Jefferson was actively championing assimilation. "In truth, the ultimate point of rest and happiness for them [Indians] is to let our settlements and theirs meet and blend together, to intermix, and become one people," he wrote in his "Policy of Civilization and Assimilation" in 1803. "Incorporating themselves with us as citizens of the United States, this is what the natural process of things will, of course, bring on, and it will be better to promote than to retard it. Surely it will be better for them to be identified with us, and preserved in the occupation of their lands, than be exposed to the many casualties which may endanger them while a separate people." Unlike most Kentuckians, who presumed that through either death or displacement, Indians would fade from the trans-Appalachian landscape, Jefferson imagined racial amalgamation as the way to make a culturally distinct people vanish.

Jeffersonian assimilation never rooted in Kentucky's imagination, even though assimilated Indians resided in the state. Referring to one of his slaves, Samuel Hopkins noted in 1807 that "Fanny has a handsome Indian for her spouse, and seems much pleased with him." Hopkins was exceptional, however. Decades of terror and Indian hatred had so poisoned the Kentucky mind that most residents could not imagine living beside their former enemies. They refused to forget when the "war whoop of the savage was heard on every hill and through every valley of our State, and when the cold-blooded butchery of the wives and children of our fathers was a daily and hourly occurrence." Nothing distinguished the anti-Indian rhetoric of the 1790s and early 1800s from that of the War of 1812, except possibly the amplification.

After the War of 1812, however, presumably permanently freed from the Indian threat, Kentuckians began to re-imagine their former enemies. John Bradford's "Notes on Kentucky," published in the mid-1820s, provided a narrative that was almost nostalgic about the contest for control of Kentucke. The battlefield on which white-Indian relations had played out between the 1770s and 1810s was cast as what "was then called by the Indians in their language, the 'Dark or Bloody Grounds.'" One narrative of Blackfish's meeting with Daniel Boone during the siege of Boonesborough elaborated, "Black-Fish then said 'brother there is a heavy cloud hanging over this country.—This is called the *Bloody land*, you know;—we have had much war.'" The imagery of a bloodied land became central to regional memory. An 1820 immigrants' guide exported the ideal to Europe: "If any part of the inhabited earth could be said to have been peopled in 'tears and blood,' that was, emphatically, Kentucky." As one folk song about the Battle of Blue Licks expounded:

> Then had the Indians their revenge,
> Their foes were rash and few;
> The waters gurgled red with blood

Their mossy basin through;
Scarce was a white man left to tell,
What hand his clansmen slew.

Quite a contrast to the celebratory tone of "The Hunters of Kentucky," sung not only after the victorious Battle of New Orleans but after the Indians had vanished from Kentucky. As in a trial by fire, only through the bloodying of Kentucky could the landscape be whitened as well. As one late-nineteenth-century writer put it, "the Indians' path of incursion in the West was moistened with Kentucky blood—our battlefields are white with Kentucky bones."

The idea of the Vanishing Indian was particularly salient for two early scientists who made Kentucky their field laboratory— John D. Clifford and Constantine Rafinesque. Like most migrants traveling down the Ohio River who passed the ancient Indian mounds, Clifford wondered at the stories of the mound builders. In a series of letters published in Lexington's *Western Review and Miscellaneous Magazine* in the 1810s, he set out to prove that the "manners and customs of our present Native American Indians are so totally incompatible with the characteristics displayed in these laborious constructions, that we cannot suppose their ancestors concerned in the formation of them." Drawing upon regional myths of the Allegewis, Clifford concluded that the mound builders had been the same stock as the Aztecs, Mayans, Incas, and Hindus—all categorized as great mound builders themselves. For many white Americans, the mound builder theory provided an antiquity to the new nation, a historical legacy comparable to England's Stonehenge, Egypt's pyramids, and the Hindus' temples. When combined with the Mammoth Cave mummy, considered by many to be as impressively embalmed as those unearthed in Egypt, the mounds—what Rafinesque proclaimed as the "Ancient Monuments of North America"—suggested a great culture in prehistoric North America, one that rivaled the ancient civilizations of Asia, Africa, and Europe.

Rafinesque, a self-taught man of Enlightenment science, accepted the professorship in botany and natural history at Transylvania University in 1818, at Clifford's urging. He shared his friend's fascination with the mounds, but Rafinesque was immersed in a larger scientific controversy—the debate over whether all humans arose from a single act of creation (a scripturally based monogenic theory) or whether each race was created separately (a polygenic theory increasingly popular with natural historians such as Louis Agassiz). In the eighteenth century, Enlightenment racial theories had stressed the monogenic theory, making feasible the notion that "all men are created equal," even conceivably assimilated Indians and, according to the most radical proponents of monogenism, African Americans. While recognizing great differences (including racial differences) among specific people, most eighteenth-century thinkers insisted on the unity of humanity, believing that all people could develop progressively toward a "civilized" state. Jefferson fully accepted such theories in conceptualizing assimilation as his Indian policy.

The rise of scientific reasoning and nineteenth-century racial classification, however, challenged monogenism. If proven, polygenism would have legitimized racial differences: whites, blacks, and Indians would have been classified as different species, and categories of superiority and inferiority would have been easier to justify. Rafinesque rejected polygenism, and strongly disapproved of the enslavement of blacks and displacement of Indians. For example, in reaction to the pejorative use of "red" to describe Indians, he asserted that "there is not a Red man (nor ever was) in this continent. There are humans of many colors, but none red, unless painted!" So Rafinesque initiated a series of archaeological and linguistic investigations to demonstrate humankind's monogenic origins.

In 1824, he published his findings as *Ancient Annals of Kentucky*, an account of the region's mounds. Like Clifford, Rafinesque accepted the mound builder theory and their identity as the Allegewis, a superior civilization related to the peoples of ancient India and displaced by less-advanced peoples known to nineteenth-century Americans as Indians. The connections of India to North America evinced an ancient unity of humanity and verified for Rafinesque the monogenic origins of humankind. Differences among human groups he attributed to environmental causes: "The white man became tawny by constant exposure, brown in warm climates, coppery in cold regions, and black in the sands of India and Africa." His scientific methods and racial assumptions of the cultural primacy of whiteness aside, Rafinesque pushed forward monogenism as the foundation on which human equality could be argued.

Having dismissed any connection between the mound builders and contemporary Native Americans, however, Rafinesque felt obliged to justify better treatment of Indians. Through a statistical study of domesticated animals, he argued that Native American husbandry excelled that of other "civilized" peoples in Europe, Asia, and Indonesia. But his promotion of the mound builder theory in public orations, local and national publications, and the classrooms of Transylvania University reinforced what most Kentuckians already knew: Native Americans no longer mattered in Kentucky. Indians were not vanishing; they had vanished. Instead of bleeding over the earth, they were already buried in the earth; and their mounds and mummies validated arguments for reclaiming the rest of the continent from "that Indian race / Whose lease to this majestic land, misused, / It hath pleased God to cancel," as one poet put it. For destroying the great mound-building civilization and for wasting the North American continent, the Shawnees and Creeks, Wyandots and Chickamaugas, Wabash and Chickasaws deserved, like the mummies of Lexington, to burn in the fire that accentuated their redness and ultimately destroyed it.

Characterizing contemporary Indians as the destroyers of ancient American civilization magnified their malevolence. In his epic "The Mountain Muse," Daniel Bryan demonized Indians as spellbound by Satan into believing that white Americans would take their lands and destroy their game:

> M'Bride and Finley and their valiant bands,
> Who erst had visited in friendly guise
> The "DARK AND BLOODY GROUND"; first waked the fire
> Of Indian jealousy; which now the Fiends
> Of nether darkness fed with secret fuel,
> And fan'd into a flame of furious rage.
> To FANTASIES
> TRANSFOM'D, IN MIDNIGHT DREAMS,

> They crouded Wizard-Horrors through the brain
> Of the fierce Natives, representing Death
> As whetting the "LONG KNIFE" to exterminate
> Their tribes, where from its mighty blade huge streams
> Of Indian blood in smoking sluices gush'd!
> They saw their Groves and flowery Forests fall,
> And desolating Conflagrations sweep
> Their cany Vales and wig-wam Villages.
> They saw their Deer, their Bears and Buffalos die,
> And swarms of Whitemen covering all the plains,
> Which from great Allegany's base extend,
> To where MISSOURI's thundering surges roll!

It mattered not that white Americans *had* taken the Indians' land and destroyed their game. The poet, too, could remake history: Bryan dismissed the past by casting it as fantasy. But like Bryan's epic, the Vanishing Indian was just fantasy. When John A. McClung published *Sketches of Western Adventure* in 1832, he revealed the sad reality of the dispossessed: "Indians, from fierce and numerous tribes, were gradually melting down to a few squalid wanderers, hovering like restless spirits around the scenes of their former glory, or driven, with insult, from the doors of settlers, where they were perpetually calling for food and rum."

The Battle for History

Like Jackson and Shelby, Thomas Randolph, and Daniel Bryan, many Americans of the early republic demonstrated little use for history, for it ideologically bound them to the colonial past and their Old World origins. Fielding Bradford, editor of the *Kentucky Gazette* in 1821, condemned the colonial generations for at least their naiveté and at most their ignorance: those people "drowned and burned *witches* and stood with their hats under their arms at the doors of great men." Superstition and deference were the lessons of the American past, and like other early-nineteenth-century Americans, Bradford was ready to discard those lessons for the excitement of democracy and progress.

Rafinesque's and Clifford's fascinations with the Vanishing Indian, however, evidenced another vein of thought on history's usefulness. In their cases, the purpose was to apply history to contemporary racial debates. Fielding Bradford's brother, John, similarly considered history an ideological weapon. Founder of the *Kentucky Gazette* and the *Kentucky Almanac*, John Bradford was probably Kentucky's greatest promoter of "American" history. Both the newspaper and the almanac became vehicles for patriotic republican rhetoric. The timing of Kentucky's development held particular relevance: its history paralleled the formation of a nation, evidenced annually in the almanac with a chronology of "national" events since 1774 (not coincidentally, the year of Kentucke's first permanent white settlement) and culminating with Kentucky statehood in 1792 as if it were the rational conclusion to the American Revolution. Frontispieces in the almanac typically read "xth year of American Independence, xth of our Federal Government, xth of this Commonwealth," a practice that underscored how Kentuckians' ability to identify as Americans depended upon their participation in and their inheritance of the events that created the nation.

Yet, the tensions that had existed between Kentucky and the federal government in the 1780s, 1790s, and early 1800s left Kentuckians feeling as outsiders, and they had no historical markers by which they could affirm their patriotism. Daniel Drake recalled how "father and mother emigrated from a densely settled part of New Jersey, and had passed through the stirring scenes of the Revolution, in which their native State so largely participated." There was no stirring scene of the Revolution in Kentucky. The Battle of Blue Licks had been a disaster and hardly worth commemoration. Yet, by contextualizing the battle (and the larger Indian war of which it was a part) as a theater of the Revolutionary War, Kentuckians incorporated the disaster into collective memory. Having the tale related to him time and again as he traveled from Maysville to Lexington in 1806, Fortesque Cuming mused that "there was not a half mile of the road between the two places unstained by human blood!" While a history of frontier Kentucky existed, it did so in the vernacular folklore and legends passed among the people.

Humphrey Marshall believed that Kentucky was in need of a more official historical narrative. "There is not probably, any thing which more distinctly marks the difference between savage and civilized states, than the want, or possession of history," he explained in 1812. Marshall fired the first shot in the battle over who would define Kentucky's frontier narrative when he wrote *The History of Kentucky* (1812). There had been previous "histories"— John Filson's *Discovery, Settlement, and Present State of Kentucky* (1784), Gilbert Imlay's *A Topographical Description of the Western Territory of North America* (1792), and Harry Toulmin's *The Western Country in 1793: Reports on Kentucky and Virginia* (1793). Still, as authors of promotional tracts, Filson, Imlay, and Toulmin were less concerned with reflecting on Kentucke's meaning than selling Kentucke's land. Marshall's was the first reflective and analytical history written by a survivor of the Kentucke frontiers.

Sensitive about westerners' marginalization in the United States, Marshall argued Kentucky's case for national relevance. After assessing the ancient republics of Greece and Rome, he queried, "But Kentucky! brought forth in obscurity; laped in simple industry; raised up in peace, after a few predatory alarms, and simple invasions of savages; what has she in common with the countries, just reviewed? what splendid subjects for history does her short period of existence display? How shall the historian fill his empty page?" His answer was the image of a "sylvan empire"—God's anointed Eden, rich with "nature's creative energy" and offering the greatest hope for true republicanism. As *History of Kentucky* unfolded, however, Marshall's readers discovered that, rather than an Edenic republic, Kentucky had become a paradise lost.

Marshall did not hide his disappointment, frustration, and anger that the region had not evolved as a land where men of status and wealth, disinterested in their own needs, ruled with the consent of and on behalf of the masses. Instead, he argued that in the 1792 constitution, George Nicholas had acquiesced to the rude majority and established "a representative democracy—instead of a real republic, as all governments should be." Condemning the notion that "all men are equal when they form the social compact," Marshall the Federalist declared "'THAT ALL MEN ARE BY NATURE UNEQUAL;' that from the same source, they have each a claim to happiness; and in order to ensure it, in the social state, for which that inequality has fitted them, and to which they have a common right, they therefore agree to submit to be governed by a constitution." The constitution had not provided political and economic opportunity, however, and Marshall saw that as tragedy, given the rich and abundant promise that Kentucke had once offered: "No wood had been felled; no field cleared; no human habitation raised; even the red man of the forest had not put up his wigwam of poles and bark."

But that is where Marshall ceased the Edenic metaphor, for Kentucky was no Eden and had not been settled by chosen people. Its future had been usurped by the wrong sort of Americans: "Nor has Kentucky, been without her wars, revolutions, conspiracies— She too, has had her generals, statesmen, patriots—and traitors!!!" As a politician and historian, Marshall did not hide his disdain for certain "traitors." In the 1790s, through a series of letters to *The Western World*, he had accused Harry Innes of treasonous complicity in James Wilkinson's Spanish Conspiracy. "Men who should live in mutual confidence and friendship, were taught to suspect, and to hate each other," he lamented; "Thirty thousand people were to renounce the benefits of the American union, with their neighbors—their natural connexions—and their political friends—to forfeit their peace—and to incur the terrors of civil war." Additionally, Innes's devotion to common law and jury trials represented the very democratic appeals that Marshall loathed; and the judge had been the foremost impediment to Uncle Thomas Marshall's collection of whiskey taxes in the 1790s. In response to Marshall's attacks in *The Western World*, Democratic-Republican William Littell wrote *A Narrative of the Settlement of Kentucky and Political Transactions in and Concerning Kentucky* (1806) to exonerate Innes. In 1807, however, Marshall was elected to the state assembly, which he interpreted as a vote of confidence, an indictment of Innes, and a rejection of Littell's apology. He began working on the manuscript that would become *History of Kentucky*, convinced that it would not appeal to "*conspirators* and *intriguers*," but would please "honest, and liberal minds."

Marshall also retained some venom for Henry Clay, who had successfully defended Burr and thereby undermined Marshall's accusations of Innes's treason by association. Antagonisms between Clay and Marshall became so intense that in January 1809 their verbal quarrel devolved into a duel. Clay's bullet grazed Marshall above the navel, and Marshall's shot struck Clay's right thigh. Officially, the state assembly censured both men; unofficially they were proclaimed "cool, determined, and brave in the highest degree."

Personal honor aside, the conflict between Clay and Marshall embodied the contest between democracy and history found throughout the early American republic. Clay represented the democratic order of increased individualism, political equality, and economic accessibility. Marshall saw himself as guardian of the deferential republican ideals of the Revolutionary generation. *History of Kentucky*, then, was no simple smear campaign on Marshall's behalf. He went out of his way to vilify those men whom he directly associated with damaging the integrity of republicanism and the intentions of the Founding Fathers.

Marshall believed that history was a powerful tool, and that his book might succeed where his politics had not. "[O]ur government is but in its infancy—that it has much to reform," he explained, "and that the only way, by which it can attain perfection, is, impartially to detect its errors, see whence they flow, and then, with a sound discernment and honest intention, correct them." The rise to adulthood and political power by Clay's generation of Kentuckians demanded vigilance:

> Should he [the historian] trace the revolutions of ancient states, and develop their causes; should he single out the ambitious demagogue, who from time, to time, deluded the credulous people, under the mask of *patriotism*, and the name of REPUBLICAN, and thence pursue him to the usurped, and the despot, he would have full scope for moral reflections, and political admonition.

Marshall had touched on a sad revelation: with the rise of a new generation of Kentucky heroes—Richard Mentor Johnson, Henry Clay, and the "Hunters from Kentucky" among them—the Revolutionary generation and the earliest of Kentucky's settlers became increasingly irrelevant, as did the institutions that had buttressed their world.

In the mid-1820s, Marshall found a new and more engaged readership when he revised his *History of Kentucky*. Much had changed since the first printing of his volume. The War of 1812 had inspired rabid patriotism in Kentucky. Economic crises of the late 1810s, including the Panic of 1819, injured thousands of Kentuckians and forced thousands more to migrate out of the state. An unstable economy raised anxieties throughout the West. "Everyone is afraid of bursting the bubble," reported one visitor, but the bubble did burst, and a relief war ensued that challenged the legitimacy of the state's supreme court and led to a constitutional crisis. Kentuckians were furious.

Yet, the moneyed classes that Clay represented not only seemed to weather the storm, they consolidated their hold on Kentucky's political power and industrial and agricultural wealth. In general, although some entrepreneurs suffered as much as farmers and laborers, merchants and lawyers found many opportunities to purchase land and businesses in the late 1810s and early 1820s as less-wealthy Kentuckians begged for relief to save their farms. With the 1812 edition of *History of Kentucky*, it may have been that the public just could not get enough of Marshall's inspired castigations of fellow politicians, but the popularity of the 1826 edition was certainly Marshall's emphatic proclamation of a paradise lost. He reminded readers that guardians of actual republican principles (including himself) had warned against too enthusiastic an entry into the War of 1812, and the ensuing economic crisis confirmed their counsel.

An aging John Bradford rejected Marshall's portrait of regional declension and denunciations of democracy. Hoping to vindicate the state's founders and the society they had created, he took back his editorial position at the *Kentucky Gazette* in 1825 and began the first of sixty-six historical reminiscences collectively known as "Notes on Kentucky," intended to remind Kentuckians of their heritage by celebrating individualism, opportunity, and the success of the early settlers in defeating the twin threats of Indians and wilderness. Bradford also claimed that pioneer energies and patriotic passions continued to define Kentuckians for the good. Like so many of his generation, he feared that younger Americans would forget the founders' ordeals and virtues. The War of 1812 not only energized patriotism in Kentucky, but many younger Kentuckians claimed to "have taught their elders practical patriotism," a boast that certainly troubled men like Bradford. "Notes on Kentucky" reinforced the ideals of the Founding Fathers and the sacrifices of pioneer culture, depicting early settlers as great heroes who, with each skirmish and every attack on isolated cabins, demonstrated uncommon valor and fortitude in the face of the Indian threat.

Explorer James Smith, for example, who traveled central Kentucky in 1766 with his young slave Jamie, epitomized frontier heroism in Bradford's work. Hobbled by a stab wound to his foot, Smith taught his companion how to make "Indian medicine" from tree bark, construct a cane shelter, and shoot and jerk buffalo. Smith read the *Psalms* and a collection of *Watt's Prayers* to his companion, and composed a song that ended,

> This doleful circumstance cannot
> My happiness prevent,
> While peace of conscience I enjoy,
> Great comfort and content.

Even Daniel Boone, so often portrayed as a republican stoic in the wilderness, would have been hard-pressed to match Smith as forest philosopher.

As in the Smith story, Bradford made a point of joining individual destinies across racial and gendered lines. When a Native American breached the doorway of one isolated cabin in Bradford's history, the "negro seized the Indian who had entered, and threw him down, when the white woman seizing an axe which happened to be in the house, beat out his brains." There is no hint that bubbling under the surface was white patriarchal paranoia over the proximity of black men to white women or the impropriety of housewives crushing Indians' skulls with household tools. Bradford emphasized the beauty and desirability of the western landscape, and the inherent rightness and goodness of those who wanted to settle it—patterns of eighteenth-century sentimentalism that exalted the myth that Kentucky's frontier environment had made all whites equal. (Importantly, all blacks and white women found in "Notes in Kentucky" are cooperative, loyal, dependent, and, by implication, unequal.)

The cooperative demands of frontier life provide a recurring theme in Bradford's "Notes on Kentucky," and he regularly emphasized how failure to work together led to death. In "The Tragedy at the Blue Licks," he chastised the rash hot-head Hugh McGary, who had led confused young militiamen to their deaths. Their impetuousness resulted in an inglorious end and brought only pain to their families:

> No sound was uttered but the cry of the gorged vulture hovering over their heads. Those who were drawn by affection to the horrid spectacle, with the hope of saving some relic of hair or garment from a lost father, brother or friend, were denied this favour. The remains of the mangled bodies were so distended by the excessive heat of the weather, or so disfigured by the tomahawk, vultures and wild beasts, that it was impossible to distinguish one individual from another.

Bradford impressed upon his readers the demanding, collective ordeal of founding a good life—a hardship few of them had endured.

Since "Notes on Kentucky" were found in the weekly newspaper, Bradford reached a substantially larger readership than did Marshall. In 1827, an Ohioan republished the first twenty-three columns as *The Western Miscellany*, taking the lessons of Kentucke to a more regional audience. But it was Kentuckians for whom Bradford spun his tales of heroism, responsibility, and cooperation. After years of economic strife, Kentuckians needed reconciliation, and Bradford offered the standards of the past as a corrective for the present.

The popularity of Marshall's and Bradford's histories evidenced a cultural awakening under way by the 1820s and early 1830s. The War of 1812 had facilitated Kentuckians' participation in national development and inheritance of its revolutionary origins. They felt fully American, and as the founding generation died in the decades following the War of 1812, Kentuckians joined their fellow Americans in rediscovering the national past. The

United States Congress authorized the printing of the *Secret Journals of the Confederation* in 1820. The following year, *Secret Proceedings and Debates of the Convention Assembled at Philadelphia, in the Year 1787* were also published. Charles Wilson Peale's Philadelphia Museum was incorporated in 1821. State historical societies opened in New Hampshire, Connecticut, Rhode Island, Maine, and Pennsylvania between 1822 and 1825. New Englanders dedicated the Bunker Hill Monument in 1825; the same year that John Trumbull completed his four Revolutionary-themed portraits on the United States capitol rotunda. Individual Americans purchased portraits of Washington, Jefferson, Franklin, Lafayette, and Boone as decorative arts for their homes. There was, as well, a flurry of historical writing, most notably John Drayton's *Memoirs of the American Revolution* (1821) and Washington Irving's popular *Sketch-Book* collection (1819–20), but also hundreds of lesser-known authors on an incredible breadth of topics. Possibly most significant were James Fenimore Cooper's *The Pioneers* (1823) and *Last of the Mohicans* (1826), both situated in historical American contexts. In 1828, John Augustus Stone's *Metamora*, a play about the seventeenth-century Indian conflict known as King Philip's War, became the foundation on which the great actor Edwin Forrest hoped to "give my country, by fostering the exertions of our literary friends, something like what might be called an American national drama."

Kentucky joined in this cultural awakening. Greater availability of books and more widespread literacy led the state assembly to consider comprehensive education and establish a literary fund, allowing larger and more diverse audiences to contemplate and appreciate history. It also led to the Kentucky Historical Society, established in 1836 with the expressed objective to "celebrate in such a manner as shall be deemed most expedient, the anniversary of the first settlement of Kentucky on the spot where that settlement was made." The founding resolution limited society membership to "native citizens of Kentucky, or such as may have intermarried with families born in the State, and of those citizens who may have emigrated to it prior to June 1st, 1792, when the Constitution went into effect." In essence, the

society meant to preserve the lineage of Kentucke's frontiers as they faded from memory.

In their emphases on the current disintegrating morality and on preserving the best of the past, Kentucky's early historians were similar to other literary figures of the age, but their affinity for making frontier morality the standard by which their own generations and the American future were to be judged was almost uniquely Kentuckian, at least initially. Seeking to retain the moral purpose of storytelling through the print culture of the early republic, Kentucky's historians cast the region's history as a "frontier" epic that promoted ideals of heroism, hardship, and enterprise. As a future generation of historians such as Lewis Collins and Frederick Jackson Turner digested these histories, they perpetuated the centrality of the frontier to understanding Kentucky's and indeed America's past and present.

The forging of a national memory and culture, however, exposed tensions between the past and the present. In 1816, Thomas Jefferson declared, "I like the dreams of the future better than the history of the past," and most Americans seemed to agree. As Fielding Bradford knew, history celebrated superstitions, deference, and the traditions that underlay them—traditions that he believed could not survive in an increasingly democratic society. As the United States Congress debated a memorial for George Washington in the early 1830s, John Quincy Adams declared, "Democracy has no monuments. It strikes no medals. It bears the head of no man upon a coin. Its very essence is iconoclastic." By the 1820s, the republican ideals of the founding generation seemed to be dying out, and the inheritors of the Revolution did not seem particularly mournful.

Boone as Kentucke

Simultaneous with Kentuckians' coming to terms with their frontier past was Americans' appropriation of Kentucky into a larger national history. Kentucky was the first true "American" state: its population was an amalgamation of settlers from every other state in the union, and until populations began pouring onto the

Great Plains, it was geographically situated in the center of the nation. Following the War of 1812, Americans became infatuated with Kentucke and its hero: Daniel Boone.

As early as 1784, Filson had appended a glowing biography of Boone to his *Discovery, Settlement and Present State of Kentucke*. Marshall, however, had been critical of Boone as land surveyor and military leader and, while willing to grant Boone a certain stature, portrayed him less a Moses leading the chosen people to the promised land than an Abraham who left the land of his forefathers to venture into the wilderness and sacrificed his own sons, James and Israel, on the altar of the Indian wars. In 1823, when James Fenimore Cooper published *The Pioneers* and thrust his hero Nathaniel "Natty" Bumppo into the national imagination, everyone knew it was Boone who modeled the wilderness philosopher and Indian fighter. Cooper specifically related Bumppo to Boone, proclaiming the latter "the patriarch of Kentucky." John Bradford took Cooper's lead and situated Boone as a central character in the first fifteen tales of "Notes of Kentucky," making the frontiersman integral to the myth of frontier Kentucke.

Celebration of Boone made him the hero of the western wilderness in the enlarging pantheon of great Americans. In the typical mode of the hero, the immortalized Boone demonstrated courage and cunning against powerful antagonists while on his long hunts. By placating his restlessness through finding courage, self-responsibility, and identity on the quest, Boone fulfilled the basic motif of the hero. In an age consumed with Parson Weems's tales of George Washington and Washington Irving's Knickerbocker stories, Boone's adventures quickly became American legend. In *Westward Ho!* (1832), one of the most popular novels of the day, James Kirke Paulding credited the tales about Boone as the impetus for America's continuing westward movement. Such claims irritated Daniel Drake, who, having grown up in Kentucke, condemned "the failure of Mr. Cooper in his *Prairie*, and Mr. Paulding in his *Westward Ho*, as conclusive evidence, that in delineating the West, no power of genius, can supply the want of opportunities for personal observation on our natural and social

aspects." According to Drake, "no western man can read those works with interest." But thousands of Americans did, and they imagined that all Kentuckians were like Boone.

The romanticized version of Boone came to represent Kentucke's frontier in the American mind, and was literally engraved into the national consciousness. When planning the United States capitol rotunda in the 1820s, architects commissioned four bas-reliefs to ornament the doorways. Three drew upon themes of seventeenth-century Indian-white relations: *Preservation of Captain Smith by Pocahontas* (1825), *Landing of the Pilgrims* (1825), and *William Penn's Treaty with the Indians* (1827). The fourth relief—Enrico Causici's *Conflict of Daniel Boone and the Indians* (1826)—was different, representing the late eighteenth century and, more importantly, overturning the interracial cooperation portrayed in the other reliefs. James Fenimore Cooper praised the relief as a "personal recontre of Colonel Boon, the patriarch of Kentucky, with the savages," but in contrast to Boone's insistence that he had never harbored violent intentions toward Native Americans and had killed only three in his lifetime, the relief commemorated the violence of Kentucke, and of Boone.

In *Conflict of Daniel Boone and the Indians*, Boone has already killed one Indian, whose body takes up the entire space of the ground and from whose stab wound blood drops to the soil below. With no space left, Boone and a second Indian stand over him, weapons raised. The result of the conflict is known: the Indian will join his dead brother on the forest floor. And so Kentucky was imagined by the nation. As representative of the colonial past (and as represented in the other bas-reliefs), Virginia, Massachusetts, and Pennsylvania had been places of peace where Indians saved white lives and sold land. As the first western state, Kentucke had been a place of war, where Indians had to be killed for whites to advance.

Causici's *Conflict of Daniel Boone and the Indians* added to the apotheosis of Boone as a symbol of western America, a theme drawn upon by Horatio Greenough when he designed *The Rescue* in the 1840s to sit on the main staircase of the United States capitol. The statue displayed a larger-than-life white man over-

Figure 8.1. In 1826, Enrico Causici created the bas-relief *Conflict of Daniel Boone and the Indians* for display in the rotunda of the national capitol. Based upon a wood-cut print from Timothy Flint's *Biographical Memoir of Daniel Boone* (1833), the image was meant to symbolize the nation's sense of Manifest Destiny. Courtesy of the Architect of the Capitol, Washington, D.C.

whelming a nearly naked Indian. The latter held a tomahawk, but the pioneer restrained his arms and rendered him impotent. At the pioneer's feet are the objects he sought to protect: a wife and child, huddled in fear. "You see the exposure and suffering of the female emigrant," praised one critic, "the ferocious and destructive instinct of the savage, and his easy subjugation under

the superior manhood of the new colonist." The white man in *The Rescue* did not look or dress at all like Boone, but the statue became commonly known as "Daniel Boone Protects His Family."

While he had seldom demonstrated himself a family man, Boone as hero meant Boone as domestic protector. In 1823, he rejected the emerging mythology: "Many heroic actions and chivalrous adventures are related to me which exist only in the regions of fancy. With me the world has taken great liberties, and yet I have been but a common man." In no circumstances was that more true than in the literature and art that portrayed Boone as the über-paterfamilias. In his 1833 *Biographical Memoir of Boone*, Timothy Flint depicted his protagonist, upon discovering his daughter Jemima's captivity, as swearing "By the Eternal Power that made me a father, if my daughter lives, and is found, I will either bring her back, or spill my life blood"—a line that Edwin Forrest most certainly would have loved to perform on stage. "In an age of chivalry—during the Crusades—Boone would have been a knight errant, equally fearless and gentle," declared southern novelist William Gilmore Simms in 1845 as he transformed Boone in the quintessence of antebellum southern manhood: "That he would have been much of a Squire or Dames, is very uncertain—but he loved his wife, and he risked his scalp more than once to rescue beauty from the clutches of the savage." With the exception of Jemima's rescue, however, Boone had never been in a situation to "rescue beauty." But by the mid-nineteenth century, the historical Boone no longer mattered. The metaphorical Boone had become *the* American man—conqueror of the West, killer of Indians, knight errant, rescuer of beauty.

Following the War of 1812, Kentucky became the toast of American culture. Flint's *Biographical Memoir of Daniel Boone* became the most widely read biography of the era, going through fourteen editions over the next thirty-five years. He exaggerated Boone's exploits, having him escape Indians by swinging on vines, fighting hand-to-paw against a bear, and shooting a panther off the back of a buffalo that it had attacked. These were tall tales worthy of American legends, teaching Americans that Boone was not just the epitomic Kentuckian but the iconic American. The song "The Hunters of Kentucky," immensely popular in the 1820s and serving as Andrew Jackson's campaign song in 1828, made all Kentuckians into Boones:

We are a hardy, free-born race,
Each man to fear a stranger;
Whate'er the game we join in chase,
Despoiling time and danger
And if a daring foe annoys,
Whate'er his strength and forces,
We'll show him that Kentucky boys
Are alligator horses.

In the 1820s, New Orleans minstrel actor Noah Ludlow dressed in a fringed buckskin jacket and moccasins as he recited the stanzas and chorus of "Hunters of Kentucky." Unable to find a beaver hat like Boone had worn, he donned a coonskin cap. As he neared the end of the song, he threw his hat to the floor, knelt down and raised his rifle as if to shoot over the audience, and drew a standing ovation. The popularity of Ludlow's performances influenced a young Davy Crockett to adopt the persona. When, in 1830, James Kirke Paulding wrote the play *The Lion of the West*, loosely based on Ludlow's characterization of the old Kentucky hunter, the new Whig Party tried to bolster the political fortunes of their rising star Crockett by arguing that the main character was fashioned after him. The Hunter of Kentucky, then, no longer represented Kentucky but could be appropriated by any self-proclaimed hunter, explorer, or Indian killer. By 1852, the Kentuckian had become a caricature: "Why, thar's more real satisfaction in sarcumventing and scalping one o' them red heathen, than in all the amusement you could scare up in a thick-peopled peaceable settlement in a life time," he declared in Emerson Bennett's *Ella Barnwell* (1853).

The Hunter of Kentucky caricature was a powerful, chivalrous, larger-than-life man, and his believability required a terrified and diminutive woman. In fact, when *The Rescue* was pieced together by capitol architect Robert Mills, he apparently situated the mother and child section on the wrong corner of the pedestal, eliciting sharp objections from the sculptor's family. If assembled correctly, "the group told its story of the peril of the American wilderness, the ferocity of our Indians, the superiority of the whiteman, and why and how civilization crowded the Indian from his soil, with the episode of woman and infancy and the sentiments that belong to them," appealed a family representative. "Now all this is perverted, the mother and child are removed from this peril, which is the *causa causans* of the action of the piece and she is looking unconcernedly away from it."

Why had civilization crowded the Indian from his soil? For the sake of women and families was the answer provided by *The Rescue*. Consequently, frontier women no longer could be cast as capable, independent survivors. Rebecca Boone could not be viewed as the woman who, when Daniel left for prolonged trips, found sexual satisfaction in another man's bed. She had to be the woman cowering behind him as he destroyed the threatening Indian. In the 1813 epic poem "The Mountain Muse," readers learned of Rebecca's newly remade image:

> The tenderest eloquence of mourning love
> At length broke from the sweet impassion'd lips
> Of his affectionate spouse. "My Boon!" She cried,
> And press'd him to her groaning breast; "My Boone!"
> How can you leave your Home, your Wife and Babes,
> Your life in bloody woods to jeopardize,
> Among the murdering Indians' cruel tribes?
> My God! The horrid thought I cannot bear!
> How shall I rest in peace, when dangers watch
> To take away my dear Companion's life?

Rebecca Boone, like all frontier women, was helpless without her husband.

When they were not relegated to a supporting role, frontier women were altogether ignored. One of the more famous episodes of true frontier women's bravery arose from the 1782 siege of Bryan's Station. Out of water, the settlers desperately needed to refill buckets at a spring several hundred yards outside the station walls. As historian John McClung related the story in his 1832 *Sketches of Western Adventure*, the men induced the women to go out to the spring, to which the women observed "that *they* were not bullet-proof, and that the Indians made no distinction between male and female scalps!" Assuring them that the Indians would not want to "unmask themselves for the sake of firing

Figure 8.2. William Greenhough designed *The Rescue* (1851) to convey the triumph of white civilization. *The Rescue* both depicted the vulnerability of American civilization—represented by the woman and child—and legitimated the use of force against Native Americans. Courtesy of the Architect of the Capitol, Washington, D.C.

at a few women, when they hoped, by remaining concealed a few moments longer, to obtain complete possession of the fort," the men convinced several women to leave the fort walls. The women succeeded, proving themselves courageous beyond call, but their story warranted very little historical attention as historians elevated frontier manhood at the expense of frontier womanhood. McClung's story is by far the longest at three sentences. Marshall ignored the story completely, and Flint and Bradford each acknowledged it with a single sentence.

The frontier had demonstrated women's capacity for courage, but for the sake of American manhood, it was not to be celebrated. Just as Kentucky's courts, legislature, and churches had attempted to restrain unruly frontier women in the 1790s and early 1800s, Kentucky's historians of the 1820s and 1830s reined in women's roles in western conquest and settlement. The image of docile, domestic, and dependent women was not needed just in Kentucky, however. Throughout the early republic, Americans increasingly measured manhood as the protection of helpless and often hapless women.

Slavery and the Continuity of Terror

In late 1840, John Dabney Shane began a twenty-year project of collecting pioneer accounts of the Ohio River Valley. Six weeks into the process, he wrote to his brother: "Since I saw you, I have written in the book you sent me near 6,000 lines, besides rode some 150 miles, and made many visits. . . . You can form no idea of how absorbing & enthusiastic a nature my present pursuit is, especially as is sped on by uninterrupted success." Shane not only collected books and documents, but he recorded the oral histories of hundreds of Kentuckians. He met with former frontiersmen and frontierswomen, took notes of their memories, transcribed the interviews into his notebooks, and then revisited the interviewees to read his entries and make any final corrections or additions. In an era when popular culture celebrated the great men of the Revolutionary Era, Shane's interviews comprised a unique acknowledgment of the fortitude and fortune of ordinary people in extending American civilization. The only exception was that out of over four hundred interviewees, none was black, even though one of six Kentuckians in 1790 had been African American.

Shane's oversight was more than just happenstance, for it would have been impossible for him not to see blacks on his travels. In the 1840s, when Daniel Drake returned to Mayslick to visit the village in which he grew up, slaves were ubiquitous. "New investments are constantly made in land and negroes," he complained about the diminishing white population, "and hence the soil is always passing from the many to the few. Slaves take the place of freemen, 'negro quarters' replace the humble habitations of happy families." Despite their visibility in homes, fields, and churches, blacks were hidden in plain sight, just as they had been in Kentucke.

The ways in which white Kentuckians remembered (or neglected) stories of frontier slaves reflected an important cultural trend under way in early- to mid-nineteenth-century Kentucky. The wave of historical interest that swept the early American republic was part of a larger cultural whitening of America. As they defined and shaped a national culture, artists, writers, scientists, and others found it impossible to conceive American identity without also thinking about everything it was not—the Other. By highlighting Indian savagery or black enslavement, white Americans identified themselves as civilized and free, and in the process, racialized themselves as white. In the white mind of Kentucky and throughout America, to admit that blacks enslaved or free had shared in the freedom, self-reliance, and rugged manliness or womanliness of the frontier was to deny that westward expansion was providential and manifest for white America.

Consequently, the argument had to be suggested that blacks just had not mattered on the frontier. Shane's nostalgic pioneers seldom mentioned blacks, and the grander histories of Marshall and Bradford, McClung and Flint, reduced blacks to supporting-actor roles in the drama of Kentucke. Recall Bradford's story of Jamie, the young slave who aided the hobbled James Smith in 1766; or the slave who held down an invading Indian so that a white woman could axe him to death. Almost every tale that included a slave relegated the black to a subservient role. With few exceptions, oral and written stories portrayed black heroism as a consequence of white guidance and instruction. When blacks ignored whites' warnings of frontier danger, they most often died or disappeared forever. Even though blacks were a central component of Kentucke's frontier, they were increasingly absent from the narratives that constructed public memory of it.

Racializing Kentucke's frontier history also reflected the continuing debate over slavery in Kentucky. As much of the South embraced John C. Calhoun's "slavery as positive good" theory in the late 1820s, an older "slavery as necessary evil" theory remained powerful in Kentucky. The premise should sound familiar: with two races coexisting in the same space, the resulting racial hatred and competition would induce violence and retaliation by the "inferior" race. It had once pertained to Indian-white relations, but as white Kentuckians grew fearful of a new racial threat, they applied the same logic to black-white relations, consequently accepting slavery as necessary although many believed it to be contrary to religious and moral teachings. An 1830s migrant to Kentucky "talked with rich and poor alike on the subject, and find them alike, would be glad if there was not a slave in the state." As long as slaves remained, however, white self-preservation required complete control over the necessary evil, even in historical memory.

The constitutional debates of 1799 had elicited much discussion about the racial differences between blacks and whites. Gone were the frontier days of "the black white man." "The sable colour of the Africans . . . completely frightens us," wrote one contributor to *The Mirror*, while an editorialist in the *Kentucky Gazette* contemplated, "Observe their shape and color. The flatness of their noses evidently discovers their want of sense—their thick lips appear as if made to be buffeted—their crooked legs seem as if already pressed under the burden—and from their color, it is plain they were never designed to lie upon beds, but by the fire among the ashes." At the very least, the repeated racialization of the Other enhanced whites' claims to the rights and privileges of whiteness. More critically, however, by defining blacks as "Ugly,

Black, Flatnosed, Thick-lipped, Wooly-headed, Ignorant, Savage Heathens," whites justified preempting the threat that the different Other posed.

As white Kentuckians defined themselves in opposition to blacks and as slavery hardened the racial line between them, blacks viewed whites as the violent Other. Kentucky's slave patrols and watch houses provided the symbols of violence, making slaves fearful in even the most innocent of circumstances. "The black men protested that their wives were held under the water longer than the white women," recalled former slave Francis Fedric about a group baptism in the early 1800s, "although there was not a shade of difference in the time of immersion." Blacks were as suspicious of whites as whites were of blacks. "It is a saying among the masters, the bigger fool the better nigger," explained Fedric. Henry Bibb opened his memoirs of slavery: "I was bought up in the Counties of Shelby, Henry, Oldham, and Trimble. Or, more correctly speaking, . . . I was *flogged up*; for where I should have received moral, mental, and religious instruction."

Slave reminiscences relate a lot about individual slaves' perspectives, but it is nearly impossible to know how early-nineteenth-century black Kentuckians remembered Kentucke. Still, in descriptions of their relationships with whites, blacks employed language similar to what whites had used in describing their own relations with Indians on the frontier. The terror of frontier life may have begun subsiding for whites with the Battle of Fallen Timbers, but it persisted as a theme of African American life. Only the antagonists and protagonists changed. Like those who withstood the terror of the frontier, enslaved blacks were aware of their own vulnerability and determined to survive the fear that framed their lives.

For example, the security of the family cabin was illusionary. At any moment day or night, men could crash through the door, grabbing residents and pulling them outside, where slave patrols determined whether the absence of passes warranted public floggings. On occasion, when the patrols sought specific slaves for punishment, the scenario was reminiscent of Indian attacks. Francis Fedric remembered a corn shucking in the 1820s during which over one hundred white men terrified the slaves by whoop-

ing and shooting guns as they raided a barn to find two slaves
who had talked back to their master. The two men were dragged
out and flogged as women and children screamed in horror. One
was beaten "until the poor fellow was one mass of blood and
raw flesh." This was not enough for some of the patrollers, who
wanted to put one "on a blacksmith's fire, and have the slaves
to hold him until I blew the bellows to roast him alive," and the
other "ought to be tied to a tree and burnt alive." The terror employed against slaves made the possibility of physical harm, even
death, a constant threat.

So too was the possibility of captivity. Families could not be
stable under the threat that fathers, mothers, or children would
be ripped away, never to be seen again. "Licentious white men,
can and do, enter at night or day the lodging places of slaves;
break up the bonds of affection in families; destroy all their domestic and social union for life," explained Bibb. Fedric remembered "men and women down on their knees begging to be purchased to go with their wives or husbands . . . children crying
and imploring not to have their parents sent away from them; . . .
Still, after so many years, their wailings and lamentations and
piercing cries sound in my ears." And, of course, slaves *were*
captives—from Africa, from parents and grandparents, and from
wives, husbands, and children.

In Kentucke, reaction to threats of death and captivity had
been frenzies of mean fear. When terror invaded their homesteads, white and black pioneers violently struck back. Not surprisingly, then, in Kentucky, whites expected blacks to respond
with similar reactionary violence against the terror imposed upon
them. Rumors of slave insurrections circulated regularly, but they
were an aberration of the white mind, a side effect of the paranoia
that slaveholding created. When a factory or barn burned down,
immediately the cry of slave rebellion echoed across Kentucky.

Most certainly, many slaves wanted to react. Milton Clarke
remembered how, upon discovering the master injuring Clarke's
mother and whipping his sister, he "became completely frantic,
and ran and caught an axe, and intended to cut him down at a
blow." Generally speaking, however, slaves just did not have the
weapons to strike back in mean fear. The state had eliminated

black gun ownership as the frontier faded. "The only weapon of self defence that I could use successfully, was that of deception," recalled Henry Bibb. So, from breaking shovels to stealing food, slaves undermined daily work and complicated white family life in thousands of little ways that may have provided momentary satisfaction but in no way reduced the terror.

For some, the best alternative was to escape. As Mary Draper Ingles had realized in the 1760s, forests were liminal spaces between captivity and escape, fear and security. In the early 1800s, blacks also took to the forests to flee the terror of slavery. Some imagined going farther, across the Ohio River to freedom. "I have stood upon the lofty banks of the river Ohio," lamented Henry Bibb, "and I thought of the fishes of the water, the fowls of the air, the wild beasts of the forest, all appeared to be free, to go just where they pleased, and I was an unhappy slave!" For Kentucky's slaves, the Ohio River remained the line between savagery and civilization.

The terror faced by Kentucky's slaves was by no means identical to or a consequence of the terror of frontier Kentucke. American racial slavery and the fear and intimidation used to create and enforce it had a long history well before Kentucky was born. Yet, the greater security and stability that the Battle of Fallen Timbers and the Treaty of Greenville had initiated for white Kentuckians just did not resonate with enslaved and free blacks. The terrors of scalping, captivity, and extirpation were replaced by the terrors of physical mutilation and dismemberment, the separation and sale of families, and enslavement in perpetuity.

EPILOGUE

Regardless of what one might think of Frederick Jackson Turner's "frontier thesis," there is an inherent truth in Turner's placement of the frontier at the center of American identity development. The frontier narrative *is* a foundational drama on which American society is constructed. Kentucke's frontiers were among the first national frontiers. Its settlers continued patterns not only of touching America as it is but of assaulting it in frenzies of mean fear that had characterized the earliest Atlantic colonial frontiers and would continue as Americans crossed the Plains, claimed the Great West, filled in the continent, and confronted the rest of the world.

Contemporary historians' efforts to redefine the frontier as a cultural zone have brought significant insight into the complicated dynamics of Indian-white-black relations. As one anthology introduction claimed of its contributors: "They see them [frontiers] as contested spaces, not as a stage in the progress of the world according to Europeans." But white Europeans and Americans who actually settled the West saw the frontier both as contested space *and* as a stage for "civilized" progress. Reconceptualizing the frontier as contested spaces without continued recognition of the frontier as a line that separated "civilization" from "savagery"—as Americans of the eighteenth and nineteenth centuries imagined it—minimizes the sense of God-ordained entitlement that most whites felt about conquering the frontier and the American future: settlement of western lands was considered a moral right, and impediments to that right were by definition wrong.

The children and grandchildren of Kentucke's earliest generation of settlers heard the stories of frontier life, and as they recorded it in the nineteenth century, Kentucke's frontier narrative became one of conflict with malevolent, racialized Others who hid in the wilderness, living not as "civilized" nations but in poorly defined tribal and village entities, refusing to abide by "civilized" rules of military engagement, and indiscriminately waging war against American families—men, women, and children. It is true that in their desires to keep their lands, Indians employed brutal and savage tactics to instill terror among enemy civilians. It is equally true that settlers became equally savage as they ripped those lands from the Indians. Historically, however, savagery as an ethnic characteristic was ascribed to native peoples, even as the same tactics employed by white settlers were justified as vengeance or strategic.

Categorizing the native enemy in this manner was not specifically an American trait: it was and remains characteristic of all Western imperialism. As psychopathologist of colonization Franz Fanon once argued, "the settler paints the native as a sort of quintessence of evil. . . . It is not enough for the colonist to affirm that those values have disappeared from, or still better never existed in, the colonial world. The native is declared insensible to ethics; he represents not only the absence of values, but also the negation of values." One need only consider the mound-builder theorists' condemnation of contemporary Indians as the destroyers of greater civilized cultures to see the validity of this argument. Because their imperialism—military, cultural, gendered, and racial—was part of a larger effort to define national identity in the late eighteenth and nineteenth centuries, white Americans did not easily or quickly abandon demonizing the Others, even as natives were pushed farther and farther westward. Frontier memories, from the most educated, like Humphrey Marshall, to the least literate, like some of John Dabney Shane's interviewees, sanctified a narrative in which "the settler was making history; his life is an epoch, an Odyssey," as Fanon continued; "He is the absolute beginning: 'This land was created by us'; he is the unceasing cause: 'If we leave, all is lost, and the country will go back to the Middle Ages'. . . . The settler makes history, and is conscious of it."

Not only did settlers make history, but they acted upon those constructed histories. White Americans who pioneered trans-Appalachia took with them the stories of colonial Indian wars and savagery, and their own children and grandchildren did not forget the lessons of Kentucke. As historian June Namias concluded, along the frontiers where loss of family was a constant peril, "The retelling of these stories of loss marked each American generation during the first three centuries of North American life. These tales constituted significant childhood memories, so significant that in their telling we find the education of the next generation of historians who pass the word along." When Kentucke's settlers finished their wars with the Shawnees and Miamis, Wyandots and Wabash, Cherokees, Chickamaugas, and Chickasaws, the fear and the terror that had fomented in Kentucke added to those memories deep in the American psyche.

Celebration of the heroic frontier narrative, then, neglects those memories and fears. When John F. Kennedy championed the New Frontier and when Ronald Reagan compared the *Challenger* crew to hardy western pioneers, they praised the enduring heroism of the American frontier narrative. So too should we concede the less celebrated but no less significant frenzies of mean fear that also continue to frame the American narrative. While it is always risky to draw modern analogies from history, the long-term consequences of fear and terror on the American mind and American culture are always worth consideration. As social commentator Susan Faludi so provocatively suggested,

Sept. 11 cracked the plaster on that master narrative of American prowess because it so exactly duplicated the terms of the early Indian wars, right down to the fecklessness of our leaders and the failures of our military strategies. Like its early American antecedents, the 9/11 attack was a homeland incursion against civilian targets by non-European, non-Christian combatants who fought under the flag of no recognized nation. Like the "different type of war" heralded by President Bush, the 17th and 18th century "troubles" [and I would add Kentucke's late-eighteenth-century Indian conflict] . . . seemed to have no battlefield conventions, no constraints and no end.

In many ways, the eighteenth- and early-nineteenth-century world that we believed we had lost with the rise of modernism remains with us.

Thomas Jefferson was prophetic when he wrote George Rogers Clark in 1779 that the "same world will scarcely do for them and us." In order to secure the continent, white Americans created other worlds for "them": removal, reservations, and extermination. Unable to protect their homes and families from assault and terror, Kentucke's guardians—from frontiersmen such as Boone and Clark to local, state, and national political leaders— fashioned racial suspicions into a morality play in which the actions of dark Others, threatening white women and children, required constant vigilance and immediate retaliation. The end of the Indian threat in the mid-1790s did not alleviate terror. Instead, blacks assumed the role of dark Other in the white Kentuckian mind. In order to secure their families and futures, white Kentuckians created another world for "them": enslavement. As Kentucky became an Old South frontier, making slavery a critical element of social identity, whites repackaged their fear of Indian attacks into anticipatory anxieties of slave insurrection. Unlike Native Americans, few blacks had the resources or freedom to actually pose threats. But African Americans were ubiquitous in Kentucky, and their omnipresence unsettled whites. As whites employed terror against slaves and free blacks to keep a real threat from manifesting, they too became dangerous Others in the eyes of their black neighbors.

Notably, the terror that played out in Kentucke as it transformed into Kentucky was intimate. Whether it was the Indians trying to inspire excessive fear among frontier settlers so that they would abandon Kentucke, or whites employing excessive fear among blacks so that they would stay submissive, very often the victims knew their antagonists. The Indians who captured Mary Draper Ingles had visited Draper Valley before on friendlier terms, and the men who nightly patrolled Louisville's streets to find and punish errant blacks knew their targets as co-workers in smithies and carriage houses. Terror works by instilling fear and inducing a sense of helplessness—nothing could have been more terrifying than looking into the face of a neighbor, co-worker, or even friend and knowing that a dangerous Other might be hiding inside. That is why Indian attacks and slave patrol raids were random: the more indiscriminate antagonists were in selecting their victims, the better it suited the desired results of fear, compliance, and immobility.

The heroic way of touching America, in this context, then becomes not the absence of fear but the ability to cope with fear. On Kentucke's frontiers, black slaves who risked their lives to scoop up white babies from the forest floor, white women who left forts in the midst of Indian sieges to gather water, and Indians who held off Kentucke militias while their wives and children fled to safety were as heroic as Boone, Clark, or any Hunter from Kentucky. Only when the frontier had passed did white men who had interpreted Kentucke as an opportunity to regenerate their lives, their fortunes, and their honor monopolize heroism as an underpinning of white manhood—they made history.

In dissecting this "great central myth of initiation into a new world and a new life that is at the core of the American experience," Richard Slotkin concluded that white male regeneration required a male counterpart who represented savagery and a white female who required protection. The story of nineteenth-century Kentucky and America is one of more virulent racism, hardening patriarchy, and greater violence, as the stages on which white masculinity had traditionally been proven began to disappear. When in 1893 Frederick Jackson Turner declared the end of the frontier, he correspondingly pronounced the end of American manhood as it had been defined since 1607. With the abolition of slavery in the 1860s, the end of the Indian wars in the 1880s, and the acceleration of the women's suffrage movement, the privileges of white manhood seemed more and more empty as the nineteenth century progressed, requiring "civilized" men to seek out new antagonists who would define and regenerate white manhood. A mid-century Kentucky minister understood well: "When God confers great privileges on a nation, he holds her responsible for all she enjoys, and that where great privileges are abused, sometimes they are turned into the heaviest curses."

Citations and Essays on Sources

The essays that follow do not offer comprehensive treatment of all the books and articles relevant to the history of the Kentucke frontiers and the eras in which they developed. I have concentrated on citing important works that framed this study. In the interest of avoiding repetition, only occasionally did I cite a work more than once, trying to place it where it specifically influenced this narrative. A note on editing: I have elected to present quotes exactly as they read in the sources without correction of spelling or editorial interference.

Abbreviations

AHR	*American Historical Review*
DMC	Draper Manuscript Collection, University of Wisconsin, Madison
FCHQ/FHQ	*Filson Club Historical Quarterly/Filson Historical Quarterly*
FHS	Filson Historical Society, Louisville, Ky.
OVH	*Ohio Valley History*
RKHS	*Register of the Kentucky Historical Society*
UKSC	Department of Special Collections and Archives, Margaret I. King Library, University of Kentucky, Lexington
WMQ	*William and Mary Quarterly*

Preface

"There are two ways of being American . . ."
  —D. H. Lawrence, "American Heroes," *The Nation* 112 (April 14, 1926): 413

"Because of my research . . ."
  —Robert Remini, "The Early Heroes of Kentucky," *RKHS* 90 (1992): 226

"We think back . . ."
—Ronald Reagan, Speech on the *Challenger* Disaster, January 28, 1986, available at www.reaganlibrary.com/reagan/speeches/challenger.asp

"From the lands that stretch . . ."
—John F. Kennedy, Democratic National Convention Nomination Acceptance Address, July 15, 1960, available at www.americanrhetoric.com/speeches/jfk1960dnc.htm

"The horror and fear flowed . . ."
—Peter Silver, *Our Savage Neighbors: How Indian War Transformed Early America* (New York: W. W. Norton, 2007), xviii

"atmosphere of terror . . ."
—Richard Slotkin, *Regeneration through Violence: The Mythology of the American Frontier, 1600–1860* (Norman: University of Oklahoma Press, 1973), 158

"Lie still and go to sleep . . ."
—Elizabeth Shotwell Drake, in Daniel Drake, *Pioneer Life in Kentucky, 1785–1800*, ed. Emmet Field Horine (New York: Henry Schuman, 1948), 20

"It is impossible to conceive . . ."
—W. J. Cash, *Mind of the South* (1941; reprint, New York: Vintage Books, 1991), 10

"on the one hand were the needs . . ."
—Malcolm J. Rohrbough, *The Trans-Appalachian Frontier: People, Societies, and Institutions, 1775–1850* (New York: Oxford University Press, 1978), 63

"Take a lesson from your old pa . . ."
—Robert Schenkkan, *The Kentucky Cycle* (New York: Plume Books, 1993), 47

Frontier Kentucky has been well studied. Older notable surveys include Lewis Collins, *Historical Sketches of Kentucky* (Cincinnati: J. A. and U. P. James, 1847); Robert S. Cotterill, *History of Pioneer Kentucky* (Cincinnati: Johnson and Hardin, 1917); vol. 1 of Charles Kerr, ed., *History of Kentucky*, 5 vols. (New York: American Historical Society, 1922); vol. 1 of Temple Bodley, *History of Kentucky*, 4 vols. (Chicago: S. J. Clarke, 1928); Thomas D. Clark, *History of Kentucky* (Lexington: University of Kentucky Press, 1954); George M. Chinn, *Kentucky Settlement and Statehood, 1750–1800* (Frankfort: Kentucky Historical Society, 1975); Otis K. Rice, *Frontier Kentucky* (Lexington: University Press of Kentucky, 1975). The early chapters of Lowell H. Harrison and James C. Klotter, *A New History of Kentucky* (Lexington: University Press of Kentucky, 1997), and chapters 2 and 3 of Malcolm J. Rohrbough, *Trans-Appalachian Frontier: People, Societies, and Institutions, 1775–1850* (1978; reprint, Bloomington: Indiana University Press, 2007) are useful as well. For an overview of the historiography of frontier Kentucky, see Craig Thompson Friend, "Introduction: The Buzzel about Kentuck," in *The Buzzel about Kentuck: Settling the Promised Land,* ed. Craig Thompson Friend (Lexington: University Press of Kentucky, 1999), 1–23.

The last two decades have seen a flurry of historical scholarship on early Kentucky, and many of the doctoral dissertations produced during this time have emerged as monographs. The most notable are Stephen Aron, *How the West Was Lost: The Transformation of Kentucky from Daniel Boone to Henry Clay* (Baltimore, Md.: Johns Hopkins University Press, 1996); Elizabeth A. Perkins, *Border Life: Experience and Memory in the Revolutionary Ohio Valley* (Chapel Hill: University of North Carolina Press, 1998); Ellen Eslinger, *Citizens of Zion: The Social Origins of Camp Meeting Revivalism* (Knoxville: University of Tennessee Press, 1999); and Craig Thompson Friend, *Along the Maysville Road: The Early American Republic in the Trans-Appalachian West* (Knoxville: University of Tennessee Press, 2005).

Among the fine dissertations that have not been published as books are Fredrika Johanna Teute, "Land, Liberty, and Labor in the Post-Revolutionary Era: Kentucky as the Promised Land" (Ph.D. diss., Johns Hopkins University, 1988); Gail S. Terry, "Family Empires: A Frontier Elite in Virginia and Kentucky, 1740–1815" (Ph.D. diss., College of William and Mary, 1992); Todd Harold Barnett, "The Evolution of 'North' and 'South': Settlement and Slavery on America's Sectional Border, 1650–1810" (Ph.D. diss., University of Pennsylvania, 1993); Matthew G. Schoenbachler, "The Origins of Jacksonian Politics: Central Kentucky, 1790–1840" (Ph.D. diss., University of Kentucky, 1996); Patrick Lee Lucas, "Realized Ideals: Grecian-Style Building as Metaphors for Democracy on the Trans-Appalachian Frontier" (Ph.D. diss., Michigan State University, 2002); John H. Wigger, "Born of Water and Spirit: Popular Religion and Early American Baptists in Kentucky, 1776–1860" (Ph.D. diss., University of Missouri–Columbia, 2003); Honor R. Sachs, "Not the Best Poor Man's Country: The Social World of the Eighteenth-Century West" (Ph.D. diss., University of Wisconsin–Madison, 2006); Marion C. Nelson, "Power in Motion: Western Success Stories of the Jeffersonian Republic" (Ph.D. diss., University of Pennsylvania, 2006).

On definitions and redefinitions of "frontier," see Frederick Jackson Turner, *The Frontier in American History* (New York: Henry Holt, 1920); Thomas Slaughter, *The Whiskey Rebellion: Frontier Epilogue to the American Revolution* (New York: Oxford University Press, 1986); Patricia Nelson Limerick, *The Legacy of Conquest: The Unbroken Past of the American West* (New York: W. W. Norton, 1987); Gregory H. Nobles, "Breaking into the Backcountry: New Approaches to the Early American Frontier," *WMQ* 46 (October 1989): 641–70; Richard White, *The Middle Ground: Indians, Empires, and Republics in the Great Lakes Region, 1650–1815* (New York: Cambridge University Press, 1991); William Cronon, George Miles, and Jay Catlin, eds., *Under an Open Sky: Rethinking America's Western Past* (New York: W. W. Norton, 1992); Elliott West, "American Frontier," in *The Oxford History of the American West*, ed. Clyde A. Milner II, Carol A. O'Connor, and Martha A. Sandweiss (New York: Oxford University Press, 1994), 115–49; Alan Taylor, *William Cooper's Town: Power and Persuasion on the Frontier of the Early American Republic* (New York: Alfred A. Knopf, 1995); Gregory H. Nobles, *American Frontiers: Cultural Encounters and Continental Conquest* (New York: Hill and Wang, 1997); Jeremy Adelman and Stephen Aron, "From Borderlands to Borders: Empires, Nation-States, and the Peoples in between in North American History," *AHR* 104 (1999): 814–41. For Kentucky's role in defining frontier, see Stephen Aron, "The Significance of the Kentucky Frontier," *RKHS* 91 (1993): 298–323.

1. The Indians' Frontiers

"we were attacked . . ."
—George Washington to Governor Robert Dinwiddie, July 18, 1755, in *The Great Events by Famous Historians: A Comprehensive and Readable Account of the World's History, Emphasizing the More Important Events, and Presenting These as Complete Narratives in the Master-Words of the Most Eminent Historians*, ed. Charles F. Stone et al., 22 vols. (New York: National Alumni, 1904–11), 13: 177

"do not might that they come here . . ."
—Peter Schuyler to New York Council, September 6, 1692, in *The Livingston Indian Records 1666–1723*, ed. Lawrence H. Leder (Gettysburg: Pennsylvania Historical Association, 1956), 168

"Since you have not hearkened . . ."
—Shawnee Chiefs to Governor Gordon, 1732, *Pennsylvania Archives* 1 (1852): 329

"All the world knows . . ."
—Chief Tachanoontia speech at Lancaster, 1744, in *Christopher Gist's Journals*, ed. William M. Darlington (1893; reprint, New York: Argonaut Press, 1966), 143

"all the lands within the said colony . . ."
—Deed, July 2, 1744, Colonial Papers, Library of Virginia, Richmond

"sort of republic . . ."
—French correspondence of 1748–49, in "The French Regime in Wisconsin," *Collections of the State Historical Society of Wisconsin*, ed. Reuben Gold Thwaites, 31 vols. (Madison: Wisconsin Historical Society, 1855–1931), 18: 20–22

"stand the brunt of Peter Chartier . . ."
—John Ellis to William Gooch, May 10, 1746, in Lucien Beckner, "Eskippakithiki: The Last Indian Town in Kentucky," *FCHQ* 6 (1932): 370

"Laurel Trees marked with Crosses . . ."
—Thomas Walker, *Journal of an Exploration in the Spring of the Year 1750* (Boston: Little, Brown, 1888), 57

"Settlements of British subjects . . ."
—Treaty of Logstown, 1752, Papers of Walker, his son, Francis Walker, and the Walker and Page families, 1742–1886, Special Collections, University of Virginia Library, University of Virginia, Charlottesville

"fourteen hundred of our men will be here . . ."
—William Trent journal, reprinted in Charles A. Hanna, *The Wilderness Trail; or, The Ventures and Adventures of the Pennsylvania Traders on the Allegheny Path, with Some New Annals of the Old West, and the Records of Some Strong Men and Some Bad Ones*, 2 vols. (New York: G. P. Putnam's Sons, 1911), 2: 297

My understanding of native societies has been largely shaped by sources such as White, *The Middle Ground*; Francis Jennings, *The Founders of America: From the Earliest Migrations to the Present* (New York: W. W. Norton, 1993); Theda Perdue, *Cherokee Women: Gender and Culture Change, 1700–1835* (Lincoln: University of Nebraska Press, 1998); Daniel K. Richter, *Facing East from Indian Country: A Native History of Early America* (Cambridge, Mass.: Harvard University Press, 2001); Robbie Ethridge and Charles Hudson, eds., *The Transformation of the Southeastern Indians, 1540–1760* (Oxford: University Press of Mississippi, 2002).

Prehistoric cultures and their evolution into historical Indian nations are addressed in Henry R. Dobyns, *Their Number Became Thinned: Native American Population Dynamics in Eastern North America* (Knoxville: University of Tennessee Press, 1983); Peter H. Wood, "The Changing Population of the Colonial South: An Overview by Race and Region, 1685–1790," in *Powhatan's Mantle: Indians in the Colonial Southeast*, ed. Peter H. Wood, Gregory A. Waselkov, and M. Thomas Hartley (Lincoln: University of Nebraska Press, 1989), 35–103; Chester B. DePratter, *Late Prehistoric and Early Historic Chiefdoms in the Southeastern United States* (New York: Garland Press, 1991); Russell Thornton, Jonathan Warren, and Tim Miller, "Depopulation in the Southeast after 1492," in *Disease and Demography in the Americas*, ed. John W. Verano and Douglas H. Ubelaker (Washington, D.C.: Smithsonian Institution Press, 1992), 187–95; and Richard W. Jeffries, "Hunters and Gatherers after the Ice Age," in *Kentucky Archaeology*, ed. R. Berry Lewis (Lexington: University Press of Kentucky, 1996), 39–78.

For the indigenous peoples of Kentucke and the Ohio River valley, see A. Gwynn Henderson, *Kentuckians before Boone* (Lexington: University Press of Kentucky, 1992); idem, "Dispelling the Myth: Seventeenth- and Eighteenth-Century Indian Life in Kentucky," *RKHS* 90 (1992): 1–25; Jimmy A. Railey, "Woodland Cultivators," in Lewis, ed., *Kentucky Archaeology*, 79–126; R. Barry Lewis, "Mississippian Farmers," in Lewis, ed., *Kentucky Archaeology*, 127–60; William E. Sharp, "Fort Ancient Farmers," in Lewis, ed., *Kentucky Archaeology*, 161–82; and A. Gwynn Henderson, "Middle Fort Ancient Villages and Organization Complexity in Central Kentucky" (Ph.D. diss., University of Kentucky, 1998).

On Indian trails, see William E. Meyer, *Indian Trails of the Southeast* (Nashville: Blue and Gray Press, 1971); Helen Hornbeck Turner, "The Land and Water Communication Systems of the Southeastern Indians," in Wood, ed., *Powhatan's Mantle*, 27–42; Neal O. Hammon, "Pioneer Routes in Central Kentucky," *FCHQ* 74 (2000): 125–43; Karl Raitz, Nancy O'Malley, Dick Gilbreath, and Jeff Levy, *Kentucky's Frontier Trails: Warrior's Path, Boone's Trace, and Wilderness Road* (Lexington: Gyula Pauer Center for Cartography and GIS, University of Kentucky, 2008).

The Shawnees' forced departure from the Ohio River valley and eventual return occurred within larger themes of eighteenth-century Indian cultural conflict. Among the sources used to reconstruct this story were Lucien Beckner, "Eskippakithiki: The Last Indian Town in Kentucky," *FCHQ* 6 (1932): 355–82; Randolph C. Downes, *Council Fires* on the Upper Ohio: A Narrative of Indian Affairs in the Upper Ohio Valley until 1795 (Pittsburgh: University of Pittsburgh Press, 1940); Jerry E. Clark, The Shawnee (Lexington: University Press of Kentucky, 1977); Francis Jennings, The Ambiguous Iroquois Empire: The Covenant Chain Confederation of Indian Tribes with English Colonies from its beginnings to the Lancaster Treaty of 1744 (New York: W. W. Norton, 1984); Gregory Evans Dowd, A Spirited Resistance: The North American Indian Struggle for Unity, 1743–1815 (Baltimore, Md.: Johns Hopkins University Press, 1992); Michael N. McConnell, A Country Between: The Upper Ohio Valley and Its Peoples, 1724–1774 (Lincoln: University of Nebraska Press, 1992); A. Gwynn Henderson, "The Lower Shawnee Town: Sustaining Native Autonomy in an Indian 'Republic,'" in The Buzzel about Kentuck: Settling the Promised Land, ed. Craig Thompson Friend (Lexington: University Press of Kentucky, 1999), 26–55; Colin G. Calloway, The Shawnees and the War for America (New York: Penguin Books, 2007).

On the initial stages of the French and Indian War, see William Blake Hindman, The Great Meadows Campaign and the Climactic Battle of Fort Necessity (Leesburg, Va.: Potomac Press, 1967); Matthew C. Ward, "Fighting the 'Old Women': Indian Strategy on the Virginia and Pennsylvania Frontier, 1754–1758," Virginia Magazine of History and Biography 103 (1995): 297–320; Frank W. Brecker, Losing a Continent: France's North American Policy, 1753–1763 (Westwood, Conn.: Greenwood Press, 1998); Fred Anderson, Crucible of War: The Seven Years' War and the Fate of Empire in British North America, 1754–1766 (New York: Vintage Books, 2001).

For English colonials' early contact with the Kentucke hunting lands, see Lee Pendleton, Indian Massacres in Montgomery County, 1755–1756: Drapers Meadow Massacre Retold, also Fort Vause and its Traditions (n.p., 1973); Allen Powell, Christopher Gist, Frontier Scout (Shippensburg, Pa.: Burd Street Press, 1992); David M. Burns, Gateway: Dr. Thomas Walker and the Opening of Kentucky (Middlesboro, Ky.: Bell County Historical Society, 2000).

On the land companies, see William M. Darlington, ed., Christopher Gist's Journals (1893; reprint, New York: Argonaut Press, 1966); J. Stoddard Johnston, First Explorations of Kentucky (Louisville, Ky.: Filson Club, 1898); Archibald Henderson, Dr. Thomas Walker and the Loyal Land Company of Virginia (Worcester, Mass.: American Antiquarian Society, 1931); Thomas Perkins Abernethy, Western Lands and the American Revolution (New York: Appleton-Century, 1937); Kenneth P. Bailey, The Ohio Company of Virginia and the Westward Movement,

1748–1792: A Chapter in the History of the Colonial Frontier (Glendale, Calif.: Arthur H. Clark, 1939).

2. Colonial Kentucke

"as men we cannot but thank heaven . . ."
—William Hunter, "Observations on the bones, commonly supposed to elephant's bones, which have been found near the river Ohio in America," February 23, 1768, in *The American Museum, or Repository of Ancient and Modern Fugitive Pieced, andc. Prose and Poetical*, 6 vols. (Philadelphia: Mathew Carey, 1789), 5: 155

"what system, or hypothesis . . ."
—Peter Collison, "An Account of some very large fossil teeth, found in North America," n.d., in *The American Museum*, 5: 156

"in ancient times a herd of them . . ." and "[The Great Spirit] made man . . ."
—W. Winterbotham, *A Historical, Geographical, Commercial and Philosophical View of the American United States and the European Settlements in the America and the West-Indies*, 4 vols. (London: J. Ridgway, 1795), 3: 138

"We found everywhere abundance . . ."
—Daniel Boone, in John Filson, *Adventures of Daniel Boon, one of the Original Settlers of Kentucky: containing the wars with the Indians on the Ohio, from 1769 to the present time, and the first establishment and progress of the settlements on that river* (Windsor, Vt.: Alden Spooner, 1793), 2

"Now, brothers, go home . . ."
—Will Emery, in Lyman Cooper Draper, "The Life of Daniel Boone," DMC 2B188

"eyes like two balls of fire . . ."
—Thomas Jefferson, "A Memoir of the Discovery of Certain Bones of a Quadruped of the Clawed Kind in the Western Parts of Virginia," March 10, 1797, *Transactions of the American Philosophical Society* 4 (1799): 253–54

"We were in a dangerous . . ."
—Boone, in Filson, *Adventures of Daniel Boon*, 17

"his hardships and adventures . . ."
—John B. Roark to Lyman Cooper Draper, March 30, 1885, DMC 16C81

"2300 deer skins . . ."
—in Thomas D. Clark, *A History of Kentucky* (Ashland, Ky.: Jesse Stuart Foundation, 1988), 33

"I am sent with my people . . ."
—Thomas Bullitt, speech to the chief of the Shawanoe Nation, June 9, 1773, in *The Life and Times of Robert B. McAfee and His Family and Connections*, part 3: Summer 1773, at www.drizzle.com/~jtenlen/mcafee/life/life4.html

". . . our young men to be friendly . . ."
—Chief Cornstalk, response to Bullitt's speech, June 10, 1773, in *The Life and Times of Robert B. McAfee*

"I do assure you . . ."
—Richard Butler to unknown, June 10, 1773, in *The Life and Times of Robert B. McAfee*

"a temporary expedient . . ."
—George Washington to William Crawford, September 21, 1767, in Account Book 2, George Washington Papers, 1741–1799, Series 5: Financial Papers, Manuscript Division, Library of Congress, Washington, D.C.

"the Opportunity we have . . ."
—William Preston, in *Documentary History of Dunmore's War, 1774*, ed. Reuben G. Thwaites and Louise P. Kellogg (Madison: Wisconsin Historical Society, 1905), 93

"In the course of the last year . . ."
—"Logan's Lament," October 1774, in Peter Force, ed., *American Archives: consisting of a collection of authentick records, state papers, debates, and letters and other notices of publick affairs, the whole forming a documentary history of the origin and progress of the North American colonies; of the causes and accomplishment of the American revolution; and of the Constitution of government for the United States, to the final ratification thereof*, ser. 4, 6 vols. (Washington, D.C.: M. St. Clair Clarke and Peter Force, 1837–46), 1: 1020

"the love of Liberty . . ."
—Fort Gower Resolves, November 5, 1774, in Force, *American Archives*, ser. 4, 1: 962–63

"the operation carried on . . ."
—George Washington, in Archibald Henderson, "The Creative Forces in Westward Expansion: Henderson and Boone," *AHR* 20 (1914): 100

"You, Carolina Dick . . ."
    —deposition of Samuel Watson, DMC 1CC161

"is something in that affair . . ."
    —George Washington, in William Stewart Lester, *The Transylvania
    Colony* (Spencer, Ind.: S. R. Guard, 1935), 41

"some walking, others loping . . ."
    —Felix Walker, "Narrative of His Trip with Boone from Long Island to
    Boonesborough in March 1775," in George W. Ranck, *Boonesborough*
    (Louisville, Ky.: Filson Club, 1901), 166

"the Indians should do us a favor . . ."
    —Richard Henderson to partners, June 12, 1775, DMC 4B16

"Every Kentuckian ought to try her gait . . ."
    —John Dabney Shane interview with Nathaniel Hart Jr., DMC 17CC195

"settle somewhere . . ."
    —Journal of Richard Henderson, DMC 3B199

On fossils and early myths surrounding Kentucke, see Reuben T. Durrett, *Traditions of the Earliest Visits of Foreigners to North America, the First Formed and First Inhabited of the Continents*, Filson Club Publication No. 23 (Louisville, Ky.: J. P. Morton, 1908); Thomas D. Clark, *The History of Laurel County* (London, Ky.: Laurel County Historical Society, 1989); Adreinne Mayor, *Fossil Legends of the First Americans* (Princeton, N.J.: Princeton University Press, 2005). For the relationship between such myths and the Edenic description, see Henry Nash Smith, *Virgin Land: The American West as Symbol and Myth* (Cambridge, Mass.: Harvard University Press, 1950); Lester H. Cohen, "Eden's Constitution: The Paradisiacal Dream and Enlightenment Values of Late Eighteenth-Century Literature on the American Frontier," *Prospects: An Annual of American Cultural Studies* 3 (1977): 83–109.

On Kentucke's bison, see Julian J. N. Campbell, "Present and Presettlement Forest Conditions in the Inner Bluegrass of Kentucky" (Ph.D. diss., University of Kentucky, 1980); Ted Franklin Belue, *The Long Hunt: Death of the Buffalo East of the Mississippi* (Mechanicsburg, Pa.: Stackpole Books, 1996). On the Long Hunters, see Harriet Simpson Arnow, *Seedtime on the Cumberland* (New York: Macmillan, 1960); Ted Franklin Belue, *The Hunters of Kentucky: A Narrative History of America's First Far West, 1750–1792* (Mechanicsburg, Pa.: Stackpole Books, 2003).

Daniel Boone's earliest excursions into Kentucke have been recounted many times. For my version of the Boone story, I have relied heavily on John Mack Faragher, *Daniel Boone: The Life and Legend of an American Pioneer* (New York: Macmillan, 1993); Lyman Copeland Draper, *The Life of Daniel Boone*, ed. Ted Franklin Belue (Mechanicsburg, Pa.: Stackpole Press, 1998); Michael A. Lofaro, *Daniel Boone: An American Life* (Lexington: University Press of Kentucky, 2003); Robert Morgan, *Boone: A Biography* (Chapel Hill, N.C.: Algonquian Books, 2007). For a unique interpretation of the Boone legend, see Richard Slotkin, "Narrative into Myth: The Emergence of a Hero (1784)," in *Regeneration through Violence*, 269–312.

Boone was only the biggest of frontier big men. On James Harrod, see Kathryn Harrod Mason, *James Harrod of Kentucky* (Baton Rouge: Louisiana State University Press, 1951). On Benjamin Logan, see Charles Gano Talbert, *Benjamin Logan: Kentucky Frontiersman* (Lexington: University of Kentucky Press, 1962). On Simon Kenton, see Thomas D. Clark, *Simon Kenton: Kentucky Scout* (New York: Farrar and Rinehart, 1943); Patricia Jahns, *The Violent Years: Simon Kenton and the Ohio-Kentucky Frontier* (New York: Hastings House, 1962).

On the Wilderness Road, see William Allen Pusey, *The Wilderness Road to Kentucky* (New York: George H. Doren, 1921); Robert L. Kincaid, *The Wilderness Road* (Indianapolis: Bobbs-Merrill, 1947); Thomas L. Connelly, "Gateway to Kentucky: The Wilderness Road, 1748–1792," *RKHS* 59 (1961): 109–32; and Neal Owen Hammon, "Early Roads into Kentucky," *RKHS* 68 (1970): 91–133. On traveling the Wilderness Road versus traveling the Ohio River, see Ellen Eslinger, "Introduction," in *Running Mad for Kentucky: Frontier Travel Accounts* (Lexington: University Press of Kentucky, 2004), 1–67.

On western land surveying, see Samuel M. Wilson, *Kentucky Land Warrants, for the French, Indian, and Revolutionary Wars* (1917; reprint, n.p.: Southern Historical Press, 1994); Stephen A. Aron, "Pioneers and Profiteers: Land Speculation and the Homestead Ethic in Frontier Kentucky," *Western Historical Quarterly* 23 (1992): 179–98; Daniel M. Friedenberg, *Life, Liberty, and the Pursuit of Land: The Plundering of America* (Buffalo, N.Y.: Prometheus Books, 1992); Andro Linklater, *Measuring America: How an Untamed Wilderness Shaped the United States and Fulfilled the Promise of Democracy* (New York: Walker, 2002). Neal O. Hammon has been tireless in exploring land laws, surveying, and claims; see "The First Trip to Boonesborough," *FCHQ* 45 (1971): 249–63; "Fincastle Surveyors in the Bluegrass, 1774," *RKHS* 70 (1972): 277–95; "The Fincastle Surveyors at the Falls of the

Ohio, 1774," *FCHQ* 47 (1973): 268–83; "Settlers, Land Jobbers, and Out-lyers: A Quantitative Analysis of Land Acquisition on the Kentucky Frontier," *RKHS* 84 (1986): 241–62; and especially *Early Kentucky Land Records, 1773–1780* (Louisville, Ky.: Filson Club, 1992).

3. Revolutions

"all indented Servants, Negroes, or others"
—Proclamation of Earl of Dunmore, November 7, 1775, Special Collections, University of Virginia Library

"good, loyal, and useful subjects . . ."
—James Otis, *The Rights of the British Colonies Asserted and Proved*, 1764, in *Pamphlets of the American Revolution, 1750–1776*, ed. Bernard Bailyn, 2 vols. (Cambridge, Mass.: Harvard University Press, 1965), 1: 455

"There are thousands . . ."
—Thomas Paine, *Common Sense* (Philadelphia: W. and T. Bradford, 1776), 50

"He has excited domestic insurrections . . ."
—Declaration of Independence, July 4, 1776

"a body of people . . ." and "if we do not act . . ."
—James Hogg, in Force, ed., *American Archives*, ser. 4, 4: 544, 545

"And as we are anxious . . ."
—"The Petition of the Inhabitants, and some of the intended Settlers, of that part of NORTH-AMERICA now denominated TRANSYLVANIA," in Force, ed., *American Archives*, ser. 4, 6: 1528

"Hundreds of wretches come down . . ."
—John Floyd to William Preston, May 27, 1776, DMC 33S2968

"If valuable conditions . . ."
—George Rogers Clark to Jonathan Clark, in Temple Bodley, *History of Kentucky*, 2 vols. (Chicago: S. J. Clarke, 1928), 1: 209–10

"We could hardly get along . . ."
—John Dabney Shane interview with William Clinkenbeard, DMC 11CC66

"I am afraid to lose sight . . ."
—John Todd to William Preston, June 22, 1776, in Draper, "The Life of Daniel Boone," DMC 2B188

"a civil war among the people . . ."
—John Floyd to William Preston, May 27, 1776, DMC 33S296-297

"I'm worried to death almost . . ."
   —Todd to Preston, June 22, 1776

"The Virginians are haughty . . ."
   —Henry Hamilton to General Guy Carleton, November 30, 1775, DMC
   45J101

"Our study had been . . ."
   —John Floyd to William Preston, July 21, 1776, DMC 4C20

"Several who called . . ."
   —David Ramsey, *History of the Revolution of South Carolina* (Trenton,
   N.J.: Isaac Collins, 1785), 141

"When God created this World . . ."
   —Speech of Cornstalk, November 7, 1776, in *Iroquois Indians: A Documentary History of the Diplomacy of the Six Nations and Their
   League*, ed. Francis Jennings et al., 50 reels (Woodbridge, Conn.: Research Publications, 1985), reel 32

"I think more than 300 men . . ."
   —Floyd to Preston, July 21, 1776

"it was out of my power . . ."
   —George Rogers Clark, in William H. English, *Conquest of the Country
   Northwest of the River Ohio 1778–1783 and the Life of Gen. George
   Rogers Clark*, 2 vols. (Indianapolis: Bowen-Merrill, 1896), 1: 75

"the validity of the titles . . ."
   —Virginia Convention Resolution, June 24, 1776, in Force, ed., *American
   Archives*, ser. 4, 4: 1044

"few hot headed rash young Men . . ."
   —Mss PP4, William Fleming Papers, Special Collections, Leyburn Library,
   Washington and Lee University, Lexington, Va.

"to march against and attack . . ."
   —English, *Conquest of the Country Northwest of the River Ohio*, 1: 92–93

"What I have in View . . ."
   —Patrick Henry to George Rogers Clark, January 2, 1778, in *George Rog-
   ers Clark Papers*, ed. James Alton James, 2 vols. (Springfield: Illinois
   State Historical Library, 1912–24), 1: 36

"when the weather will be warm . . ."
   —Daniel Boone, in John Dabney Shane interview with Joseph Jackson,
   DMC 11C62

"This is the last speech . . ."
—George Rogers Clark, in Ross F. Lockridge, *George Rogers Clark, Pioneer Hero of the Old Northwest* (Yonkers-on-the-Hudson, N.Y.: World Book, 1927), 87–88

"to excel them in barbarity . . ."
—George Rogers Clark, in "Clark-Leyba Papers," ed. Lawrence Kinnaird, *AHR* 41 (1935): 101

"he had just come . . ."
—English, *Conquest of the Country Northwest of the River Ohio*, 1: 342

"is an enemy so execrable . . ."
—Thomas Jefferson to Patrick Henry, March 27, 1779, in *The Writings of Thomas Jefferson*, ed. Andrew A. Lipscomb and Albert Ellery Bergh, 20 vols. (Washington, D.C.: Thomas Jefferson Memorial Association, 1903–1904), 4: 54

"The indiscriminate murder . . ."
—Thomas Jefferson to Theodorick Bland Jr., June 7, 1779, in *The Works of Thomas Jefferson*, ed. Paul L. Ford, 12 vols. (New York: G. P. Putnam's Sons, 1904–1905), 3: 44

"our Enemies the Chickasaws . . ."
—George Rogers Clark to Thomas Jefferson, September 23, 1779, in James, ed., *George Rogers Papers*, 1: 365

"those tribes of Indians . . ."
—Thomas Jefferson to George Rogers Clark, January 1, 1780, in *The Papers of Thomas Jefferson*, ed. Julian Boyd et al., 34 vols. (Princeton, N.J.: Princeton University Press, 1950–), 3: 258

"Destitute of every other Hope, . . ."
—Boonesborough petition, March 1780, in James, *George Rogers Clark Papers*, 1: 400

"The Indians have this year . . ."
—John Floyd to George Rogers Clark, May 22, 1781, in James, *George Rogers Clark Papers*, 1: 557

"We see ourselves weak . . ."
—Chief Wryneck, in *Collections and Researches Made by the Michigan Pioneer and Historical Society*, 40 vols. (Lansing, Mich.: Wynkoops Harrenbeck Crawford, 1874–1929), 10: 464

"and our numbers seem to decrease . . ."
—Floyd to Clark, May 22, 1781

"Shawnees were almost gold-yellow . . ."
—John Dabney Shane interview with Sarah Graham, c. 1840, DMC 12CC49

"a sort of yellow man"
—John Dabney Shane interview with William Clinkenbeard, c. 1840, DMC 11CC59

"a yellow man, who staid at the Fort"
—John Dabney Shane interview with Nathaniel Hart Jr., 1843, DMC 17CC192

"a 'copper' snake struck . . ."
—unknown, in *History of the Upper Ohio Valley*, 2 vols. (Madison, Wis.: Brant and Fuller, 1890–91), 1: 356

"rowed by naked Copper colored men . . ."
—David Meade to Ann Randolph, September 1, 1796, in "The Westward Migration of a Planter Pioneer in 1796," ed. Bayard Still, *WMQ* 21 (1941): 331

"nearly all my troubled or vivid dreams . . ."
—Drake, *Pioneer Life in Kentucky*, 28

"It seemed strange to me . . ."
—David Jones, *A Journal of Two Visits Made to Some Nations of Indians on the West Side of the River Ohio, in the Years 1772 and 1773* (1774; reprint, New York: Joseph Sabin, 1865), 88

"Emedeately Old Reddle cryed . . ."
—Daniel Trabue, in *Westward into Kentucky: The Narrative of Daniel Trabue*, ed. Chester Raymond Young (Lexington: University Press of Kentucky, 1981), 140

"white savage"
—John G. E. Heckewelder, *A Narrative of the Mission of the United Brethren among the Delaware and Mohegan Indians; from its Commencement, in the year 1740, to the Close of the Year 1808* (Philadelphia: M'Carty and Davis, 1820), 192

"Brothers, the Long Knives . . ."
—Simon Girty, in John Bradford, *The Voice of the Frontier: John Bradford's Notes on Kentucky*, ed. Thomas D. Clark (Lexington: University Press of Kentucky, 1993), 49–50

"Some [blacks] have been . . ."
—Thomas Jefferson, *Notes on the State of Virginia* (1781; reprint, New York: Library of America, 1984), 266

"take dat to 'member Ben . . ."
—Lewis Collins, *Historical Sketches of Kentucky* (Cincinnati: J. A. and
U. P. James, 1948), 300

"dark mulatto"
—John Redd, "Reminiscences of Western Virginia," *Virginia Magazine of
History and Biography* 6 (1899): 339

"We saw them . . ."
—John Dabney Shane interview with Henry Parvin, DMC 11CC173

"the inroads of the Savages"
—Harrodsburg Memorial to the Virginia Convention, June 20, 1776, DMC
14S11-12

"We Virginians . . ."
—Daniel Boone, in *Audubon and His Journals*, ed. Maria R. Audubon,
2 vols. (New York: Charles Scribner's Sons, 1897), 2: 241

On the Revolutionary War in Kentucke and the Ohio River valley,
see George W. Ranck, *Boonesborough: its founding, pioneer struggles,
Indian experiences, Transylvania days, and revolutionary annals*
(Louisville, Ky.: J. P. Morton, 1901); Reuben Gold Thwaites and Louise
Phelps Kellogg, eds., *The Revolution on the Upper Ohio, 1775–1777*
(Madison: Wisconsin Historical Society, 1908); Reuben Gold Thwaites
and Louise Phelps Kellogg, eds., *Frontier Defense on the Upper Ohio,
1777–1778* (Madison: Wisconsin Historical Society, 1912); Louise Phelps
Kellogg, ed., *Frontier Advance on the Upper Ohio, 1778–1779* (Madison:
Wisconsin Historical Society, 1916); idem, ed., *Frontier Retreat on the
Upper Ohio, 1779–1781* (Madison: Wisconsin Historical Society, 1917);
Randolph C. Downes, "Indian War on the Upper Ohio, 1779–1782,"
Western Pennsylvania History Magazine 17 (1934): 93–115; Charles G.
Talbert, "Kentucky Invades Ohio—1780," *RKHS* 52 (1954): 291–300;
idem, "Kentucky Invades Ohio—1782," *RKHS* 53 (1955): 288–97; Neal
Hammon and Richard Taylor, *Virginia's Western War, 1775–1786* (Mechanicsburg, Pa.: Stackpole Press, 2002).

For the intersection of race and revolution, see David B. Davis, *The
Problem of Slavery in the Age of Revolution, 1770–1823* (New York: Oxford University Press, 1975); Sylvia R. Frey, *Water from the Rock: Black
Resistance in a Revolutionary Age* (Princeton, N.J.: Princeton University Press, 1991); Alfred F. Young, *The Shoemaker and the Tea Party:
Memory and the American Revolution* (Boston: Beacon Press, 1999);
Richter, *Facing East from Indian Country*. For the Ethiopian Regiment,

see Benjamin Quarles, *The Negro in the American Revolution* (Chapel Hill: University of North Carolina Press, 1961); Donald R. Wright, *African Americans in the Colonial Era: From African Origins though the American Revolution* (Wheeling, Ill.: Harlan Davidson, 1990).

On the deterioration of backcountry relations with Native Americans as the Revolutionary War opened, see John Richard Alden, *John Stuart and the Southern Colonial Frontier: A Study of Indian Relations, War, Trade, and Land Problems in the Southern Wilderness, 1774–1775* (1944; reprint, New York: Gordian Press, 1966); Tom Hatley, *The Dividing Paths: Cherokees and South Carolinians through the Era of Revolution* (New York: Oxford University Press, 1993); Colin G. Calloway, *The American Revolution in Indian Country: Crisis and Diversity in Native American Communities* (New York: Cambridge University Press, 1995); J. Russell Snapp, *John Stuart and the Struggle for Empire on the Southern Frontier* (Baton Rouge: Louisiana State University Press, 1996); Colin G. Calloway, "The Continuing Revolution in Indian Country," in *Native Americans and the Early Republic*, ed. Frederick E. Hoxie, Ronald Hoffman, and Peter J. Albert (Charlottesville: University Press of Virginia, 1999), 3–36.

On George Rogers Clark and the Illinois country campaigns, see Temple Bodley, *George Rogers Clark: His Life and Public Services* (New York: Houghton Mifflin, 1926); James A. James, *The Life of George Rogers Clark* (Chicago: University of Chicago Press, 1928); Lowell H. Harrison, *George Rogers Clark and the War in the West* (Lexington: University Press of Kentucky, 1976); William Dodd Brown, "Dangerous Situation, Delayed Response: Col. John Bowman and the Kentucky Expedition of 1777," *RKHS* 97 (1999): 137–58.

On the Other and identity, see Eve Kornfield, "Encountering 'the Other': American Intellectuals and Indians in the 1790s," *WMQ* 52 (1995): 287–314; Richard White, "'Although I am dead, I am not entirely dead. I have left a second of myself': Constructing Self and Persons on the Middle Ground of Early America," in *Through a Glass Darkly: Reflections on Personal Identity in Early America*, ed. Ronald Hoffman, Mechal Sobel, and Fredrika J. Teute (Chapel Hill: University of North Carolina Press, 1997), 404–18; Matthew Frye Jacobson, *Whiteness of a Different Color: European Immigrants and the Alchemy of Race* (Cambridge, Mass.: Harvard University Press, 1998); William B. Hart, "Black 'Go-Betweens' and the Mutability of 'Race,' Status, and Identity on New York's Pre-Revolutionary Frontier," in *Contact Points: American Frontiers from the Mohawk Valley to the Mississippi, 1750–1830*, ed. Andrew R. L. Cayton and Fredrika J. Teute (Chapel Hill: University of

North Carolina Press, 1998), 88–113; Perkins, *Border Life*; Nancy Shoe-maker, *A Strange Likeness: Becoming Red and White in Eighteenth-Century America* (New York: Oxford University Press, 2004); Colin G. Calloway, *White People, Indians, and Highlanders: Tribal Peoples and Colonial Encounters in Scotland and America* (New York: Oxford University Press, 2008). On the conflation of Other with animal character-izations, see Winthrop Jordan, *White over Black: American Attitudes toward the Negro, 1550–1812* (New York: W. W. Norton, 1968); Barbara J. Fields, "Of Rogues and Geldings," *AHR* 108 (2003): 1397–1405. On the tensions between identity shaped through community and identity shaped by individualism, see Michael Zuckerman, "The Fabrication of Identity in Early America," *WMQ* 34 (1977): 83–124.

On Simon Girty, see George Washington Ranck, "Girty, the White Indian: A Study in Early Western History," *Magazine of American History* 15 (1886): 33–59; Daniel P. Barr, "'A Monster So Brutal': Simon Girty and the Degenerative Myth of the American Frontier, 1783–1900," *Essays in History* 40 (1998), http://etext.virginia.edu/journals/EH/EH40/barr40.html.

On blacks in early Kentucky, see J. Winston Coleman, *Slavery Times in Kentucky* (Chapel Hill: University of North Carolina Press, 1940); Marion B. Lucas, *A History of Blacks in Kentucky*, vol. 1: *From Slavery to Segregation, 1760–1891* (Frankfort: Kentucky Historical Society, 1992); Ellen Eslinger, "The Shape of Slavery on the Kentucky Frontier, 1775–1800," *RKHS* 92 (1994): 1–23; Marion B. Lucas, "African Ameri-cans on the Kentucky Frontier," *RKHS* 95 (1997): 121–34.

4. Peopling Kentucke

"Brothers, the intruders . . ."
   —Simon Girty, in Bradford, *Voice of the Frontier*, 49–50

"Them that ain't cowards . . ."
   —John Dabney Shane interview with Jacob Stevens, DMC 12CC134

"did not know how many . . ."
   —John Dabney Shane interview with Sarah Graham, DMC 12CC50

"We have nothing . . ."
   —Benjamin Harrison to George Rogers Clark, December 20, 1781, DMC 51J101

"I can with truth say . . ."
   —Harry Innes, in *American State Papers: Indian Affairs*, 2 vols. (Washington, D.C.: Gales and Seaton, 1832–61), 1: 88

"when the Indians relate . . ."
—John Heckewelder, *History, Manners, and Customs of the Indian Nations Who Once Inhabited Pennsylvania and the Neighbouring States,* ed. William C. Reichel (Philadelphia: Historical Society of Pennsylvania, 1876), 216

"fineshed . . . and let him lie . . ."
—Trabue, in Young, *Westward into Kentucky,* 153

"cut him up and fed him . . ."
—John Dabney Shane interview with Jacob Stevens, DMC 12CC136

"Savages killing and scalping . . ."
—"Franklin and Lafayette's List of Prints to Illustrate British Cruelties," May 1779, in *The Papers of Benjamin Franklin,* ed. Leonard W. Labaree, 35 vols. (New Haven, Conn.: Yale University Press, 1959–), 29: 591–92

"we were struck with Horror . . ."
—"Supplement to the Boston Independent Chronicle," in Labaree, *The Papers of Benjamin Franklin,* 37: 187–88

"lying tomahawked . . ."
—Donald F. Carmony, ed., "Spencer Records' Memoir of the Ohio Valley Frontier, 1766–1795," *Indiana Magazine of History* 55 (1959): 336

"wishd he could come up . . ."
—Trabue, in Young, *Westward into Kentucky,* 45

"yet reeking with the blood . . ."
—Henry Hamilton, in "The Haldiman Papers," *Michigan Pioneer and Historical Collections* 9 (1886): 501–502

"The savages are not . . ."
—Joseph Reed to Daniel Brodhead, April 29, 1780, in *Pennsylvania Archives* 8 (1853): 218

"that Spirit which is so necessary . . ."
—Joseph Reed to Joseph Montgomery, April 8, 1780, in McKinney et al., *Pennsylvania Archives* 8: 170

"upon the principle of *revenge* . . ."
—Harry Innes to the Secretary of War, July 7, 1780, in *American State Papers: Indian Affairs,* 1: 88

"same world will scarcely do . . ."
—Thomas Jefferson to George Rogers Clark, January 1, 1779, in Boyd et al., *Papers of Thomas Jefferson,* 3: 259

"We wish to learn you . . ."
  —Speech to Jean Baptist Ducoigne, June 1, 1781, in Boyd et al., *Papers of Thomas Jefferson*, 6: 63

"the depredatory mode of war . . ."
  —Innes, in *American State Papers: Indian Affairs*, 1: 88

"against those who are our enemies . . ."
  —Thomas Jefferson to George Rogers Clark, January 29, 1780, in Boyd et al., *Papers of Thomas Jefferson*, 3: 276

"looked as much like an Indian . . ."
  —John Dabney Shane interview with William Clinkenbeard, DMC 11CC66

"He left his plough . . ."
  —John Dabney Shane interview with Asa Farrar, DMC 13CC1 (emphasis added)

"Hardly one wek pass . . ."
  —John Floyd to William Preston, May 31, 1780, DMC 17CC127

"keep themselves as united . . ."
  —Jefferson County Court Records, 1779, DMC 51J104

"the Terror it had on me . . ."
  —Rosanna Wallace to Anne Fleming, October 23, 1784, Bullitt Family Papers, FHS

"Nothing less than the preservation . . ."
  —Petition from the Inhabitants of Boonesborough to Clark, March 10, 1780, in James, *George Rogers Clark Papers*, 1: 398

"A woman dare not go . . ."
  —John Dabney Shane interview with John Dyal, DMC 13CC228

"They was a couragus people . . ."
  —Trabue, in Young, *Westward into Kentucky*, 61

"about with a rake . . ."
  —John Dabney Shane interview with Mary Perkins, John Day Caldwell Papers, Cincinnati Historical Society, Cincinnati, Ohio

"I was not made for a fighter . . ."
  —John Dabney Shane interview with John Gass, DMC 11CC13

"It is easy to fight Indians . . ."
  —Jane Sprowl, in Carmony, "Spencer Records' Memoir of the Ohio Valley Frontier," 357

"was trying to lift the slabs . . ."
—John Dabney Shane interview with Martin Wymore, DMC 11CC130

"had learned on purpose . . ."
—John Dabney Shane interview with Levisa McKinney, DMC 9CC12

"moulded bullets . . ."
—Cephas Washburn, *Reminiscences of the Indians*, ed. J. W. Moore
(1869; reprint, New York: Johnson Reprint, 1971), 206

"My party, 27 in number . . ."
—John Floyd to George Rogers Clark, September 16, 1781, DMC 17CC34
(emphasis added)

"The Country has been . . ."
—John May to Samuel Beall, April 15, 1780, John May Papers 1779–1780, FHS

"spirit of speculation . . ."
—David Rice, in Robert H. Bishop, ed., *An Outline of the History of the
Church in the State of Kentucky, During a Period of Forty Years: Containing the Memoirs of Rev. David Rice, and Sketches of the Origin
and Present State of Particular Churches, and of the Lives and La-
bours of a Number of Men Who Were Eminent and Useful in Their Day*
(Lexington: Thomas T. Skilman, 1824), 36

"You would be surprised . . ."
—John Floyd to William Preston, May 5, 1780, DMC 17CC127

"desired my brother . . ."
—John May to Samuel Beall, August 30, 1779, Beall-Booth Papers, FHS

"some of them having entered . . ."
—John May to Samuel Beall, April 15, 1780, John May Papers

"The whole dirt and filth . . ."
—"Journal of Colonel William Fleming," in *Travels in the American
Colonies*, ed. Newton D. Mereness (New York: Antiquarian Press,
1961), 630

"continually Harrased . . ."
—"Statement of Grievances by the inhabitants of Kentucky and a request
either for a better government or independence from Virginia," May 30,
1782, in *Petitions of the Early Inhabitants of Kentucky to the General
Assembly of Virginia, 1769 to 1792*, ed. James Rood Robertson (Louisville: J. P. Morton, 1914), 63

"live so near each other . . ."
—Drake, *Pioneer Life in Kentucky*, 13–14

"any land that sells now . . ."
　　—William Christian to Thomas Madison, March 30, 1786, Bullitt Family
　　Papers

"As we are very near . . ."
　　—William Christian to sister, November 4, 1785, Bullitt Family Papers

"Wm. Whitley I am your Horn . . ."
　　—in W. M. Beauchamp, "Rhymes from Old Powder Horns II," *Journal of
　　American Folk-Lore* 5 (1892): 286

"When I got me a family . . ."
　　—James Wade, in "Buffaloes in the Corn: James Wade's Account of Pio-
　　neer Kentucky," ed. Roseann R. Hogan, *RKHS* 89 (1991): 31

"I have suffered much . . ."
　　—unknown to unknown, January 30, 1780, FHS

"You had better have staid . . ."
　　—John Dabney Shane interview with Stephen Cooper, 1889, DMC 11C101

"Oh what troubles . . ."
　　—Ann Christian to Ann Fleming, 1786, Bullitt Family Papers

"old aunt Sarah . . ."
　　—John Dabney Shane interview with William Moseby, DMC 11CC272

"the yard was full of Indians . . ."
　　—Alfred Henderson to Lyman Copeland Draper, February 12, 1853, DMC
　　24C38

"lie still and go to sleep . . ."
　　—Elizabeth Shotwell Drake, in Drake, *Pioneer Life in Kentucky*, 25

"the axe and scythe . . ."
　　—Drake, *Pioneer Life in Kentucky*, 24

"Broad Ax and Bar of Iron"
　　—Isaac Hite to Abraham Hite, April 26, 1783, FHS

"taunted each other . . ."
　　—John Dabney Shane interview with Thomas Metcalf, DMC 11CC185

"I stood at the little gate . . ."
　　—John Dabney Shane interview with William Niblick, DMC 11CC84

"the western people . . ."
　　—George Mason, in *The debates in the several state conventions on the
　　adoption of the federal Constitution, as recommended by the general*

convention at Philadelphia, in 1787, ed. Jonathan Elliot, 2nd ed.,
5 vols. (Philadelphia: J. B. Lippincott, 1836–59), 5: 458

"They made good soldiers"
—John Dabney Shane interview with William McBride, DMC 11CC262

"let him in and put out Bob"
—John Dabney Shane interview with Sarah Graham, DMC 12CC47

"It was believed from the sign . . ."
—John Dabney Shane interview with James Wade, DMC 123CC38

"send a parcel of poor slaves . . ."
—Thomas Hart to Nathaniel Hart, August 3, 1780, in "Shane Collection
of Documents: The Hart Paper," *Journal of the Presbyterian Historical
Society* 14 (1931): 343–44

"You will not be displeased . . ."
—Robert Daniel to William Christian, October 27, 1784, Robert Emmett
McDowell Collection, FHS

"I am oblige to give . . ."
—Robert Daniel to William Christian, January 7, 1784, Robert Emmett
McDowell Collection

"Time desires me . . ."
—Annie Christian to Elizabeth Christian, April 12, 1787, Hugh Blair
Grigsby Papers, Virginia Historical Society, Richmond

"fell in with some worthless . . ."
—John May to Samuel Beall, December 9, 1780, Beall-Booth Family Papers

"A large House . . ."
—"Franklin and Lafayette's List of Prints to Illustrate British Cruelties,"
May 1779, in Labaree, *Papers of Benjamin Franklin*, 29: 591

"he must make use . . ."
—unknown to unknown, January 30, 1780

"unless you can sell . . ."
William Christian to mother, December 12, 1785, Hugh Blair Grigsby
Papers

"purchase young Negroes . . ."
—A. Drummond to John Coles, April 5, 1780, Carter-Smith Papers, Special Collections, University of Virginia Library

"7 or 8 Negroes . . ."
—Samuel McDowell to Andrew Rich, July 13, 1791, Samuel McDowell
Papers, FHS

"removal to the state . . ."
—"An Act concerning Slaves," October 1785, in *The Statutes at Large; being a collection of all the Laws of Virginia*, ed. William W. Hening, 13 vols. (Richmond: George Cochran, 1823), 12: 182–83

"An Act concerning . . ."
—"An Act concerning the importation of slaves, into the district of Kentucky," October 1788, in Hening, *Statutes at Large*, 12: 713–14

"by neglecting to take the Oath . . ."
—Petition of Benjamin Stevenson, October 28, 1780, in Robertson, *Petitions*, 125

"Any observations of your own . . ."
—Thomas Jefferson to George Rogers Clark, November 26, 1782, in Boyd et al., *Papers of Thomas Jefferson*, 6: 204

"suppose our country"
—Jefferson, *Notes on the State of Virginia*, 203

"*new colony* on the *back* of Virginia . . ."
—Thomas Paine, *Public Good*, in *Thomas Paine: Collected Writings* (New York: Library of America, 1995), 279, 282, 284

"have absolutely been hitherto . . ."
—John Floyd to Thomas Nelson, October 5, 1781, in James, *George Rogers Clark Papers*, 19: 3

"almost the whole of the lands . . ."
—Petition to Congress, 1780, Papers of the Continental Congress, 1774–1789, National Archives, Washington, D.C.

"Without the interposition . . ."
—*Maryland Journal*, December 3, 1783, DMC 3JJ114

"The British had call'd . . ."
—Benjamin Harrison to George Rogers Clark, January 13, 1783, DMC 52 J73

"They treat us . . ."
—Francisco Cruzat to Estevan Miró, August 23, 1784, in Carl J. Ekberg, *Colonial Ste. Genevieve: An Adventure on the Mississippi Frontier* (Gerald, Mo.: Patrice Press, 1985), 93

"will enable [Virginia] to economize . . ."
—James Monroe to George Rogers Clark, October 19, 1783, in James, *George Rogers Clark Papers*, 19: 250

"It is for the interest . . ."
—Thomas Jefferson to James Madison, February 20, 1784, in Boyd et al., *Papers of Thomas Jefferson*, 6: 547

"The spirit of emigration . . ."
—George Washington to the President of Congress, December 14, 1784, in *The Writings of George Washington*, ed. John C. Fitzpatrick et al., 39 vols. (Westport, Conn.: Greenwood Press, 1934–70), 28: 12

"propogators of false news . . ."
—Humphrey Marshall, *The History of Kentucky, Exhibiting An Account of the Modern Discovery; Settlement; Progressive Improvement; Civil and Military Transactions; and the Present State of the Country*, 2 vols. (1812; reprint, Frankfort: George S. Robinson, 1824), 1: 186

"That you have enemies . . ."
—Thomas Jefferson to George Rogers Clark, November 26, 1782, in Boyd et al., *Papers of Thomas Jefferson*, 6: 204–205

"Many of the inhabitants . . ."
—James Speed to Benjamin Harrison, May 22, 1784, General Correspondence, Accounts and Vouchers, 1776–1795, George Rogers Clark Papers, Library of Virginia

"I hope our petitioning . . ."
—Daniel Boone to William Christian, August 16, 1785, Emmer Collection, Rare Books and Manuscript Division, New York Public Library

"a Revolution in this Country . . ."
—Walker Daniel to Benjamin Harrison, May 21, 1784, in *Calendar of Virginia State Papers*, ed. William P. Palmer et al., 11 vols. (Richmond: Virginia State Library, 1875–93), 3: 584, 588

"There is much Reason . . ."
—Samuel Purviance to Richard Henry Lee, December 20, 1784, Arthur Campbell Papers, 1743–1811, FHS

"I feel myself called upon . . ."
—Benjamin Harrison to George Rogers Clark, July 2, 1783, DMC 32J80

"family is quite safe . . ."
—William Christian to William Fleming, September 25, 1785, Virginia Historical Society

"the Legislative Body . . ."
—Levi Todd to Edmund Randolph, April 30, 1787, in Palmer et al., *Calendar of Virginia State Papers*, 4: 277

"The injries done to the Indens . . ."
—Daniel Boone to Patrick Henry, August 16, 1785, DMC 32C8

On the Battle of Blue Licks, see Samuel M. Wilson, *Battle of the Blue Licks, August 19, 1782* (Lexington: n.p., 1927); Michael C. C. Adams, "An Appraisal of the Blue Licks Battle," *FHQ* 75 (2001): 181–203.

On scalping and bodily mutilation, see James Axtell, "Scalping: The Ethnohistory of a Moral Question," in *The European and the Indian: Essay in the Ethnohistory of Colonial North America* (New York: Oxford University Press, 1981), 207–41; Ruth Richardson, *Death, Dissection, and the Destitute* (Chicago: University of Chicago Press, 1987); Nancy Isenberg, "Death and Satire: Dismembering the Body Politic," in *Mortal Remains: Death in Early America*, ed. Nancy Isenberg and Andrew Burstein (Philadelphia: University of Pennsylvania, 2003), 71–90. On terror as a weapon, see Walter Laqueur, *Terrorism* (Boston: Little, Brown, 1977). On Daniel Trabue's interpretation of the Indian threat, see Marco Sioli, "Hugenot Traditions in the Mountains of Kentucky: Daniel Trabue's Memories," *Journal of American History* 84 (1998): 1313–33.

On stations and forts, see Nancy O'Malley, *Stockading Up* (Lexington: Kentucky Heritage Council, 1987); idem, *Searching for Boonesborough* (Lexington: University Press of Kentucky, 1990); Clay Lancaster, *Antebellum Architecture in Kentucky* (Lexington: University Press of Kentucky, 1991), ch. 1; Nancy O'Malley, "Frontier Defenses and Pioneer Strategies in the Historic Settlement Era," in Friend, *The Buzzel about Kentuck*, 57–76; Neal O. Hammon, "Kentucky Pioneer Forts and Stations," *FHQ* 76 (2002): 523–86.

On women and family life on the frontier, see Margaret Ripley Wolfe, "Fallen Leaves and Missing Pages: Women in Kentucky History," *RKHS* 90 (1992): 64–89; Kenneth C. Carstens, *Women on Kentucky's Western Colonial Frontier* (Frankfort: Kentucky Historical Society, 1996); Perkins, *Border Life*. For family structures in the backcountries, see David Hackett Fischer, *Albion's Seed: Four British Folkways in America* (New York: Oxford University Press, 1989); Warren R. Hofstra, "Land, Ethnicity, and Community at the Opequon Settlement, Virginia, 1730–1800," *Virginia Magazine of History and Biography* 98 (1990): 423–48; David Hackett Fischer and James C. Kelly, *Bound Away: Virginia and the Westward Movement* (Charlottesville: University Press of Virginia, 2000). On the changing nature of marriage in the eighteenth century, see Daniel Blake Smith, *Inside the Great House: Planter Family Life in Eighteenth-Century Chesapeake Society* (Ithaca, N.Y.: Cornell University Press, 1986).

On land acquisition and the 1779 land law, see Abernethy, *Western Lands and the American Revolution;* Hammon, *Early Kentucky Land*

Records. For information on specific land surveys and warrants, see the Kentucky Land Office website at www.sos.ky.gov/land/.

On Kentucky's relationship to Virginia and the path to separation, see Patricia Watlington, "Discontent in Frontier Kentucky," *RKHS* 65 (1967): 77–93; Peter S. Onuf, *The Origins of the Federal Republic: Jurisdictional Controversies in the United States, 1775–1787* (Philadelphia: University of Pennsylvania Press, 1983); L. Scott Philyaw, *Virginia's Western Visions: Political and Cultural Expansion on an Early American Frontier* (Knoxville: University of Tennessee Press, 2004).

On frontier imagery, see Slotkin, *Regeneration through Violence;* Daniel Blake Smith, "'This Idea in Heaven': Image and Reality on the Kentucky Frontier," in Friend, *The Buzzel about Kentuck,* 77–99; Thomas Hallock, *From the Fallen Tree: Frontier Narratives, Environmental Politics, and the Roots of National Pastoral, 1749–1826* (Chapel Hill: University of North Carolina Press, 2003).

On Kentucke slavery, see Lucas, *A History of Blacks in Kentucky,* vol. 1; Clement Eaton, "Slave-Hiring in the Upper South: A Step toward Freedom," *Mississippi Valley Historical Review* 46 (1960): 663–78; Gail S. Terry, "Sustaining the Bonds of Kinship in a Trans-Appalachian Migration, 1790–1811," *Virginia Magazine of History and Biography* 102 (1994): 455–76; Ellen Eslinger, "The Shape of Slavery on Virginia's Kentucky Frontier, 1775–1800," in *Diversity and Accommodation: Essays on the Cultural Composition of the Virginia Frontier,* ed. Michael J. Puglisi (Knoxville: University of Tennessee Press, 1997), 172–93.

5. Seeking Security and Stability

"We hold it as a self evident . . . ,"
  —Temple Bodley, ed., *Reprints of Littell's Political Transactions in and Concerning Kentucky; Letter of George Nicholas to his friend in Virginia; General Wilkinson's Memorial* (Louisville: J. P. Morton, 1926), 63

"We conceive the people . . ."
  —Caleb Wallace to James Madison, July 12, 1785, James Madison Papers, Library of Congress

"not leave to the Western country . . ."
  —Answers to Démeunier's First Queries, January 24, 1786, in Boyd et al., *Papers of Thomas Jefferson,* 10: 14

"no interval whatever . . ."
  —James Madison to Richard Henry Lee, July 7, 1785, in *The Papers of*

James Madison, ed. William T. Hutchinson et al., 13 vols. (Chicago: 1962–), 8: 314

"meet them upon their own ground . . ."
—George Washington to Thomas Jefferson, Sept. 6, 1785, in Fitzpatrick, *Writings of George Washington*, 28: 280

"the whole of the party . . . ,"
—Journal of General Butler, in *The Olden Time*, ed. Neville B. Craig, 2 vols. (Pittsburgh: Wright and Charlton, 1848), 2: 512–13

"They conceived us . . ."
—Ebenezer Denny, *Military Journal of Ebenezer Denny* (Philadelphia: J. B. Lippincott, 1860), 69

"I find that many . . ."
—Journal of General Butler, January 17, 1786, 2: 416 (emphasis original)

"God gave us this country . . ."
—Journal of General Butler, January 30, 1786, 2: 522

"The U.S. will take . . ."
—Journal of General Butler, January 20, 1786, 2: 424–25

"devious mischievous"
—Speech of Chief Molunthy, March 20, 1786, Papers of the Continental Congress, 1774–89, National Archives

"a banditti of refugees . . ."
—Robert Patterson to Walter Finney, July 12, 1786, Papers of the Continental Congress

"I don't think this country . . ."
—George Rogers Clark to Patrick Henry, May 1786, in Palmer et al., *Calendar of Virginia State Papers*, 4: 122

"in case any person . . ."
—Benjamin Logan, DMC 12S136-37

"It may require some management . . ."
—George Washington to Henry Lee, June 18, 1786, in Fitzpatrick, *Writings of George Washington*, 28: 461

"an act declaring and acknowledging . . ."
—"Request of the inhabitants of Jefferson, Fayette, Lincoln, and Nelson Counties for an act acknowledging the independence of Kentucky from Virginia," in Robertson, *Petitions*, 81

"fear that the people of Kentucky . . ."
   —Thomas Jefferson to A. Stuart, January 25, 1786, in Lipscomb and
      Bergh, *Writings of Thomas Jefferson* 5: 259

"and to the end that no interval . . ."
   —"An Act making further provision for the erection of the district of Ken-
      tuckey into an independent state," in Hening, *Statues at Large*, 12: 242

"the value of land here . . ."
   —John May to Samuel Beall, April 15, 1780, John May Papers

"There are many ambitious . . ."
   —George Washington to Henry Lee, July 26, 1786, in Fitzpatrick, *Writ-
      ings of George Washington*, 28: 484

"Whenever the new states . . ."
   —George Washington to Henry Lee, June 18, 1786, in Fitzpatrick, *Writ-
      ings of George Washington*, 28: 460

"the Western people had nothing . . ."
   —Harry Innes to John Brown, December 7, 1787, Papers of Harry Innes,
      Library of Congress

"the direction of the current . . ."
   —Isaac Dunn to Esteban Miró, June 14, 1788, in Charles Gayarré, *History
      of Louisiana*, 4 vols. (New Orleans: A Hawkins, 1885), 3: 212

"Money there is none . . ."
   —William Christian to William Fleming, September 25, 1785, Virginia
      Historical Society

"There has gone such a Train . . ."
   —John Breckinridge to Lettice Breckinridge, February 9, 1783, Breckin-
      ridge Family Papers, Library of Congress

"Kentucky is the greatest field . . ."
   —John Breckinridge to James Breckinridge, January 29, 1786, James
      Breckinridge Papers, University of Virginia Library

"First: That the American Settlements . . ."
   —Wilkinson's Memorial and Expatriation Declaration, September 23,
      1787, in Bodley, *Reprints of Littell's Political Transactions*, cxxv–cxxvii

"that my principles and . . ."
   —Bodley, *Reprints of Littell's Political Transactions*, cxxxix

"these articles being intended . . ."
   —*Kentucky Gazette*, December 15, 1787

"for some time all the trade . . ."
—Daniel Clark, *Notes from the Proofs of the Corruption of Gen. James Wilkinson and of His Connexion with Aaron Burr* (Philadelphia: Wm. Hall, Jun. and Geo. W. Pierie, 1809), 9

"This is the first Armada . . ."
—*New York Journal and Weekly Register*, March 15, 1789

"if the Constitution is adopted . . ."
—Harry Innes to John Brown, February 20, 1788, Harry Innes Papers, FHS

"The only danger I apprehend . . ."
—James Madison to George Washington, April 10, 1788, in Gaillard Hunt, ed., *The Writings of James Madison*, 9 vols. (New York: G. P. Putnam's Sons, 1900–1910), 5: 115n1

"Are not the United States . . ."
—George Nicholas, in Jonathan Elliot, ed., *The Debates in the Several State Conventions of the Adoption of the Federal Constitution, as recommended by the general convention at Philadelphia, in 1787*, 2nd ed., 5 vols. (Philadelphia: J. B. Lippincott, 1836–59), 3: 261

"If nine states give it away . . ."
—William Grayson, in Elliot, *Debates in the Several State Conventions*, 3: 350

"The people of Kentucky . . ."
—Patrick Henry, in Elliot, *Debates in the Several State Conventions*, 3: 353

"I think that Kentucky . . ."
—George Nicholas, in Elliot, *Debates in the Several State Conventions*, 3: 361–62

"the impression of Kentucky . . ."
—James Madison to George Washington, April 10, 1788, in Hunt, *Writings of James Madison*, 5: 116

"if Kentucky will declare . . ."
—John Brown to George Muter, July 10, 1788, in Thomas Marshall Green, *The Spanish Conspiracy* (Cincinnati: R. Clarke, 1891), 170

"told us that he did not . . ."
—Thomas Marshall to George Washington, February 12, 1789, in Dorothy Twohig, ed., *The Papers of George Washington: Presidential Series*, 13 vols. (Charlottesville: University Press of Virginia, 1987–2007), 1: 294

"touched the key . . ."
   —Harry Innes to George Washington, December 18, 1788, Harry Innes
      Papers

"The people of this country . . ."
   —Thomas Marshall to George Washington, February 12, 1789

"so that it is entirely . . ."
   —Alexander S. Bullitt to the Governor of Virginia, May 16, 1787, Bullitt
      Family Papers

"In Fayette there are parties . . ."
   —William Fleming to his wife, December 3, 1789, William Fleming
      Papers

"in the habit of retaliation . . ."
   —Arthur St. Clair to George Washington, September 14, 1789, in William
      Henry Smith, ed., *The St. Clair Papers*, 2 vols. (Cincinnati: R. Clarke,
      1882), 2: 124

"some of the inhabitants . . ."
   —Henry Knox, "Relative to the Northwestern Indians," June 15, 1789, in
      American State Papers: Indian Affairs, 2: 13

"this Kentuck affair . . ."
   —John Hamtramck to Josiah Harmar, August 14, 1789, letter book B,
      Harmar Papers, William Clements Library, University of Michigan,
      Ann Arbor

"The angry passions . . ."
   —Henry Knox to the President of the United States, May 23, 1789, in
      American State Papers: Indian Affairs, 2: 53

"will united with the hostile . . ."
   —Arthur St. Clair to the President of the United States, September 14,
      1789, in *American State Papers: Indian Affairs*, 2: 58

"the sword of the republic . . ."
   —Knox, "Relative to the Northwestern Indians," 2: 13

"what the Officers . . ."
   —January 25, 1790, *Diaries of George Washington*, ed. Donald Jackson,
      6 vols. (Charlottesville: University Press of Virginia, 1976), 6: 15

"the people of Kentucky . . ."
   —John Hamtramck to Arthur St. Clair, December 2, 1790, in Smith,
      St. Clair Papers, 2: 198

"four moccasin tracks . . ."
—Brigadier General Harmar to the Secretary of War, June 9, 1790, in *American State Papers: Indian Affairs*, 2: 91

"killed a girl of twelve years old . . ."
—Deposition of Joseph Barnett, June 8, 1790, in *American State Papers: Indian Affairs*, 2: 90

"the Kentucky militia appeared . . ."
—Ebenezer Denny, *Military Journal of Ebenezer Denny* (Philadelphia: J. B. Lippincott, 1860), 344

"we shall give them . . ."
—Thomas Jefferson to Charles Carroll, April 15, 1791, in Boyd et al., *Papers of Thomas Jefferson*, 20: 214

"depredations and murders . . ."
—"An Act to authorize and direct the commanding officers of certain counties within the district of Kentuckey, to order our guards for certain purposes," October 1790, in Hening, ed., *Statutes at Large*, 13: 202

"The recital of your happiness . . ."
—John Filson, *The Discovery, Settlement, and Present State of Kentucke* (Wilmington, Del.: James Adams, 1784), 392–93

"not pleased with the Splendid Dress . . ."
—Caleb Wallace to James Madison, September 25, 1785, James Madison Papers

"discarded the complimentary style . . ."
—"Statement of grievances by the inhabitants of Kentucky and a request for a better government or independence from Virginia," in Robertson, *Petitions*, 65, 62–63

"the two great points . . ."
—James Madison, *Federalist No. 10*

"Ideas of that System . . ."
—James Wilkinson to James Hutchinson, June 20, 1785, *Pennsylvania Magazine of History and Biography* 12 (1888): 60

"A Free Trade . . ."
—James Wilkinson to James Hutchinson, June 20, 1785

"I am unfortunate . . ."
—James Wilkinson to Harry Innes, February 29, 1792, Harry Innes Papers

"In a free government . . . ,"
—Thomas Speed, *The Political Club: Danville, Kentucky, 1786–1790*
(Louisville: John P. Morton, 1894), 125, 120, 134, 151

"the fertility of the soils . . ."
—Caleb Wallace to James Madison, July 12, 1785, in Hutchinson, *Papers of James Madison*, 8: 321

"Down the Mississippi . . ."
—"To the Honourable House, of Assembly, for the State of Virginia," October 14, 1779, in Robertson, *Petitions*, 46

"possessed of twenty-five acres . . ."
—"An act concerning election of members of general assembly," October 1785, in Hening, *Statutes at Large*, 12: 120

"remain valid and secure"
—"An act concerning the erection of the district of Kentucky into an independent state," October 1788, in Hening, *Statutes at Large*, 12: 789

"every cast and denomination . . ."
—*Kentucky Gazette*, October 8, 1791

"Politically Mad . . ."
—Alexander Scott Bullitt to William Fleming, March 8, 1792, Bullitt Family Papers

"Peasantry are perfectly mad . . ."
—Harry Innes to Thomas Jefferson, August 27, 1791, Thomas Jefferson Papers

"There is a wide difference . . ."
—*Kentucky Gazette*, March 1, 1788

"novices who will only be able . . ."
—*Kentucky Gazette*, October 8, 1791

"We have a great clamor . . ."
—Frances Ransdell Slaughter to John Ransdell, June 6, 1792, FHS

"They have given a very serious alarm . . ."
—Harry Innes to Thomas Jefferson, August 27, 1791, Thomas Jefferson Papers

"What a Buzzel is this . . ."
—John Brown Sr. to William Preston, May 5, 1775, DMC 4QQ15

"They seemed absolutely infatuated . . ."
—Wade Hall, ed., "Along the Wilderness Trail: A Young Lawyer's 1785 Letter from Danville, Kentucky to Massachusetts," *FCHQ* 61 (1987): 288–95.

"Heaven is a Kaintuck . . ."
—Timothy Flint, *Recollections of the Last Ten Years, Passed in Occasional Residences and Journeyings in the Valley of the Mississippi* (Boston: Cummings, Hilliard, 1826), 64

"Canaan of the West"
—Samuel Rogers, *Autobiography of Elder Samuel Rogers*, ed. Elder John Rogers (Cincinnati: Standard Publishing, 1880), 3

"With a view and expectation . . ."
—in A. C. Quisenberry, "Five Hundred Kentucky Pioneers," *RKHS* 10 (1912): 41

"subscribe to and support . . ."
—Low Dutch Company Articles of Agreement, Jane Bergen Beers Collection, 1784–1927, FHS

"in one minute a gang of men . . ."
—Joseph Craig, *A Sketch of a journal of the Rev. Joseph Craig in which is contained his experience* (Lexington: Thomas Skillman, 1813), 23

"Great sorrows of late . . ."
—John Waller, 1781, in Craig, *A Sketch of a journal*, appendix

"Their camp-meetings . . ."
—Drake, *Pioneer Life in Kentucky*, 194

"In a despotic country . . ."
—Drake, *Pioneer Life in Kentucky*, 212

"inviting the Baptists . . ."
—William Warren Sweet, *Religion on the American Frontier*, vol. 2: *The Presbyterians, 1763–1840: A Collection of Source Materials* (New York: Harper, 1936), 135

"pass for free men"
—*Kentucky Gazette*, September 1, 1792

"Beside a lamp . . ."
—*Kentucky Gazette*, May 31, 1794

"Disorder cannot be countenanced"
—"A Copy of the First Minutes of Bryan Station Church, Fayette County, Kentucky 1786–1895," June 1792, UKSC

"How do you do sister . . ."
—John Taylor, *Baptists on the American Frontier: A History of Ten Baptist Churches*, ed. Chester Raymond Young, 3rd ed. (Macon, Ga.: Mercer University Press, 1995), 189

On Moluntha's death, see Colin G. Calloway, "Maquachake: The Perils of Neutrality in the Ohio Country," in *The American Revolution in Indian Country: Crisis and Diversity in Native American Communities* (New York: Cambridge University Press, 1995), 158–81.

On efforts to commercially connect trans-Appalachia to the East, see Douglas R. Littlefield, "The Potomac Company: A Misadventure in Financing an Early American Internal Improvement Project," *Business History Review* 58 (1984): 562–85; Peter S. Onuf, "Liberty, Development, and Union: Visions of the West in the 1780s," *WMQ* 43 (1986): 179–213; John Lauritz Larson, *Internal Improvements: National Public Works and the Promise of Poplar Government in the Early United States* (Chapel Hill: University of North Carolina Press, 2001).

On salt and saltpeter production, see Thomas D. Clark, "Salt, a Factor in the Settlement of Kentucky," *FCHQ* 12 (1938): 42–53; Robert E. McDowell, "Bullitt's Lick: The Related Saltworks and Settlements," *FCHQ* 30 (1956): 241–69; Burston Faust, "The History of Saltpeter Mining in Mammoth Cave, Kentucky," *FCHQ* 41 (1967): 5–20; Carol A. Hill and Duane DePaepe, "Saltpeter Mining in Kentucky Caves," *RKHS* 77 (1979): 247–62.

On early agrarian promotions and developments, see Thomas D. Clark, *Agrarian Kentucky* (Lexington: University Press of Kentucky, 1977); Lee Soltow, "Kentucky Wealth at the End of the Eighteenth Century," *Journal of Economic History* 43 (1983): 617–33; Steven A. Aron, "Significance of the Frontier in the Transition to Capitalism," *History Teacher* 27 (1994): 263–88; Craig Thompson Friend, "'Work and Be Rich': Economy and Culture on the Bluegrass Farm," in Friend, *The Buzzel about Kentuck*, 125–51.

On Jenny Wiley's captivity, see C. Mitchell Hart, *Jenny Wiley Country: A History of the Big Sandy Valley in Kentucky's Eastern Highlands and Genealogy of the Region's People*, 4 vols. (Kingsport, Tenn.: Kingsport Press, 1972).

On the political landscape of the late 1780s and early 1790s, see Thomas Speed, *The Political Club: Danville, Kentucky* (Louisville: John P. Morton, 1894); Patricia Watlington, *The Partisan Spirit: Kentucky Politics, 1779–1792* (New York: Atheneum, 1972); Teute, "Land, Liberty, and Labor in the Post-Revolutionary Era"; Lowell H. Harrison, *Kentucky's Road to Statehood* (Lexington: University Press of Kentucky, 1992); Harry S. Laver, "'Chimney Corner Constitutions': Democratization and Its Limits in Frontier Kentucky," *RKHS* 95 (1997): 337–67.

On religious groups in early Kentucke, see Bayly Ellen Marks, "The Rage for Kentucky: Emigration from St. Mary's County, 1790–1810," in

Geographical Perspectives on Maryland's Past, ed. Robert D. Mitchell and Edward K. Muller, University of Maryland Occasional Papers in Geography 4 (College Park: Dept. of Geography, University of Maryland, 1979): 108–28; George W. Ranck, "The Travelling Church: An Account of the Baptist Exodus from Virginia to Kentucky in 1781," *RKHS* 79 (1981): 240–65; Vincent Akers, *The Low Dutch Company: A History of the Holland Dutch Settlement of the Kentucky Frontier* (Bargersville, Ind.: privately printed, 1982); Ellen Eslinger, "Some Notes on the History of Cane Ridge Prior to the Great Revival," *RKHS* 91 (1993): 1–23. Also see Rhys Isaac, *The Transformation of Virginia, 1740–1790* (New York: W. W. Norton, 1982) for the shifting religious atmosphere in Revolutionary-era Virginia.

6. From Kentucke to Kentucky

"persons, living on . . ."
—George Nicholas to James Madison, November 2, 1789, in Hutchinson, et al., *Papers of James Madison*, 12: 444–45

"Must we suffer our Inhabitants . . ."
—George Thompson to James Madison, June 1, 1790, in Hutchinson et al., *Papers of James Madison*, 13: 237

"assert its own power . . ."
—*Kentucky Gazette*, May 7, 1791

"the taking of so many prisoners . . ."
—George Nicholas to James Madison, June 20, 1791, in Hutchison et al., *Papers of James Madison*, 14: 32–33

"The Indians are spreading Fire . . ."
—George Rogers Clark to Jonathan Clark, May 11, 1792, George Rogers Clark Papers, Library of Virginia

"mounted Volunteers of Kentucky . . ."
—Henry Knox to Anthony Wayne, April 20, 1793, Anthony Wayne Papers, Historical Society of Pennsylvania, Philadelphia

"Nothing shall induce me . . ."
—Anthony Wayne to Henry Knox, June 20, 1793, Anthony Wayne Papers

"Let the Legion be completed . . ."
—Anthony Wayne to Henry Knox, November 15, 1793, Anthony Wayne Papers

"surrounded by a rugged desart . . ."
 —"Petition of the Inhabitants of the State of Kentucky to the Congress of
 the United States of America," December 4, 1793, Breckinridge Family
 Papers

"We have every reason to expect . . ."
 —Isaac Shelby to Henry Knox, January 10, 1794, Isaac Shelby Papers,
 1750–1826, FHS

"I fully expect that we shall be attacked . . ."
 —Isaac Shelby to Henry Knox, February 10, 1794, Isaac Shelby Papers

"Wou'd to God that . . ."
 —Anthony Wayne to Henry Knox, May 26, 1794, Anthony Wayne Papers

"Kentuckey is more full of Mony . . ."
 —William Blount to John Gray Blount, January 21, 1794, in Alice Barnwell and William Masterson, eds., *The John Gray Blount Papers*,
 3 vols. (Durham, N.C.: Christian Printing, 1952–65), 2: 350

"Our existence almost depends . . ."
 —Hubbard Taylor to James Madison, January 3, 1793, in Hutchinson et
 al., *Papers of James Madison*, 14: 435–36

"Ending Kentucky's Indian Menace"
 —"Ending Kentucky's Indian Menace," January 16, 1829, in Bradford,
 Voice of the Frontier, 318

"All men, when they form a social compact, are equal"
 —"Journal of the First Constitutional Convention of Kentucky Held in
 Danville, Kentucky, April 2 to 19, 1792" (Lexington: State Bar Associa-
 tion of Kentucky, 1942), sec. 19, art. 12

"the sentiments of warm attachment . . ."
 —Message to Congress, December 8, 1790, in *American State Papers*, 1: 13

"Kentucky to the Union given . . ."
 —James Schouler, *History of the United States under the Constitution*,
 rev. ed., 7 vols. (New York: Dodd, Mead, 1880–1917), 1: 164

"all persons are born equally free . . ."
 —Vermont Constitution (1777), ch. 1, art. 1

"The People of Kentucky are mere Fanatics . . ."
 —Harry Innes to William Fleming, August 14, 1791, William Fleming Papers

"Let no man, or set of men, . . ."
 —*Kentucky Gazette*, October 8, 1791

"obstruct the suffrage of the people . . ."
—*Kentucky Gazette*, December 3, 1791

"We know of no distinctions among men . . ."
—*Kentucky Gazette*, October 15, 1791

"Government must be strong enough"
—George Nicholas, "Speech in the Kentucky Convention," George
Nicholas Papers, Reuben T. Durrett Collection, Special Collections,
Joseph Regenstein Library, University of Chicago

"The most serious reflection . . ."
—George Nicholas to James Madison, May 2, 1792, in Hutchinson et al.,
Papers of James Madison, 14: 296

"If a man is poor . . ."
—George Nicholas, Right of Suffrage, 1792, George Nicholas Papers

"exclusion not from the Legislature only . . ."
—John Hughes to Charles Simms, March 20, 1792, in *Early Chapters in
the Development of the Patomac Route to the West*, ed. Corra Bacon-
Foster (Washington, D.C.: Columbia Historical Society, 1912), 262

"resolve UNCONDITIONALLY . . ."
—David Rice, *Slavery Inconsistent with Justice and Good Policy, Proved
by a Speech Delivered in the Convention, Held at Danville, Kentucky*
(New York: Isaac Collins and Sons, 1792), 43

"Oh come the time, and haste the day . . ."
—*Kentucky Gazette*, July 19, 1788

"Excluding slaves . . ."
—"Speech on Slaves," George Nicholas Papers

"Just get all the Negroes asleep, . . ."
—Memoir of Rev. James Gallaher, DMC 15CC224

"I view the blacks as part of the human species, . . ."
—*Kentucky Gazette*, July 2, 1791

"as this measure will not add . . ."
—George Nicholas to James Madison, May 2, 1792, in Hutchinson et al.,
Papers of James Madison, 14: 296–97

"whenever the United States shall be invaded . . ."
—Militia Act of 1792, May 2, 1792, sec. 1, Second Congress, Session I

"America has fixed in the minds . . ."
—George Nicholas to James Madison, May 2, 1792, in Hutchinson et al.,
Papers of James Madison, 14: 298

"The adoption of the constitution for the State of Kentucky . . ."
    —Address of the House of Representatives to the President, November 9,
    1792, in Hutchinson et al., *Papers of James Madison*, 14: 403–404

"The fact is that there seems to be a foundation . . ."
    —George Nicholas to James Madison, September 5, 1792, in Hutchinson
    et al., *Papers of James Madison*, 14: 358–59

"with as little formality and legal criticisms as possible . . ."
    —*Stewart's* (Lexington) *Kentucky Herald*, January 14, 1795

"in the state 2 years, or the county . . ."
    —Kentucky Constitution, 1792, sec. 1, art. 3

"How many poor unfortunate fellow creatures . . ."
    —*Kentucky Gazette*, January 31, 1798

"the office was set on fire . . ."
    —Asa Farrar interview, DMC 13CC3

"mutually and by our own consent"
    —*Kentucky Gazette*, July 27, 1793

"treated her inhumanely . . ."
    —*Acts of a Local, or Private Nature, Passed at the Second Session of the
    Sixth General Assembly for the Commonwealth of Kentucky* (Frank-
    fort, Ky.: John Bradford, 1798), 44

"By marriage, the husband and wife . . ."
    —William Blackstone, *Commentaries on the Laws of England*, 4 vols.
    (Oxford: Claredon Press, 1765–69), 1: 442

"may at their discretion make such order . . ."
    —"An Act to amend and reduce into one act the several acts concerning
    Bastardy," December 1795, William Littell and Jacob Swigert, *A Digest
    of the Statute Law of Kentucky*, 2 vols. (Frankfort, Ky.: Kendall and
    Russell, 1822), 1: 282–84

"if either of the parties intending to marry . . ."
    —"Marriages," February 3, 1798, in Littell and Swigert, *Digest of the
    Statute Law of Kentucky*, 1: 878

"If any *feme sole*, of the age of twelve . . ."
    —"Marriages," February 3, 1798, in Littell and Swigert, *Digest of the
    Statute Law of Kentucky*, 1: 879

"Negros hire very well in this country"
    —Samuel Meredith to John Breckenridge, May 17, 1792, Breckinridge
    Family Papers

"great wagons, laden with merchandise . . ."
—Drake, *Pioneer Life in Kentucky*, 176

"under last will and testament . . ."
—"An Act concerning the Importation and Emancipation of Slaves," December 1794, in Littell and Swigert, *Statute Law of Kentucky* 1: 247

"any gun, powder, shot . . ."
—"Slaves," February 14, 1798, in Littell and Swigert, *Digest of the Statute Law of Kentucky*, 1: 1150–51

"other than their own complexion . . ."
—"Master and Servant," January 16, 1798, in Littell and Swigert, *Digest of the Statute Law of Kentucky*, 1: 882

"If the Indians whip . . ."
—David Barrow Diary, July 11, 1795, FHS

"gave him the right hand of Christian affection . . ."
—Bishop, *Outline of the History of the Church*, 233

"teach every slave . . ."
—Extracts from the Minutes of the Transylvania Presbytery, 1786–1837, in Sweet, *Religion on the American Frontier*, vol. 2: *The Presbyterians*, 147

"Is slavery a moral evil?"
—Extracts from the Minutes of the Transylvania Presbytery, 1786–1837, in Sweet, *Religion on the American Frontier*, vol. 2: *The Presbyterians*, 169–70

"temper his intercourse with all men . . ."
—Extracts from the Minutes of the Transylvania Presbytery, 1786–1837, in Sweet, *Religion on the American Frontier*, vol. 2: *The Presbyterians*, 179

"passions for domination . . ."
—*Kentucky Gazette*, October 17, 1787

"republicans, patriots, friends to the American revolution . . ."
—David Barrow, *Involuntary, Unmerited, Perpetual, Absolute, Hereditary, Slavery Examined on the Principles of Nature, Reason, Justice, Policy, and Scripture* (Lexington, Ky.: D. and C. Bradford, 1808), 21

"under the same order and Disciplin . . ."
—Records of Severn's Valley Church, Kentucky, 1788–90, in William Warren Sweet, *Religion on the American Frontier*, vol. 1: *The Baptists, 1783–1830* (New York: Henry Holt, 1936), 250

"Make the Deed in the Space of one year"
—Records of Severn's Valley Church, Kentucky, 1788–90, in Sweet, *Religion on the American Frontier*, vol. 1: *The Baptists*, 253

"fornication viz of being with child . . ."
—Records of Severns Valley Church, Kentucky, 1788–90, in Sweet, *Religion on the American Frontier*, vol. 1: *The Baptists*, 267

"with his bounties . . ."
—Barrow Diary, June 15, 1795

"slaves were received by the congregation . . ."
—William Hickman, in G. C. Downing, "Forks of Elkhorn Church," *RKHS* 4 (1906): 35–42

"whether it is lawful for a slave . . ."
—Minutes of the Elkhorn Baptist Association, in Sweet, *Religion on the American Frontier*, vol. 1: *The Baptists*, 437

"No mother's smiles . . ."
—William Hayden, *Narrative of William Hayden, Containing a Full Account of His Travels for a Number of Years, Whilst a Slave, in the South* (Cincinnati: n.p., 1846), 20

"if the Indians was at peace . . ."
—Hubbard Taylor to James Madison, May 23, 1793, in Hutchinson et al., *Papers of James Madison*, 15: 20

"take the whole of Louisiana . . ."
—George Rogers Clark to the French minister, February 5, 1793, in "Correspondence between Clark and Genet," ed. Frederick Jackson Turner, *Reports of the Historical Manuscripts Commission of the American Historical Association, 1896* (Washington, D.C.: Government Printing Office, 1897), 967

"Louisiana groaning under tyranny . . ."
—"Old Fashioned Republican," n.d., Breckinridge Family Papers

"Our all is at stake . . ."
—George Nicholas to James Madison, December 15, 1793, in Hutchinson et al., *Papers of James Madison*, 15: 136–38

"enticing officers and soldiers . . ."
—Jefferson's memorandum, July 5, 1793, in *The Anas of Thomas Jefferson*, ed. Franklin B. Sawvel (1903; reprint, New York: Da Capo Press, 1970), 130

"Such information might call their attention . . ."
—James Brown to Isaac Shelby, February 16, 1794, "Selections from the Draper Collection . . . to Elucidate the Proposed French Expedition under George Rogers Clark against Louisiana, in the Years 1793–94," *Annual Report of the American Historical Association for the Year 1896* (Washington, D.C.: Government Printing Office, 1897), 1041

"invading and plundering . . ."
—Washington Proclamation, March 24, 1794, in Fitzpatrick, *Papers of George Washington*, 33: 304–305

"if the General Government . . ."
—"Remonstrance to the Citizens West of the Allegheny Mountains to the President and Congress of the United States," December 1793, in *The Democratic-Republican Societies, 1790–1800: A Documentary Sourcebook of Constitutions, Declarations, Addresses, Resolutions, and Toasts*, ed. Philip S. Foner (Westport, Conn.: Greenwood Press, 1976), 365

"The spirit of it must be . . ."
—George Nicholas to James Madison, September 16, 1791, in Hutchinson et al., *Papers of James Madison*, 14: 75

"Nature has done everything for us . . ."
—John Breckinridge to Samuel Hopkins, September 15, 1794, Breckinridge Family Papers

"What if the Government . . ."
—Edmond Randolph to Thomas Jefferson, August 28, 1794, Thomas Jefferson Papers, Library of Congress

"most inflammatory and invective language"
—Anthony Wayne to Henry Knox, June 11, 1794, in *The Papers of Hamilton*, ed. Harold Syrett, 17 vols. (New York: Columbia University Press, 1961–87), 16: 589

"Do you think it is unjust to subject us . . ."
—George Nicholas to James Madison, June 20, 1791, in Hutchinson et al., *Papers of James Madison*, 14: 32–33

"it was apprehended by several . . ."
—Caleb Wallace to Harry Innes, June 6, 1807, Harry Innes Papers

"attachments to governments . . ."
—"To the President and Congress of the United States of America," January 6, 1793, in "The Democratic Societies of 1793 and 1794 in Kentucky, Pennsylvania and Virginia," *WMQ* 2 (1922): 245

"had the session continued . . ."
—*The* (Frankfort) *Palladium*, August 27, 1798

"I have at present not a doubt . . ."
—John Breckinridge to James Monroe, August 12, 1798, James Monroe
Papers, New York Public Library

"There was a Barbacue . . ."
—Robert B. McAfee, "Life and Times of Robert B. McAfee and His
Family and Connections," *RKHS* 25 (1927): 217

"resolutions praying for an appeal . . ."
—*Kentucky Gazette*, August 25, 1798

"If these sagacious and learned citizens . . ."
—*Porcupine's Gazette*, September 21, 1798

"a mass of talents . . ."
—Thomas Jefferson to Wilson Cary Nicholas, September 6, 1799, in Ford,
Works of Thomas Jefferson, 9: 80

"mad and wicked schemes . . ."
—George Nicholas to Isaac Shelby, December 27, 1798, Shelby Family Papers, Library of Congress

"Where is the difference . . ."
—"At a meeting of a large number of the Farmers and Planters of the
County of Fayette at the Big Spring," broadside, April 28, 1798, Printed
Ephemera Collection, Library of Congress

"Thieves, Robbers and beardless boys"
—*Kentucky Gazette*, April 11, 1799

"if there is an inconsistency . . ."
—George Nicholas, "To the Freemen of Kentucky," March 30, 1799,
Broadside Collection, Library of Congress

"All America acknowledges . . ."
—"To the Electors of Fayette County," *Kentucky Gazette*, April 25, 1798

"unless he have either a tract . . ."
—*Kentucky Gazette*, March 7, 1799

"Ignorant Savage Heathens . . ."
—*The* (Washington, Ky.) *Mirror*, April 5, 1799

"would wade to his knees in blood . . ."
—Drake, *Pioneer Life in Kentucky*, 209

"I would not advise Slaveholders . . ."
—David Meade to William Bolling, May 6, 1798, William Bolling Papers, Special Collections, Duke University, Durham, N.C.

"all *free* men, when they form . . ."
—Kentucky Constitution, 1799, sec. 2, art. 8

On the federal military in the Northwest Territory, see Paul David Nelson, "General Charles Scott, the Kentucky Mounted Volunteers, and the Northwest Indian Wars, 1784–1794," *Journal of the Early Republic* 6 (1986): 219–51; Andrew R. L. Cayton, "'Separate Interests' and the Nation-State: The Washington Administration and the Origins of Regionalism in the Trans-Appalachian West," *Journal of American History* 79 (1992): 39–67; idem, "'Noble Actors' upon 'the Theatre of Honour': Power and Civility in the Treaty of Greenville," in Cayton and Teute, *Contact Points*, 235–69; Alan Taylor, *The Divided Ground: Indians, Settlers, and the Northern Borderland of the American Revolution* (New York: Alfred A. Knopf, 2006); David Andrew Nichols, *Red Gentlemen and White Savages: Indians, Federalists, and the Search for Order on the American Frontier* (Charlottesville: University of Virginia Press, 2008). On Kentucky's militias, see G. Glenn Clift, *The "Corn Stalk" Militia of Kentucky, 1792–1811* (Frankfort: Kentucky Historical Society, 1957); Richard G. Stone, *A Brittle Sword: The Kentucky Militia, 1776–1912* (Lexington: University Press of Kentucky, 1977); Harry S. Laver, *Citizens More Than Soldiers: The Kentucky Militia and Society in the Early Republic* (Lincoln: University of Nebraska Press, 2007).

On the constitution of 1792, see Joan Wells Coward, *Kentucky in the New Republic: The Process of Constitution Making* (Lexington: University Press of Kentucky, 1979); Penny N. Miller, *Kentucky Politics and Government: Do We Stand United?* (Lincoln: University of Nebraska Press, 1994); Robert M. Ireland, *The Kentucky State Constitution: A Reference Guide* (Westport, Conn.: Greenwood Press, 1999).

On the legal and social ordering of Kentucky in the 1790s, see Ethelbert D. Warfield, "The Constitutional Aspect of Kentucky's Struggle for Autonomy—1784–92," *Papers of the American Historical Association* 4 (1889): 23–39; Richard E. Ellis, *The Jeffersonian Crisis: Courts and Politics in the Young Republic* (New York: W. W. Norton, 1971); Robert M. Ireland, *The County Courts in Antebellum Kentucky* (Lexington: University Press of Kentucky, 1972). On transformations in the marriage narrative, see Sachs, "Not the Best Poor Man's Country"; idem,

"The Myth of the Abandoned Wife: Married Women's Agency and the Legal Narrative of Gender in Eighteenth-Century Kentucky," *OVH* 3 (2003): 3–20. On the strengthening of patriarchy in the late-eighteenth- and early-nineteenth-century South, see Victoria E. Bynum, *Unruly Women: The Politics of Social and Sexual Control in the Old South* (Chapel Hill: University of North Carolina Press, 1992); Stephanie McCurry, *Masters of Small Worlds: Yeoman Households, Gender Relations, and the Political Culture of the Antebellum South Carolina Low Country* (New York: Oxford University Press, 1995); Peter W. Bardaglio, *Reconstructing the Household: Families, Sex, and the Law in the Nineteenth-Century South* (Chapel Hill: University of North Carolina Press, 1998).

On the village West, see Alexander D. Finley, *The History of Russellville and Logan County, Ky., which is to some extent a history of Western Kentucky* (Russellville, Ky.: O. C. Rhea, 1878); R. S. Cotterill, "The Old Limestone Road: Pioneer Trade and Settlements along a Celebrated Kentucky Highway," *Kentucky Magazine* 1 (1916): 616–20; G. Glenn Clift, *History of Maysville and Mason County* (Lexington, Ky.: Transylvania Printing, 1936); Richard C. Wade, *The Urban Frontier: Pioneer Life in Early Pittsburgh, Cincinnati, Lexington, Louisville, and St. Louis* (Chicago: University of Chicago Press, 1964); Clay Lancaster, *Vestiges of the Venerable City: A Chronicle of Lexington, Kentucky, Its Architectural Development and Survey of Its Early Streets and Antiquities* (Lexington, Ky.: Lexington-Fayette County Historic Commission, 1978); George H. Yater, *Two Hundred Years at the Falls of the Ohio: A History of Louisville and Jefferson County* (Louisville: Filson Club, 1987); Nancy O'Malley, *A New Village Called Washington* (Lexington: Kentucky Humanities Council, 1987); Richard C. Brown, *A History of Danville and Boyle County, Kentucky, 1774–1992* (Danville, Ky.: Bicentennial Books, 1992); Darrett Rutman with Anita Rutman, "The Village South," in *Small Worlds, Large Questions: Explorations in Early American Social History, 1600–1850* (Charlottesville: University Press of Virginia, 1994), 231–72; Kim M. Gruenwald, *River of Enterprise: The Commercial Origins of Regional Identity in the Ohio Valley, 1790–1850* (Bloomington: Indiana University Press, 2002); Friend, *Along the Maysville Road.*

On Kentucke's relationship to the national government, see Archibald Henderson, "Isaac Shelby and the Genet Mission," *Mississippi Valley Historical Review* 6 (1920): 451–69; E. Merton Coulter, "The Efforts of the Democratic Societies of the West to Open the Navigation of the Mississippi," *Mississippi Valley Historical Review* 11 (1925): 376–

89; Lowell H. Harrison, "John Breckinridge and the Kentucky Constitution of 1799," *RKHS* 57 (1959): 209–33; Robert Pettus Hay, "A Jubilee for Freemen: The Fourth of July in Frontier Kentucky, 1788–1916," *RKHS* 64 (1966): 169–95; James Morton Smith, "The Grass Roots Origins of the Kentucky Resolutions," *WMQ* 27 (1970): 221–45; Mary K. Bonsteel Tachau, "The Whiskey Rebellion in Kentucky: A Forgotten Episode of Civil Disobedience," *Journal of the Early Republic* 2 (1982): 239–59; Matthew Schoenbachler, "Republicanism in the Age of Democratic Revolution: The Democratic-Republican Societies of the 1790s," *Journal of the Early Republic* 18 (1998): 237–61; Marion Nelson Winship, "Kentucky *in* the New Republic: A Study of Distance and Connection," in Friend, ed., *The Buzzel about Kentuck*, 101–24.

On economic opportunity for white women and blacks, see Elizabeth A. Perkins, "The Consumer Frontier: Household Consumption in Early Kentucky," *Journal of American History* 78 (September 1991): 486–510; Friend, *Along the Maysville Road*. The merchants' ledgers employed in the economic analysis of this study are Benedick Leonard's store ledger (Washington, Ky.), December 1790–November 1791, Research Library, Mason County History Museum, Maysville, Ky.; John Moylan's store ledger (Lexington, Ky.), January 1792–November 1794, UKSC; John W. Hunt's daybook (Lexington, Ky.), July 1790–September 1796, UKSC; James McDonald and Charles Thruston's account books (Louisville, Ky.), 1794–97, FHS; Daniel Halstead's account books (Lexington, Ky.), 1806, FHS; William Tureman's daybook (Washington, Ky.), January–March 1807, Research Library, Mason County History Museum; Edmund Martin's journal (Maysville), vol. B., July 1800–February 1810, Research Library, Mason County History Museum.

On evangelicalism's challenge to patriarchy, see Anne Loveland, *Southern Evangelicals and the Social Order, 1800–1860* (Baton Rouge: Louisiana State University Press, 1980); Barbara Leslie Epstein, *The Politics of Domesticity: Women, Evangelicalism, and Temperance in Nineteenth-Century America* (Middletown, Conn.: Wesleyan University Press, 1981); Jay Fliegelman, *Prodigals and Pilgrims: The American Revolution against Patriarchal Authority, 1750–1800* (New York: Cambridge University Press, 1982).

7. An Old South Frontier

You are in a genteel, agreeable neighborhood . . ."
    —John Breckinridge to Samuel Meredith, August 7, 1796, Breckinridge
    Family Papers

"the Western people . . ."
—"To the Citizens of Western America," *Kentucky Gazette*, July 25, 1798

"Times are greatly changed . . ."
—James Morrison to John Breckinridge, February 27, 1802, Breckinridge Family Papers

"the existence of slavery in Kentucky . . ."
—Drake, *Pioneer Life in Kentucky*, 209

"New comers can be at no loss . . ."
—David Meade to Ann Randolph, September 1, 1796, 341

"In various parts of the state . . ."
—Toulmin, "Comments on America and Kentucky," 100

"the time is not far distant when . . ."
—"The Senate Debate on the Breckinridge Bill for the Government of Louisiana, 1804," *AHR* 22 (1917): 345

"I can assure you that ther . . ."
—Charles Scott to Henry Dearborn, July 1804, Charles Scott Papers, UKSC

"the Slaves in the South are . . ."
—Lexington Trustees Minute Book, June 22, 1802, UKSC

"Our climate is not favorable . . ."
—Barthelemi Tardiveau to Hector St. John de Crevécouer, October 7, 1789, Barthelemi Tardiveau Miscellaneous Files, FHS

"The blacks who are slaves . . ."
—*Annals of Congress*, 8th cong., 1st sess., 554–55

"certain citizens of this Commonwealth possessing slaves . . ."
—*Journal of the Senate of the Commonwealth of Kentucky* (Frankfort: State Printer, 1811–12), 184

"united by commercial interests . . ."
—François André Michaux, *Travels to the West of the Allegheny Mountains, in the States of Ohio, Kentucky, and Tennessee, and Back to Charleston, by the Upper Carolines*, in *Early Western Travels, 1748–1846*, ed. Reuben Gold Thwaites, 32 vols. (Cleveland: Arthur H. Clark, 1904), 3: 252

"No price has been talked of . . ."
—Benjamin Howard to John Breckinridge, January 12, 1803, Breckinridge Family Papers

"Most people calculate on war"
   —John Allen to John Breckinridge, December 18, 1802, Breckinridge
      Family Papers

"Armies, Sieges, and Storms . . ."
   —Henry Clay to John Breckinridge, November 21, 1803, Breckinridge
      Family Papers

"our present administration . . ."
   —*Kentucky Gazette*, August 16, 1803

"patriotism, republicanism . . ."
   —*National Intelligencer*, December 18, 1803

"The future inhabitants . . ."
   —Thomas Jefferson to John Breckinridge, August 12, 1803, in Ford, *Works
      of Thomas Jefferson*, 8: 244

"We who have long been from our very hearts . . ."
   —James Brown to John Breckinridge, January 13, 1803, Breckinridge
      Family Papers

"perpetuity to the union . . ."
   —*Kentucky Gazette*, March 15, 1803

"if he calculated on withdrawing the affections . . ."
   —*Kentucky Gazette*, November 3, 1805

"The plot is laid wider than you imagine . . ."
   —Joseph Hamilton Daviess to Thomas Jefferson, January 10, 1806, in
      Marshall, *The History of Kentucky*, 2: 400

"Having left Kentucky . . ."
   —Henry Clay to Thomas M. Prentiss, February 15, 1807, in *The Private
      Correspondence of Henry Clay*, ed. Calvin Colton (New York: A. S.
      Barnes, 1855), 6

"I often heard of Shakers while . . ."
   —"Samuel Hoosier's Hymn," in Daniel W. Patterson, *The Shaker Spiri-
      tual* (Mineola, N.Y.: Courier Dover Publications, 2000), 147

"Let Shakerism predominate . . ."
   —James Smith, *Shakerism Detected; Their Erroneous and Treasonous
      Proceedings and False Publications, Contained in Different News-
      papers; Exposed to Public View, by the Depositions of Ten Different
      Persons Living in Various Parts of the States of Kentucky and Ohio,
      Accompanied by Remarks* (Paris, Ky.: Joel R. Lyle, 1810), 35

"Several times while dancing they hallow . . ."
—"South Union, 1810, Nourse-Chapline Letters," *RKHS* 31 (1933): 166

"We humbly conceive they ought . . ."
—*Kentucky Gazette*, July 17, 1810

"I have brought forward the falling down . . ."
—George Baxter to Mr. Davis, September 4, 1803, Special Collections, Leyburn Library, Washington and Lee University Library

"Becca Bell—who often fell . . ."
—John Lyle Diary, October 5, 1801, Lyle Family Papers, UKSC

"church members [should] carefully avoid . . ."
—List of Article and Faith, 1800, Six Mile Christiansburg Church, Baptist Churches Records, FHS

"Is it not a matter worthy of Exclusion . . ."
—May–June 1807, Forks of Elkhorn Baptist Church Minutes, Kentucky, 1788–1831, Southern Baptist Theological Seminary, Louisville, Ky.

"Sister Rogers hath been guilty . . ."
—Minute Book of Mount Tabor Baptist Church, June–October 1809, Southern Baptist Theological Seminary

"I'll be Goddamned if . . ."
—Grand Jury Indictment, *Commonwealth v. Jesse Glasscock*, March 1813, Caldwell Circuit Court Papers, Caldwell County Circuit Clerk's Office, Princeton, Ky.

"preaching the doctrine of emancipation . . ."
—"Minutes of the North-District Association of Baptists, Held . . . in Bath County, state of Kentucky . . . July . . . 1817" (Lexington: Thomas T. Skilman, 1817), 3

"improper for ministers . . ."
—resolution, in Sweet, *Religion on the American Frontier*, vol. 1: *The Baptists*, 82

"We are now distinguished . . ."
—"Minutes of the Baptized Licking-Locust Association, Friends of Humanity," in Sweet, *Religion on the American Frontier*, vol. 1: *The Baptists*, 566–67

"Let it not be supposed . . ."
—circular letter, 1810, South District Association, in Sweet, *Religion on the American Frontier*, vol. 1: *The Baptists*, 86

"once thought it her duty . . ."
—May 1806, Forks of Elkhorn Minutes Baptist Church Minutes

"exposing to sale . . ."
—Minutes of the Synod of Kentucky, 1802–11, in Sweet, *Religion on the American Frontier*, vol. 2: *The Presbyterians*, 378

"With his consent . . ."
—John Taylor, *A History of Ten Baptist Churches* (1823; reprint, New York: Arno Press, 1980), 103

"Shall we not be as comfortable . . ."
—*Kentucky Gazette*, November 12, 1787

"many opulent and some Genteel people . . ."
—David Meade to Ann Randolph, September 1, 1796, 341

"This *equality*, my Love . . ."
—Margaretta Brown to John Brown, March 8, 1802, Brown Family Papers, FHS

"God must be prospering you . . ."
—Polly Davis to Thomas Davis, November 6, 1792, in *Virginia Magazine of History and Biography* 12 (1905): 436

"dollars at any time . . ."
—*The Mirror*, November 18, 1797

"seven-tenths of the manufactured articles . . ."
—Michaux, *Travels to the West*, 203

"the merchant's *dwelling* . . ."
—*Kentucky Gazette*, September 20, 1803

"the Philadelphia of Kentucky"
—Lewis Condict, "Journal of a Trip to Kentucky in 1795," *Proceedings of the New Jersey Historical Society* 4 (1919): 120

"in less than twelve months . . ."
—John James Audubon, *John James Audubon: Writings and Drawings*, ed. Christopher Irmscher (New York: Library of America, 1999), 791

"the strap, gentlemen . . ."
—Humphrey Marshall, in James Redpath, *The Roving Editor, Or Talks with Slaves in the Southern States* (New York: A. B. Burdick, 1859), 60

"These men who were dirtying . . ."
—*Kentucky Gazette*, July 19, 1808

"It gave us pleasure on this occasion . . ."
  —*Kentucky Reporter*, July 8, 1809

"You may as well call the revolutionary war . . ."
  —*Kentucky Gazette*, December 7, 1811

"the hour is at hand . . ."
  —*Kentucky Gazette*, September 15, 1812

"Indians have not . . ."
  —Samuel Hopkins, "Resolution," in *Journal of the House of Representatives of the Commonwealth of Kentucky, 1811–1812* (Frankfort: State Printer, 1812), 106

"inciting the savages to murder . . ."
  —*Niles' Weekly Register*, January 11, 1812

"The eternal dread . . ."
  —Carter Tarrant, *The Substance of a Discourse Delivered in the Town of Versailles, Woodford County, State of Kentucky, 20 April 1806* (Lexington, Ky.: Daniel Bradford, 1806), 9–10

"a Lesson for Negroes for setting fire to . . ."
  —*American Republic* (Frankfort), May 31, 1811

"We must prove to the Union at large . . ."
  —Millersburg, Ky., residents to Isaac Shelby, August 31, 1812, UKSC

"something ten thousand times more valuable . . ."
  —*Kentucky Reporter*, December 7, 1811

"are a spirited people . . ."
  —Richard Johnson to James Madison, July 24, 1812, in "The Letters of Colonel Richard M. Johnson of Kentucky," ed. James A. Padgett, *RKHS* 38 (1940): 189

"hearing of the girls getting married . . ."
  —Thomas Bedford to Elizabeth Kennedy, November 12, 1812, Edwin Green Bedford Papers, 1812–1902, UKSC

"a country's gratitude . . ."
  —*Niles' Weekly Register*, December 28, 1811

"Let the spinning wheel, the loom . . ."
  —*Kentucky Gazette*, September 15, 1812

"*The Kentucky fair* . . ."
  —*Kentucky Gazette*, August 3, 1813

"The American fair . . ."
—*Kentucky Gazette*, July 11, 1814

"The spirit of your fathers aroused you . . ."
—*Niles' Weekly Register*, February 20, 1813

"they are the most patriotic people . . ."
—*Niles' Weekly Register*, supplement to vol. 8 (Baltimore, Md.: Franklin Press, 1815), 178–79

"Until those *civilized allies* . . ."
—*Kentucky Gazette*, April 14, 1812

"The Hunters of Kentucky" lyrics
—"The Hunters of Kentucky" (New York: Andrews, n.d.)

"You have done your duty . . ."
—*Kentucky Gazette*, March 13, 1815

On the Harpes, see Otto A. Rothert, *The Outlaws of Cave-in-Rock* (Cleveland: Arthur H. Clark, 1924); W. D. Snively Jr. and Louanna Furbee, *Satan's Ferrymen, a True Tale of the Old Frontier* (New York: Frederick Unger, 1968); J. T. Gooch, *Stories of the Pennyrile* (Mt. Vernon, Ind.: Windmill Publishing, 1990).

On demographic shifts in the 1790s and early 1800s, see Thomas L. Purvis, "The Ethnic Descent of Kentucky's Early Population: A Statistical Investigation of American and European Sources of Emigration, 1790–1820," *RKHS* 80 (1982): 253–66; Lee Shai Weissbach, "The Peopling of Lexington, Kentucky: Growth and Mobility in a Frontier Town," *RKHS* 81 (1983): 115–33; Todd Harold Barnett, "The Evolution of 'North' and 'South': Settlement and Slavery on America's Sectional Border, 1650–1810" (Ph.D. diss., University of Pennsylvania, 1993). For the effects of demographic shifts on slavery, see Emil Pocock, "Slavery and Freedom in the Early Republic: Robert Patterson's Slaves in Kentucky and Ohio, 1804–1819," *OVH* 6 (2006): 3–26. On economic shifts, see W. F. Axton, *Tobacco and Kentucky* (Lexington: University of Kentucky Press, 1975); John Solomon Otto, *The Southern Frontiers, 1670–1860: The Agricultural Evolution of the Colonial and Antebellum South* (Westport, Conn.: Greenwood Press, 1989).

On the Green River country, see Juliet E. K. Walker, *Free Frank: A Black Pioneer on the Antebellum Frontier* (Lexington: University Press of Kentucky, 1983); Boynton Merrill, *Jefferson's Nephews: A Frontier Tragedy* (Lexington: University Press of Kentucky, 1987); Suzanne Marshall, *Violence in the Black Patch of Kentucky and Tennessee* (Columbia: University of Missouri Press, 1994); Christopher Waldrep, "Opportunity on the Frontier South of the Green," in Friend, *The Buzzel about Kentuck*, 153–74. On the Green River region's relationship to Tennessee, see John Finger, *Tennessee Frontiers: Three Regions in Transition* (Bloomington: Indiana University Press, 2001); Kristofer Ray, *Middle Tennessee, 1775–1825: Progress and Popular Democracy on the Southwestern Frontier* (Knoxville: University of Tennessee Press, 2007). On Appalachia, see Willard Rouse Jillson, *The Big Sandy: A Regional History Prior to the Year 1850* (Louisville, Ky.: John P. Morton, 1923); Henry P. Scalf, *Kentucky's Last Frontier* (Pikeville, Ky.: Pikeville College Press, 1972); Wilma A. Dunaway, *The First American Frontier: Transition to Capitalism in Southern Appalachia, 1700–1860* (Chapel Hill: University of North Carolina Press, 1996).

On portable planters, see David Hackett Fischer, *Bound Away: Virginia and the Westward Movement* (Charlottesville: University of Virginia Press, 2000); Nelson, "Power in Motion." On the movement of plantation families, see Joan E. Cashin, *A Family Venture: Men and Women on the Southern Frontier* (Baltimore, Md.: Johns Hopkins University Press, 1991); Terry, "Family Empires."

On the Burr episode, see Samuel M. Wilson, "The Court Proceedings of 1806 in Kentucky against Aaron Burr and John Adair," *Filson Club Historical Quarterly* 10 (1936): 31–40; Mary K. Bonsteel Tachau, *Federal Courts in the Early Republic: Kentucky, 1789–1816* (Princeton, N.J.: Princeton University Press, 1978). On Breckinridge's political career, see Lowell H. Harrison, *John Breckinridge: Jeffersonian Republican* (Louisville: Filson Club, 1969); James C. Klotter, *The Breckinridges of Kentucky, 1760–1981* (Lexington: University Press of Kentucky, 1986). On Clay's political career, see Robert V. Remini, *Henry Clay: Statesman for the Union* (New York: W. W. Norton, 1991).

On slave patrols, see Sally Hadden, *Slave Patrols: Law and Violence in Virginia and the Carolinas* (Cambridge, Mass.: Harvard University Press, 2001); Anthony E. Kaye, *Joining Places: Slave Neighborhoods in the Old South* (Chapel Hill: University of North Carolina Press, 2007).

On Kentucky Shakerism, see Julia Neal, *By Their Fruits: The Story of Shakerism in South Union, Kentucky* (1947; reprint, Philadelphia: Porcupine Press, 1975); Samuel W. Thomas and Mary Lawrence Young, "The Development of Shakertown at Pleasant Hill, Kentucky," *FCHS* 49 (1975): 231–55; Stephen J. Stein, *The Shaker Experience in America: A History of the United Society of Believers* (New Haven, Conn.: Yale University Press, 1994); Tom Kanon, "'Seduced, Bewildered, and Lost':

Anti-Shakerism on the Early Nineteenth-Century Frontier," *OVH* 7 (2007): 1–30. On revivalism, see John B. Boles, *Religion in Antebellum Kentucky* (Lexington: University Press of Kentucky, 1976); Nathan O. Hatch, *The Democratization of American Christianity* (New Haven: Yale University Press, 1989); Paul K. Conkin, *Cane Ridge: America's Pentecost* (Madison: University of Wisconsin Press, 1990); Christine Leigh Heyrman, *Southern Cross: The Beginnings of the Bible Belt* (New York: Knopf, 1997); Ellen Eslinger, *Citizens of Zion: The Social Origins of Camp Meeting Revivalism* (Knoxville: University of Tennessee Press, 1999).

On revivalism's impact on Kentucky society, see Christopher Waldrep, "The Making of a Border State Society: James McGready, the Great Revival, and the Prosecution of Profanity in Kentucky," *AHR* 99 (1994): 767–84; Blair A. Pogue, "'I Cannot Believe the Gospel That Is So Much Preached': Gender, Belief, and Discipline in Baptist Religious Culture," in Friend, *The Buzzel about Kentuck*, 217–42; Ellen Eslinger, "The Beginnings of Afro-American Christianity among Kentucky Baptists," in Friend, *The Buzzel about Kentuck*, 197–216; Andrew Lee Feight, "James Blythe and the Slavery Controversy in the Presbyterian Churches of Kentucky, 1791–1802," *RKHS* 102 (2004): 13–38; Monica Najar, "'Meddling with Emancipation': Baptists, Authority, and the Rift over Slavery in the Upper South," *Journal of the Early Republic* 25 (2005): 157–86.

On patterns of refinement, see Lee Soltow, "Kentucky Wealth at the End of the Eighteenth Century," *Journal of Economic History* 43 (1983): 617–33; Richard Bushman, *The Refinement of America: Persons, Houses, Cities* (New York: Vintage, 1993). On homespun, see Laurel Thatcher Ulrich, *The Age of Homespun: Objects and Stories in the Creation of an American Myth* (New York: Alfred A. Knopf, 2001). On Kentucky merchants, see Gary A. O'Dell, "The Trotter Family, Gunpowder, and Early Kentucky Entrepreneurship, 1784–1833," *RKHS* 88 (1990): 394–430; Craig Thompson Friend, "Merchants and Markethouses: Reflections on Moral Economy in Early Kentucky," *Journal of the Early Republic* 17 (1997): 553–74; idem, "Trotter and Sons: Merchants of the Early West," in *The Human Tradition in Antebellum America*, ed. Michael A. Morrison (Wilmington, Del.: Scholarly Resources, 2000), 35–52.

On Native American–white relations on the eve of the War of 1812, see David R. Edmunds, *The Shawnee Prophet* (Lincoln: University of Nebraska Press, 1983); Gregory Evans Dowd, *A Spirited Resistance: The North American Indian Struggle for Unity, 1745–1815* (Baltimore,

Md.: Johns Hopkins University Press, 1993). On Kentuckians' participation in the War of 1812, see Anderson Chenault Quisenberry, *Kentucky in the War of 1812* (Frankfort: Kentucky State Historical Society,
1915); G. Glenn Clift, *Remember the Raisin! Kentucky and Kentuckians in the Battles and Massacres at Frenchtown, Michigan Territory,
in the War of 1812* (Frankfort: Kentucky Historical Society, 1961); James
Wallace Hammock, *Kentucky and the Second American Revolution:
The War of 1812* (Lexington: University Press of Kentucky, 1976).

8. Remembering

"military to the nth degree . . ."
> —G. Glenn Clift, *A History of Maysville and Mason County*, 2 vols. (Lex-
> ington: Transylvania Printing, 1936), 1: 158–59

"Evry thing was *Lafayette* . . ."
> —Frances L. S. Dugan and Jacqueline P. Bull, eds., *Bluegrass Crafts-
> man: Being the Reminiscences of Ebenezer Hiram Stedman, Paper-
> maker, 1808–1885* (Lexington: University of Kentucky Press, 1959), 75

"We are powerful . . ."
> —Henry Clay, January 20, 1819, in *Annals of Congress*, 15th cong., 2nd
> sess., 639

"barbarism has . . . been receding . . ."
> —Thomas Jefferson to William Ludlow, September 6, 1824, in Lipscomb
> and Bergh, *Writings of Thomas Jefferson*, 16: 75

"This land comes within 7 miles . . ."
> —Matthew Lyon to James Munroe, May 12, 1811, FHS

"perpetuate that peace and harmony . . ."
> —Treaty with the Chickasaw, September 20, 1816, in *Indian Affairs: Laws
> and Treaties*, ed. Charles J. Kappler et al., 5 vols. (Washington, D.C.:
> Government Printing Office, 1904–72), 2: 135

"valor and patriotism . . ."
> —*Journal of the House of Representatives of the Commonwealth of Ken-
> tucky, 1811–1812* (Frankfort: State Printer, 1812), 106

"necessary measure of precaution . . ."
> —Thomas W. Randolph to the Governor of Kentucky, n.d., FHS

"stands nearly on the site of an old Indian town . . ."
> —Thomas Ashe, *Travels in America Performed in 1806: For the Purpose
> of Exploring the Rivers Alleghany, Monongahela, Ohio, and Missis-*

sippi, and Ascertaining the Produce and Condition of Their Banks and Vicinity (London, Eng.: R. Phillips, 1808), 158–61

"Shawnees, Delawares, Mingoes . . ."
—*The Mirror*, August 29, 1807

"an infant, of nine or twelve months old . . ."
—"Letter from Charles Wilkins to Samuel Burnside, dated 2 October 1817," *Archaeologia Americana: Transactions and Collections of the American Antiquarian Society* 1 (1820): 362

"a race of beings, who acknowledge no laws, human or divine . . ."
—*Kentucky Gazette*, May 7, 1791

"Thoughts on the present Indian War . . ."
—"H. H. Brackenridge on the Indian Problem," *Kentucky Gazette*, October 26, 1827, in Bradford, *Voice of the Frontier*, 177

"In truth, the ultimate point of rest and happiness for them . . ."
—Thomas Jefferson to Benjamin Hawkins, February 18, 1803, in Ford, *Writings of Thomas Jefferson*, 10: 363

"Fanny has a handsome Indian for her spouse"
—Samuel Hopkins to Walter Alves, February 1807, Walter Alves Family Papers, Southern Historical Collection, Wilson Library, University of North Carolina, Chapel Hill

"war whoop of the savage . . ."
—*Kentucky Gazette*, June 11, 1805

"was then called by the Indians . . ."
—"Opening the Way West," August 25, 1826, in Bradford, *Voice of the Frontier*, 3

"Black-Fish then said 'brother . . .'"
—"A Wilderness Ordeal," in Bradford, *Voice of the Frontier*, 16

"If any part of the inhabited earth . . ."
—Daniel Boone, *A Geographical, Historical, Commercial, and Agricultural View of the United States of America* (London: Edwards and Knibb, 1820), 593.

"Then had the Indians their revenge . . ."
—DMC 31C3

"The Indians' path of incursion in the West . . ."
—Isaac Smucker, "1750—Kentucky History—1800," *Magazine of Western History* 10 (September 1889): 504

"manners and customs of our present Native American Indians . . ."
  —John D. Clifford, "Letter II: Their Builders Descended from the Same
    Race as the Hindus," in *John D. Clifford's Indian Antiquities*, ed.
    Charles Boewe (Knoxville: University of Tennessee Press, 2000), 7

"Ancient Monuments of North America"
  —Constantine Rafinesque, "Ancient Monuments of North America," in
    Boewe, *John D. Clifford's Indian Antiquities*, 128

"there is not a Red man (nor ever was) . . ."
  —*Saturday Evening Post*, June 7, 1828

"The white man became tawny by constant exposure . . ."
  —*Cincinnati Literary Gazette* 2 (1824): 203

"that Indian race/Whose lease . . ."
  —William Ross Wallace, "Daniel Boone," in *Poets and Poetry of the West*,
    ed. William T. Coggeshall (New York: Follett, Foster, 1860), 228

"M'Bride and Finley . . ."
  —Daniel Bryan, *The Mountain Muse: Comprising the Adventures
    of Daniel Boone; and the Power of Virtuous and Refined Beauty*
    (Harrisonburg, Va.: Davidson and Bourne, 1813), 115–16

"Indians, from fierce and numerous tribes . . ."
  —John A. McClung, *Sketches of Western Adventure, Containing an Ac-
    count of the Most Interesting Incidents Connected with the Settlement
    of the West, from 1755 to 1794; with an Appendix* (1832; reprint, Louis-
    ville: Richard H. Collins, 1879), 288–89

"drowned and burned *witches* and . . ."
  —*Kentucky Gazette*, September 17, 1821

"xth year of American Independence . . ."
  —*Kentucky Almanac* (Lexington, Ky.: John Bradford, 1794), UKSC

"through the stirring scenes . . ."
  —Drake, *Pioneer Life in Kentucky*, 177

"there was not a half mile of the road . . ."
  —Fortesque Cuming, *Sketches of a Tour to the Western Country through
    the States of Ohio and Kentucky*, in Thwaites, *Early Western Travels*,
    4: 177

"There is not probably, any thing . . ."
  —Marshall, *History of Kentucky*, 1: iii

"But Kentucky! brought forth in obscurity . . ."
—Marshall, *History of Kentucky*, 1: v

"a representative democracy . . ." and "That all men are by nature
unequal . . ."
—Marshall, *History of Kentucky*, 2: 414–15

"No wood had been felled . . ."
—Marshall, *History of Kentucky*, 1: 5

"Nor has Kentucky, been without her wars . . ."
—Marshall, *History of Kentucky*, 1: v, vi

"Men who should live in mutual confidence . . ."
—Marshall, *History of Kentucky*, 1: 347

"conspirators and *intriguers* . . ."
—Marshall, *History of Kentucky*, preface

"cool, determined, and brave . . ."
—James Johnson to Henry Clay, January 28, 1809, in *The Papers of
Henry Clay*, ed. James F. Hopkins et al., 10 vols. (Lexington: Univer-
sity Press of Kentucky, 1959–91), 1: 401

"[O]ur government is but in its infancy . . ."
—Marshall, *History of Kentucky*, 2: iii–iv

"Should he [the historian] trace the revolutions of ancient states . . ."
—Marshall, *History of Kentucky*, 1: iv–v

"Everyone is afraid of bursting the bubble"
—James Flint, *Letters from America*, in Thwaites, *Early Western Travels*, 9: 136

"have taught their elders practical patriotism"
—*Eagle* (Maysville, Ky.), July 4, 1817

"This doleful circumstance cannot . . ."
—"The Long Hunters," in Clark, *Voice of the Frontier*, 6–7

"negro seized the Indian who had entered . . ."
—Retaliation and a Step toward Statehood," in Clark, *Voice of the Frontier*, 59

"No sound was uttered but the cry of the gorged vulture . . ."
—Tragedy at the Blue Licks," in Clark, *Voice of the Frontier*, 56–58

"give my country, by fostering . . ."
—James Rees, *The Life of Edwin Forrest with Reminiscences and Personal Recollections* (Philadelphia: T. B. Peterson, 1874), 104

"celebrate in such a manner . . ." and "native citizens of Kentucky, or such . . ."
——resolution in regard to the formation of the Kentucky Historical Society, in J. W. Townsend, "History of the Kentucky Historical Society," *RKHS* 4 (September 1906): 50

"I like the dreams of the future . . ."
——Thomas Jefferson to John Adams, August 1, 1816, in *The Adams-Jefferson Letters*, ed. Lester J. Capon (Chapel Hill: University of North Carolina Press, 1959), 485

"Democracy has no monuments . . ."
——"Introductory Remarks by Brooks Adams," in Daniel Munro Wilson, *John Quincy: Master of Mount Wollaston* (Cambridge, Mass.: Harvard University Press, 1909), 13

"the patriarch of Kentucky"
——James Fenimore Cooper, *The Prairie: A Tale* (1827; reprint, New York: Signet Books, 1964), vii

"the failure of Mr. Cooper in his *Prairie* . . ."
——Daniel Drake, *Discourse on the History, Character, and Prospects of the West* (Cincinnati: Truman and Smith, 1834), 55

"personal recontre of Colonel Boon James . . ."
——James Fenimore Cooper, *Notions of the Americans: Picked Up by a Travelling Bachelor*, 2 vols. (London, Eng.: H. Colburn, 1828), 2: 36

"You see the exposure and suffering . . ."
——*Bulletin of the American Art-Union* (September 1851), 97

"Many heroic actions . . ."
——*National-Republican* (Cincinnati), August 19, 1823, DMC 16C67

"By the Eternal Power . . ."
——Timothy Flint, *The First White Man of the West: Life and Exploits of Col. Dan'l Boone, the First Settler of Kentucky; Interspersed with Incidents in the Early Annals of the Country* (Cincinnati: Applegate, 1856), 87

"In an age of chivalry . . ."
——William Gilmore Simms, *Views and Reviews of American Literature, History and Fiction* (London, Eng.: Wiley and Putnam, 1846), 120

"We are a hardy, free-born race . . ."
——"The Hunters of Kentucky" (New York: Andrews, n.d.)

"Why, thar's more real satisfaction . . ."
——Emerson Bennett, *Ella Barnwell: A Historical Romance of Border Life* (Cincinnati: U. P. James, 1853), 10

"the group told its story . . ."
  —Edward G. Loring to James Pearce, February 1859, Montgomery Meigs
    Letterbook, Records of the Architect of the Capitol, National Archives

"The tenderest eloquence . . ."
  —Bryan, *The Mountain Muse*, 56

"that *they* were not bullet-proof . . ."
  —John A. McClung, *Sketches of Western Adventure: containing an ac-
    count of the most interesting incidents connected with the settlement
    of the West, from 1755 to 1794* (1832; reprint, Covington, Ky.: Richard
    H. Collins, 1872), 68–69

"Since I saw you, I have written . . ."
  —John Dabney Shane to Charles G. Shane, February 11, 1841, Shane Col-
    lection 1716–1860, Presbyterian Historical Society, Philadelphia

"New investments are constantly made . . ."
  —Drake, *Pioneer Life in Kentucky*, 182

"talked with rich and poor alike . . ."
  —John Irwin to John Irwin Sr., February 26, 1839, John Irwin Papers, FHS

"The sable colour of the Africans . . ."
  —*The Mirror*, April 5, 1799

"Observe their shape and color . . ."
  —*Kentucky Gazette*, March 21, 1799

"Ugly, Black, Flatnosed . . ."
  —*The Mirror*, April 5, 1799

"the black men protested . . ."
  —Francis Fedric, *Slave Life in Virginia and Kentucky; or, Fifty Years of
    Slavery in the Southern States of America* (London, Eng.: Wertheim,
    Macintosh, and Hunt, 1863), 25

"It is a saying among the masters . . ."
  —Fedric, *Slave Life in Virginia and Kentucky*, 18

"I was bought up in the Counties . . ."
  —Henry Bibb, *Narrative of the Life and Adventures of Henry Bibb, An
    American Slave* (1850; reprint, New York: Negro Universities Press,
    1969), 13

"until the poor fellow . . ."
  —Fedric, *Slave Life in Virginia and Kentucky*, 31

"Licentious white men . . ."
  —Bibb, *Narrative of the Life and Adventures of Henry Bibb*, 38

"men and women down . . ."
 —Fedric, *Slave Life in Virginia and Kentucky*, 14–15

"became completely frantic . . ."
 —Lewis Clarke, *Narratives of the Sufferings of Lewis and Milton Clarke* (Boston: Bela Marsh, 1846), 74

"The only weapon of self defence . . ."
 —Bibb, *Narrative of the Life and Adventures of Henry Bibb*, 17

"I have stood on the lofty banks . . ."
 —Bibb, *Narrative of the Life and Adventures of Henry Bibb*, 29–30

On celebrations of nationalism, see Len Travers, *Celebrating the Fourth: Independence Day and the Rites of Nationalism in the Early Republic* (Amherst: University of Massachusetts Press, 1997); David Waldstreicher, *In the Midst of Perpetual Fetes: The Making of American Nationalism, 1776–1820* (Chapel Hill: University of North Carolina Press, 1997). On the collision between tradition and democracy, see Lucas, "Realized Ideals." On literary styles and their employment of frontier themes, see E. Douglas Branch, *The Sentimental Years, 1836–1860* (New York: D. Appleton-Century, 1934); Arthur K. Moore, *The Frontier Mind* (Lexington: University Press of Kentucky, 1957); Warren Motley, *The American Abraham: James Fenimore Cooper and the Frontier Patriarch* (New York: Cambridge University Press, 1987); Lewis Perry, *Boats against the Current: American Culture between Revolution and Modernity, 1820–1860* (New York: Oxford University Press, 1993).

On the hero, see Joseph Campbell, *The Power of Myth* (New York: Anchor Books, 1988), ch. 5.; Michael Allen, *Western Rivermen, 1763–1861: Ohio and Mississippi Boatmen and the Myth of the Alligator Horse* (Baton Rouge: Louisiana State University Press, 1990); "Appendix I: Wildfire and the *Life*," in James Atkins Shackford, *David Crockett: The Man and the Legend*, ed. John B. Shackford (Lincoln: University of Nebraska Press, 1994); Daniel J. Herman, "The Other Daniel Boone: The Nascence of a Middle-Class Hunter Hero, 1784–1860," *Journal of the Early Republic* 18 (1998): 429–58; and Richard Taylor, "Daniel Boone as American Icon: A Literary View," *RKHS* 102 (2004): 513–33.

Among the novels that venerate the Kentucky/American pioneer are James Kirke Paulding, *Westward Ho! A Tale*, 2 vols. (New York: J. and J. Harper, 1832), and James Fenimore Cooper's Leatherstocking Tales—*The Pioneers* (1823), *The Last of the Mohicans* (1826), *The Prairie* (1827), *The Pathfinder* (1840), and *The Deerslayer* (1841).

On the Vanishing Indian, see C. F. Rafinesque, *Ancient History, or*

Annals of Kentucky: with a survey of the ancient monuments of North America, and a tabular view of the principal languages and primitive nations of the whole earth (Frankfort, Ky.: privately printed, 1824); E. G. Squirer and E. H. Davis, *Ancient Monuments of the Mississippi Valley* (New York: Bartlett and Welford, 1848); Brian W. Dippie, *The Vanishing American: White Attitudes and U.S. Indian Policy* (Lawrence: University Press of Kansas, 1982); John F. Sears, "Mammoth Cave: Theater of the Cosmic," in *Sacred Places: American Tourist Attractions of the Nineteenth Century* (Amherst: University of Massachusetts Press, 1998); Anthony F. C. Wallace, *Jefferson and the Indians: The Tragic Fate of the First Americans* (Cambridge, Mass.: Harvard University Press, 1999); Alan Trachtenberg, *Shades of Hiawatha: Staging Indians, Making Americans, 1880–1930* (New York: Hill and Wang, 2004); Steven Conn, *History's Shadow: Native Americans and Historical Consciousness in the Nineteenth Century* (Chicago: University of Chicago Press, 2004); Judy A. Kertész, "Skeletons in the American Attic: Curiosity, Science, and the Appropriation of the American Indian Past, 1776–1846" (Ph.D. diss., Harvard University, 2010).

On assimilationist policies, see Francis Paul Prucha, *American Indian Policy in the Formative Years: The Indian Trade and Intercourse Acts, 1790–1834* (Lincoln: University of Nebraska Press, 1962). On the rotunda reliefs, see Vivien Green Fryd, *Art and Empire: The Politics of Ethnicity in the United States Capitol, 1815–1860* (New Haven, Conn.: Yale University Press, 1992).

On history and the "whitening" of America in the mid-nineteenth century, see Reginald Horsman, *Race and Manifest Destiny: The Origins of American Racial Anglo-Saxonism* (Cambridge, Mass.: Harvard University Press, 1981); Bridget T. Heneghan, *Whitewashing America: Material Culture and Race in the Antebellum Imagination* (Oxford: University of Mississippi Press, 2003); Amy S. Greenberg, *Manifest Manhood and the Antebellum American Empire* (New York: Cambridge University Press, 2005); John Van Houten Dippel, *Race to the Frontier: "White Flight" and Westward Expansion* (New York: Algora Publishing, 2005). On Kentuckians' greater appreciation for history, see J. Winston Coleman Jr., "John Bradford and *The Kentucky Gazette*," *FCHQ* 34 (1960): 24–34; Neils Sonne, *Liberal Kentucky 1780–1828* (Lexington: University of Kentucky Press, 1968); Thomas E. Stephens, "'A Glorious Birthright to Guard': A History of the Kentucky Historical Society," *RKHS* 101 (2003): 7–44.

On slavery and black life, see Jeffrey Brooke Allen, "The Origins of Proslavery Thought in Kentucky, 1792–1799," *RKHS* 77 (1979): 75–90; Harold D. Tallant, *Evil Necessity: Slavery and Political Culture in*

Antebellum Kentucky (Lexington: University Press of Kentucky, 2003); Alex Bontemps, *The Punished Self: Surviving Slavery in the Colonial South* (Ithaca, N.Y.: Cornell University Press, 2008).

Epilogue

"They see then as contested . . ."
—Andrew R. L. Cayton and Fredrika J. Teute, "Introduction: On the Connection of Frontiers," in *Contact Points*, 2

"the settler paints the native . . ."
—Franz Fanon, *The Wretched of the Earth*, trans. Constance Farrington (New York: Grove Weidenfeld, 1963), 41, 51

"The retelling of these stories . . ."
—June Namias, *White Captives: Gender and Ethnicity on the American Frontiers* (Chapel Hill: University of North Carolina Press, 1993), 268

"Sept. 11 cracked . . ."
—Susan Faludi, "America's Guardian Myths," *New York Times*, September 7, 2007

"great central myth of initiation . . ."
—Slotkin, *Regeneration through Violence*, 17
—Jacob Young, *Autobiography of a Pioneer; Or, the Nativity, Experience, Travels, and Ministerial Labors of Rev. Jacob Young, with Incidents, Observations, and Reflections* (Cincinnati: L. Swormstedt and A. Poe, 1857), 244

On Frederick Jackson Turner and the frontier thesis, see Ray Allen Billington, *The Genesis of the Frontier Thesis: A Study in Historical Creativity* (San Marino, Calif.: Huntington Library, 1971); Martin Ridge, ed., *Frederick Jackson Turner: Wisconsin's Historian of the Frontier* (Madison: State Historical Society of Wisconsin, 1986); Michael A. Flannery, "The Significance of the Frontier Thesis in Kentucky Culture: A Study in Historical Practice and Perception," *RKHS* 92 (1994): 239–66; John Mack Faragher, *Rereading Frederick Jackson Turner: "The Significance of the Frontier in American History" and Other Essays* (New Haven, Conn.: Yale University Press, 1998).

For further consideration of the long-term consequences of frontier fear and the atmosphere of terror on the frontiers, see Namias, *White Captives*; Jill Lepore, *The Name of War: King Philip's War and the Origins of American Identity* (New York: Vintage Books, 1998); Susan Faludi, *The Terror Dream: Fear and Fantasy in Post-9/11 America* (New York: Metropolitan Books, 2007).

Index

CRAIG THOMPSON FRIEND

is Professor of History at North Carolina State University, author of *Along the Maysville Road: The Early American Republic in the Trans-Appalachian West*, and editor of *The Buzzel about Kentuck: Settling the Promised Land*.

Printed in the USA
CPSIA information can be obtained
at www.ICGtesting.com
JSHW060156191023
50101JS00036B/9